CW01432525

Dread Danger

When confronted with the abject fear of going into battle, Civil War soldiers were expected to overcome the dread of the oncoming danger with feats of courage and victory on the battlefield. The Fire Zouaves and the 2nd Texas Infantry went to war with high expectations that they would perform bravely; they had famed commanders and enthusiastic community support. How could they possibly fail? Yet falter they did, facing humiliating charges of cowardice thereafter that cast a lingering shadow on the two regiments, despite their best efforts at redemption. By the end of the war, however, these charges were largely forgotten, replaced with the jingoistic rhetoric of martial heroism, a legacy that led many, including historians, to insist that all Civil War soldiers were heroes. *Dread Danger* creates a fuller understanding of the soldier experience and the overall costs and sufferings of war.

Lesley J. Gordon is the Charles G. Summersell Chair of Southern History at the University of Alabama. Her publications include *General George E. Pickett in Life and Legend* (Chapel Hill, NC: University of North Carolina Press, 1998) and *A Broken Regiment: The 16th Connecticut's Civil War* (Baton Rouge, LA: Louisiana State University Press, 2014).

Dread Danger

Cowardice and Combat in the American Civil War

LESLEY J. GORDON
The University of Alabama

CAMBRIDGE
UNIVERSITY PRESS

CAMBRIDGE
UNIVERSITY PRESS

Shaftesbury Road, Cambridge CB2 8EA, United Kingdom

One Liberty Plaza, 20th Floor, New York, NY 10006, USA

477 Williamstown Road, Port Melbourne, VIC 3207, Australia

314–321, 3rd Floor, Plot 3, Splendor Forum, Jasola District Centre,
New Delhi – 110025, India

103 Penang Road, #05–06/07, Visioncrest Commercial, Singapore 238467

Cambridge University Press is part of Cambridge University Press & Assessment,
a department of the University of Cambridge.

We share the University's mission to contribute to society through the pursuit of
education, learning and research at the highest international levels of excellence.

www.cambridge.org
Information on this title: www.cambridge.org/9781108492287

DOI: 10.1017/9781108679367

© Lesley J. Gordon 2025

This publication is in copyright. Subject to statutory exception and to the provisions
of relevant collective licensing agreements, no reproduction of any part may take
place without the written permission of Cambridge University Press & Assessment.

When citing this work, please include a reference to the DOI 10.1017/9781108679367

First published 2025

A catalogue record for this publication is available from the British Library.

A Cataloging-in-Publication data record for this book is available from the Library of
Congress.

ISBN 978-1-108-49228-7 Hardback
ISBN 978-1-108-72919-2 Paperback

Cambridge University Press & Assessment has no responsibility for the persistence
or accuracy of URLs for external or third-party internet websites referred to in this
publication and does not guarantee that any content on such websites is, or will
remain, accurate or appropriate.

Contents

Maps and Figures

Acknowledgments

The idea of this book began years ago, originating with my continued interest in the antiheroic, non-triumphant approach to war. Its early roots also stemmed from my exploration of wartime myths and the creation of historical narratives. I see it reemphasizing the complicated lived experience of Civil War soldiers that did not (and does not) always fit widely held popular expectations, then as much as now.

Through the years of researching and writing, I have amassed a good deal of debt to students, fellow scholars, librarians, archivists, friends, and family. For helping me to gather research, transcribe documents, and proof drafts, I thank Sean Briody, Trace Brusco, Susan Burneson, Shane Evans, Melissa Franson, Josh Keil, Brian Martin, Moyra Schauffler, Liz Stovall, and Luke Voyles. Andrew Deaton skillfully and efficiently translated several issues of a German newspaper for me; Bradley Smith helped create a roster and images of flags for this volume and designed the book's cover. A special callout to my University of Alabama graduate advisees, "the Little Regiment," for their encouragement and enthusiasm for this project, too.

Archivists who tracked down primary materials and provided copies, often from afar, include Carmelita G. Martinez, from the South Texas Archives & Special Collections, James C. Jernigan Library, at Texas A&M University – Kingsville; Gina Radandt, at the Kenosha Public Museum, Kenosha, Wisconsin; Trevor Plante, at the National Archives and Records Administration in Washington, DC; and Mary Ann Schneider, at the Texas Heritage Museum, at Hill College.

National Park historians and rangers were vital to this project from the start. They include Stacy Allen, John Castaldo, John Hennessy, Jennifer Leasor, Shannon Rowe, and Patrick Schroeder.

Fellow scholars and friends who listened, offered thoughtful commentary, and read (sometimes multiple) drafts include Kevin Adams, Steve Berry, Keith Bohannon, Peter Carmichael, Carole Emberton, Alice Fahs, Sarah Gardner, Judy Giesberg, David Gleeson, Megan Kate Nelson, Kenneth Noe, Mike Parrish, George Rable, Anne Sarah Rubin, David Silkenat, Diane Miller Sommerville, Chris Stowe, Amy Murrell Taylor, Patrick Troester, Chris Walsh, Sam Watson, Tim Williams, and Susannah Ural. I know this book has benefitted immensely from their input. A special thanks to Harry Smeltzer, who first suggested I look at the Fire Zouaves as a possible subject for this project. He was right!

I was fortunate to receive financial support from the General and Mrs. Matthew B. Ridgway Research Grant to travel and conduct research at the US Army Heritage and Education Center at the Army War College, Carlisle Barracks, PA in the summer of 2016. An Andrew W. Mellon Short-Term Research Fellowship allowed me to spend an incredibly productive month at the Huntington Library in San Marino, CA. I have benefitted, too, from the research funds allotted to me as the Charles G. Summersell Chair of Southern History at the University of Alabama.

I am also appreciative for the opportunity to present parts of this book to audiences throughout the United States and abroad, including the American History workshop at the University of Edinburgh; America's Civil War Museum in Richmond, VA; Auburn University; Mississippi State University; University of Southern Mississippi; Southern Methodist University; the University of Alabama; and West Virginia University.

Steve Harp, from my former institutional home the University of Akron, remains a dear friend and mentor. Kari Frederickson and Andrew Huebner at the University of Alabama have been great colleagues and supporters in the latter stages of the book.

The seed of this book began in 2002 when the late Michael Fellman was starting a new series at Johns Hopkins University Press on War, Culture, and Society. I ended up moving the project to Cambridge University Press after Michael's death, initially working with Debbie Gershenowitz, and then Cecelia Cancellaro. Cecilia helped shepherd the manuscript to completion, and I am very grateful for her support, especially through the pandemic. Victoria Phillips at Cambridge also assisted me with the final stages of the manuscript.

Finally, I thank my family: my parents, Fran and Robert Gordon; my husband, John, who expertly edited several drafts; and my children, Colin and Caitlyn, who have grown into funny, smart, kind, and amazing adults alongside of it. Our family dog Jupiter, too, deserves recognition for providing me with companionship during weeks and months of early morning writing. Juppy, we can take that walk now.

Abbreviations

ADAH	Alabama Department of Archives and History, Montgomery, AL
AGNY	*Annual Report of the Adjutant General of the State of New York for the Year 1899*
ALPL	Abraham Lincoln Presidential Library
CCWIC	Corinth Civil War Interpretive Center
CMSR	Compiled Military Service Records
DBC	Dolph Briscoe Center for American History
JCCW	Joint Committee on the Conduct of War
LOC	Library of Congress
MNHS	Minnesota Historical Society
NARA	National Archives and Records Administration
NYHS	New York Historical Society
NYSA	New York State Archives
NYSL	New York State Library
NYSMM	New York State Military Museum and Veterans Research Center
OR	*Official Records of the Union and Confederate Armies*
ORN	*Official Records of the Union and Confederate Navies*
OWCC	Old Warren County Courthouse
RM	The Rosenbach Museum
SNMP	Shiloh National Military Park
THM	Texas Heritage Museum
TSLAC	Texas State Library and Archives Commission

INTRODUCTION

"Almost Enough to Make Cowards of the Bravest Men"

On June 20, 1863, William Lovelace Foster, the regimental chaplain for the 35th Mississippi Infantry Regiment, wrote a long letter to his wife, Sarah, offering a detailed and firsthand account of the Vicksburg siege. By mid-June, Confederates were huddled in trench lines, knowing that time was not on their side; soldiers and civilians were growing desperate with little fresh water, food, or other basic supplies. Union forces inched closer, tightening their hold on the city, and seeking to wrest control of what was once considered the "Gibraltar of the Confederacy." Rifle and artillery fire was incessant, raging all day and into the night, for days and then weeks. Chaplain Foster reflected on the dire condition of the men as they tried to withstand the enemy's deadly fire but had to hold back from returning fire due to the scarcity of ammunition. It was a grueling and deadly waiting game. "Nothing is more painful – nothing is more demoralizing," he contended, "than to lie under a galling fire without the power of replying. It is enough to strike terror in the bravest heart – almost enough to make cowards of the bravest men!" Instead, he told his wife that when soldiers were "rushing to the charge or engaged in active conflict with the enemy, the stimulus of action & the engagedness of the mind hide from view the dread danger that returns." Having to lie and wait, however, exposed to such constant peril, and "at the mercy of those most terrible engines of destruction, the mind contemplates the danger without any stimulus of counteracting influence whatever." This wretched condition "was almost unbearable."[1]

---

[1] "William Lovelace Foster's Letter," June 20, 1863, in Kenneth Trist Urquhart, ed., *Vicksburg: Southern City under Siege: William Lovelace Foster's Letter Describing the*

Foster contemplated how the terror and trauma of battle could make even the bravest men cowards. For the Mississippi chaplain, it was the waiting and worrying and feeling defenseless that was so demoralizing. As a noncombatant, he no doubt spoke for himself as a white southern man as much as the soldiers he served. The label "coward" was freely applied to enemies, but also to one's own troops. The epithet shamed soldiers as much as it inspired action. It was a disgraceful insult to be sure, and a serious military crime according to both Confederate and US Articles of War, potentially punishable by death.[2] But beyond its military significance, it had greater impact. An 1863 letter to *The New York Times* explained: "The world has always specially honored courage and stigmatized cowardice. To be brave is as essential for a man as to be chaste is for a woman, and a coward among men is in as poor repute as a prostitute among women."[3]

"SECRET HISTORY OF THE FIGHT"

Civil War soldiers themselves certainly thought a good deal about what makes a man a coward, a skulker, or a croaker – all common

Defense and Surrender of the Confederate Fortress on the Mississippi (New Orleans, LA: The Historic New Orleans Collection, 1980), 10. At Vicksburg, the 35th Mississippi Infantry Regiment served alongside the 2nd Texas Infantry Regiment – one of the two units focused on in this book. Foster's letter begins on June 20, 1863, but then combines diary entries prior to that date, extending until the Confederate surrender on July 4, 1863.

[2] The US and Confederate *Articles of War* specified that misbehavior "before the enemy" could include a soldier or officer running away, "shamefully" abandoning one's post, or inducing others to do the same. The punishment, if found guilty, was death, "or such other punishment as shall be ordered by the sentence of a general court martial." See Section I, Article 52, Confederate States of America War Department, *Articles of War for the Government of the Army of the Confederate States* (Montgomery, AL: Barrett, Wimbish, Printers and Binders, 1861), 11. The same language appears in the US version. In 1863, the US War Department extended the punishment of "commissioned officers" "cashiered for cowardice" stipulating that "the crime, name, and place of abode, and punishment of the delinquent be published in the newspapers in and about the camp, and of the particular State from which the offender came, or where he usually resides; after which it shall be deemed scandalous for an officer to associate with him." See Appendix, Article 85, United States War Department, *Revised United States Army Regulations, 1861. With an Appendix Containing the Changes and Laws Affecting Army Regulations and Articles of War to June 25, 1863* (Washington; Government Printing Office. 1863), 498; see also Section I, Article 52, 493.

[3] "The Crime of Cowardice," "EBH" to the Editor, *The New York Times*, March 13, 1863. See also Lesley J. Gordon, "'Deeds of Brave Suffering and Lofty Heroism': Martialised Rhetoric and Kentucky Soldiers," *Register of the Kentucky Historical Society* Vol. 117, No. 2 (Spring 2019): 179–195.

contemporary synonyms for the term – and what makes a hero. They worried about it incessantly, not just green troops, but hardened veterans. As James McPherson observes in *For Cause and Comrades*: "Civil War soldiers wrote much about courage, bravery and valor – the three words meant the same thing." Yet he admitted that they "wrote even more about cowardice – the mark of dishonor."[4] Civil War soldiers, most historians affirm, subscribed to the mantra "Death before dishonor."[5] In his seminal book *Embattled Courage*, Gerald Linderman argues that there was a prevalent belief, especially early in the war, that "the brave would live and the cowardly would die."[6]

But relatively little has been published about the topic of cowardice in combat. Scholars who have examined the subject in any depth contend that nineteenth-century Americans grappled with the concept, struggling to differentiate it from lapses in moral character, physiological failings, or psychological weakness. As Chris Walsh explains, "a man who was a coward in war would be a coward everywhere else."[7] While the ignominy of being called a coward seemed nearly impossible to escape, definitions and understandings of this concept were clearly in flux. Central, too, to shifting definitions of manly courage and cowardice were acts of violence: withstanding them, performing them, and stoically witnessing them. Civil War soldiers could best vanquish allegations of cowardice through violent behavior. The notion of redemption through violence was a powerful one to mid-nineteenth-century Americans affected so deeply by the Christian revivalism of the Second Great Awakening. Many believed that suffering could be sublime and bring them purity, peace, and redemption from sin. Perhaps, then, it is not surprising that units (or individuals) accused of cowardice sought redemption through violence – displaying their fighting mettle in the field.[8]

[4] James McPherson, *For Cause and Comrades: Why Civil War Soldiers Fought in the Civil War* (New York: Oxford, 1997), 77.

[5] McPherson, *For Cause and Comrades*, 77.

[6] Gerald F. Linderman, *Embattled Courage: The Experience of Combat in the American Civil War* (New York: Free Press, 1987), 61.

[7] Chris Walsh, "'Cowardice Weakness or Infirmity, Whichever It May Be termed': A Shadow History of the Civil War," *Civil War History* Vol. 59, No. 4 (December 2013), 501. In 2015, Joseph Cook similarly observed that the "causes and effects of breakdowns in courage have rarely been explored" by Civil War scholars. See Joseph Cook, "The Future of Civil War Soldier Studies: The Failure of Courage," *Saber and Scroll* Vol. 3, Issue 4 (Fall 2014), 26.

[8] Walsh notes the direct tie between violence and redemption, in "Cowardice Weakness or Infirmity," 501; 500. Carole Emberton explores the implications of W.E.B. Du Bois' observation that for Black men to prove their manhood and bravery, they had to commit

Manly bravery manifested itself in ways other than the act of combat. It was also in soldiers' battle scars. Tattered flags, depleted ranks, and visible wounds: these were all concrete ways to quiet suspicions of skulking. Regiments with higher casualty numbers proudly proclaimed themselves "heroes." As William Fox explains in his *Regimental Losses in the American Civil War*: "Wars and battles are considered great in proportion to the loss of life resulting from them." "Bloodless battles," he writes, "excite no interest."[9]

Studying cowardice in any depth has just not proven to be satisfying or interesting to most Civil War historians. Bell Wiley wrote in 1943: "Cowardice under fire, being a less gratifying subject than heroism has not received much attention from those who have written or talked of the Confederate Army."[10] Chris Walsh, who in 2014 published the first monograph-length study on cowardice in American history and culture, bemoaned that "cowardice remains starkly underrepresented and under analyzed."[11] It is not that some occasional attention to the issue is entirely absent in the scholarship. Joseph Glatthaar in his 2008 study of General Lee's Army describes "large portions or entire regiments" of Confederates who broke and ran, for example, during the Seven Days Campaign. But Glatthaar, who admits to the shock and disaffection such behavior wrought, rather quickly dismisses instances of it. He concludes that cowardice was most upsetting to the men "who remained behind" and did "their duty."[12] Nonetheless, Glatthaar's book provides revealing insight. At one point, he quotes Col. Alfred H. Colquitt in a letter to a friend: "I witnessed acts of cowardice that is [sic] disgraceful to Southern character." Colquitt felt "discouraged and demoralized." He admitted, though, that few would ever learn about it publicly: "This is the secret history of the fight," he predicted, "which you will not see published."[13]

---

violence. See Carole Emberton, "'Only Murder Makes Men': Reconsidering the Black Military Experience," *Journal of the Civil War Era* Vol. 2, No. 3 (September 2012): 369–393.

[9] William F. Fox, *Regimental Losses in the American Civil War, 1861–1865: A Treatise on the Extent and Nature of the Mortuary Losses in the Union Regiments, with Full and Exhaustive Statistics Compiled from the Official Records on File in the State Military Bureaus and at Washington* (Albany, NY: Albany Publishing, 1889), 1.

[10] Bell I. Wiley, *The Life Of Johnny Reb, The Common Soldier of the Confederacy* (Indianapolis, IN: Bobbs-Merrill, 1943), 83.

[11] Chris Walsh, *Cowardice: A Brief History*, (Princeton, NJ: Princeton University Press, 2014), 14.

[12] Joseph T. Glatthaar, *General Lee's Army: From Victory to Collapse* (New York: The Free Press, 2008), 141.

[13] Quoted in Glatthaar, *General Lee's Army*, 142.

Colquitt's prediction proved prescient. To be sure, historians dating as far back as Bell Wiley have *acknowledged* the shirker, the croaker, and the skulk; but most, including Wiley, as well as Earl Hess, Joseph Glatthaar, and Aaron Sheehan-Dean, among others, have insisted that these instances encompassed a minority of soldiers, and thus do not merit serious extended discussion.[14] Hess contends that even something that looked like shirking really was not that at all: soldiers routinely "made a show of charging then stopped after their bravery could be verified by their commanders," erasing any hint that men felt fear or panic. This was a "common phenomenon in warfare," he argues, "the insistence by

[14] The general consensus among historians is that the majority of all Civil War soldiers fought well and behaved heroically in battle. For example, see James I. Robertson, Jr., *Soldiers Blue and Gray* (Columbia, SC: University of South Carolina Press, 1988); Earl J. Hess, *The Union Soldier in Battle: Enduring the Ordeal of Combat* (Lawrence, KS: University Press of Kansas, 1997); and McPherson, *For Cause and Comrades*. Gerald Linderman explores changing notions of courage and cowardice in *Embattled Courage*, but since his sources are mainly postwar and printed ones, it does make some of his conclusions suspect. Margaret Creighton sought to expand the definition of courage to include women, African Americans, and immigrant troops in *The Colors of Courage: Gettysburg's Forgotten History: Immigrants, Women, and African Americans in The Civil War's Defining Battle* (New York: Basic Books, 2005). Edward Ayers critiques the generalized and largely triumphant narrative accepted by scholars and the general public best in his piece "Worrying about the Civil War," in Karen Halttunen and Lewis Perry, eds., *Moral Problems in American Life: New Perspectives in Cultural History* (Ithaca, NY: Cornell University Press, 1998), 145–165. Ayers notes that the popular and dominant interpretation of the war stresses the "common bravery and hardships of soldiers North and South." See Ayers, 146. Glatthaar's *General Lee's Army* argues that the select group of men in Lee's Army were uniquely courageous, proudly independent, honor-bound, and fierce fighters. While acknowledging a handful of cowards and deserters, he is impressed there was not more disaffection given the odds Confederate faced. Aaron Sheehan-Dean also insists that a core group of Virginia soldiers fought defiantly and bravely until the very end. Both studies add to the perception that Confederate soldiers were uncommonly courageous, especially compared to their Union counterparts. See Aaron Sheehan-Dean, *Why Confederates Fought: Family and Nation in Civil War Virginia* (Chapel Hill, NC: University of North Carolina Press, 2007). In regard to Union soldiers faltering in battle, Earl Hess contends: "All the collateral evidence indicates the numbers were small and the incidents infrequent." see Hess, *The Union Soldier in Battle*, 82–93. Quote from 91. Mark A. Weitz acknowledges some volunteers in both armies who performed badly in battle, especially green troops, but still contends that "most Civil War soldiers performed admirably in combat." See Mark A. Weitz, "Drill, Training and the Combat Performance of the Civil War Soldier: Dispelling the Myth of the Poor Soldier, Great Fighter," *Journal of Military History* Vol. 62, No. 2 (April 1998): 269–270. See also Dora L. Costa and Matthew E. Kahn, *Heroes and Cowards: The Social Face of War* (Princeton, NJ: Princeton University Press, 2008). Costa and Kahn conflate desertion broadly defined with cowardice and only focus on Union soldiers. Joseph Cook also reflects on these gaps in the historiography and the distorted portrait it produces of a triumphant, exceptional American past, in "The Future of Civil War Studies," 33–34.

common soldiers that they had a right to decide how far they could be pushed into the cauldron." There were, he suggests, self-imposed and accepted "limits" to their bravery.[15] Authors of one of the most systematic examinations of Shiloh and the erratic performance of soldiers there conclude that, although there were many examples of battlefield coward-ice, these experiences had little lasting effect on the men or the armies at large. Joseph Allen Frank and George Reeves in *Seeing the Elephant: Raw Recruits At the Battle of Shiloh* explain soldiers' faltering in combat to be caused by their inexperience, ineffective weaponry, exposed flanks, fatigue, and paralyzing fear. Nonetheless, they insist that "no unit panicked to a man" and that in the end, "seeing the elephant" was not "such a wrenching experience that they would be forever transformed by its horrors."[16]

There are even some scholars who caution that studying this topic in any substantive way is irresponsible. Gary Gallagher and Kathryn Shively warn that cowardice is "a behavior very difficult to categorize in many ways," implying that trying to do so (and thus contributing to the sup-posed "dark turn" in the field of Civil War history) somehow makes soldiers helpless "victims." "The analytical risk of overemphasizing the dark side," they argue, "is that readers who do not know much about the war might infer that atypical experiences were in fact normative ones."[17] The implication from Gallagher, Shively, and other critics of the "dark turn" is that such scholarly focus somehow projects presentism and politicized agendas onto the past, distorting what actually happened.[18]

This study certainly does not contend that the majority of Civil War soldiers were cowards. Nonetheless, trepidation about the dreaded danger of mortal combat was an understandable and common

---

[15] Earl J. Hess, *Storming Vicksburg: Grant, Pemberton and the Battles of March 19–22, 1863* (Chapel Hill, NC: University of North Carolina Press, 2020), 292; and Hess, *Union Soldiers in Battle*, 82–88.

[16] Joseph Allen Frank and George Reeves, *Seeing the Elephant: Raw Recruits at the Battle of Shiloh* (Westport, CT: Greenwood Press, 1989), 114, 181. Larry J. Daniel mentions the allegations against the 2nd Texas at Shiloh described in this book without comment in *Shiloh: The Battle that Changed the Civil War* (New York: Simon and Schuster, 1997), 273. Wiley discusses the 2nd Texas and other units at Shiloh (and other battles) as "playing the coward," but he, too, concludes that these men were a minority. See Wiley, *Johnny Reb*, 80–89, quote from 84. Thus, even when cowardice is acknowledged, readers get little sense of the repercussions or broader context of such accusations or behavior.

[17] Gary W. Gallagher and Kathyrn Shively Meier, "Coming to Terms with Civil War Military History," *Journal of the Civil War Era* Vol. 4, No. 4 (December 2014): 492.

[18] The term "dark turn" seems to originate from Michael C.C. Adams' book *Living Hell: The Dark Side of the Civil War* (Baltimore, MD: Johns Hopkins University Press, 2014).

psychological response to their predicament. For mid-nineteenth-century Americans, the word "coward" suggested a failure or lack of manhood, and it was frequently applied to immigrants and Black men as inherent character flaws, with the expectation that white native-born males were naturally courageous; foreign-born and African Americans were not. For southern white men there was added meaning: equating southern courage with white male honor was intrinsic to upholding the powerful social structures of a patriarchal, slaveholding society, which historians have delineated as personal, often violent, and frequently enforced by fear of shame. Diane Miller Sommerville, in her important work on suicide, notes "extreme cases," where "the burden of anxiety about manly and honorable performance under fire" caused some southern white men to consider taking their own lives, rather than risk being labeled a coward.[19]

Two Civil War Regiments

This book looks at two regiments, one Union and one Confederate, both sent to war with sky-high expectations that they would fight bravely but found themselves instead tainted with the humiliating accusations of cowardice in combat. The 11th New York Volunteer Infantry consisted of city firemen, "known for their physical prowess, reckless bravery, courage, and swaggering bravado."[20] Raised by Col. Elmer E. Ellsworth, who had gained fame for his touring Chicago Zouaves the summer prior, these Fire Zouaves seemed destined for martial success. Confidence in the 2nd Texas Infantry was equally strong. These were white southern men and Texans, including veterans from the Texas Revolution. The eldest son of Governor Sam Houston was a private in the unit. Early in their service, however, both regiments faced shameful and very public charges

Besides Gallagher and Shively, critics of this approach include Peter S. Carmichael, "Relevance, Resonance, and Historiography: Interpreting the Lives and Experiences of Civil War Soldiers," *Civil War History* Vol. 62, No. 2 (June 2016): 170–185; and Wayne Hsieh, "'Go to Your Gawd Like a Soldier': Transnational Reflections on Veteranhood," *Journal of the Civil War Era* Vol. 5, No. 4 (December 2015): 551–577. See also Yael Sternhell's seminal article about a perceived anti-war shift in the field: Yael A. Sternhell, "Revisionism Reinvented? The Antiwar Turn in Civil War Scholarship," *The Journal of the Civil War Era* Vol. 3, No. 2 (June 2013): 239–256.

[19] Diane Miller Sommerville, "'A Burden Too Heavy to Bear': War Trauma, Suicide and Confederate Soldiers," *Civil War History*, Vol. 59, No. 4 (December 2013), 455, 462.

[20] Brian Pohanka, "Forward," in Brian C. Pohanka and Patrick A. Schroeder, eds., *With the 11th New York Fire Zouaves in Camp, Battle, and Prison: The Narrative of Private Arthur O'Neil Alcock in the New York Atlas and Leader* (Lynchburg, VA: Schroeder, 2011), 9.

of cowardice: the Fire Zouaves at the First Battle of Bull Run in July 1861, and the 2nd Texas Infantry at the Battle of Shiloh in April 1862. Rather than underplaying or ignoring these allegations, I take them seriously as the men did themselves, exploring their origins and lasting impact. And unlike historians who want to disregard such episodes or claim that they do not really matter, I contend that they mattered (and still do), since these indictments directly affected their regimental effectiveness, reputation, and ultimate fate as a unit.

In many ways these regiments shared similar histories. Both were raised early in the war, during the spring, summer, and fall of 1861. Both had devoted and impassioned colonels whose lives became intertwined with their commands and whose dramatic deaths became martyrized. Elmer E. Ellsworth was shot and killed in Alexandria, Virginia, by a civilian only a few weeks after departing with his men to the front; and William P. Rogers died in combat, leading his regiment against the fortifications at Corinth, Mississippi. In each regiment, members relied on and utilized the press to advocate for them and defend their reputations. For the Fire Zouaves, the influential New York media acted as both boosters and harsh critics. For the 2nd Texas, the *Weekly Telegraph* and its outspoken editor E. H. Cushing were mostly supportive, but there were cracks in that positive coverage, too.

Their differences were equally significant. Ellsworth's Fire Zouaves lasted for just over a year, eventually "disbanding itself" in June 1862.[21] The 2nd Texas served throughout the war, but after their capture and parole at Vicksburg, they were a shell of the original unit; a small contingency of the "Bloody 2nd" surrendered in June 1865, its ranks ravaged by disease, death, and demoralization.[22] The 11th New York faced harsher political attacks than the 2nd Texas, coming under formal investigation by Congress; while the 2nd Texas had powerful political leaders eager to defend them when public censure occurred. The 11th New York also included a good number of Irish immigrants, helping to fuel the criticism

---

[21] Charles McKnight Leoser, (n.d), 11th New York Volunteer Infantry, Regimental Returns, Volunteer Organizations, Office of the Adjutant General, Record Group 94, National Archives and Records Administration, Washington, DC. Hereafter referred to as RG 94, NARA. There were two New York City Fire Zouave regiments; Ellsworth's was the first, and the second (formerly designated the 73rd New York Infantry Regiment), mustered into service in July 1861, participated in active campaigning until the war's end, including fighting prominently at the Battle of Gettysburg.

[22] "Bloody 2nd" from William P. Rogers to Martha Rogers, April 18, 1862, in Eleanor Damon Pace, ed. "The Diary and Letters of William P. Rogers, 1846–1862," *Southwestern Historical Quarterly* Vol. 37, No. 4 (April 1929): 286.

against it from nativists and anti-Catholic detractors. The 2nd Texas originally included immigrants too, a company of German-born soldiers, but its identity was more closely tied to what Ashbel Smith, one of the founding members of the regiment, declared the "destiny allotted to the Anglo Saxon race."[23]

By concentrating on two regiments to study broader questions of war, this work continues an assertion I made in my book *A Broken Regiment: The 16th Connecticut's Civil War*, namely that we need to re-envision regimental histories and how to use them.[24] Too many academic historians have been quick to dismiss them as an amateur genre valued only for the source material that might be mined from them. This book narrates the stories of each regiment separately but with the larger themes of cowardice and heroism in mind. With that said, this book is not meant to be a comprehensive history of either unit. Instead, I use the accusations made concerning their cowardice in combat as a starting point to construct a new narrative, recounting their histories in two parallel sections with three chapters each. I describe the regiments' origins and leadership, then first battle, and the subsequent aftermath of the allegations. Sources are wide-ranging, including unpublished manuscripts, government records, contemporary newspapers, and official reports, as well as postwar regimentals and modern histories.

Although my focus is on these two regiments, individuals are important to this study, most notably officers. As elite white men, they provide a good deal of the primary source materials for this book, and by the nature of their power and positions, they helped shape the personalities and reputations of their regiments. They also bore the brunt of the criticism. In both the 2nd Texas and 11th New York, their slain colonels became permanently associated with them. Ellsworth's Fire Zouaves went to

---

[23] Ashbel Smith, *An Address Delivered in the City of Galveston on the 22d of February,1848, The Anniversary of the Birth Day of Washington and the Battle of Buena Vista* (Galveston, TX: News Office, 1848), 7; 11. Emphasis from original.

[24] Lesley J. Gordon, *A Broken Regiment: The 16th Connecticut's Civil War* (Baton Rouge, LA: Louisiana State University Press, 2014). See also Lesley J. Gordon, "Civil War Regiments," in Jon Butler, ed., *Oxford Research Encyclopedia of American History* (Oxford: Oxford University Press, 2021), accessed via oxfordre.com/americanhistory. Susannah Ural further discusses the significance of unit histories and ways to reimagine them as a genre. See Susannah J. Ural, *Hood's Texas Brigade: The Soldiers and Families of the Confederacy's Most Celebrated Unit* (Baton Rouge, LA: Louisiana State University Press, 2017). Another study that seeks to reconsider the unit history is Eric Michael Burke, *Soldiers from Experience: The Forging of Sherman's Fifteenth Corps, 1862–1863* (Baton Rouge, LA: Louisiana State University Press, 2022).

battle without their leader, yet their affiliation with him may have sealed their fate. Ellsworth was famous but he was also a polarizing figure, earning the disdain of professional army officers and New York Democrats for his avid support of and close relationship to Lincoln. His death at the hands of a civilian with a shotgun seems senseless and decidedly unsoldierly, even though he became a national martyr. His Fire Zouaves never really recovered from his loss. The 2nd Texas' original colonel, John C. Moore, was a blunt man who did not mince words when he felt his authority was challenged. But he struggled to clear his association with the shameful allegations from Shiloh. His successor, William P. Rogers, died what many called a hero's death leading a charge to atone for his regiment's soiled reputation as much as his own; yet there is also evidence of irrepressible fear and moral ambiguity in the final moments of his life.

"War Stories"

This reconsideration of two Civil War regiments allows for an exploration of the creation and dissemination of what historian Drew Gilpin Faust calls "war stories." Faust explains: "War and narrative in some sense create one another. Fighting is reconceived as war because of how humans write and speak about it; it is framed as a story with a plot that imbues its actors with both individual and shared purpose and is intended to move toward victory for one or another side. To rename violence as war is to give it teleology." Faust further observes that war "assumes a trajectory towards victory," and yet armed combat is fundamentally non-linear and chaotic; stories and histories are created to make order out of chaos. But not just any order; order that as Faust suggests leads to triumph and inspiration. This is the "highly conventionalized heroic account of combat" that remains in American popular culture and has, as Faust maintains, "shaped not just the rhetoric and assumptions of military history, but more powerfully and more dangerously, the understanding and seduction of war itself." Faust states: "Tales of glory, honor, manhood and sacrifice enhance war's attraction and mobilize men and armies."[25]

[25] Drew Gilpin Faust, "Telling War Stories: Reflections of a Civil War Historian," National Endowment for the Humanities Lecture (2011), www.neh.gov. Faust's observations, however, are not necessarily true for all times and places. Holly Furneaux, for example, in her work on British soldiers and civilians during the Crimean War argues there were competing narratives challenging the "normalized hyper-aggressive tale" of soldiers killing without reflection and describes a "very different rhetorical and narratological

Such tales saturated the world which these men inhabited and can, at times, appear overly jingoistic and superficial.[26] But as Faust recognizes, this rhetoric of martial heroism had a practical purpose in motivating men to go to war. And once one starts to look, it is not difficult to find frequent mentions of cowardice, sometimes in contrast to that very same rhetoric. Battle reports, drafted by officers soon after the fight, were some of the first efforts to seek to "organize the violence of the battlefield" and craft those war stories.[27] It is here that we can find a good deal of discussion about cowardice, as much as bravery. Commanders sometimes hesitated to single out individuals for praise, maintaining that by doing so, they might overlook someone just as worthy. Confederate Brig. Gen. Albert Rust spoke for many when he stated after Corinth: "When all behaved so well the commanding general will not hazard injustice to others by mentioning those who particularly attracted his notice."[28] Singling out cowards by name or by unit, however, was more common than one might expect; certainly more than many historians would lead us to believe. But as Confederate Brig. Gen. John S. Bowen wrote in his report of Corinth: "I know of no better way of rewarding the 2,000 brave men than by casting out the two or three cowards who happened to be among them." He went on to name soldiers from the 15th Mississippi Infantry, demanding that the commissioned officer be "dismissed in disgrace" and that three men in the ranks to be "drummed out of service and their names published, with the sentence attached."[29]

Admittedly, this is not the story of actors without a voice; mainly my focus here are white men with authority and agency. It is not that one cannot find evidence of their failings – there are examples readily available in the historical record. Still, due to the societal expectations of manhood and the demands of a state at war, portions of their military

---

impulse" at work "in which tales of violence are swiftly rerouted into ameliorative stories of healing and restoration, physical and emotional." See Holly Furneaux, *Military Men of Feeling: Emotion, Touch and Masculinity in the Crimean War* (Oxford: Oxford University Press, 2016), 1–2.

[26] Jason Phillips offers an insightful essay on the topic of overgeneralizing common soldiers' experiences in "Battling Stereotypes: A Taxonomy of Commons Soldiers in Civil War History," *History Compass* Vol. 6, No. 6 (November 2008): 1407–1425.

[27] James Dawes, *The Language of War: Literature and Culture in the U.S. from the Civil War through World War II* (Cambridge, MA: Harvard University Press, 2005), 40.

[28] Albert Rust to Edward Ivy, October 13, 1862, *War of the Rebellion: A Compilation of the Official Records of the Union and Confederate Armies*: 128 vols (Washington, DC: Government Printing Office, 1880–1901), Ser. 1, Vol. 17, pt. 1, 409. Hereafter referred to as OR.

[29] John S. Bowen to Edward Ivy, October 12, 1862, OR, Ser. 1, Vol. 17, pt. 1, 413–14.

records were muted; specific charges quickly challenged and often expunged from public memory. In this light, it is not surprising then that most scholarly and public accounts of Civil War soldiers fail to acknowledge cowardice or, if they do, they explain or dismiss it as an anomaly.

These allegations mattered. We know this because people of the time told us. Survivors of the Fire Zouaves returned home to New York City despondent and despairing that they would be attacked so viciously in print. Col. William P. Rogers wrote his wife in shock that there were rumors that his Texans had behaved badly at Shiloh. Public accusations of cowardice undeniably humiliated the men of the 11th New York and 2nd Texas. All of this added another layer to the trauma soldiers endured from combat. Members fervently sought to expunge the insult to their reputation as men and as soldiers. And in some ways, they were successful: their "secret histories" have been largely forgotten and overlooked by historians. Still, there was a cost to those efforts: reputations destroyed, and lives sacrificed in order to redeem themselves with what novelist Stephen Crane famously called a "red badge of courage."[30]

Overall, then, cowardly behavior and accusations were part and parcel of the Civil War battlefield experience, happening with greater frequency than historians typically have been willing to acknowledge. In this regard, it is not unreasonable to suggest that the terror and trauma of violent war was enough to make "cowards of the bravest men" on much more than a few isolated occasions. Individuals faltered in combat, but so too did large numbers of men, even entire units. The impact was significant not only on battle plans and the war effort but on soldiers' subsequent lives – their well-being and their reputations, not to mention the effect it also had on their families and communities. In any event, to explore the complexities surrounding this issue in some depth is not to demonize the soldiers, units, or regiments accused of such actions; if anything, it is meant to provide a fair hearing to their predicaments, to humanize their struggles by delving into the mental challenges and moral ambiguities that informed them. By recognizing this unvarnished reality, we can understand more fully the Civil War soldier experience.

---

[30] Stephen Crane, *The Red Badge of Courage: An Episode of the American Civil War* (New York: D. Appleton, 1895). A recent exploration of the novel's lasting significance is Kevin J. Hayes, *At War with the Red Badge of Courage: A Critical and Cultural History* (Rochester, NY: Camden House, 2021).

PART I

THE 11TH NEW YORK VOLUNTEER
INFANTRY REGIMENT

"Soldiers, and Yet Not Soldiers": New York and Washington, DC

"Instant Service"

On April 18, 1861, an article appeared in the *New York Tribune* announcing the formation of a "Zouave Regiment," modeled after the colorfully uniformed North African troops known for their gymnastic aptitude, fearless swagger, and elite fighting abilities.[1] Less than a week prior, Fort Sumter had fallen to the Confederacy, President Lincoln called for 75,000 militia volunteers to quell the rebellious South, and Virginia seceded from the Union. Regiments north and south formed quickly, and war seemed imminent, with most Americans convinced that any sort of armed conflict would be quick and relatively bloodless. For this new unit of Zouaves, however, only a certain class of men qualified: New York City

---

[1] The First New York Fire Zouaves or 11th New York Volunteer Infantry was one of more than seventy Union regiments (and some twenty-five Confederate units) raised during the Civil War that tried in varying ways to adopt the dress, manner, and drill of the original North Algerian and then French-born Zouaves. For an overview of Zouave Civil War regiments, see Michael Kalu, "Fierce and Colorful: Zouave Regiments in the Civil War," War History Online, www.warhistory.com. For more on Zouaves and Americans' attraction to them, see Timothy Marr, *The Cultural Roots of American Islamicism* (Cambridge: Cambridge University Press, 2006), 265–266, 294. Gerald Wheeler notes that Zouave units attracted men who wanted to appear in an "elite regiment." Yet he states, "this very sense of selectiveness made discipline a major problem." See Gerald E. Wheeler, "D'Epineuil's Zouaves," *Civil War History* Vol. 2, No. 4 (December 1956): 99. See also Carol E. Harrison and Thomas J. Brown, *Zouave Theaters: Transnational Military Fashion and Performance* (Baton Rouge, LA: Louisiana State University Press, 2024); Daniel J. Miller, *American Zouaves, 1859–1959: An Illustrated History* (Jefferson, NC: McFarland, 2019). Parts of this chapter and Chapter 2 previously appeared in "'Novices in Warfare': Elmer E. Ellsworth and Militia Reform on the Eve of Civil War," *Journal of Civil War Era* Vol. 11, No. 2 (June 2021): 194–223, published by the University of North Carolina Press.

volunteer firemen.[2] The *Tribune* attested that firemen possessed the perfect combination of physical and mental prowess: "As men of steady nerves, unflinching courage, of the cool temper which the habit of facing danger alone can give, built up with muscles of steel, and of an indomitable power of endurance, they are just the men for that service." They were, the *Tribune* described, "soldiers, and yet not soldiers; men who had just drill enough for the habit of it, but without any that would interfere with the acquisition of new tactics."[3] Leaders of the city's fire department quickly joined the call, urging their members to "turn out" and "join a regiment of firemen who can sustain the name of the New York Fire Department under any and all circumstances."[4] Nearly every fire station became a recruiting office, and hundreds of men excitedly signed up to serve.[5] In just over a week, thousands of dollars were raised, uniforms procured, and the Fire Zouaves, as they were quickly known, had more than 1,000 volunteers in their ranks.[6] In a letter pledging funds from individual members of the

---

[2] Additional qualifications called for: "Men between the ages of twenty-one and thirty-five, and over five feet two and a half inches, and under five feet ten inches." See *The New York Times*, April 21, 1861. Not every member of the unit was a fireman, but the majority were. It is also significant that most of the officers were firemen, with the notable exceptions of Elmer E. Ellsworth, Adjutant Charles McKnight Leoser, a recent West Point graduate, and nearly all the first lieutenants, who were former Chicago Zouaves.

[3] *New York Tribune*, April 18, 1861.

[4] *New York Herald*, April 19, 1861. Fire Department Chief John Decker and several other assistant engineers signed this appeal. Decker, as chief engineer, was elected every three years by the volunteers. See Augustine E. Costello, *Our Firemen: A History of the New York Fire Department* (New York: Augustine E. Costello, 1887), 126.

[5] There were 123 firehouses in New York City with more than 4,000 members in 1861. See John Mulligan, "'Trial by Fire,' the Story of the Fire Zouaves," *WNYF: With the New York Firefighters* Vol. 48 (1987): 8; New York Military Museum, Saratoga Springs, NY (hereafter referred to as NYSMM). Costello calculates 4,227 members of the Fire Department's "working force" in 1860. See Costello, *Our Firemen*, 140.

[6] *The New York Times*, April 27, 1861; *New York Leader*, April 27, 1861. The Zouave Fire Regiment Fund Committee quickly formed with Adolphus F. Ockerhausen as chairman, George F. Nesbitt as secretary, and James Kelly as treasurer. Kelly got to work writing letters to men well connected with the city's fire department, inviting them to his home on the night of April 19 to help organize the regiment and raise funds. By April 24, the committee had raised $12,000, including $1,000 from the "New York Board of Brokers." See James Kelly to Henry B. Venn, April 19, 1861; Minutes of April 24, 1861 meeting; William Wright to James Kelly, April 20, 1861; James Kelly to George F. Nesbit, April 19, 1861, all in the Folder 2, Box 8, Administrative Correspondence Files, Series A4111, Bureau of Military Statistics, New York State Archives, Albany, NY (hereafter referred to as NYSA). See also *New York Tribune*, April 22, 1861. Adolphus F. Ockerhausen was a "well-known and wealthy sugar refiner," who died in 1877. See *Railroad Gazette* (New York, NY), Vol. 9 (April 27, 1877): 189.

New York Stock Exchange, William Irving Graham expressed his and his fellow brokers' appreciation for "our red shirt" and "gallant friends," confident that the firemen would "never prove unworthy of the generosity extended to them."[7] The regiment of "brave firemen" was, the press declared, "ready for instant service."[8]

Elmer E. Ellsworth, the Fire Zouaves' twenty-four-year-old commander, already had a national reputation as the "finest drill officer of his age."[9] During the summer of 1860, he toured the country exhibiting his Chicago Zouaves, an elite company of militia volunteers who perfected gymnastic-like drills and carefully coordinated maneuvers. Clad in flamboyant uniforms, Ellsworth and his cadets impressed audiences and received mostly rave reviews from the press. Their performances, which lasted hours, attracted tens of thousands of spectators. When they visited Washington, DC, in August 1860, *The Baltimore Sun* described the Zouaves executing "the finest display of manual exercise ever witnessed here." President James Buchanan praised them as models of citizen soldiery. "I wish you prosperity and happiness in peace," Buchanan told the cadets; "should war come I know where you will be."[10]

Now Civil War *had* come, and Ellsworth rushed to participate. He had been dreaming of being a soldier since he was a boy in upstate New York. His family had struggled to make ends meet, and as a teen he had ventured off to New York City and later Chicago to support himself and his parents.[11] Still, the military beckoned. Ellsworth initially

---

[7] See W. Irving Graham to George Nesbit, April 24, 1861, Folder 2, Box 8, Administrative Correspondence Files, Series A4111, Bureau of Military Statistics, NYSA.

[8] "brave firemen" from the *New York Herald*, April 19, 1861; "ready for instant service" from the *New York Daily Tribune*, April 20, 1861. Ellsworth won the endorsement of *New York Tribune* editor Horace Greeley, who helped him with a "well planned system of placarding" to stir enlistments. See William D. Kelley, "The Assassination of Ellsworth," *The Graphic News* (Cincinnati, OH) Vol. 1, No. 4 (July 21, 1886), in Newspaper Clippings, Frank E. Brownell Papers, Minnesota Historical Society, St. Paul, MN (hereafter referred to as MNHS). Kelley was long-serving Pennsylvania Republican congressman.

[9] *Chicago Tribune*, March 20, 1861.

[10] *Baltimore Sun*, August 6, 1860.

[11] Ellsworth's biographers emphasize his modest beginnings and the impoverishment of his parents, apparently struck hard by the Panic of 1837. See, for example, Charles Ingraham, *Elmer E. Ellsworth and the Zouaves of '61* (Chicago, IL: University of Chicago Press, 1925), 5; Ruth Painter Randall, *Colonel Elmer Ellsworth: A Biography of Lincoln's Friend and First Hero of the Civil War* (Boston, MA: Little, Brown, 1960), 11–12.

sought an appointment to the United States Military Academy at West Point, but lacking political connections or adequate education to pass the qualifying exams, he turned toward the volunteer militia. By the age of twenty, he served as a drill instructor to various militia companies in Illinois and Wisconsin. In 1858, he sought to raise a unit of volunteers to fight in what looked like a war with Mormons in Utah territory, and in September 1859, he gained appointment as Assistant Adjutant General and Paymaster for the State of Illinois. In the meantime, he was accumulating political connections, too, including, most notably, the soon-to-be president Abraham Lincoln. The outbreak of war seemed to position Ellsworth in an ideal situation, with the right contacts and experience to secure a commission and make his dream of military command a reality.[12]

Ellsworth had also developed an elaborate plan that was as much about reforming young white working-class men like himself as it was about revitalizing the volunteer militia. The Chicago Zouaves had to follow his own strict "Golden Resolutions," which banned alcohol, profanity, and other perceived sinful behaviors. In essence, he wanted to mold men as much as transform the militia system and reconfigure the volunteer American soldier as respectable as any other professional class. In his proposed legislation, which he first tried at the state level, and then nationally, the militia would be not only more efficient in times of crisis, but more valued and admired. In doing so, Ellsworth was revisiting a perennial question of US military policy: Could the citizen soldier be relied upon for national defense?[13]

Ellsworth fervently believed that he could single-handedly transform Americans' attitudes toward citizen soldiers. With the outbreak of the Civil War, it seemed that his moment had come.

---

[12] Biographical details on Ellsworth can be found in Randall, *Colonel Elmer Ellsworth*; and Ingraham, *Elmer E. Ellsworth*. These works are decidedly hagiographical, yet they contain valuable insights into his life, particularly his boyhood and struggles as a young man. A more recent and somewhat better-balanced biography of Ellsworth is Meg Groeling, *First Fallen: The Life of Colonel Elmer Ellsworth, the North's First Civil War Hero* (El Dorado Hills, CA: Savas Beatie, 2021).

[13] Ellsworth detailed his "Militia Bill" in an interview with the *New York Herald*, February 16, 1861. For more on the citizen-soldier ideal, militias, and attitudes toward them in American antebellum society, see Russell Weigley, *The American Way of War: A History of United States Military Strategy and Policy* (New York: Macmillan, 1973), 54; also Marcus Cunliffe, *Soldiers and Civilians: The Martial Spirit in America, 1775–1865* (Boston, MA: Little, Brown, 1968). I expand on Ellsworth's prewar ambitions to reform the militia in Gordon, "'Novices in Warfare,'" 194–223.

"AFFECT RECKLESSNESS"

Ellsworth did not return to Chicago to command his original company. Instead, he did something entirely new: he raised his regiment of New York City Firemen, intending to train them to be Zouaves.[14] There are conflicting accounts about whether Ellsworth went to New York with "orders, without assistance or authority" or had Lincoln's approval.[15] Nonetheless, he had apparently been thinking about this idea for some time, assuming that firemen would make excellent soldiers.[16] Ellsworth "had this fire brigade on the brain," his friend and fellow Chicago Zouave Edward B. Knox explained, "and nothing would stop him." To Ellsworth, "the New York firemen were his beau ideals of soldiers in embryo."[17]

This "class of men," Ellsworth presumed, would be, in the words of a postwar account, "best adapted from their accustomed exposure to privations, for the Zouave discipline."[18] "I want the New York Firemen," he

[14] As already mentioned, Ellsworth's Fire Zouaves were not the only Zouave unit raised that spring of 1861 and styled after his original Chicago company. Rush C. Hawkins, who created the "First Regiment New York Zouaves," claimed to be the "first organizer of a Zouave company in this city." See *New York Herald*, April 19, 1861. See also *The Daily True Delta* (New Orleans, LA), January 23, 1861, which includes a story about raising a "Military Organization of the Firemen" in New Orleans. Another reason why Ellsworth did not return to Chicago may have been dissent within his original company and continuing resentments toward his command style. See E. M. Coates to Elmer Ellsworth, February 11 and 14, 1861, Box 1; John C. Revere Reynolds to Elmer E. Ellsworth, March 6 and 14, 1861, Box 2, Elmer Ellsworth Papers, Brown University, Providence, RI.

[15] Eugene Arus Nash, *History of the Forty-Fourth New York Volunteer Infantry in the Civil War, 1861–1865* (Chicago, IL: R. R. Donnelley, 1911), 4. For more on Ellsworth's decision to go to New York and raise a regiment of firemen, see Henry Wisner, "Annals of the War: Chapters of Unwritten History How Ellsworth Fell, The Tragic Episode in Alexandria at the Outbreak of War," in the *Weekly Times* (Philadelphia, PA), December 29, 1883; New York State, *Fifth Annual Report of the Chief of the Bureau of Military Statistics* (Albany, NY: C. Van Benthuysen Steam Printing House, 1868), 173–174; "Zouaves of Years Ago," the *Chicago Herald* reprinted in the *Troy Observer*, (Troy, NY) June 5, 1887, from Newspaper Clippings, Brownell Papers, MNHS; *Chicago Tribune*, May 29, 1887. According to novelist Henry Morford, Ellsworth "made many valuable acquaintances in New York" during his 1860 tour with the Chicago Zouaves, and "witnessed the bravery, agility and rattling character of the New York firemen." Henry Morford, *Days of Shoddy: A Novel of the Great Rebellion in 1861* (Philadelphia, PA: J. B. Person & Brothers, 1863), 142.

[16] *Chicago Tribune*, May 25, 1861; reprinted in the *Illinois Daily State Journal* (Springfield, IL), May 28, 1861.

[17] *Chicago Tribune*, May 29, 1887, Newspaper Clippings, Brownell Papers, MNHS.

[18] "11th Regiment, New York Volunteer Infantry Historical Sketch," in State of New York, *Third Annual Report of the Bureau of Military Record of the State of New York* (Albany, NY: G. Wendell Printer, 1866), 105–106.

explained, "for there are no more effective men in the country, and none with whom I can do so much. They are sleeping on a volcano at Washington and I want men who can go into a fight now."[19] Others agreed. The *New York Daily Tribune*, for example, proclaimed: "No better material for soldiers than our firemen can be found in the world."[20] Thus, despite Ellsworth's years of experience as a drill master, and his repeated insistence that intensive training and strict discipline made effective soldiers, he now claimed he could transform these volunteers into "efficient Zouaves" in a matter of days.[21]

In his impatience to form the regiment, though, Ellsworth failed to make allowance for how challenging it would be to train them quickly.[22] To assist him, Ellsworth recruited several of his original Chicago Zouaves to serve as first lieutenants; however, the men in the ranks selected their company captains, and "seemed to consider the only qualifications necessary for the office were their ability to do considerable 'heavy swearing' and put out fires."[23] Company E initially did not have one of the original Chicago Zouaves assigned to it. The company's first lieutenant was William R. W. Chambers, a popular fellow fireman, but tardy in joining the regiment due to the death of his young daughter. Pvt. Harrison H. Comings insisted though that this was an advantage for the company, motivating them to work all the more earnestly "to perfect themselves" in its complexities without an officer familiar with the drill to instruct them.[24]

---

[19] Quoted in Ingraham, *Elmer E. Ellsworth*, 127. I have been unable to find contemporary corroboration of this quote, so it may be apocryphal.

[20] *New York Daily Tribune*, April 30, 1861.

[21] *New York Daily Tribune*, April 18, 1861. See also *The New York Times*, April 18, 1861.

[22] Morford, *Days of Shoddy*, 142.

[23] E. B. Knox, "How Ellsworth Died," *Sunday Herald* (Chicago, IL), May 24, 1885, in Newspaper Clippings, Brownell Papers, MNHS. Former Chicago Zouaves in the 11th New York included 1st Lt. E. B. Knox (Co. A), 1st Lt. Lucius Larrabee (Co. B), 1st Lt. Edwin M. Coates (Co. C), 1st Lt. Freeman Conner (Co. D), 1st Lt. Frank Yates (Co. G), Charles A. Bell (Co. H), 1st Lt. George Harris Fergus (Co. K), and 1st Lt. Stephen Stryker (Co. B). See "Eleventh Infantry," roster included in the *Annual Report of the Adjutant General of the State of New York for the Year 1899. Registers of the Sixth, Seventh, Seventh Veterans, Eighth, Ninth, and Eleventh Regiments of Infantry Transmitted to the Legislature February 5, 1900.* Serial No. 18 included in *Documents of the Assembly of the State of New York, One Hundred and Twenty-Third Session* Vol. X, No. 58, Part 3. (Albany, NY: James B. Lyon, State Printer, 1900), 1078, 1096, 1099, 1121, 1154, 1155, 1205, 1222 (hereafter referred to as AGNY). All ten of the company captains were members of the fire department. See Costello, *Our Fireman*, 718.

[24] Harrison H. Comings, *Personal Reminiscences of Co. E, N.Y. Fire Zouaves Better Known as Ellsworth's Fire Zouaves.* (Malden, MA: J. Gould Tilden, 1886), 4. The death of

Firemen frequently had to rush headlong into danger, refusing to show or admit any trepidation. In many ways, they seemed to epitomize widely held idealized conceptions of nineteenth-century white male courage.[25] Firemen also had a reputation for rabblerousing, bravado, and willfulness. Critics likened them to ruthless street gangs, fiercely competing against one another to put out fires that plagued the city.[26] The fact that a sizable contingency was Irish Catholic and working class only added to their perceived unfettered virility.[27] The English novelist Charles Dickens,

Chambers' two-year-old daughter, Minnie Eloise, who died on April 29, and chronic illness caused Chambers' continued absence in camp. Nonetheless, Company E would later gain recognition from Gen. William B. Franklin as the best company in the regiment. See William B. Franklin to S. Williams, August 9, 1861, 11th New York, Muster Rolls, Returns, Regimental Papers, RG 94, NARA. For more on Chambers, see *The New York Times*, April 30, 1861; *New York Daily Tribune*, May 2, 1861; A. O. Alcock, Letter to the Editor, May 29, 1861; *New York Leader*, June 1, 1861; A. O. Alcock, Letter to the Editor, June 19, 1861; *New York Leader*, June 1861 in Pohanka and Schroeder, eds., *With the 11th New York*, 92, 120. In the 1860 census, Chambers is listed as twenty-nine years old and a clerk with two children (including Minnie). He and his wife Mary ran a boarding house. See Eighth Census of the United States, 1860: Population Schedule, New York Ward 10 District 4, New York, Records of the Bureau of the Census, RG 29, NARA, accessed via ancestry.com. Chambers' younger brother Thomas was private in Co. E and killed at the Battle of Bull Run. See AGNY, 1094; and Costello, *Our Firemen*, 489.

[25] Scholars have noted competing notions of manhood in flux during the long nineteenth century, demarcated by class, race, and ethnicity. See Gail Bederman, *Manliness and Civilization: A Cultural History of Gender and Race in the United States, 1880–1917* (Chicago, IL: University of Chicago Press, 1995). Amy Greenberg, *Manifest Manhood and the Antebellum American Empire* (Cambridge: Cambridge University Press, 2005); Lorien Foote, *The Gentleman and the Roughs: Violence, Honor and Manhood in the Union Army* (New York: New York University Press, 2010).

[26] Pohanka, "Foreword," in Pohanka and Schroeder, eds., *With the 11th New York Fire*, 9. Problems with the "disreputable element" of the firemen can be traced to their early beginnings in the late eighteenth century. In an 1887 history of the New York City Fire Department, the author recognized "the existence of a rowdy crowd" within the ranks, which remained despite repeated efforts to weed them out. This fighting between companies and "spirit of rowdyism" impaired "its character and efficiency." See Costello, *Our Firemen*, 115–116. Costello also maintained that a "superior class of men" composed the volunteer fire department (148).

[27] For more on Irish immigrants and their service in the Union army, see Susannah Ural Bruce, *The Harp and the Eagle: Irish American Volunteers and the Union Army, 1861–1865* (New York: New York University Press, 2006); Damian Shiels, *The Irish in the American Civil War* (Dublin: The History Press of Ireland, 2013). David T. Gleeson offers an examination of Irish Confederates and a list of common Irish surnames in his appendix. Based on his list, there were approximately 208 men with Irish surnames in the 11th New York or just under 20 percent of the regiment. See David T. Gleeson, *The Green and the Gray: The Irish in the Confederate States of America* (Chapel Hill, NC: University of North Carolina Press, 2013), 225–227. For these Irish members, their identity seemed layered as immigrants, firemen, and Zouaves. No doubt, some of the negative attention they garnered came from the anti-Catholic and anti-immigrant sentiment of the time.

who observed them during a visit to the city, reasoned that "fireman's service" as compared to that of the militia was more popular because it was "not so restrained and monotonous as that of the militiaman's." Noting their red flannel shirts, "leather helmet bound with brass," black handkerchiefs tied in "jaunty tailor knots," Dickens wrote: "It is evidently the manner with them to affect recklessness, so as not to appear to be drilled or drummed about to the detriment of their brave democratic freedom uniform."[28]

Dickens sensed the very real challenges in trying to make soldiers out of firemen. They were fearless; no one doubted that, and their bravery seemed to be part of their moral constitution. But that recklessness, so central to their self-identity, would prove to be a detriment to their wartime service. In his famous exposition of the golden mean in the *Nicomachean Ethics*, the Classical Greek philosopher Aristotle noted that an excess of fearlessness was actually rashness, and thus not properly modulated and genuine courage at all. In effect, just as a lack of courage could result in cowardice, too much boldness could get one into trouble, recklessly exacerbating a dangerous situation rather than effectively resolving it. In this regard, while these men were initially lauded for their fearless behavior as firemen, later concerns would emerge about their moral disposition and judgment – particularly their unruliness, their disobedience, and their impatience.[29] For instance, a later account of the unit explained that they would have been fine in the fight; it was the tediousness of camp life and drilling that was problematic for them: "To select such a regiment composed of elements so peculiar and so thoroughly permeated with the spirit of intrepid bravery – a spirit that regards the most heroic deeds in the light of everyday achievements – for the dull routine of permanent garrison duty, was a blunder."[30]

In truth, bold and brash men did not, and do not, always make effectual soldiers. This was a lesson yet to be learned in the early months of the Civil War. In April 1861, before any real fighting had commenced, it appeared

---

[28] Charles Dickens, "American Volunteer Fireman," *All the Year Round*, March 16, 1861. For more on the political and economic culture of volunteer firemen, see Amy Greenberg, *Cause for Alarm: The Volunteer Fire Department in the Nineteenth-Century City* (Princeton, NJ: Princeton University Press, 1998).

[29] Aristotle, *Nicomachean Ethics* (1115b.7 to 1116a.15), from "What Is Courage and How It Stands between Cowardice and Rashness," Aristotelian Philosophy, translated by George Kotsalis, www.aristotelianphilsophy.com. See also Walsh, *Cowardice*, 5.

[30] Costello, *Our Firemen*, 722–723.

uncontested that men already proven to be fearless in peacetime would easily translate that same valor to the battlefield.[31]

"RESTLESS SPIRITS"

Soldiers, even the most seemingly courageous, require basic necessities: guns, uniforms, and rations for starters. Ellsworth had promised brand new Sharps rifles, bowie knives, and bright ostentatious uniforms, like that of "the famous Imperial Zouaves."[32] Yet, obtaining these items quickly, and in adequate numbers and good quality, proved a serious challenge for local and state officials. The country was hastening to war at breakneck speed, but few Americans really had any experience at all dealing with the basic logistics of arming and preparing tens of thousands of volunteers for the battlefront.[33] One private likened their original uniform to a "butterfly costume," cheaply made with inadequate insulation for cool nights or dewy mornings.[34] When crates of used, rusty muskets were delivered to the regiment, the men balked at unpacking them. Colonel Ellsworth had to request assistance from Chester A. Arthur, New York's assistant quarter-master, who called in the local police and allegedly "put the ringleaders under arrest." The muskets were unpacked but never used.[35]

[31] In August 1860, there had been an attempt to create a Zouave militia unit of New York City firemen soon after the Chicago Zouaves' performance there. The "military duties" were not to "interfere with the business of extinguishing fires, but are intended to afford innocent amusement to the firemen; and by creating direct social intercourse between the members it is thought it would break down those strong company distinctions and animosities which now exist," to make them "more united, and harmonious." As the *New York World* explained, the purpose of such a unit "is to keep men out of the rum-shops," and "break them of playing cards" and "cursing and swearing." See *New York World*, August 14, 1860. As mentioned in my introduction, the opposite was also assumed to be true: cowards in peace would be cowards in war. See Walsh, "'Cowardice Weakness or Infirmity,'" 501.

[32] *The New York Times*, April 18, 1861. Sharps rifles were breech-loading guns with relatively long-range accuracy, designed for rapid firing and maneuvering. They proved expensive to manufacture and thus ended up reserved for elite sharpshooting units. See Fred Ray, "Picketing, Skirmishing and Sharpshooting," Essential Civil War Curriculum, www.essentialcivilwarcurriculum.com.

[33] A few days before their departure south, the regiment was also short on funds despite the thousands of dollars raised. See *The New York Times*, April 27, 1861.

[34] A. O. Alcock complained about the lack of proper clothing and arms repeatedly in his published letters to New York newspapers. See, for example, A. O. Alcock, Letter to the Editor, May 10, 1861, *New York Leader*, May 11, 1861, in Pohanka and Schroeder, eds., *With the 11th New York*, 53–54.

[35] This story about the Fire Zouaves refusing to open boxes of muskets is repeated in biographies of Arthur, including the most recent by Scott S. Greenberger, *The*

FIGURE 1.1 "Colonel Ellsworth's New York Fire Zouaves." Image courtesy of *Harper's Weekly*, May 18, 1861.

As they waited for their promised Sharps rifles, there were reports that "great dissatisfaction exists among our gallant volunteer firemen, that no arms have been furnished them." *The New York Times*, though, insisted: "They will never desert – no fireman would do that – but they declare they will not go on till they have something better than their bare fists to fight with."[36]

Unexpected President: The Life and Times of Chester A. Arthur (New York: DeCapo Press, 2017), 52. These biographers claim that Arthur called in local police, but this is not verified by any contemporary sources. See also "Ellsworth Was a 'Golden Boy': Death Made Him a Martyr of the North," in *New York State and the Civil War* Vol. 2, No. 1 (June 1962): 10.

[36] *The New York Times*, April 29, 1861.

Public pressure was mounting to leave quickly for Washington. *The New York Sunday Mercury* demanded that the regiment be placed "in the position they ask for. That is – *the nearest to the enemies of their country* and face to foe with the bragging, yellow-faced Southern traitors, if they *dare* to face honest men! We fear not the result."[37] Ellsworth himself pleaded with local officials to allow his regiment to head south immediately. Brig. Gen. Charles Gates, who had warned New York Governor Edwin D. Morgan to hold off dispatching volunteers too hastily, made an exception for the Fire Zouaves, reasoning that "it is composed of many enthusiastic, restless spirits who will be governed much better out of the city of New York than in it."[38]

It was also starting to prove a mixed blessing that the regiment had a close relationship with the city's major newspapers on all sides of the political spectrum. Ellsworth had shown himself quite adept at manipulating his own public persona when he led the Chicago Zouaves, although he sometimes withstood vicious attacks by the press, too.[39] The Fire Zouaves counted five "Fire Editors" and two special artists in their ranks, including one who was a correspondent for *Frank Leslie's Illustrated Newspaper*.[40] Pvt. Arthur O. Alcock served as Fire Editor for two separate Democratic newspapers, the *New York Leader* and the *New York Atlas*, both influential Democratic broadsides. Using two different pseudonyms, Alcock drafted lengthy letters to the papers

[37] *New York Sunday Mercury*, April 28, 1861. Emphasis from the original.
[38] Charles Gates to Edwin D. Morgan, April 26, 1861, quoted in "Ellsworth was a 'Golden Boy,'" 10.
[39] The Democratic press harshly criticized Ellsworth as pompous, uncouth and a greedy office-seeker. See Randall, *Col. Elmer Ellsworth*, 225–226; *Boston Herald*, March 6, 1861. No doubt much of this was due to his close affiliation with Lincoln.
[40] See *New York Daily Tribune*, April 29, 1861. A. O. Alcock mentioned that a "Leslie's artist" was "a member of Company C." See A. O. Alcock, Letter to the Editor, April 30, 1861; *New York Atlas*, May 5, 1861, in Pohanka and Schroeder, eds., *With the 11th New York*, 32. This was probably William F. or Wilbur F. Osler, who enlisted on April 20, 1861, but deserted on August 1, 1861. See AGNY, 1184. A drawing "sketched on the spot by Wilber F. Osler," "The Ellsworth Zouaves Routing the Black Horse Cavalry" appeared in the *New York Illustrated News*, August 5, 1861. *Frank Leslie's* referenced its "artists in the field" on June 1, 1861, including Wilber F. Osler. See *Frank Leslie's Illustrated Newspaper*, June 1, 1861. Sgt-Maj. Thomas F. Goodwin was also a "special artist" making sketches of the regiment. Alcock identified Goodwin as a "special artist" in his Letter to the Editor (May 13, 1861), *New York Atlas*, May 19, 1862 in Pohanka and Schroeder, eds., *With the 11th New York*, 63; see also AGNY, 1130. Goodwin was "Ex-Foreman for H and L Co. No. 15" and according to Alcock "thought much of by all." See his Letter to the Editor, April 30, 1861, *New York Atlas*, May 5, 1861, in Pohanka and Schroeder, eds., *With the 11th New York*, 37.

from the regiment's early beginnings.[41] Two more reporters, Henry J. Wisner, with the conservative Republican *New York Times*, who was also Ellsworth's acting aide-de-camp, and Edward House, with the Democratic *New York Herald*, were essentially embedded within the unit.[42]

With so many papers tracking them, the Fire Zouaves became avid consumers of news themselves. One member demanded copies of the *New York Sunday Mercury*: "The boys can't do without it. If you forget it, and I am shot; I will haunt you."[43] Another soldier, Pvt. John A. Smith (Co. H), "an ex-knight of the quill," agreed, stating that the *Mercury* in particular was "in great demand here." He explained: "It is meat and drink to the boys."[44] With the added media attention came a new nickname: Ellsworth's "Pet Lambs." Its origin is unclear, but the moniker circulated widely among the men themselves and beyond New York

[41] Alcock was Welsh, born around 1820, enlisting in the 11th New York as a private. He was captured at the First Battle of Bull Run, imprisoned, and paroled. He later served in the 10th New York Volunteer Infantry, also known as "The National Guard Zouaves," suffering a leg wound at Spotsylvania Courthouse on May 10, 1864, and dying a month later in a Washington hospital. For additional biographical details about Alcock, see Pohanka, "Forward," to Pohanka and Schroeder, eds., *With the 11th New York*, 11–16. Led by Democratic editor John Clancy, the *New York Leader* became the principal organ of Tammany Hall. See Tyler Anbinder, *Five Points: The Nineteenth Century New York City Neighborhood* (New York: Simon and Schuster, 2012), 171. John Clancy further had served in the fire department. See Castello, *Our Firemen*, 166. The *New York Atlas*, which Alcock wrote for too, was also a Sunday-only paper with a Democratic bent. Walt Whitman was an early contributor, but he eventually fell out of favor with its editors. One of those editors, Anson Herrick, later became a Democratic congressman. See Frederic Hudson, *Journalism in the United States, from 1690–1872* (New York: Harper and Brothers, 1873), 338–339; Zachary Turpin, "'Manly Health and Training' and the *New York Atlas*," Ed Folsom and Kenneth M. Price, eds., The Walt Whitman Archive, www.whitmanarchive.org.

[42] Pohanka and Schroeder, eds., *With the 11th New York*, 82. Henry Wisner later recalled that Ellsworth "impressed me also into his service" as his "military secretary, with the rank and uniform of first lieutenant" soon after his arrival in New York city. See Wisner, "Annals" in *Weekly Times* (Philadelphia, PA), December 29, 1883. However, Wisner is not listed on the 11th New York's roster, nor is there any other proof that he had a formal commission with the unit, although it may be that it was delayed (like other commissions) and he left the unit before receiving it.

[43] "Company C., Ellsworth's Fire Zouaves," Letter to the Editors, *New York Sunday Mercury*, May 8, 1861, in William B. Styple, ed., *Writing and Fighting the Civil War: Soldier Correspondence to the New York Sunday Mercury* (Gettysburg, PA: Belle Grove, 2000), 19.

[44] John A. Smith, Letter to the Editors, *New York Sunday Mercury* (May 9, 1861), in Styple, ed., *Writing and Fighting the Civil War* 18. "ex-knight of the quill," from *The New York Times*, August 20, 1861. Smith briefly served as secretary to Colonel Leoser after Bull Run. He resigned in October with the rank of second lieutenant. See AGNY, 1201.

City.[45] Contrasted with the Fire Zouaves' repute for impudence, "pet lambs" implied innocence and coddling; but the term also conveyed a chilling foreboding: lambs, even pet ones, can be sacrificed and slaughtered.

The media attention, both positive and negative, heightened the regiment's eagerness to rush to war. It had only been a matter of weeks, but Ellsworth and his Zouaves were convinced they were ready for war.

"PLAYING SOLDIER LONG ENOUGH"

On the morning of Sunday, April 28, a large and boisterous crowd gathered in front of the regiment's temporary headquarters on Canal Street. The "entire Fire Department" turned out to escort their comrades through the city to board a steamer heading south. But there was bureaucratic "red tapeism," and the men still lacked guns and other accouterments.[46] Chafing at the delay, Ellsworth pronounced that his regiment had "been playing soldier long enough" and he deemed them ready to begin "the actual duties of a soldier's life."[47]

The next day, they were off, their departure creating a memorable spectacle.[48] The Republican *New York Daily Tribune* proclaimed it: "a proud day for the New-York Firemen." More than 1,000 Fire Zouaves,

---

[45] For example, on May 13, 1861, *The Sun* stated: "The 'Pet Lambs' is the soubriquet by which the New York Fire Zouaves are favorably known in Washington. They are fast improving in discipline and their officers predict that the 'Pet Lambs' will make their mark in the military history of the country." See *The Sun* (New York), May 13, 1816. See also John A. Smith, Letter to the Editors, *New York Sunday Mercury*, May 9, 1861, in Styple, ed., *Writing and Fighting the Civil War*, 18; "L.B.," Letter to the Editor, *New York Herald*, May 12, 1861. Later, they would be called "Lincoln's pet lambs." See *The Daily Pittsburgh Gazette*, May 23, 1861. Brian Pohanka claims that Ellsworth himself dubbed the regiment his "pet lambs," but this author has not found any evidence of this. See Pohanka, "Forward," Pohanka and Schroeder, eds., *With the 11th New York*, 10.

[46] "Red tapeism" from *The New York Times*, April 30, 1861. Although George Strong described seeing the regiment fully armed with "Sharp's rifles and revolvers," by the time they departed New York on April 29, members later complained that they never received them in their list of grievances after Bull Run. See *The New York Times*, August 15, 1861; and Allan Nevins and Milton Halsey Thomas, eds. *The Diary of George Templeton Strong: The Civil War, 1860–1865* (New York: Macmillan, 1952), April 29, 1861, 137. See also Robert Campbell to Charles G. Myers, April 1861, Telegrams Sent and Received by the Governor's Office, 1861–1862, Box 1, Series A4149, Bureau of Military Statistics, NYSA. *New York Daily Tribune*, April 28 and 29, 1861; *New York Herald*, April 28 and 29, 1861.

[47] *New York Daily Tribune*, April 29, 1861.

[48] All the major New York newspapers commented on the parade (and its initial delay). See for example the *New York Tribune*, April 28, 1861; and the *New York Herald*, April 28, 1861.

"the bone and sinew of the city," marched smartly through the city streets, escorted by police and some 5,000 fellow firemen.[49] Clad in loose-fitting gray uniforms, with bright red shirts and red kepis, they stepped in cadence past cheering crowds. In their rear followed fourteen "colored servants" "attached to the regiment," assisting with menial tasks and chores.[50] The sense of exhilaration and expectation was palatable. *The New York Times* described the firemen "in their highest animal spirits, and all seemed happy at the prospect of soon having a set-to with the Secessionists."[51] "You can scarcely conceive," one private later recalled, "the excitement that occurred in New York at this time."[52] George Templeton Strong, who watched the parade from atop an omnibus, was unimpressed with their marching, yet judged the regiment "a rugged set" who "will fight hard if judiciously handled."[53]

At various locations, the Fire Zouaves halted to ceremoniously receive stands of colors, including a white silk banner from the Fire Department, displaying "all the implements pertaining to the fireman's calling – hooks, ladders, trumpets, hats, lanterns, torches &c."[54] There were also specially designed banners from Augusta Astor, the wife of wealthy financier and real estate magnate John Jacob Astor III, and one from the actress Laura Keene.[55] There seemed enough flags, the *New York Daily Tribune* observed, for the men to "wrap themselves up in American flags if they

[49] There were also police, a "melodious band," and miscellaneous citizens marching along-side them. Descriptions of the parade from the *New York Daily Tribune*, April 30, 1861, and the *New York Herald*, April 30, 1861.

[50] *New York Daily Tribune*, April 30, 1861. It is unclear who these "servants" were, their purpose nor their eventual fate, but Brownell later wrote that Ellsworth had a personal "colored servant" who helped dress him. See Brownell quoted in unnamed newspaper clipping, February 2, 1886, Newspaper clippings, Brownell Papers, MNHS. For more on the Zouaves' original uniform, see Richard Warren and Roger Sturckle, "The 11th New York Volunteer Infantry (Ellsworth's First New York Zouaves), 1861–62," *Military Collector & Historian* Vol. 39 (1987): n.p.

[51] *The New York Times*, April 30, 1861.

[52] Comings, *Personal Reminiscences*, 1.

[53] Nevins and Thomas, eds., *Diary of George Templeton Strong*, April 29, 1861, 137. Strong also observed: "As a regiment of the line, they will be weak, but they are the very men to deal with the mob of Baltimore."

[54] *New York Daily Tribune*, April 30, 1861. See also Christopher S. Morton, "'The Star Spangled Banner in Triumph Shall Wave': The New York City Fire Department's Presentation Color Carried by Ellsworth's New York Zouaves, 1861," *Military Collector and Historian* Vol. 57, No. 2 (Summer 2005): 58–60.

[55] The flag from Laura Keene had the inscription: "From Captain Laura Keene to her Brother Zouaves." Keene's New York theater featured a play called the "Seven Sisters" which included twenty-five women performing Ellsworth's stylized Zouave drill with Keene as commander. See *New York Daily Tribune*, April 30, 1861.

choose."[56] The martial pageantry fit the pattern Ellsworth had mastered with his Chicago Zouaves on their national tour the year prior: it was a public celebration of citizen soldiery.

Military officials, local politicians, and leaders of the fire department addressed the men with rousing speeches.[57] W. H. Wickham, the Fire Department President, professed: "You have established a character for noble daring which has received the admiration and the tribute of the people." He urged them to "go forth to exhibit your gallantry and your energies in another field," and enter "where the fight is the thickest and the bullets fly the fastest."[58] Kentuckian Cassius M. Clay recounted a visit to Russia where he was asked: "how was it that a government as extensive as ours could be conducted without the aid of a standing army?" Clay responded that the United States had in fact the "largest standing army in the world," in its citizenry. "We are all soldiers here," he proclaimed, "ever ready to defend the honor for the flag under which we live."[59]

A noticeably tired Ellsworth spoke too, declaring his pride in commanding "such a gallant body of men" despite the short association he had had with them. "He knew," he told the crowd, "that brave hearts beat within their breasts and felt confident that if the opportunity offered, they would do credit not only to the firemen but to the city of New York." Accepting one of the banners, he vowed: "So long as any of us live – so long as one single arm responds to the promptings of the heart – this flag will not be disgraced by any act of the New York Fire Zouaves." He admitted that his men would "go into [the] field without discipline, it is true, without drill." Nevertheless, he assured the crowd that they would more than compensate for these deficiencies and make the city and fire department proud. He promised to return from war with their "colors as pure and unsullied as they are now."[60]

Most press accounts were glowing. "No class of men," the *New York Herald* declared, "could be better calculated to go through the fatigue of campaign than Colonel Ellsworth's Zouaves. Thick set, rugged and tough

[56] *New York Daily Tribune*, April 30, 1861.

[57] Speakers included: Gen. John A. Dix, Kentucky politician Cassius M. Clay, and "Board of Fire Commissioners, Supervisors, Councilmen and others." See *New York Daily Tribune*, April 30, 1861; also *New York Herald*, April 29, 1861.

[58] *New York Herald*, April 30, 1860. Wickham later became Democratic mayor of New York City. See *The New York Times*, January 14, 1893. See also *New York Leader*, April 30, 1861.

[59] Ellsworth invited Clay to address the regiment. See *New York Herald*, April 30, 1861.

[60] Varying versions of Ellsworth's remarks appeared in the *New York Herald*, April 30, 1861; *The New York Times*, April 30, 1861; and the *New York Herald*, April 30, 1861.

fellows they are; capable of bearing any amount of hardship." As brave and hardy men, they would, the *Herald* predicted, excel in battle; and if they failed, it would not be for lack of valor.[61] Novelist and journalist Henry Morford later affirmed that the intention was for the Fire Zouaves, "to be *picked men*, ready for any service and capable of reflecting honor on the city that sent them forth." Other regiments, "composed of miscellaneous material and of men whose courage and endurance had never been proved, might cover themselves with glory or fall into comparative disgrace"; but firemen were a proven commodity and there was no questioning their bravery; at least that was what nearly everyone assumed at the time.[62]

Still, alongside these effusive public testimonies affirming the Fire Zouaves' gallantry were disquieting accounts of illicit behavior and challenges to their loyalty. Their insubordination over unpacking the crates of muskets was just one example. Fire Editor A. O. Alcock recognized that there were some in the city hoping to see the firemen disgrace "themselves in some way." But, he attested, except for a handful of "black sheep," the unit as a whole was strong and ready for the fight.[63] The *New York Leader*, in response to the doubters, noted the large number of enlistments in the unit as a counter to anyone that questioned the firemen's patriotism. "They know," the paper affirmed, "the hardship they are expected to endure. They offer their lives, and look to the citizens of New York for the means to get them into active service."[64]

It was becoming clear that Ellsworth's Zouaves represented more than the city's volunteer fire department: in those early, heady days of war, they seemed to embody the city's patriotism and devotion to the Union cause. *The New York Herald* had predicted that the regiment would "reflect the infinite credit on the great commercial metropolis of the United States, whether in a bold and daunted front against the enemy, or as good citizens and respectable members of society."[65] This was both a boon and burden,

[61] *New York Herald*, April 30, 1861.
[62] Morford, *Days of Shoddy*, 197–198.
[63] A. O. Alcock, Letter to the Editor, April 30, 1861, *New York Atlas*, published May 5, 1861, in Pohanka and Schroeder, eds., *With the 11th New York*, 36. Alcock later referred to a handful of soldiers in the guardhouse, calling them "black sheep," and claimed that they never belonged to the Fire Department. See A. O. Alcock, Letter to the Editor, *New York Atlas*, May 16, 1861, published May 19, 1861, in Pohanka and Schroeder, eds., *With the 11th New York*, 70. For another reference to the "misconduct of a few black sheep" from the regiment, see *The New York Times*, May 12, 1861.
[64] *New York Leader*, April 27, 1861.
[65] *New York Herald*, April 22, 1861.

and something, at least on the surface, the men of the unit welcomed and celebrated. Private Alcock encapsulated this sentiment when he described "the whole country" watching them, expecting "great things."[66]

Near the end of their joyous parade, the regiment came to a sudden stop. Ellsworth had received stern orders from the Governor's office disallowing his regiment from formal mustering into service due to "an excess of men," and thus, requiring another delay in their departure.[67] The colonel quickly consulted with military officials and made a special plea to Maj. Gen. John Wool, who was reviewing the regiment as it passed from the balcony of a hotel. Wool agreed to make an exception, issuing an order "directing the mustering of the companies in Washington, notwithstanding the excess of their numbers."[68] Wool later recalled that he was loathe to be "the first to check the noble and patriotic enthusiasm of the citizens of New York."[69] The crowd cheered, and the Fire Zouaves excitedly resumed their march forward. "But for Gen. Wool," the *New York Daily Tribune* speculated, "the firemen would have been thus turned back in Broadway the other day." The paper speculated: "Who can calculate the moral effect of such a disastrous procedure?"[70]

While the *Tribune*'s remark pertained specifically to the mustering of the regiment at this early stage in their own city, it ominously foreshadowed what was to come on the battlefield; and as the question implies, calculating the moral effect of a disastrous action is not always an easy or simple matter.

"BE AS GOOD SOLDIERS AS BRAVE MEN"

Escorted to the pier, the regiment "had to run the gauntlet of firemen, every one of whom felt it to be his bounden duty to shake the hand of every soldier and remark 'Go in Lemons'" – contemporary slang for attacking

---

[66] *New York Leader*, April 27, 1861. See also A. O. Alcock, Letter to the Editor, May 2, 1861, *New York Leader*, May 4, 1861, in Pohanka and Schroeder, eds., *With the 11th New York*, 49.

[67] *New York Daily Tribune*, April 30, 1861. It was not just the excessive size of the regiment that threatened their departure, but also their lacking "the original Roll of enlistment at headquarters." See Report of the Zouave Fire Regiment Fund Committee (April 30, 1861), May 27, 1861; also Charles W. Sandford to John Meredith Read, April 29, 1861, Telegrams Received and Sent by the Governor's Office, Box 1, Series A4149, Bureau of Military Statistics, NYSA.

[68] *New York Daily Tribune*, April 30, 1861. See also *The New York Times*, April 30, 1861.

[69] Wool quoted in "Ellsworth was a 'Golden Boy,'" 11.

[70] *New York Daily Tribune*, May 3, 1861.

"with full force or earnestly."[71] After this frenzied and final farewell, the Zouaves boarded the steamship *Baltic* and began sailing southward toward Annapolis, Maryland. This vessel, originally designed as a luxury liner for transatlantic travel, was meant to accommodate 600 passengers, not 1,000 soldiers.[72] Private Alcock described his comrades having "to camp as best they could" in any space they could find.[73] Finding the air below deck "sickening in the extreme," twenty-one-year-old Pvt. Alfred Vaughn opted to sleep in the open air, with his thin government-issued blanket for cover.[74] There also were no rations; when the order came halting the regiment's departure from the city, Quartermaster Arthur had canceled stocking the ship with food. Now with hungry men swarming the ship's decks, Arthur frantically arranged to deliver the necessary supplies.[75]

Even in transport, Ellsworth sought to get better control of his raw troops. He ordered company drills on the upper deck and posted guards throughout the ship, but the men were more interested in amusing themselves. They smoked, played cards, told raucous jokes, and sang, well into the early morning hours. At one point, it appeared that an enemy boat came close to attack, but this proved a false alarm. Then a rumor spread that several Fire Zouaves had been arrested and were in irons. This, too, was untrue. By the time they debarked in Annapolis on May 2, an officer from the 13th New York Infantry observed that Ellsworth's men "seemed highly pleased to get off the vessel. Some say they have fared well on their passage, and some tell a different story." He remarked: "I have no doubt

[71] *New York Daily Tribune*, April 30, 1861; for the meaning of "Go in Lemons," see *The New Excelsior Dictionary, Containing Every Useful Word in the English Language with Its Correct Spelling, Accurate Pronunciation, and Exact Meaning According to Webster and Worcester. To which is Added an Encyclopedia of Valuable Information, Also a Complete Supplement of New Words* (Nashua, NH: C. C. Parker, 1889), 377.

[72] John H. Morrison, *History of American Steam Navigation* (New York: W. F. Sametz, 1903), 412, 419. Morrison writes that SS *Baltic* and its sister ship SS *Artic* "had large passenger accommodations, the cabins being large and roomy"; and "elaborate" "saloons." During the Civil War, these steamers were "chartered by the North Atlantic S.S. Co. to the Quartermaster's Bureau of the War Department" (419).

[73] A. O. Alcock, Letter to the Editor, April 30, 1861, *New York Atlas*, May 5, 1861, in Pohanka and Schroeder, eds., *With the 11th New York*, 32.

[74] Alfred Vaughn, Letter to the Editor, May 6, 1861, *New York Atlas*, May 12, 1861, in Pohanka and Schroeder, eds., *With the 11th New York*, 40. Twenty-one-year-old Vaughn later deserted on September 19, 1861. See AGNY, 1212. Morford claimed that the only time the unit had done any drilling prior to leaving New York was "a single and very short attempt" "in the facings." See Morford, *Days of Shoddy*, 265.

[75] "Ellsworth was a 'Golden Boy,'" 11–12.

that there are many among them who would fare well if there was any fare to be had."[76] The *Baltic*'s purser told a reporter that the New Yorkers had had a "lively time on board."[77] Ellsworth's attempts at transforming the firemen into obedient soldiers would only continue.

The regiment marched off the boat and onto the Naval Academy's parade ground for lunch. There they listened to another speaker trying to advise them on what lay ahead. The officer, identified as "Lt. Hamilton," was probably Lt. Col. Schuyler Hamilton, the grandson of Alexander Hamilton and Military Secretary to Winfield Scott. Lieutenant Hamilton told them that no one "doubted their bravery, but many feared about their order and discipline, and they must show now that they could be as good soldiers as brave men." They cheered in reply.[78]

The Zouaves packed up and resumed their journey, this time on train cars to Washington, DC. Lieutenant Hamilton's warnings proved fruitless. Just a few hours later, Private Vaughn recalled a "scene" that "makes me blush with shame to write it." As the train passed a depot manned by members of the 69th New York Infantry Regiment, a few Fire Zouaves jumped off the cars to raid the "poor men" selling various items to the passing soldiers. They returned gleefully weighed down with "boxes of cigars, loaves of bread, and anything they could lay their hands on. Not even the poor people's coffee was spared." Colonel Ellsworth quickly "paid for it all and the men were allowed to go unpunished." Vaughn, however, insisted that the culprits were not members of the Fire Department, "nor ever did; and I think it very hard that good men united in a good cause, should have their reputation and that of their Colonel and regiments ruined by evil geniuses, who go about raving pillaging, destroying and blasting the fair fruits of peace and industry, mercy to satisfy and [sic]

[76] *Brooklyn Daily Eagle*, May 7, 1861.
[77] *New York Daily Tribune*, May 3, 1861. For more on their voyage on the *Baltic* see A. O. Alcock, Letter to the Editor, May 2, 1861, *New York Leader*, May 4, 1861, in Pohanka and Schroeder, ed., *With the 11th New York*, 50–51. See also A. O. Alcock, Letter to the Editor, April 30, 1861, *New York Atlas*, May 5, 1861, in Pohanka and Schroeder, eds., *With the 11th New York*, 32, 35; and the *New York Herald*, May 5, 1861. Alcock clarified the rumor of arrests by explaining: "On Wednesday night (May 1), the store room was broken open by one of the ship's crew, who attempted to sell stolen liquor to the me at exorbitant prices. He was speedily discovered, the[n] placed in irons. No rations of whiskey were distributed at all during the passage." See A. O. Alcock, Letter to the Editor, May 2, 1861, *New York Leader*, May 4, 1861, in Pohanka and Schroeder, eds., *With the 11th New York*, 51.
[78] *The New York Times*, May 3, 1861. See also Alfred Vaughn, Letter to the Editor, May 6, 1861, *New York Atlas*, May 12, 1861, in Pohanka and Schroeder, eds., *With the 11th New York*, 41; and *New York Herald*, May 7, 1861.

insatiable thirst for that which is wrong." Vaughn, whose letter appeared in the *New York Atlas*, wanted people at home to "know that these men do not belong to the fire department, and that they may still be proud of their firemen, who are all eager to see these blackguards drummed out of the regiment."[79]

Colonel Ellsworth was finding that transforming firemen into obedient soldiers was far more difficult than he had anticipated. During the brief time he commanded the unit, he quickly gained their trust and respect. On the surface at least, he was "an excellent fit for the firemen." Private Alcock explained that his "intrepid, dashing character" suited them well: "They are used to such, and nothing else would content them." But as Ellsworth kept trying to instill "perfect discipline," he kept clashing with the firemen's distaste for conformity.[80]

"DISCREDITABLE MANNER"

The Zouaves' antics only continued during their brief stay in Washington, DC. They arrived after dark on Thursday, May 2, and marched by the White House "with a long, springing step, giving their 'Hi! Hi! Hi!' when cheered as they passed."[81] One member of the unit spotted President Abraham Lincoln watching them from a window but was unable to "distinguish his features."[82] A few days later, Ellsworth drilled his men near the Capitol building. When President Abraham Lincoln and Secretary of War William Seward came to observe them, the Zouaves crowded eagerly around the president as he shook hands and answered their inquiries.

[79] Alfred Vaughn, Letter to the Editor, May 6, 1861, *New York Atlas*, May 12, 1861, in Pohanka and Schroeder, eds., *With the 11th New York*, 41–42. The *New York Herald* reported another incident of insubordination at Annapolis where Fire Zouaves mingled with soldiers from other units: "Though under arms and in uniform the 'fire-laddie' spirit manifested itself in all its brilliancy. Dozens of them brushed by the guards stationed here and there; and in one instance, being repulsed at the bayonet's point, they raised a window, about four feet from the ground, and clambering in, fireman fashion, bolted through the building to another portion of the yard." The reporter predicted: "After a month's duty they will know better how to conduct themselves." See *New York Daily Herald*, May 7, 1861.

[80] A. O. Alcock, Letter to the Editor, April 30, 1861, *New York Leader*, May 5, 1861, Pohanka and Schroeder, eds., *With the 11th New York*, 37; and A. O. Alcock, Letter to the Editor, May 2, 1861, *New York Leader*, (May 1861), accessed via museum.dmna.ny.gov.

[81] *The Sunbury Gazette* (Sunbury, PA), May 11, 1861.

[82] Alfred Vaughn, Letter to the Editor, May 6, 1861, *New York Atlas*, May 12, 1861, in Pohanka and Schroeder, eds., *With the 11th New York*, 42; see also *New York Daily Tribune*, May 3 and 5, 1861; *New York Herald*, May 7, 1861.

Private Vaughn wrote: "He looked very well, but at the same time rather feeble."[83] The president's obvious interest in the regiment only increased public curiosity and added to already high expectations. "I doubt," one Zouave later recalled, "if any body of men ever felt the responsibility resting upon them."[84]

Within the crucible of that public pressure, the Zouaves' bad behavior worsened. Temporarily quartered in the Capitol Building, they were soon "having a good time."[85] Members held raucous mock sessions and swung from ropes from the unfinished rotunda. There were also accounts of them stealing, carousing in the city streets, and deliberately setting fires so they could put them out. The Philadelphia *Press* reported: "They have had two days of extensive, expensive and extreme fight, fun and frolic."[86] This devil-may-care attitude fueled their critics and exacerbated their officers' frustration. Gen. Winfield Scott relayed his displeasure through then Maj. Irvin McDowell, temporarily halting their shenanigans with some sort of "treaty."[87] Colonel Ellsworth tried to assure the Zouave Fire Regiment Fund Committee that "the boys have generally behaved well," admitting that there were "twenty exceptional characters" who were a problem. He predicted that, "when rid of these [we] will have a regiment creditable to your City, and I trust to myself."[88]

Less than a week later, however, Gen. Joseph K. Mansfield, commander of the Department of Washington, had to remind Colonel Ellsworth that he was "entitled to fuel," but that he would have to be "careful not to burn fences, as some have already been burnt."[89] A Pennsylvania newspaper recounted that the "quiet Massachusetts" troops quartered nearby "don't fancy them, especially as they go, eat, or sleep, where they please, 'an' mind yer don't say nuffing about it, hay!"[90] An unnamed soldier from the 71st

[83] Alfred Vaughn, Letter to the Editor, May 6, 1861, *New York Atlas*, May 12, 1861, in Pohanka and Schroeder, eds., *With the 11th New York*, 42. See also *New York Daily Tribune*, May 5, 1861.

[84] Comings, *Personal Reminiscences*, 2.

[85] "J.D.," Letter to the Editor, May 3, 1861, *New York Herald*, May 7, 1861. "J.D." was a member of the unit but there are too many names on the roster with those initials to know who he was.

[86] *The Press* (Philadelphia, PA), May 7, 1861; and *New York Daily Tribune*, May 5 and 8, 1861. See also Kelley, "The Assassination of Ellsworth," Vol. 1, No. 4 (July 21, 1886), in Newspaper Clippings, Frank E. Brownell Papers, MNHS.

[87] *The Press* (Philadelphia, PA), May 7, 1861.

[88] Elmer E. Ellsworth to James Kelly and "Gents of Committee," May 4, 1861, *The New York Times*, May 8, 1861.

[89] Joseph K. Mansfield to Elmer E. Ellsworth, May 9, 1861, Elmer Ephraim Ellsworth Papers, Abraham Lincoln Presidential Library, Springfield, IL.

[90] *The Sunbury Gazette* (Sunbury, PA), May 11, 1861.

New York Volunteer Infantry depicted more sordid behavior: "Some unworthy members of the New York Fire Zouaves are creating a great disturbance here. They break into houses, and in some instances have outraged defenseless women. So great was the disorder among them that Colonel Ellsworth was compelled to threaten some of them with death."[91] Pvt. Alfred Vaughn admitted: "Some of the men have committed outrages in the city and some are to be punished."[92]

Stories of their bad behavior made it into the Confederate press, too, only adding to their growing reputation as lowly criminals. The *Alexandria Gazette and Virginia Advertiser* noted the Fire Zouaves' arrival in Washington, DC, recognizing their ability as "efficient agents in extinguishing material combustion," but wondered if they could "subdue the concealed fires which are burning in the minds of our innocent, lawful and peaceable citizens." The paper added: "Several members of this regiment were arrested today by the police for disorderly and riotous conduct."[93] A negative story from the *Richmond Examiner*, reprinted in a Brooklyn newspaper, alleged that the Fire Zouaves were "the lowest refuse of New York city." Scoffing at their uniforms, the Confederate paper was decidedly unimpressed, dismissing them as looking dirty and "worn six months in some pork packing establishment." The *Examiner* stated: "If you were to meet one of them in a lonesome place, you would instinctively produce your wallet and hand it over. Such are the kind of men that Gen. Scott proposes to let loose upon the soil of his native South."[94] In another example, one of the "secession dailies" ridiculed the Fire Zouaves as illiterate. The *New York Leader* responded: "As our firemen went to fight for their country's honor, and not to be sneered at by a cowardly press it is rather contemptible in any man to cast slurs upon them because they cannot handle a pen as readily as a bayonet."[95] The firemen's celebrated reputation for brash fearlessness, which initially seemed to affirm their potential as soldiers, was quickly turning them into symbols of immorality.

[91] Dated May 5, 1861, this letter appeared in the *New York Herald* on May 10, 1861.

[92] Alfred Vaughn to the Editor, May 6, 1861, *New York Atlas*, May 12, 1861, in Pohanka and Schroeder, eds., *With the 11th New York*, 43.

[93] *Alexandria Gazette and Virginia Advertiser*, May 4, 1861.

[94] *Times Union* (Brooklyn, NY), May 9, 1861. The bad press cross-pollinated: For example, the *Fayetteville (NC) Observer*, May 13, 1861 reprinted a story from *The New York Times* which recounted the Fire Zouaves "ransacking the Capitol like so many rats."

[95] *New York Leader*, May 1861.

On Tuesday evening, May 7, 1861, Ellsworth's Fire Zouaves were officially mustered into service in the US Army with formal designation as the 11th New York Volunteer Infantry. Ellsworth marched the men to the parade ground near the uncompleted Washington Monument and addressed his regiment candidly in a "lengthy speech." He praised them for their "fine appearance and proficiency of drill," assuring them that promises to supply tents, new rifles, and new uniforms would be met.[96] But he also reminded the Zouaves that he had specially selected firemen because of their reputation for "bravery, intrepidity and brawn, and how much was expected of them by their country."[97] Now he sought a greater commitment from them, stipulating that they must agree to serve for the duration of the war. "Some of the men blinked," the *Tribune* recorded, "but a vast majority seemed ecstatic with delight." Ellsworth warned them: "any who didn't want to fight who would like to go home in irons and be sneered at as cowards, to stand out and he would accommodate them instanter [sic]."[98] "There were some complaints and objections," Private Alcock reported, but in the end "all but a dozen responded cheerfully to the obligation."[99] Those who refused, The New York Times pronounced, were men whose "reasons for leaving were not of a character to reflect upon their courage." "The remainder," the paper stated, "cheerfully took the oath of service for the war."[100]

Ellsworth additionally promised to discipline any members who continued to tarnish the unit's reputation. Apparently, just as he sent a squad of men to round up the guilty parties, Generals Lorenzo Thomas and Irvin

---

[96] *New York Daily Tribune*, May 8, 1861.

[97] *The New York Times*, May 11, 1861.

[98] The *Tribune* inaccurately claimed: "Nary [a] man obeyed." See *New York Daily Tribune*, May 8, 1861. This was a point of contention until the unit's disbandment in June 1862, with some claiming that, when they left New York, they were "sworn in" as a three-month regiment. This was the assumption of disgruntled members, particularly after Bull Run, but there is no documentation before their formal mustering in in May 1861. See Costello, *Our Firemen*, 718.

[99] A. O. Alcock, Letter to the Editor, May 10, 1861, *New York Leader*, May 11, 1861, in Pohanka and Schroeder, eds., *With the 11th New York*, 52. In a letter on May 29, Alcock said only three men refused to be sworn in "for the war" and were then "returned to New York, looking very small, and doubtless feeling so, amidst the jeers of their more enthusiastic and patriotic companions." See A. O. Alcock, Letter to the Editor, May 29, 1861, *New York Leader*, June 1, 1861.

[100] *The New York Times*, May 11, 1861. The *Times* described Ellsworth addressing the men in a "pithy, stirring manner upon the duties of soldiers in the present crisis, and the history and circumstances of the organization of the corps was related," and further claimed that nine men left rather than twelve.

McDowell arrived to formally swear in the regiment. President Lincoln, with his son Tad and Senators Henry Wilson and Edward Baker, also appeared to witness the mustering in and review of the troops. "The expulsion of the men" the *Tribune* reported, "was postponed."[101]

Publicly, Colonel Ellsworth and his supporters refused to concede that recruiting firemen had been a mistake. It was inevitable, he and others argued, that in a unit of more than a thousand men there would be *some* bad actors. He admitted that he had had no chance to properly screen volunteers and, thus, a small minority were "conducting themselves in a discreditable manner." "It is the intention of the regiment," he vowed publicly, "and my own determination, to free ourselves by the most summary process of all such characters, the moment we can identify them."[102] Ellsworth paid for damaged property out of his own pocket and issued new orders posting more guards and prohibiting members from roaming the streets without authorization. He further appealed to victims to come forward and identify the perpetrators.[103] When news stories circulated that more than 150 Fire Zouaves were sent home "in disgrace," Ellsworth assured his fiancée Carrie Spafford that these reports were "false." "We have sent back 6 and the men do well," adding proudly: "The President and Sec. of War say my regiment is without exception the best [in] the service of the U.S."[104]

Just who these culprits were, and what if anything happened to them, is unclear. Colonel Ellsworth claimed more than once that he had arrested the guilty parties and punished them.[105] Pvt. John Smith castigated them as "scamps, who crept into our ranks before leaving New York" who had "committed outrages here." But he also insisted, as did others, that: "they have been taken, and will be sent home in irons. Five of the vagabonds will

[101] *New York Daily Tribune*, May 8, 1861.

[102] *The Philadelphia Inquirer*, May 6, 1861. See also *The Press* (Philadelphia, PA), May 6, 1861.

[103] Elmer E. Ellsworth to Stephen W. Stryker, "Regular Orders No. 9," May 5, 1861, Elmer Ephraim Ellsworth Collection, NYSMM; See also Elmer E. Ellsworth, "Special Orders," May 6, 1861, Gilder Lehrman Institute of American History, accessed via gilderlehrman.org; *New York Daily Tribune*, May 5, 1861; Frank Brownell Interview in *St. Louis Globe-Democrat*, June 3, 1888, in Newspaper Clippings, Brownell Papers, MNHS.

[104] *Cleveland Daily Herald*, May 8, 1861; Elmer E. Ellsworth to Carrie Spafford, May 10, 1861, Ellsworth Papers, ALPL. See also Ingraham, *Elmer E. Ellsworth*, 136.

[105] Elmer E. Ellsworth to Stephen W. Stryker, "Regular Orders No. 9," May 5, 1861, Elmer Ephraim Ellsworth Collection, New York State Library, Albany, NY. See also *New York Daily Tribune*, May 8, 1861.

be turned over to the civil authorities."[106] Another Fire Zouave assured readers of the *Sunday Mercury*: "We had six bad-minded men in the regiment and they came very near disgracing us all." At least three of them disguised themselves as firemen, somehow gaining possession of the prized firemen badges. But when they were discovered, "they were drummed out of the regiment, and will be sent to New York to-morrow in irons."[107] Rosters and other surviving military documents fail to corroborate these assertions. There were a handful of men discharged or dismissed in May from the unit, some deemed unfit for active service due to physical disabilities, but nothing points to formal arrests (civil or military), court-martials, or other punitive proceedings.[108]

Ellsworth continued to do his utmost to ensure that his regiment was free of any miscreants. He still clung to the notion that firemen made the best soldiers and that all they needed was the chance to show it.

"NOT DANDY SOLDIERS"

Soon an opportunity arose to prove the Fire Zouaves' worthiness, albeit not on the field of battle. A few days after their arrival in the capital, a fire broke out in the middle of the night in a building adjacent to the famed Willard's Hotel. General Mansfield, who happened to be staying there, hurriedly sent a plea for help to Ellsworth. Some 300 firemen sprang into action, with "deliberation and bravery," breaking open the doors of the district's fire stations and rushing to extinguish the flames.[109] Their

[106] John A. Smith, Letter to the Editors, (May 9, 1861), *New York Sunday Mercury*, in Styple, ed., *Writing and Fighting the Civil War*, 18.

[107] "Company C., Ellsworth Fire Zouaves," Letter to the Editors, *New York Sunday Mercury*, May 8, 1861, in Styple, ed., *Writing and Fighting the Civil War*, 19. This soldier's identity is unknown.

[108] Discharges included: William Cashier (Co. G); Theodore Dakin [or Dacin] (Co. H); James McColgan [or Colligan] (Co. G); A. W. Renson, (Co. E). George Stevens (Co. G) is listed as "discharged 1861 by civil authority" but there is no additional explanation. See AGNY, 1093, 1107, 1165, 1191, 1204. On May 10, 1861, Alcock reported: "We sent home to-morrow (Thursday) several who are unfitted for active service, among whom is one of our military secretaries who has been in the hospital since our arrival here." See A. O. Alcock, Letter to the Editor, May 10, 1861, *New York Leader*, May 11, 1861, in Pohanka and Schroeder, eds., *With the 11th New York*, 54.

[109] Quote from *New York Herald*, May 10, 1861; see also *The New York Times*, May 11, 1861. It is unclear just how many members of the regiment participated in putting out the fire. *The New York Times* claimed that one hundred were originally ordered out, but then "nearly the whole Regiment" sprang into action. See *The New York Times*, May 10, 1861; also *The Evening Star* (Washington, DC), May 9, 1861; State of New York, *Third Annual Report of the Chief of the Bureau of Military Record*, 107;

quick action prevented the blaze from spreading and causing more damage. Ellsworth used a brass trumpet to direct the firemen and, as *The New York Times* correspondent Henry J. Wisner reported, "marched them back to quarters, none looking in any manner fatigued after two hours of as hard labor as ever, probably, fell to their lot."[110]

Their uniforms were torn and soiled, but the men were heartened by the episode. Pvt. John A. Smith described being "cheered heartily" as they marched back to their camp at the Capitol building. "Some of our detractors here," he attested, "have found out that we are fit for any kind of duty, and ask nothing but a 'clear field and no favors.'"[111] General Mansfield addressed the regiment from the balcony of Willard's with "an enthusiastic speech," predicting that if they performed as "well in actual warfare as they had in battling with that fire[,] they would render an excellent account of themselves."[112]

Indeed, the Fire Zouaves and their supporters hoped saving Willard's Hotel would silence their critics. Their "gallant behavior" was, according to one member, "the talk of the town" and managed to cover up "a multitude of sins."[113] Accounts of their handiwork appeared in major newspapers, including *Harper's Weekly*, which featured a front-page illustration of the Zouaves forming a human ladder to reach the heights of the buildings, with one member held upside down so he could spray water through an open window.[114] This "exhibition," Wisner with *The*

Brownell Interview, *St. Louis Daily Globe-Democrat*, June 3, 1888 in Newspaper clippings, Brownell Papers, MNHS.

[110] Report of the fire in *The New York Times* was attributed to H.J.W.–Henry J. Wisner serving as "acting aide-de-camp for Ellsworth." See *The New York Times*, May 11, 1861; also Pohanka and Schroeder, ed., *With the 11th New York*, 82. Wisner recalled first meeting Ellsworth in 1855 when Ellsworth was seventeen and seeking appointment to West Point. See Wisner, "Annals" in *Weekly Times* (Philadelphia), December 29, 1883. For more on Wisner as a war correspondent, see J. Cutler Andrews, *The North Reports the Civil War* (Pittsburgh, PA: University of Pittsburgh Press, 1955), 72.

[111] John A. Smith, Letter to the Editors, *New York Sunday Mercury*, (May 9, 1861), in Styple, ed., *Writing and Fighting the Civil War*, 18.

[112] Comings, *Personal Reminiscences*, 3. See also *New York Herald*, May 10, 1861. The Willard brothers gave the regiment $500 as a reward for saving their hotel from the fire, "with the idea of buying badges for the whole regiment." Years later, those funds, which had accumulated interest, helped pay for a monument to Ellsworth in Mechanicville, New York. See *Chicago Tribune*, July 16, 1872; and *Exercises Connected with the Unveiling of the Ellsworth Monument at Mechanicville, May 27, 1874* (Albany, NY: Joel Munsell, 1875). There was also talk of using some of this money to dedicate a monument to Noah Farnham, who succeeded Ellsworth as colonel, but that did not occur.

[113] A. O. Alcock, Letter to the Editor, May 10, 1861, *New York Leader*, May 11, 1861, in Pohanka and Schroeder, eds., *With the 11th New York*, 56.

[114] *Harper's Weekly*, May 25, 1861.

FIGURE 1.2 "Willard's Hotel Saved by the New York Fire Zouaves." Image courtesy of *Harper's Weekly*, May 25, 1861.

New York Times contended, should "retrieve the character of the regiment from the disgrace cast upon [them] by the excesses of the few rogues who have been turned out of its ranks." It was a "disgrace," Wisner lamented, "which was very unjustly cast upon it in consequences of the habit of some newspapers have of exaggerating and magnifying small offences into grave outrages."[115]

[115] *The New York Times*, May 11, 1861.

A change of location also seemed a possible solution to the regiment's ongoing problems. The day after the fire, Ellsworth moved his regiment to "Camp Lincoln," along the heights southwest of town as part of the capital's defenses. On their first night in their new camp, there was a heavy rain, and the men "slept on muddy ground."[116] Despite the bad weather, Wisner insisted, "The post to which the regiment has been assigned is a very important one, and the honor is fully appreciated."[117]

Here, Colonel Ellsworth once again sought to instill at least some semblance of order. He housed the men in Sibley tents and instigated five to six hours of daily drill and dress parades, even on Sundays, disallowing the regimental chaplain, George W. Dodge, from giving sermons.[118] Ellsworth was starting to realize, though, that he could not rely solely on his former Chicago Zouaves or his own skills as drillmaster; he needed more help. Assistance soon came in the form of Lt. Col. Noah L. Farnham and Adj. Charles McKnight Leoser. Farnham, thirty-one years old and nicknamed "Pony" for his small stature, was well familiar with the firemen, having served as an assistant engineer, and he was a member of the 7th New York State Militia. Like Ellsworth, Farnham had studied military tactics as a teen and excelled at fencing. "Pony Farnham is every inch a soldier," a Fire Zouave maintained, "and after the boys earn his worth and military abilities, will not stop at liking him – they will love him."[119] A. O. Alcock was also initially impressed, writing that Farnham "already made a good impression on the members of the regiment who are personally unacquainted with him; and as a

[116] A. O. Alcock, Letter to the Editor, May 16, 1861, *New York Atlas*, May 19, 1861, in Pohanka and Schroeder, eds., *With the 11th New York*, 65; see also 60. Their encampment was located on Insane Asylum Hill, across from the Navy Yard.

[117] *The New York Times*, May 11, 1861.

[118] Alcock complained that he and his comrades "believe in keeping the Sabbath day holy," and despite the demands of training, they should still have the "benefit" of a sermon from their chaplain. See A. O. Alcock, Letter to the Editor, May 23, 1861, *New York Atlas*, May 26, 1861, in Pohanka and Schroeder, eds., *With the 11th New York*, 75.

[119] "Company G," Letter to the Editors, *New York Sunday Mercury*, May 13, 1861, in Styple, ed., *Writing and Fighting the Civil War*, 20. Farnham met Ellsworth during the Chicago Zouave tour in 1860, and organized his own Zouave company in the city. See *Brooklyn Evening Star*, May 30, 1861; and *New York Herald*, June 9, 1861. He resigned from the 7th New York State Militia, writing Ellsworth on May 6 that he would "report for duty as soon as I am relieved from guard." See Noah L. Farnham to Elmer E. Ellsworth, May 6, 1861, Elmer E. Ellsworth Papers, Folder Ams 811/2.6, The Rosenbach Museum, Philadelphia, PA (hereafter referred to as RM). For more on Farnham see *The New York Times*, August 16, 1861 and *New York Daily Tribune*, August 16, 1861.

disciplinarian he will prove inestimable to us."[120] Leoser, only twenty-one years old, graduated West Point that May, and brought his professional education to the regiment.[121]

Ellsworth further sought to resolve the unit's continued supply problems: there still were not enough guns, and uniforms were wearing thin.[122] Chief Decker visited them from New York, impressing upon them yet again "the necessity of obedience and discipline."[123] There was some noticeable improvement – at least General Mansfield thought so when he reviewed the regiment at Camp Lincoln, complimenting them on their "progress" in drilling.[124]

Despite these improvements, with stricter rules and new officers, the men had, according to one Fire Zouave, "plenty of amusements here, more than a person would think." There were daily visitors from Washington and New York, including "many ladies," and Wallace's Band performed regularly, cheering the men with "its enlivening strains."[125] "Just imagine to yourself," one member recounted, "a thousand men playing leap frog; dancing, groups of singers, card-players, smoking, cooking, washing, growling, [and] talking fire."[126] The regiment, though, was restless for

---

[120] A. O. Alcock, Letter to the Editor, May 10, 1861, *New York Leader*, May 11, 1861, in Pohanka and Schroeder, eds., *With the 11th New York*, 54.

[121] Biographical information from Pohanka, "Forward," in Pohanka and Schroeder, eds., *With the 11th New York*, 11, 5n; *New York Tribune*, April 28, 1861; and "Charles McKnight Leoser," findagrave.com. Leoser impressed Alcock, who judged the young officer as intelligent, well-mannered, and a gentleman. See A. O. Alcock, Letter to the Editor, May 16, 1861, *New York Atlas*, May 19, 1861, in Pohanka and Schroeder, eds., *With the 11th New York*, 68. See also "R.W." Letter to the Editors, *New York Sunday Mercury*, May 18, 1861, in Styple, ed., *Writing and Fighting the Civil War*, 21.

[122] See A. O. Alcock, Letter to the Editor, May 17, 1861, *New York Leader*, May 18, 1861, in Pohanka and Schroeder, eds., *With the 11th New York*, 56.

[123] A. O. Alcock, Letter to the Editor, May 17, 1861, *New York Leader*, n.d., accessed via museum.dmna.ny.gov.

[124] A. O. Alcock, Letter to the Editor, May 16, 1861, *New York Atlas*, May 19, 1861, in Pohanka and Schroeder, eds., *With the 11th New York*, 69. Various accounts mention not just the insufficiency of arms, but the poor condition of the guns that were provided. See State of New York, *Third Annual Report of the Chief of the Bureau of Military Record*, 107.

[125] Letter to the Editor, May 16, 1861, *New York Herald*, May 19, 1861. Visitors included the Astors, Simeon Draper, Chief Decker, Engineers Baulch and Mccosker, Aldermen Brady and Henry. See also A. O. Alcock, Letter to the Editor, May 17, 1861, *New York Leader*, n.d., accessed via museum.dmna.ny.gov; and A. O. Alcock, Letter to the Editor, May 16, 1861, *New York Atlas*, May 19, 1861, in Pohanka and Schroeder, eds., *With the 11th New York*, 69.

[126] "M.C. Company G," Letter to the Editors, *New York Sunday Mercury*, May 13, 1861, in Styple, ed., *Writing and Fighting the Civil War*, 20.

real action. "Here," a member bemoaned, "we remain, in dull inactivity, rusting for want of excitement."[127] Some soldiers were intent on finding their own excitement, easily slipping past guards, and venturing into the city.[128]

The Zouaves' antics were still making national news. For example, *The Weekly Sun* from Vincennes, Indiana, reported that thirty women were discovered in their camp soon after they arrived in DC. The women were sent home, but the paper observed: "The Zouaves, we fear, are not at all of the highest moral character."[129] An article in the *Philadelphia Press* targeted seventy-five members of the unit as part of a "class whose irrepressible propensities for mischief cause themselves and their friends no little trouble." The paper described members scattering through the capital's streets, looking for "amusements, novel, exciting, and dangerous and otherwise." Several Fire Zouaves "amused themselves in feats of jumping" "over a six foot iron rail around the grounds of the Smithsonian." Colonel Ellsworth, the paper alleged, planned to return 100 men back to New York City to be rid of the bad influence. This would leave the regiment "orderly, noble and brave men as ever were called together for military duty."[130]

This was a pattern that had developed from the initial founding of the regiment. Lurid stories of the Fire Zouaves' bad behavior circulated in the press and then there was a rush to defend them, with claims that the stories were exaggerated or that only a handful of men were culprits and would be duly punished. Their "unenviable notoriety," one New Yorker insisted, was simply due to "the pranks of a few unruly members."[131] Ellsworth

[127] "R.W.," Letter to the Editors, *New York Sunday Mercury*, May 18, 1861, in Styple, ed., *Writing and Fighting the Civil War*, 20. "R.W." could be Pvt. Robert Waldron (Co. E); Pvt. Robert F. Wallace (Co. I); Pvt. Richard Warner (Co. A) or Pvt. Richard Wilson (Co. B).

[128] Alcock described: "Last night the Colonel sent a detachment to the city to pick up stragglers. It seems that about a dozen, tired of being kept in camp, crossed the river in fishing-boats, and were seen in the streets of Washington. Word was immediately sent to the camp, and probably all will be arrested before morning as deserters." See A. O. Alcock, Letter to the Editor, May 17, 1861, *New York Leader*, n.d., accessed via museum.dmna.ny.gov.

[129] *The Weekly Sun*, (Vincennes, IN), May 17, 1861.

[130] *The Press* (Philadelphia, PA) excerpted in *The Advance* (Ogdensburgh, NY), May 17, 1861.

[131] "L.B.," Letter to the Editor, *New York Herald*, May 12, 1861. "L.B." could be Sgt. Levi Bennett, (Co. A); later commissioned 2nd Lt.; Lloyd W. Berry, 2nd Lt in Co. E; or Pvt. Lawrence Brown, (Co. G). See AGNY, 1079, 1086.

dismissed the bad press out of hand, writing his fiancée Carrie: "Stories you hear about [the] Regt [are] all false."[132]

Fire Editor and Pvt. A. O. Alcock wrote a lengthy defense of his regiment to the *New York Leader* on May 10: "You have probably heard," he told his readers, "of the alleged disgraceful conduct of a few of our members and in common with our friends in New York have felt aggrieved." Alcock echoed Ellsworth when he reasoned that the hurried nature of the regiment's formation meant that there were men in the ranks "whom had never met before they were mustered into service." Thus, to expect "them to be all saints would have been too much, and we all knew that if there were any bad or vicious natures in the ranks, they would soon make themselves known through their activities." Like others, Alcock insisted that the "few derelictions committed were traced to less than a dozen men, six of whom have been publicly disgraced and dismissed from the regiment." Except for these few men, Alcock declared, the regiment consisted of "good material" who behaved "as orderly as any members of any company now in Washington." He characterized most of the accusations as "rumors and exaggerated stories," some of them "manufactured out of whole cloth" by reporters who failed to understand the ways and manners of firemen. It was true, Alcock admitted, that the men were still lacking in mastering the manual of arms. But their "evolutions and marching are not excelled." "All the members of the Regiment are anxious and willing to do their duty, and discipline among volunteers is not learned in a day." He avowed: "The Fire Zouaves are not dandy soldiers, full of smirking politeness, but rugged and vigorous warriors, who do not deserve the severe criticism that has been showered upon them."[133]

That severe criticism would not abate; it only seemed to increase the longer the Fire Zouaves remained idle.

"WE WANT THE CREDIT FOR IT"

On May 17, the 11th New York moved again, two more miles further down on the banks of the Potomac. They were now quartered on the sprawling property of George Washington Young, a large slave and landowner, and according to Alcock "not the most reliable friend that

---

[132] Elmer E. Ellsworth to Carrie Spafford, (May 1861), Ellsworth Papers, ALPL.

[133] A. O. Alcock, Letter to the Editor, May 10, 1861, *New York Leader*, May 11, 1861, in Pohanka and Schroeder, eds., *With the 11th New York*, 52–54.

Union men have in these times." The men christened their new location "Camp Decker" to honor their popular Fire Chief.[134] The firemen's rocky transformation from civilian to soldier continued. They had to give up their band due to its expense. But Alcock maintained it was an unnecessary luxury. "We are not," he proclaimed, "holiday soldiers, and care nothing for show, or for thirty days but 'FOR THE WAR,' we willingly leave the 'lascivious pleading of the lute,' for the 'stern alarms,' until we can return to those we love, crowned with victory."[135] While at Camp Decker the men also received new guns: "splendid Minie Rifles." Alcock reported confidently that "if our boys ever get into action with the beautiful weapons they now possess, they will make [a] mark that will distinguish the Firemen's Zouaves forever."[136] A fellow Zouave affirmed: "We will be immediately initiated in the grand mystery of using them."[137]

The close ties between the city and the regiment persisted. Alcock candidly declared that the Fire Zouaves had to "*depend on our men at home*" to ensure they had the necessary supplies and armaments. The regiment's "friends in New York" have, Alcock stated, "pledged themselves to us, and we have plighted our honors to them, that we will faithfully represent the Fire Department in any and everything we may

[134] A. O. Alcock, Letter to the Editor, May 23, 1861, *New York Atlas*, May 26, 1861, in Pohanka and Schroeder, eds., *With the 11th New York*, 73–74. According to the 1860 Slave Schedule, George W. Young owned a total of sixty slaves, ages seven months to seventy years old. See Eighth Census of the United States, 1860: Population and Slave Schedule, Washington Ward 4, Washington, DC, Records of the Bureau of the Census, RG 29, NARA; accessed via ancestry.com. See also Kenneth J. Heineman, *Civil War Dynasty: The Ewing Family of Ohio* (New York: New York University Press, 2012), 93; Louise Daniel Hutchinson, The *Anacostia Story, 1608–1930* (Washington, DC: US Govt. Printing Office, 1977), 61–62; and "R.W.," Letter to the Editors, *New York Sunday Mercury*, May 18, 1861, in Styple, ed., *Writing and Fighting the Civil War*, 21.

[135] A. O. Alcock, Letter to the Editor, May 23, 1861, *New York Atlas*, May 26, 1861, Pohanka and Schroeder, eds., *With the 11th New York*, 75.

[136] A. O. Alcock, Letter to the Editor, May 23, 1861, *New York Atlas*, May 26, 1861, in Pohanka and Schroeder, eds., *With the 11th New York*, 77.

[137] Letter to the Editor, May 16, 1861, *New York Herald*, May 19, 1861. This soldier claimed the new rifles arrived at Camp Lincoln, but Alcock alleged they arrived later at Camp Decker. Frank Brownell, however, stated that the regiment did not receive new rifles until the day before they departed for Alexandria (May 23). See *The Budget* (Troy, NY), September 20, 1891, in Newspaper Clippings, Brownell Papers, MNHS. Ron Field, however, maintains that the 11th New York "received Model 1855 rifle-muskets – although the two flank companies (A and K) continued to carry Model 1855 rifles with sword bayonets." See Ron Field, *Union Infantryman vs Confederate Infantryman: Easter Theater 1861–65* (Oxford: Osprey, 2013), 42.

be called upon to do. We know them – they know us, – and neither will be disappointed."[138] In addition, the firemen expected the city to take care of their loved ones left at home. On May 19, three representatives of the Fire Department "deputized by the Committee of the Board of Trustees of the Fire Department," Alcock explained, "to attend to the wants of the firemen in our regiment, and those of the families left behind."[139]

Published letters from the regiment sought to counter the relentless negative publicity about them. One soldier insisted: "We are all in the best of health and spirits, with the best of provisions to eat and plenty of good water to drink. The common reports to the contrary in the newspapers are entirely without foundation."[140] Capt. John B. Leverich (Co. E) wrote directly to the *New York Herald* to defend his men: "We were hurriedly organized, and instead of being, as stated, unfortunate in the selection of men, we have been remarkably fortunate. Out of one thousand and fifty men, we can find but five who have acted disgracefully, and even these cases are not as bad as represented." "No regiment," Leverich stated, "that has left the city has had less disorderly men than ours. The reports against the regiment are injurious, and as we are on our good behavior, we want the credit of it; we value a good name at home, and will strive to deserve it, and ask your assistance."[141]

As with Ellsworth's earlier letter to his fiancée, such an assessment is perhaps understandable as a defensive reaction against public condemnation. Yet it clearly requires an element of denial as an attempt to gloss over and cover up transgressions. It would prove an ironic foreshadowing of what was to come in the aftermath of the regiment's first battle: the public magnification and censoring of their actions that will serve to incriminate them to the public.

---

[138] A. O. Alcock, Letter to the Editor, May 23, 1861, *New York Atlas*, May 26, 1861, in Pohanka and Schroeder, eds., *With the 11th New York*, 77.

[139] The three Fire Department representatives were Owen W. Brennan, Andrew Craft, and John R. Platt. Brennan was an assistant engineer with two brothers who also served in the department; Craft had been a member of the NYC Fire Department since 1829 and served as Fire Commissioner. Platt, whom Costello called the "*beau ideal* of a fireman," had been foreman of three different companies and president of the Fire Department. See Costello, *Our Firemen*, 499, emphasis from original; also 109, 425, 460. See also A. O. Alcock, Letter to the Editor, May 23, 1861, *New York Atlas*, May 26, 1861, in Pohanka and Schroeder, eds., *With the 11th New York*, 77.

[140] *New York Herald*, May 21, 1861.

[141] *New York Herald*, May 21, 1861. Leverich was member of Hose 7 in the NYC Volunteer Fire Department. See Costello, *Our Firemen*, 718.

It had been just over a month since those exhilarating days in New York when the Fire Zouaves first formed. Serious problems continued in the ranks, with desertions and a growing number of soldiers on the sick rolls. A few days before the regiment received orders to abandon Camp Decker, twenty-five men were listed as sick, twelve of them in the "Washington Infirmary." In addition, the regimental surgeon determined that eighteen Zouaves were "unfit for service" due to a variety of ailments including pneumonia, "shortness of vision," and "Neuralgia" – defined as someone who "wants to come back."[142]

"MEN AS WELL AS SOLDIERS"

One afternoon, when the 11th New York was still stationed in Washington, DC, Pvt. Alfred Vaughn had climbed to the top of the Capitol building, ascending "a spiral staircase, which winds round and round a pillar to the dome." "It makes you dizzy," he wrote, "before you reach the top." Vaughn observed the "glorious site" of the panoramic view of Washington, but also the city of Alexandria, which was some seven miles distant. "I can," he wrote, "discern two secession flags waving, which please God, we will tear down soon."[143]

Once the regiment moved to Camp Lincoln, about three miles from the capital and closer to Alexandria, the sights and sounds of that town continued to both bemuse and annoy the men. One soldier wrote: "Our boys are opposite the city every hour of the day, and can see the movements of the people there almost with the naked eye."[144] They still took

---

[142] A. O. Alcock, Letter to the Editor, May 23, 1861, *New York Atlas*, May 26, 1861, in Pohanka and Schroeder, eds., *With the 11th New York*, 76–77. William Gorman (Co.K) who had this diagnosis remained with the regiment until mustering out in June 1862. See AGNY, 1131.

[143] Alfred Vaughn, Letter to the Editor, May 6, 1861, *New York Atlas*, May 12, 1861, included in Alcock, *With the 11th New York*, 43. There is some dispute over whether the Marshall House flag could be seen from Washington or not, but it is significant that Vaughn made this comment nearly three weeks before Ellsworth's death. See also "Ellsworth was a 'Golden Boy,'" 12. A correspondent for the *New York Commercial* mentioned another rebel flag in Alexandria allegedly also visible from the White House: "With a glass, the secession flag, which floats over the United States Custom-house at Alexandria, is visible from the President's study window." Excerpted from the *New York Commercial*, May 23, 1861, in *The Civilian and Gazette Weekly*. (Galveston, TX) May 28, 1861. It is not clear if this was the same flag atop the Marshall House or an entirely different one.

[144] "M.C Company G" to the Editors of the *New York Sunday Mercury*, May 13, 1861, in Styple, ed., *Writing and Fighting the Civil War*. It is uncertain who "M.C." was as there is

notice of one of the rebel flags, which was enormous and could clearly be viewed through field-glasses. "Is it not tantalizing to see the secession flag flying there," a Zouave asked, "and we unable, though anxious to pull it down?" Some began to plot to steal across the river and "bear it down in triumph." But Colonel Ellsworth unearthed the scheme and "positively refused to countenance it."[145]

Less than a week later, Ellsworth learned of federal plans to move into Alexandria, Virginia. The young colonel made a special plea to General Mansfield and, allegedly, President Lincoln himself, insisting that his Fire Zouaves "must go into the field," and that they "must go first."[146] His regiment would be ready to "march at 1 minutes notice," to travel by water, or if necessary by land, "twenty miles at a *rapid pace*."[147] "I would consider it as a personal affront," he told Gen. Mansfield, "if he would not allow us to have the right of the line, which is our due, as the first volunteer Regiment sworn in for the war." Mansfield acquiesced, and

no one listed on the Co. G roster who had those initials. See Adjutant General's Office, State of New York. *A Record of the Commissioned Officers, Non-Commissioned Officers and Privates, of the Regiments which were Organized in the State of New York and Called to the Service of the United States to Assist in Suppressing the Rebellion Caused by the Secession of Some of the Southern States from the Union, A. D. 1861, as Taken from the Muster-In Rolls on File in the Adjutant General's Office, State of New York*. 8 Vols. (Albany, NY: Comstock & Cassidy, Printers, 1864), Vol. 1: 256–257.

[145] "R.W.," Letter to the Editors, *New York Sunday Mercury*, May 18, 1861, in Styple, ed., *Writing and Fighting the Civil War*, 20. See also A. O. Alcock, Letter to the Editor, May 29, 1861, *New York Leader*, June 1, 1861. John Hay later stated that Ellsworth had himself spotted a large rebel flag from the window of the White House and that "the temptation to tear it down with his own hands was too much for his boyish patriotism." This story, though, may be apocryphal. See John Hay, "A Young Hero," *The World*, February 16, 1890, Newspaper Clippings, Brownell Papers, MNHS. Henry Morford also alleged that the Zouaves had in fact taken down "its predecessor from the same roof, only a few days before," but this seems highly unlikely, too. See Morford, *Days of Shoddy*, 302. The flag that Ellsworth eventually removed, stained with his blood, was fourteen feet high and twenty-four feet long. Its remnants currently reside in the New York State Military Museum in Saratoga Springs, NY.

[146] According to Brownell, Lincoln replied that the situation was delicate and he "desired to avoid all violence." Brownell further explained that this conference with the president was "unknown to the command." This author has been unable to find any corroboration that Ellsworth appealed to Lincoln, but it would be unsurprising given their close relationship. See Frank E. Brownell, "Ellsworth's Career," *Weekly Times* (Philadelphia, PA), June 18, 1881.

[147] Elmer E. Ellsworth to Joseph Mansfield, May 23, 1861, 11th New York Volunteer Infantry, Volunteer Organizations, Regimental Returns, RG 94, NARA. Emphasis from the original.

around midnight on May 24, Ellsworth summoned his regiment to announce preparations for departure.

The night was clear with a full moon "shining over the long array of glittering bayonets, lighting up the surrounding landscape," remembered Lieutenant Coates.[148] Ellsworth excitedly addressed the soldiers: "Go to your tents, lie down, and take your rest till 2 o'clock, when the boat will arrive, and we go forward to victory or death." The Zouaves were about to embark on their first mission, and, their young colonel warned them, the world was watching: "When we reach the place of destination, act as men; do nothing to shame the regiment, show the enemy that you are men as well as soldiers, and that you will treat them with kindness until they force you to use violence. I want to kill them with kindness. Go to your tents and do as I tell you."[149] He stressed, too, that this was a special honor even though there were "many regiments in a better state of drill than ourselves."[150] Lieutenant Knox well remembered Ellsworth's words that night, emphasizing "the great necessity of obedience" and assuring them that he would "never order one of you to go where I fear to lead."[151] It was nearly impossible to sleep. Private Alcock described: "little knots of men might be seen here and there, talking of our prospects in the approaching struggle – strong in their determination to do or die as became good soldiers in a just cause."[152]

Ellsworth penned a short note to his parents, predicting "it may be my lot to be injured in some manner. Whatever may happen I shall have the consolation of knowing I was engaged in the performance of a sacred

[148] E. M. Coates to Charles Coates, May 24, 1861, published in the *New York Herald*, May 27, 1861.
[149] "Ellsworth's Last Speech," in Frank Moore, ed. *The Rebellion Record: A Diary of American Events, with Documents, Narratives, Illustrative Incidents, Poetry, etc.* 12 Vols. (New York: G. P. Putnam, 1861–1868), Vol. 2 "Rumors and Incidents," 57. See also Wisner, "Annals," *Weekly Times* (Philadelphia, PA), December 29, 1883. According to Morford, the Zouaves finally received new rifles for everyone just before leaving for Alexandria. See Morford, *Days of Shoddy*, 285.
[150] E. M. Coates to Charles Coates, May 24, 1861, in the *New York Herald*, May 27, 1861.
[151] E. B. Knox, "How Ellsworth Died," *The Sunday Herald* (Chicago, IL), May 24, 1885 in Newspaper Clippings, Brownell Papers, MNHS. Another soldier described the speech as "thrilling." See Wilber A. Apgar Letter, May 30, 1861, excerpted in R. L. Murray, *"They Fought like Tigers": The 11th New York Fire Zouaves, 14th Brooklyn and Irish 69th New York at First Battle of Bull Run. Army of the Potomac Journal, Volume Two* (Wolcott, NY: Benedum Books, 2005), 13; see also *Brooklyn Daily Eagle*, May 27, 1861.
[152] A. O. Alcock, Letter to the Editor, May 29, 1861, *New York Leader*, June 1, 1861, in Pohanka and Schroeder, eds., *With the 11th New York*, 92. See also A. O. Alcock, Letter to the Editor, May 23, 1861, *New York Atlas*, May 26, 1861, in Pohanka and Schroeder, eds., *With the 11th New York*, 73.

duty."[153] To his fiancée Carrie, he similarly and ominously admitted in a letter to her that his unit may "meet with a warm reception" and with "so many careless fellows one is somewhat likely to be hit."[154] His words would prove chillingly prophetic but not in the way anyone could have anticipated.

[153] Elmer E. Ellsworth to Ephraim and Phoebe Ellsworth, May 23, 1861, printed in the *Weekly Times* (Philadelphia, PA), June 18, 1881. A typescript copy of this letter can also be found in the Ellsworth Papers, ALPL.
[154] Elmer E. Ellsworth to Carrie Spafford, May 23, 1861, Ellsworth Papers, ALPL.

2

"Effervescent Courage": Virginia

"AN ACT OF RASHNESS"

Around 4:00 AM on May 24, 1861, the Fire Zouaves boarded two steamers and set sail across the Potomac River, accompanied by the sloop-of-war USS *Pawnee*. The sun was rising and the morning sky was clear and bright. As the boats neared the shore, one Zouave reported "several sentinels who had previously been observed by us ... discharged their muskets." Some shot in the air. Others aimed toward the steamers. "[T]hen," he continued, "giving leg bail they travelled at as lively a gait up the hill as if there had been a general alarm of fire, or as if the Devil himself had been after them with a particularly sharp stick." The sight of the scurrying guards delighted the men, with many shouting, "See how they run!" "How them fellers stick in their toe-nails!" "Don't they scratch gravel!"[1] When some of the "impetuous and untrained zouaves at once began to fire upon the retreating figures," officers quickly restrained them.[2] Corporal Brownell who was standing near the colonel, inquired if he could shoot his musket in response. Ellsworth turned to him "in a manner I shall never forget," asking brusquely, "if I had so soon forgotten what he said before leaving camp – that not a shot must be fired without orders."[3]

---

[1] A. O. Alcock Letter to the Editor, May 29, 1861, *New York Leader*, June 1, 1861, in Pohanka and Schroeder, eds., *With the 11th New York*, 93.

[2] Wisner, "Annals," *Weekly Times* (Philadelphia, PA), December 29, 1883; See also E. B. Knox, "How Ellsworth Died," *The Sunday Herald* (Chicago, IL), May 24, 1885, in Newspaper Clippings, Brownell Papers, MNHS. Comings later recalled: "As we steamed down the river, Alexandria came into view, with a secession flag floating from one of the buildings." See Comings, *Personal Reminiscences*, 5.

[3] "The Avenger's Story," Interview with Frank Brownell by Walter B. Stevens, *St. Louis Daily Globe-Democrat*, June 10, 1888, Newspaper Clippings, Brownell Papers, MNHS.

The orders Colonel Ellsworth had received hours prior instructed him to "act in concert" with Col. Orlando B. Willcox "so to time their movements as to march on Alexandria simultaneously – Ellsworth by the river front and Willcox by the Washington pike."[4] Without waiting for word from Colonel Willcox or for his own troops to fully disembark, the young colonel, "springing to the dock," hastened forward into the town with a small squad of soldiers and noncombatants, including two journalists and regimental chaplain George Dodge.[5] Brownell later defended Ellsworth's failure to coordinate with Willcox, alleging that because one of the steamers, the USS *Mount Vernon*, was "in sinking condition" due to tampering by "secession sympathizers," the Fire Zouaves had to disembark quickly without delay. This, however, fails to explain why Ellsworth rushed into town ahead of the bulk of his regiment.[6] His impatience would soon prove his own undoing.

Descriptions of the 11th New York's arrival in Alexandria circulated widely in the press. See, for example, the *Evening Star* (Washington, DC), May 24, 1861; reprinted in the *Illinois State Daily Journal* (Springfield, IL), May 28, 1861. Coates gave a similar account but blamed a "man of the Seventh regiment" for aiming his rifle at the shoreline. Coates ordered him not to fire, but the man did anyway, "but no one was hit." See E. M. Coates to Charles Coates, May 24, 1861, in *New York Herald*, May 27, 1861. The 7th New York State Militia actually crossed to Alexandria via the Long Bridge. See Emmons Clark, *History of the Seventh Regiment of New York, 1806–1889*, 2 Vols. (New York: Published by the Seventh Regiment, 1890), Vol. 2: 25–26.

[4] O. B. Willcox, "Alexandria. Graphic Account of Its Capture and Occupation in 1861," *National Tribune* (Washington, DC), December 25, 1884, in Newspaper Clippings, Brownell Papers, MNHS. The original plan to advance into Alexandria included a number of other units besides the 1st Michigan and 11th New York, converging in three directions, all expected to coordinate together. See Samuel P. Heintzelman to George L. Thomas, July 20, 1863, OR, Ser. I, Vol. 2, 40–41; and *Evening Star* (Washington, DC), October 9, 1902, Newspaper Clippings, Brownell Papers, MNHS.

[5] "springing to the dock" from W.H.H. to "Dear Friend," May 25, 1861, in *Brooklyn Daily Eagle*, May 27, 1861. The letter writer was most likely Pvt. William H. Hogeboom, Co. E; See AGNY, 1142. Henry Wisner, *The New York Times* reporter, claimed that Ellsworth initially set out with no military escort, only the two reporters and the chaplain, but assented to an escort when Wisner suggested it. The squad that accompanied Ellsworth included five soldiers from Company A: Cpl. Frank Brownell, Cpl. Henry Phillips, Sgt. Frank B. Marshall, Pvt. Richard Gleason, and Pvt. James M. Brannan; also Chaplain George W. Dodge, Wisner, and *New York Tribune* reporter E. H. House. House was the only one, according to Wisner, "utterly unarmed." See Wisner, "Annals," *Weekly Times* (Philadelphia, PA), December 29, 1883; and *The Budget*, (Troy, NY), September 20, 1891, in Newspaper Clippings, Brownell Papers, MNHS; See also A. O. Alcock, Letter to the Editor, June 20, 1861, *New York Atlas*, June 23, 1861 in Pohanka and Schroeder, *With the 11th New York*, 125–126; Edward H. House, *Biography of Col. E. E. Ellsworth* (Cincinnati, OH: Mumford, 1864).

[6] State of New York, *Annual Report of the Adjutant General, Transmitted to the Legislature, January 31st, 1868.* (Albany, NY: Printing House of Charles van

The town was eerily quiet like a "cemetery," according to Frank Brownell, who remembered: "Not even a face could be seen at a shutter." The silence, he described, "was actually painful."[7] Warned of their arrival by Lt. R. B. Lowry, a naval officer on the USS *Pawnee*, nearly all the Confederate troops quickly evacuated, leaving local residents sleeping or waiting anxiously in their homes. Upon hearing of the evacuation and the claim that only women and children remained behind, Ellsworth pledged to Lowry that he and his men would "harm no one."[8] Their destination was the telegraph office, but after traversing just a few blocks, Ellsworth spotted a massive rebel flag flying over a boarding house – the same flag, it seems, that his own men had been scheming to seize when camped across the river.

There are varying versions of what Ellsworth said or did next. At some point, though, he abruptly changed direction and entered the Marshall Boarding House. He dispatched a sergeant to bring up a company in support, but instead of waiting for their arrival or conducting a reconnaissance with his small squad, he resolved to remove the flag from the roof himself. After a brusque encounter with a man on the first floor, the whole party headed to the attic where Ellsworth mounted a stepladder and cut down the banner. The boarding house's proprietor, James W. Jackson, the same person whom they had encountered on entry, confronted the Zouaves with a double-barreled shotgun as they descended the stairs. Corporal Brownell, who was leading the group, instinctively

Benthuysen, 1868), Vol. 1: 115. Brownell asserted that both steamers were leaking and thus a portion of Company E. helped bail out the boat. See "The Avenger's Story," interview with Brownell by Walter B. Stevens, *St. Louis Daily Globe-Democrat*, June 10, 1888, Newspaper Clippings, Brownell Papers, MNHS; *State of New York Annual Report of the Adjutant General 1868*, Vol. 1: 115.

[7] Brownell, "Ellsworth's Career," *Weekly Times* (Philadelphia, PA), June 18, 1881.

[8] Alexandria already had relatively few troops stationed there prior to the Federals' arrival on May 24. See William C. Davis, *Battle at Bull Run: A History of the First Major Campaign of the Civil War* (New York: Doubleday, 1977), 8–9. The warning to the Confederates, issued by USN Commander Stephen C. Rowan, and carried out by Lt. Reigert Bolivar Lowry, caused some controversy as Rowan also acted without orders. He insisted, though, that he "was actuated solely by motives of humanity." Secretary of Navy Gideon Welles chided Rowan for committing a "grave error." See the varying exchanges among Rowan, Lowry, and Welles, including Lowry recounting his conversation with Ellsworth, and quoted in *Official Records of the Union and Confederate Navies in the War of the Rebellion*, 30 Vols. (Washington, DC: Government Printing Office, 1894–1922), Ser. I, Vol. 4: 479–481 (hereafter referred to as ORN). See also George H. Terrett to Thomas Jordan, May 28, 1861, OR, Ser. 1, Vol. 2: 43; the *Richmond Enquirer*, May 28, 1861; and Brownell, "Ellsworth's Career," *Weekly Times* (Philadelphia, PA), June 18, 1881.

FIGURE 2.1 "Assassination of Colonel Ellsworth at the Marshall House." Image courtesy of *Frank Leslie's Illustrated, Newspaper*, June 1, 1861.

jumped to the foot of the stairs and sought to strike Jackson's gun down with his own. In a matter of seconds, Jackson regained his balance and re-aimed, this time firing directly at the colonel at point-blank range. "My God!" Ellsworth gasped, before collapsing dead on the stairs. Brownell responded in kind, shooting Jackson "through the head and then ran him through with his bayonet."[9]

[9] *Frank Leslie's Illustrated Newspaper*, June 1, 1861. Brownell himself described: "Jackson was shot in the corner of the left eye, through the brain. The bayonet pierced his heart." See "The Avenger's Story," interview with Brownell by Walter B. Stevens, *St. Louis Daily Globe-Democrat*, June 10, 1888, Newspaper Clippings, Brownell Papers, MNHS. Brownell, Wisner and House's eye-witness accounts differ in varying but notable ways, Wisner's postwar account centered himself more closely to Ellsworth, claiming to be the one who thought of adding a military escort, and handing the colonel a bowie knife to cut down the flag. He further maintained that he prevented soldiers from tearing pieces of the flag as "mementoes of the exploit" before Ellsworth was shot. See Wisner, "Annals," *Weekly Times* (Philadelphia, PA), December 29, 1883. Wisner's letter to *The New York Times* on May 27, 1861, defended Ellsworth as calm and brave the day of his death. See *The New York Times*, May 29, 1861. Brownell, who gave an extensive interview to the *New York Leader* within a week of the shootings, altered his story through the years, but remained a staunch defender of Ellsworth. In this early interview, he recounted (seemingly inaccurately) that at the same time Ellsworth requested the "special guard to follow him, he also directed that Company A, Captain Coyle, should overtake him as speedily as possible." Other contemporary and postwar versions (including Brownell's own postwar

It was a gruesome sight. Ellsworth's uniform, one witness remembered, "was so drenched with blood that it was almost impossible to discover the locality of his wound." The buckshot left a "cavity almost large enough to insert a clenched hand."[10] At 5:30 AM, Colonel Willcox sent word to General Mansfield, "Alexandria is ours." "I regret to say," he added, "Colonel Ellsworth has been shot by a person in a house."[11] Willcox later recollected that the "circumstances of Ellsworth's death struck us with horror and indignation."[12] Lt. Col. Noah L. Farnham, now ostensibly in command of the 11th New York, notified General Mansfield that he was "ignorant of the details of the orders issued to the regiment," and could only "await further instruction."[13] Colonel Willcox, who was processing all that had happened in a matter of mere hours, moved the Fire Zouaves a few miles out of town to Shuter's Hill. He waited until the evening to inform the rest of the regiment of their colonel's death, worried that the Fire Zouaves might burn the entire town in anger.[14]

On the surface, Ellsworth's fateful decision to enter the Marshall House appears, as one commentator later stated, "rash," and "an act contrary to the training of an officer in the regular army."[15] Novelist Henry Morford blasted: "It was a mad, reckless waste of life and desertion of command – nothing more nothing less."[16] Willcox later complained that "Ellsworth's command had treated us cavalierly, and gone its own way oblivious of orders, reckless and *debonair*, in true Zouave d'Afrique

interviews) indicate that Ellsworth ordered the company only after he spotted the flag. See *New York Leader*, June 1, 1861; House, *Biography of Col. E. E. Ellsworth*, 10; Brownell, "Ellsworth's Career," *Weekly Times* (Philadelphia, PA), June 18, 1881 from Newspaper Clippings, Brownell Papers, MNHS; For other versions of Brownell's account see *The Cleveland Leader* (Cleveland, OH), May 24, 1883; "The Avenger's Story," interview with Brownell by Walter B. Stevens, *St. Louis Daily Globe-Democrat*, June 10, 1888, Newspaper Clippings, Brownell Papers, MNHS and Correspondence and Related Papers, Brownell Collection, MNHS.

[10] Wisner, "Annals," *Weekly Times* (Philadelphia, PA), December 29, 1883.
[11] O. B. Willcox to Joseph K. Mansfield, May 24, 1861, *OR*, Ser. I, Vol. 2: 41.
[12] O. B. Willcox, "Alexandria. Graphic Account of its Capture and Occupation in 1861," *National Tribune* (Washington, DC), December 25, 1884, in Newspaper Clippings, Brownell Papers, MNHS.
[13] Noah L. Farnham to Joseph K. Mansfield, May 24, 1861, *OR*, Ser. I, Vol. 2, 41–42.
[14] Morford, *Days of Shoddy*, 299–300.
[15] E. E. Jones, "Hero of 61," unpublished manuscript, n.d., Ellsworth Papers, Folder Ams 811/2.9, RM, pp. 8–9. Another example of this criticism is Thomas M. Aldrich, *The History of Battery A, First Regiment Rhode Island Light Artillery in the War to Preserve the Union, 1861–1865* (Providence, RI: Snow & Farnham, Printers, 1904), 124.
[16] Morford, *The Days of Shoddy*, 302.

style."[17] Certainly, as a colonel with a green regiment entering an enemy location, he should have detailed his men to secure the town and not taken it upon himself to commit such a provocative act, although the flag of truce may have given him false confidence. Nonetheless, it is telling that he neglected to inform his second in command, Lieutenant-Colonel Farnham, of the full extent of his original orders, or that he set out into town with such a small escort. 1st Lt. E. M. Coates wrote his father a few hours after the killings, sitting close to the site, lamenting that his friend and commander had "fallen at the very threshold of a brilliant career, a sacrifice to that determination to be first in everything."[18]

The New York Times reporter Henry Wisner, acting as Ellsworth's military aid, felt "pained" when he began to hear of these criticisms just days after the killings. He knew, he wrote in the *Times*, that Ellsworth had been entirely "calm and self-possessed" the day they arrived in Alexandria and speculated that Jackson had raised the flag purposefully "in a spirit of bravado." Ellsworth "acted as any brave man would under similar circumstances," he asserted.[19] Years later, though, Wisner admitted, "We were all novices in warfare at the time, and I am sure not one of us was conscious of the danger which threatened us in entering the streets of a city whose people were excited and angry, and among whom were doubtless the average proportion of 'cranks,' eager to distinguish themselves." Ellsworth's death proved a "bitter experience" to teach them lessons of real war.[20]

Cpl. Frank Brownell, who soon earned the moniker "Ellsworth's Avenger," insisted that his commander's actions were intended to keep the peace and ensure that his Fire Zouaves, troops he had struggled to control, did not react violently when they encountered the banner. In an interview the corporal gave to the *New York Leader* less than a week after

---

[17] O. B. Willcox, "Alexandria," *National Tribune* (Washington, DC), December 25, 1884, in Newspaper Clippings, Brownell Papers, MNHS.

[18] E. M. Coates to Charles Coates, May 24, 1861, letter published in the *New York Herald*, May 27, 1861.

[19] Henry J. Wisner, "Special Correspondent," May 27, 1861, *The New York Times*, May 29, 1861.

[20] Wisner like Brownell believed that the flag of truce caught Ellsworth "off his guard, causing him to neglect those precautions for his personal safety which would have prevented his unhappy death." See Wisner, "Annals," *Weekly Times* (Philadelphia, PA), December 29, 1883. Alcock defended Ellsworth as "courageous, though young and consequently indiscreet." See A. O. Alcock, Letter to the Editor, May 29, 1861, *New York Leader*, June 1, 1861, in Pohanka and Schroeder, eds., *With the 11th New York*, 94.

the shootings, Brownell insisted that "there was no rash impetuosity or desire for any ostentatious display of courage on the part of Colonel Ellsworth, connected in any way with the manner of his death. No danger was apprehended in the enterprise, and if any could have been anticipated, Colonel Ellsworth was too cool and collected to have unnecessarily ventured into needless peril."[21] Brownell would go on to defend Ellsworth on multiple occasions, including at the postwar dedication of a monument to him. "It has been often charged," he acknowledged that "even by those who intend to honor Ellsworth that he lost his life while committing a very rash and reckless act," insinuating that "the young solder lacked the very principle which he exacted from others, discipline and obedience to orders." Brownell, though, countered that Ellsworth "sacrificed his life in the endeavor to preserve order and enforce discipline."[22]

Brownell, who had a blinding headache after the encounter, went to rest in the camp of the 71st New York. He did not stay long. He soon learned that the President wanted to see him. He found Lincoln distraught and pacing the floor. At one point, Lincoln lifted the cloth from Ellsworth's face and exclaimed, "My boy, my boy! Was it necessary this sacrifice should be made!"[23] Lincoln later disclosed to a reporter that Ellsworth's decision to rush into the Marshall House "was undoubtedly an act of rashness," but it displayed "the heroic spirit that animates our soldiers from high to low, in this righteous cause of ours."[24]

Lincoln's praise underscored the issue at play: acting rashly did not necessarily translate to prudent military conduct. That contrast was only becoming more clear for the Fire Zouaves.

"STIR THE FIRE"

Meantime, as Ellsworth made his ill-fated entry into the Marshall House, Company E, led by Capt. John B. Leverich, hurried at a double quick to the railroad depot. En route, they encountered a portion of the local

---

[21] *New York Leader*, June 1, 1861.

[22] Francis E. Brownell, "Address," in *Exercises Connected with the Unveiling of the Ellsworth Monument at Mechanicville, May 27, 1874* (Albany, NY: Joel Munsell, 1875), 49, 52. See also undated, unnamed paper, Newspaper Clippings, Frank Brownell Papers, MNHS; Brownell, "Ellsworth's Career," *Weekly Times* (Philadelphia, PA), June 18, 1881; and Brownell interview, *Cleveland Leader* (Cleveland, OH), May 24, 1883; both from Newspaper Clippings MNHS.

[23] Brownell, "Ellsworth's Career," *Weekly Times* (Philadelphia, PA), June 18, 1881.

[24] Abraham Lincoln quoted in the *New York Herald*, May 25, 1861.

Fairfax Cavalry, and unexpectedly, more federal troops – Willcox's men, who had arrived by land. Barely avoiding friendly fire from these additional Union troops, Captain Leverich had a sharp exchange with Colonel Willcox, who was apoplectic that Ellsworth had failed to coordinate with him.[25] The rebel cavalrymen, though, outnumbered and surrounded, quickly surrendered. Nearby, Private Comings found stark evidence of southern slavery when he "strolled into the slave pen of Alexandria," and discovered a black man "chained in the floor." Comings freed him "after some labor."[26] Private Hogeboom was well-pleased with his comrades and himself, writing home: "Thank God, I can say with truth, that not once have I flinched, even at the moment when I for the first time in all my life, absolutely believed that I stared death in the face." He maintained: "You all may be truly proud of the boys; they are all firm, unflinching and resolved to sell their lives dearly. Thank God, we are all in good health, and not yet disposed to go home."[27]

Ellsworth's body, though, was soon heading home to his native New York, accompanied by a small detachment of Fire Zouaves. First, it was transported to Washington, DC, and lay in state in the East Room of the White House before traveling by railroad cars to New York City and eventually for burial in Mechanicville. In the capital, crowds lined Pennsylvania Avenue to glimpse the fallen colonel. One congressman later remembered: "The impressive funeral services were probably attended by more persons of preeminent distinction than were present at those of any other victim of the war, however great his rank or distinguished his services might have been."[28] Diarist and lawyer George Templeton Strong observed the funeral procession in New York City, noting Brownell had borne "his rifle with fixed bayonet and the rebel flag which Ellsworth had hauled down." Strong found this "close juxtaposition of the murdered colonel with his bayonet that was red with his

---

[25] Morford, *Days of Shoddy*, 298–299.
[26] Comings, *Personal Reminiscences*, 6. Comings also described the cavalry encounter, 5–6.
[27] W.H.H. to "Dear Friend," May 25, 1862, *Brooklyn Daily Eagle*, May 27, 1861. See also E. B. Knox, "How Ellsworth Died," *The Sunday Herald* (Chicago, IL), May 24, 1885 in Newspaper Clippings, Brownell Papers, MNHS.
[28] W. D. Kelley, "The Assassination of Ellsworth," *The Graphic News* (Cincinnati, OH), Vol. 1, No. 4 (July 21, 1886), in Newspaper Clippings, Frank E. Brownell Papers, MNHS. See also George W. Sheldon, *The Story of the Volunteer Fire Department of the City of New York*. (New York: Harper & Brothers, 1882), 314. Sarah J. Purcell discusses Ellsworth's funeral and the extensive public mourning that followed in her book *Spectacle of Grief: Public Funerals and Memory in the Civil War Era* (Chapel Hill, NC: University of North Carolina Press, 2022), 45–72.

murderer's life blood forty-eight hours ago" to be "hardly appropriate" for the solemnness of the occasion. Still, he mused that Ellsworth was more valuable dead than alive: "His murder will stir the fire of every western state, and shows all Christendom with what kind of enemy we are contending."[29]

Seemingly overnight, the 11th New York's young commander became a Union martyr, and his death an "assassination."[30] For Confederates, the slayings represented the North's ruthlessness and egregious trampling of their rights. A poem entitled "Stand by Your Flag" and dedicated to Jackson's widow predicted:

> The living shall enshrine his fame,
> And little children, yet unborn,
> Will learn to lisp the martyr's name.[31]

In the North, there were poems, too, as well as songs, paintings, public speeches, and extensive coverage in newspapers.[32] In Ellsworth's home town of Mechanicville, New York, citizens passed a resolution expressing their "most profound grief and indignation," offering their sympathy to Ellsworth's grieving parents, and to his regiment: "which by this sudden affliction deplore the loss of a faithful friend and brass commander and bid them strike, in honorable battle, hard blows in Freedom's cause."[33]

There had already been a good deal of public interest in the Fire Zouaves before Ellsworth's death, but his killing only increased their notoriety.[34] The Marshall House became a shrine where curiosity-seekers, including

[29] Nevins and Thomas, eds. *The Diary of George Templeton Strong*, May 24 and 26, 1861, 146, 147.
[30] *New York Tribune*, May 25, 1861. Maj.-Gen. John Dix issued a formal statement on Ellsworth's death calling him a "victim of a double perfidy" and ordered officers in his division to "wear the usual badge of mourning for thirty days in memory of their youthful and gallant companion in arms." See "General Orders No. 4," May 25, 1861 in *New York Leader* (May 1861) accessed via museum.dmna.ny.gov.
[31] M. B. Wharton, "Stand by Your Flag," in *Richmond Dispatch*, May 31, 1861.
[32] Alice Fahs notes a "shared national culture of mourning" evidenced by the outpouring of poetry and images in response to Ellsworth's death. See Alice Fahs, *The Imagined Civil War: Popular Literature of the North and South, 1861–1865* (Chapel Hill, NC: University of North Carolina Press, 2001), 83–86. Examples of poems and songs include Thomas J. M. M'Cavily, "Zouave War-Song," May 27, 1861, *New York Atlas*, June 9, 1861 in *With the 11th New York*, 97; G. B. De Wolfe, "Columbia Mourns for Ellsworth," n.d., New York Historical Society, New York, NY (hereafter referred to as NYHS).
[33] "Resolutions Adopted by the Citizens of Mechanicville," May 26, 1861, Folder 3, Box 8, Administrative Correspondence Files (Series A4111), Bureau of Military Statistics, NYSA.
[34] *Harper's Weekly* published mostly positive stories about Ellsworth and his Zouaves in successive issues, including May 11, 18, and 25, 1861; and June 8, 15, 1861. *Frank Leslie's*

members of the 11th New York, stripped the house for relics.[35] The flag which sparked the entire incident was cut up, first by his own men, and then by others who coveted pieces of the banner as keepsakes. Eventually, the blood-stained and torn flag made its way to New York City where it was presented to the Fire Department.[36]

There were also widespread vows of revenge. The *Sunday Mercury* tied Ellsworth's death to the cause for abolition, predicting: "The whole North and North-west will rally to punish the cowards and braggart[s], who [seek] to propagate and advance the cause of human slavery."[37] The state of New York raised a new regiment known as "Ellsworth's Avengers" or the "People's Ellsworth Regiment," specially charged with vindicating the colonel's death. This unit, formally designated the 44th New York Volunteer Infantry Regiment, sought representatives from every county in the state, with requirements that they be men with "good moral character."[38]

Ellsworth's own men were seething. At first, officers tried to keep word of the colonel's killing from them, fearing their response. Upon learning the terrible news, many Zouaves were "drunk and unmanageable," threatening to burn Alexandria to ashes.[39] Private Alcock, speaking for his comrades, admitted: "we did not agree with" Ellsworth "in all things." Even so, he was confident that "we would willingly have died by his side and in his defense. As it is, we must suffer meekly the dispensation that has deprived us of a good officer, a brave man, and one in whom we trust

Illustrated Newspaper featured Ellsworth's death on the front page of its June 1, 1861 issue.

[35] George Templeton Strong visited the Marshall House less than a week after Ellsworth's death and discovered: "Flag-staff is nearly cut through; stair-banisters, all gone. Pieces of floor and stairs gouged out." See Nevins and Thomas, eds. *Diary of George Templeton Strong*, May 31, 1861, 152. A soldier from the 71st New York Volunteer Infantry also recounted visiting the house and taking a piece of a door frame. See *The New York Times*, June 1, 1861; also *New York Herald*, August 12, 1861; and *New York Daily Tribune*, August 9, 1861. A member of the 18th New York Volunteer Infantry later alleged that the entire town had suffered the regiment's wrath and that they "turned some of the houses inside out." Quote from Ryan A. Conklin, *The 18th New York Infantry in the Civil War: A History and Roster* (Jefferson, NC: McFarland, 2016), 79.

[36] *Frank Leslie's Illustrated Newspaper*, June 8, 1861. See also W.H.H. to "Dear Friend," May 25, 1862, *Brooklyn Daily Eagle*, May 27, 1861.

[37] *New York Sunday Mercury*, May 26, 1861, in Styple, ed., *Writing and Fighting the Civil War*, 21.

[38] Nash, *A History of the Forty-Fourth Regiment*, 7–12.

[39] Morford, *The Days of Shoddy*, 352.

implicitly."[40] It was only the "wiser counsels and firmness" of Lieutenant Colonel Farnham that prevented the men from turning their rage on the town and its inhabitants.[41]

If Ellsworth removed the rebel flag believing he was protecting his regiment, it is a tragic irony that his startling death as a result rekindled the reckless and unruly propensity of his men. One soldier predicted that their "burning desire for revenge" would "evince itself in the first general fight that occurs."[42] Mixed with their indignation was raw grief. One of the men in 1st Lt. E. M. Coates' company came to him sobbing, "Lieutenant say the word, and we will go down and burn every house in this place."[43] Corporal Brownell, spotted by a reporter accompanying the slain colonel's body, "fairly bit his lip through to keep from crying audibly."[44] Decades later, E. B. Knox struggled to describe how he felt when he learned that Ellsworth, his friend and commander, was gone, recalling, "I could scarcely credit my own senses."[45]

The day after Ellsworth's killing, there were two more troubling losses for the regiment. Sgt. John Butterworth was killed by one of his own men when he failed to give the countersign to a sentry stationed at their camp.[46] That same day, 2nd Lt. John Dowd killed Pvt. John F. Buckley "for insubordination and an attempt to strike his superior officer." Buckley supposedly "collared" and threatened to assault Dowd, who shot Buckley with his pistol "in self defense."[47]

[40] A. O. Alcock, Letter to the Editor, May 25, 1861, *New York Atlas*, May 26, 1861, in Pohanka and Schroeder, eds., *With the 11th New York*, 79.

[41] A. O. Alcock, Letter to the Editor, May 29, 1861, *New York Leader*, June 1, 1861, in Pohanka and Schroeder, eds., *With the 11th New York*, 95. Reports of the Fire Zouaves' vows of revenge also appeared in Confederate newspapers including the *Richmond Daily Dispatch*, May 30, 1861.

[42] *The Buffalo Commercial* (Buffalo, NY) June 15, 1861; see also *New York Sunday Mercury*, May 26, 1861, in Styple, ed., *Writing and Fighting the Civil War*, 21.

[43] E. M. Coates to Charles Coates, May 24, 1861, published in the *New York Herald*, May 27, 1861. Similarly, Pennsylvania Congressman William D. Kelley remembered encountering a straggler from the regiment in Washington. Hearing news of Ellsworth's death, the Zouave predicted "black smoke stretching all over Alexandria." See William D. Kelley, "The Assassination of Ellsworth," *The Graphic News* (Cincinnati, OH), Vol. 1, No. 4 (July 21, 1886), in Newspaper Clippings, Frank E. Brownell Papers, MNHS.

[44] *Evening Star* (Washington, DC), May 24, 1861.

[45] E. B. Knox, "How Ellsworth Died," *The Sunday Herald* (Chicago, IL), May 24, 1885 in Newspaper Clippings, Brownell Papers, MNHS.

[46] *New York Atlas*, May 26, 1819 in *With the 11th New York*, 79; A. O. Alcock, Letter to the Editor, May 29, 1861, *New York Leader*, June 1, 1861 in Pohanka and Schroeder, eds., *With the 11th New York*, 96.

[47] A. O. Alcock Letter to the Editor, May 31, 1861, *New York Atlas*, June 9, 1861, in Pohanka and Schroeder, eds., *With the 11th New York*, 101; and A. O. Alcock, Letter to the Editor, May 29, 1861, *New York Leader*, June 1, 1861 in Pohanka and Schroeder,

At some point soon after Ellsworth's death, Cpl. Edward Riley (Co.B) composed "Song of the Zouaves," trying to convey a sense of coherency and resolution within the regiment. The tune, dedicated to Capt. Edward Byrnes, included the stanza:

> Now calmly waiting we take our place;
> > With Captain Byrnes in command,
> We have no fears to contemplate,
> > For our arms are in our hands,
> And Byrnes, Stryker, and Harris
> > To lead us in the fight.
> Our cry: "Remember Ellsworth,
> > Our Country, God, and Right."[48]

The song, though, was not an accurate reflection of the Fire Zouaves' state of mind. Ellsworth's death shook the regiment to its core.

"A DISSOLUTION OF THIS FINE CORPS"

For the next several weeks, the Fire Zouaves remained at Shuter's Hill, a bluff just outside of Alexandria, christening the site "Camp Ellsworth." Under command of Gen. O. B. Willcox, they were brigaded with the 1st Michigan Infantry Regiment and 38th New York Infantry Regiment, helping to construct a line of forts and batteries in defense of Washington, DC.[49] *Frank Leslie's Illustrated Newspaper* published a sketch of the "gallant volunteers of Michigan and the Fire Zouaves" on the front page of its June 15, 1861, issue, showing the men diligently building entrenchments under the watchful eye of an engineering officer. The paper reported that a visitor to their camp found them "in the highest

---

With the 11th New York, 96. The New York State Adjutant General's roster states that Buckley was shot "for resisting an officer." See AGNY, 1087.

[48] Edward Riley, "Song of the Zouaves," "dedicated to Capt. Edward Byrnes, Assistant Foreman of Mohawk Engine Co. 10," NYHS. Edward Byrnes, age twenty-four, resigned October 4, 1861. Riley was twenty-seven years old and enlisted April 20, 1861, but later discharged for disability in December 1861. See AGNY, 1090, 1193.

[49] The volunteers were under direction of the US Army Corps of Engineers. See State of New York, *Third Annual Report of the Chief of the Bureau of Military Record*, 107–108. See also A. O. Alcock, Letter to the Editor, June 19, 1861, *New York Leader*, June 23, 1861, in Pohanka and Schroeder, *With the 11th New York*, 123; *New York Herald*, June 20, 1861; and OR Ser I, Vol. 51, 408. Company E under command of Captain Leverich remained at Alexandria. By mid-July, just before the Bull Run campaign, the 11th New York was encamped three miles from Alexandria at Campbell's Run. See A. O. Alcock, "Journal of Facts," *New York Atlas*, August 16, 1862, in Pohanka and Schroeder, eds., *With the 11th New York*, 180.

FIGURE 2.2 "The Michigan Regiment and the Ellsworth Zouaves working at the breastworks in the Outskirts of Alexandria, Va." Image courtesy of *Frank Leslie's Illustrated Newspaper*, June 15, 1861.

possible spirits and perfectly satisfied with their rations, which occasionally includes poultry fit for the table of the F.F.V.'s."[50]

[50] *Frank Leslie's Illustrated Newspaper*, June 15, 1861. See also *New York Herald*, May 30, 1861.

Things really were not so satisfactory for the 11th New York at all, though. George Templeton Strong visited the enlistees a few days after their arrival at Shuter's Hill and was "unfavorably impressed by the Zouaves." He recounted that the men "'sassed' the officers and the officers seemed loose in their notions of military subordination." One captain told Strong: "I guess we'll have the Colonel we want? If we don't, we'll let them fellows know we're about. 'We're firemen, we are." "Probably," Strong darkly predicted, "a few of the Zouaves will have to be court-martialed and shot before the regiment can be relied on."[51]

Their new colonel Noah L. Farnham was determined to change these negative perceptions. As a former Fire Department assistant engineer and officer of the celebrated 7th New York Volunteer Militia, he appeared well-suited to succeed Ellsworth. "Pony is well qualified by military experience," the *New York Leader* proclaimed, "to take charge of the boys, and his long association with a large number of them in the ranks of the Department renders him personally popular."[52] Seeking to centralize his own authority and the men's conformity, Farnham requested standard-issue uniforms from the War Department and urged the Zouave Fire Regiment Fund Committee in New York to avoid "encumbering the men with any unnecessary baggage," leaving "everything subject to further orders."[53] By June 28, Farnham wrote the Fire Department Vice President Albert J. Delatour that although "the regiment for some time after it left New York lacked a proper organization," now "all companies have their rolls, descriptive books and we are getting in good shape."[54] He further

[51] Nevins and Thomas, eds. *Diary of George Templeton Strong*, May 31, 1861, 152.

[52] *New York Leader* (June 1, 1861), accessed via museum.dmna.ny.gov. In another article on Farnham, the paper claimed that he was "personally known to almost every member of the Department, and is universally popular." See *New York Leader*, n.d., accessed via museum.dmna.ny.gov. See also the *Buffalo Courier* (Buffalo, NY), May 31, 1861. R. L. Murray, quoting from one Zouave letter, suggests that Farnham was reluctant to become colonel. He never was, it seems, formally commissioned colonel before his death. See Murray, *"They Fought like Tigers,"* 14; and AGNY, 1120.

[53] Noah L. Farnham to James Kelly, June 1, 1861, Folder 4, Box 8, Administrative Correspondence Files (Series A4111), Bureau of Military Statistics, NYSA.

[54] Noah L. Farnham to Albert J. Delatour, June 28, 1861, Folder 5, Box 8, Administrative Correspondence Files (Series A4111), Bureau of Military Statistics, NYSA; Delatour was elected vice president of the New York City Fire Department in 1860, and according to one source, he "amassed a fortune" in the "manufacture of mineral water." See Sheldon, *The Story of the Volunteer Fire Department*, 390; *The New York Times*, December 11, 1860; also Eighth Census of the United States, 1860: Population Schedule, New York Ward 17, District 4, New York, NY, Records of the Bureau of the Census, RG 29, NARA; accessed via ancestry.com.

wanted a "full corps" of drummers and fifers. "I am very anxious," he explained to the chairman of the Zouave Fire Regiment Fund Committee Adolphus F. Ockerhausen, "to have field music, because it is absolutely necessary for the perfect organization of the Regt."[55]

Private Alcock boasted to readers of the *New York Leader* that everything was progressing nicely. "The men are rapidly becoming perfect," he wrote, "and take more interest in their own improvement in this indispensable particular, than could possibly be expected of them, from their previous habits and occupation." Alcock was confident "that they will make one of the finest and most useful bodies of men in the service of the United States."[56] To be sure, there remained bad contagions plaguing the unit, but Farnham sought to be rid of them. Aware that the regiment would be marching "forward soon," he sent a list of trouble-makers to supporters in New York, explaining, "The end I want to arrive at is to keep the men together, so as to be on hand at a moment's call; and this cannot be done unless the worthless ones are publicly exposed so as to prevent their example from spreading to those who are really worth having."[57]

The 11th New York faced other changes, too. There were a good number of desertions and discharges, and officers taking furloughs or resigning entirely.[58] 1st Lt. Stephen W. Stryker, one of the original Chicago Zouaves and a close friend of Ellsworth, resigned in July to accept a commission as colonel of the newly raised "Ellsworth's People's Avengers," the 44th

---

[55] Noah L. Farnham to Alfred F. Ockerhausen, June 29, 1861, Folder 5, Box 8, Administrative Correspondence Files (Series A4111), Bureau of Military Statistics, NYSA.

[56] A. O. Alcock, Letter to the Editor, June 12, 1861, *New York Leader*, June 15, 1861, in Pohanka and Schroeder, eds., *With the 11th New York*, 116.

[57] Noah L. Farnham to (Adolphus F. Ockerhausen), July 8, 1861, Folder 6, Box 8, Administrative Correspondence Files (Series A4111), Bureau of Military Statistics, NYSA. The list is not included with the surviving letter. Morford described the Fire Zouaves' indiscipline as including drinking, brawling, and going AWOL. He further speculated that Farnham might have shaped them into effective soldiers if he had had command of them from the start and the time to train them. "But," he noted, "this is mere speculation." See Morford, *Days of Shoddy*, 351; also 361–364.

[58] The 1899 New York State Adjutant General's report lists three deserters between May 15 and July 21, 1861; twenty-nine members discharged for disability and five discharged with no reason listed. It is unclear what if anything happened to the men Farnham referenced as necessitating immediate dismissal, although Alcock wrote in late June "several of the good-for nothings, who should have always remained in New York" were discharged. See A. O. Alcock, Letter to the Editor, June 28, 1861, *New York Atlas*, June 28, 1861, in Pohanka and Schroeder, eds., *With the 11th New York*, 132. He also insisted that the "general health of the regiment is better than it has ever been since it left New York." See A. O. Alcock, Letter to the Editor, July 5, 1861, *New York Atlas*, July 7, 1861 in Pohanka and Schroeder, eds., *With the 11th New York*, 138.

New York Volunteer Infantry. Well-liked and respected, Stryker was, according to a fellow officer, "very zealous and devoted" in his "proper drill and discipline of the men."[59] Stryker's resignation was part of a steady stream of exits by officers, particularly several former Chicago Zouaves whom Ellsworth had brought with him when he created the regiment.[60] Their replacements were men who had served with Farnham in the 7th New York State Militia, and further signified the changes he sought to make in breaking free of Ellsworth's influence.[61]

Despite Farnham's efforts to take care of his men and better prepare them for battle, the failure to provide sufficient and durable Zouave uniforms was still a sore point for the regiment. "The rather jaunty and bright-looking uniforms" originally provided to the men in New York were fading and wearing thin. Unfortunately, a "close buttoned uniform of any kind" did not fit with their "ideas of firemen." They preferred the "loose Zouave dress."[62] Their supporters wrangled with the governor,

[59] Edward Byrnes to Stephen W. Stryker, July 8, 1861, Folder 6, Box 8, Administrative Correspondence Files (Series A4111), Bureau of Military Statistics, NYSA. Stryker was popular with the Fire Zouaves but his subsequent military service proved uneven. There were insinuations of dereliction of duty when he was colonel of the 44th New York Volunteer Infantry, and in 1864 he was dismissed from service as lieutenant colonel from the 18th New York Volunteer Cavalry for "perpetrating frauds upon the Government, in appropriating bounties of the state for Colored Cooks enlisted in their regiment." See *Civil War Muster Roll Abstracts of New York State Volunteers, United States Sharpshooters, and United States Colored Troops [ca. 1861–1900]*. Microfilm, 1185 rolls, New York State Archives, Albany, New York.; accessed via ancestry.com. See also Nash, *History of the Forty-Fourth New York*, 91.

[60] Ex- Chicago Zouaves who left before Bull Run included 1st Lt. George H. Fergus (Co. K), 2nd Lt. Isaac G. Seixas (Co. C), and 1st Lt. Francis E. Yates (Co. G). Edward B. Knox, Freeman Connor, and Lucius S. Larrabee, three other former Chicago Zouaves, exited on August 1, 1861. Most of these men went on to gain commissions in other units. Knox became major; Connor lieutenant-colonel and eventually colonel; and Larrabee captain, in the 44th NY. All three were singled out for their "brave conduct" with 44th NY in May 1862: See James C. Rise to E. A. Nash, May 28, 1862, OR, Ser. 1, Vol. 11, pt. 1, 731; Larrabee was killed at the Battle of Gettysburg. *U.S., Civil War Soldier Records and Profiles, 1861–1865* accessed via ancestry.com, and Nash, *History of the Forty-Fourth New York*, 5. Yates went on to serve in the 73rd New York Volunteer Infantry (the 2nd Fire Zouaves) and 18th New York Cavalry Regiment, resigning as captain in May 1865. Fergus, however, returned to Chicago and resumed his prewar occupation as printer. See *Chicago Sunday Tribune*, August 14, 1910; AGNY, 1121, 1197, 1205, 1222; and "Capt. Francis E. Yates," findagrave.com.

[61] The new officers from the 7th NYSM were Edward Bernard, Richard Bowerman, Louis Fitzgerald and Joseph E. McFarland. See Clark, *History of the Seventh Regiment*, Vol. 2: 304, 469, 491, 497.

[62] A. O. Alcock, Letter to the Editor, June 12, 1861, *New York Atlas*, June 16, 1861, in Pohanka and Schroeder, eds., *With the 11th New York*, 109.

who refused to grant an additional requisition, but allowed for new flannel red shirts.[63] By the end of June, Colonel Farnham was "satisfied" that his men, outfitted in their scarlet blouses, fez caps, and regulation blue pants, would soon be "the finest Regt in appearance near Washington."[64] Predictably, when the standard-issue blue woolen uniforms arrived, however, the Zouaves balked. "The 'lambs' almost unanimously declined to wear any part of them at all, insisting that when they enlisted as Zouaves, they had the pledge of the United States that they would be maintained as such, and as such uniformed," *The New York Times* reported.[65]

There were other reasons to be unhappy. Beyond the loss of their distinctive dress, Farnham ceased the Zouave drill, opting instead to follow the standardized Hardee and Scott manuals that he had learned as a member of the 7th New York State Militia. This further caused "great dissatisfaction among the men," with members fearing these changes would lead to "a dissolution of this fine corps."[66] The Fire Zouaves had not received any pay and some officers still had not received their commissions. Rations, too, were limited and of poor quality.[67] Men in the ranks began to worry about supporting their families. The Firemen's Zouave Fund committee complained to Rep. Francis Preston Blair, Jr., the powerful chair of the House's Military Committee, that "in many instances," soldiers' families were "left at home destitute."[68] There was nothing yet in place to formally assist soldiers' families – that would come as the war evolved and the human toll grew. Colonel Farnham expressed concern but admitted that there was little he could

[63] See James Kelly to A. J. Delatour, June 25, 1861; and Zophar Mills, "Minutes of the Zouave Fund Committee," June 25, 1861; both in Folder 5, Box 8, Administrative Correspondence Files (Series A4111), Bureau of Military Statistics, NYSA.

[64] Noah L. Farnham to Adolphus F. Ockerhausen, June 29, 1861, Folder 5, Box 8, Administrative Correspondence Files (Series A4111), Bureau of Military Statistics, NYSA.

[65] *The New York Times*, July 2, 1861. The Zouaves had better luck obtaining the briefly fashionable but wholly impractical havelocks donated by the Astor Library Ladies Army Aid Society and John C. Mather. See *New York Herald*, May 31 and June 23, 1861.

[66] "great dissatisfaction" from Comings, *Personal Reminiscences*, 7; "a dissolution" from *The New York Times*, July 2, 1861. See also "The Late Col. Farnham," Obituary, *The New York Times*, August 16, 1861.

[67] "W.N." Letter to the Editor, July 7, 1861, *New York Leader*, August 1, 1861. Most likely this "high private" was either nineteen-year-old Pvt. William Nall (Co. D), later discharged for disability in March 1862; or twenty-seven-year-old Pvt. William Nixon, Co. B, who deserted August 1, 1861. See AGNY, 1179, 1181.

[68] George F. Nesbitt to Francis Preston Blair, Jr., July 15, 1861, Folder 6, Box 8, Administrative Correspondence Files (Series A4111), Bureau of Military Statistics, NYSA.

do to assist. "My impression is that the Army Regulations make no provision but trust to the men themselves to send such portion of their pay home, [as] they please," he wrote the Committee.[69]

The Zouaves freely expressed their dissatisfaction, privately and publicly. Alcock explained, "Our men are a peculiar class, and although they are capable of and will endure all the necessary privations and hardships that any men on earth will or can, they are intelligent enough to perceive when and where a screw is loose, and will not quietly submit to be imposed upon in the most trifling degree."[70] Another Zouave reflected that since "the death of our lamented Colonel everything seems to go wrong."[71] Their confidence "was broken."[72]

In glaring contrast to the wants and needs of the men in the ranks, some officers openly flaunted their positions of power. One day in June, Capt. John Wildey (Co. I) and regimental surgeon Dr. Charles Gray entertained civilian visitors, including a "a party of ladies." Captain Wildey escorted the women through camp and then hosted "a small tea party" in front of his tent "where the delicacies of the season were distributed with a lavish hand." Dr. Gray's "little group" enjoyed lunch with their visitors, "sweetened by the smiles and gay conversation of the divinities, that was quite refreshing, and a happy relief from the monotony of our daily life at present." When Captain Byrnes returned to camp from a furlough, there was a "grand blow-out" at the NCO's tent, with several other officers in attendance and beer readily available.[73] In another instance, Captain Leverich hosted visiting guests and fellow officers with alcohol and "crackers and cheese."[74]

[69] Noah L. Farnham to Adolphus F. Ockerhausen, June 29, 1861, Folder 5, Box 8, Administrative Correspondence Files (Series A4111), Bureau of Military Statistics, NYSA; See also A. O. Alcock, Letter to the Editor (July 1861), New York Leader, July 6, 1861, in Pohanka and Schroeder, With the 11th New York, 144–145.

[70] A. O. Alcock, Letter to the Editor (July, 1861), New York Leader, July 6, 1861, in Pohanka and Schroeder, eds., With the 11th New York, 144. There were also some who dismissed these negative stories out of hand. Cpl. Thomas O'Brien, for example, on a short furlough home, visited the office of the New York Herald to insist that the regiment was well fed and "well pleased with their new colonel," and "ready to be led by him to victory or death." See New York Herald, June 9, 1861. Thomas O'Brien, age 29 (Co. A), was "discharged for disability, June 24, 1861." See AGNY, 1182.

[71] W. S. Letter, May 31, 1861 quoted in Murray, "They Fought like Tigers," 14.

[72] Comings, Personal Reminiscences, 7.

[73] A. O. Alcock, Letter to the Editor, June 12, 1861, New York Leader, June 15, 1861, in Pohanka and Schroeder, With the 11th New York, 116; Alcock, Letter to the Editor, June 19, 1861, New York Leader (June 1861), Pohanka and Schroeder, eds., With the 11th New York, 119.

[74] "Old Stock," Letter to the Editor, June 5, 1861, New York Leader (June 1861), accessed via museum.dmna.ny.gov.

Losing Ellsworth and their unique identity as Fire Zouaves only added to festering problems within the regiment. The irresponsible behavior of some of their officers was not helping.

"DO A BIG THING"

The New Yorkers still faced negative press coverage, even mockery.[75] Humorist Mortimer Thomson, under the pseudonym "Doesticks," had penned a lengthy piece entitled "The New Zouave Tactics," prior to Ellsworth's death, which ran in the *Saturday Evening Post* on June 15. Exaggerating the Zouaves' physical strength and endurance, Doesticks maintained that they trained twenty-one hours a day, mastering the "Zouave fort" and the "gallows drill." Both involved soldiers interconnecting their bodies with iron plates or ropes. "By this slight account," Doesticks concluded, "you will perceive that if you are going to send any new Zouave recruits, they must be men of the right sort." They had to "lift two tons and a half, run twenty-seven miles without stopping for breath, jump over an ordinary two-story house, and swim a mile and quarter under water."[76] The public lampooning of the Zouaves was unrelenting.

The reality of the regiment's daily routine, especially for the men in the ranks, was not this fanciful. An artist with *Harper's Weekly* drew images of them on an average day: "Cooking Dinner" and "Getting Rations" and drilling, but also cavorting and playing games.[77] Occasionally, there were

---

[75] For example, see A. O. Alcock, Letter to the Editor, July 5, 1861, *New York Atlas*, July 7, 1861 in Pohanka and Schroeder, eds., *With the 11th New York*, 136. Alcock accused the *New York Illustrated News* of printing a "diabolical caricature" of Lt. Col. John Creiger; and the *New York Herald* for "getting a bad odor among the boys, on account of the number of lies it circulates about us." See A. O. Alcock, Letter to the Editor, June 28, 1861, *New York Atlas*, June 30, 1861; and A. O. Alcock, Letter to the Editor, July 5, 1861, *New York Atlas*, July 7, 1861, in Pohanka and Schroeder, eds., *With the 11th New York*, 137.

[76] Q. K. Philander Doesticks, P.B., *Saturday Evening Post*, June 15, 1861. In another column, "Doesticks" claimed to have posed as a member of the Zouaves, helping to extinguish the fire near Willard's Hotel. He wrote of stepping on officers and getting a dog bite: "Then, I flatter myself, we all came out strong. I can only speak for myself, but I know that I came out tremendously strong." See "'Doesticks' Account of the Performances of the Fire Zouaves," in the *Bangor Daily Whig and Courier* (Bangor, ME), June 11, 1861. Alcock complained of continued "false reports" that were "scandalous and malicious" against the regiment. See A. O. Alcock, Letter to the Editor, May 31, 1861, *New York Atlas*, June 9, 1861, in Pohanka and Schroeder, eds., *With the 11th New York*, 104.

[77] "Illustrations of the Camp of Ellsworth's Zouaves at Washington," *Harper's Weekly*, June 8, 1861. The sketches probably date to their brief stay at Asylum Hill, Washington, DC, in May.

calls for "special duty." On one such occurrence, Company D marched more than four miles to help counter a brush with rebel pickets outside the town of Fairfax, Virginia. Although this movement amounted to little of any substance, a member of the company bragged that he and his comrades were "earning an enviable reputation for promptitude and subordination in the performance of their duties."[78]

Minor expeditions like this one soon, though, lost their appeal. "The boys don't like," Alcock reported, "these false alarms."[79] Picket duty offered some escape from the monotony, so much so that the men "almost came to blows for the privilege."[80] Pvt. Henry C. "Seely" Cornell convinced another soldier to allow him to go in his place. "*He was brought back a corpse*," shot while patrolling the Fairfax Road.[81] One source affirmed that "Cornell died like a brave man," attesting that "as he lay upon the ground with the life-blood gushing from his wound, he smiled at his comrades standing around him and exclaimed, 'Who would not die a soldier's death!'"[82]

This was a conventional celebration of a soldier's "Good Death": peaceful, serene, and celebratory.[83] But for the Fire Zouaves, there was something more. The same day of Cornell's burial, officers read aloud the *Articles of War* to the regiment. Pvt. John A. Smith wrote to the editors of the *New York Sunday Mercury* that he sensed special attention given to the section "which prescribes kind treatment to all prisoners of war" by Cornell's company mates. "I could not help imagining that the number of prisoners they will bring in will be very small," he predicted, while the "memory of Cornell is still fresh in their minds."[84] The implication was clear – the Fire Zouaves sought revenge, and if it meant breaking the "rules of war," they were ready to do so.

Two months earlier, when the Fire Zouaves departed New York City with cheering crowds and stirring speeches, they had been congratulated for their proven bravery as firemen; now they sought to silence their newfound critics, avenge Ellsworth's death (and young Cornell's), and

[78] *New York Leader* (June 1861), accessed via museum.dmna.ny.gov.
[79] A. O. Alcock, Letter to the Editor, June 19, 1861, *New York Leader* (June, 1861), in Pohanka and Schroeder, eds., *With the 11th New York*, 121.
[80] *The New York Times*, July 2, 1861.
[81] *The New York Times*, July 2, 1861. See also AGNY, 1101.
[82] *New York Leader* (June 1861), accessed via museum.dmna.ny.gov.
[83] The best discussion of the "Good Death" is Drew Gilpin Faust, *This Republic of Suffering: Death and the American Civil War* (New York: Knopf, 2008), 4–31.
[84] John A. Smith, Letter to the Editors, June 6, 1861, *New York Sunday Mercury*, June 16, 1861 in Styple ed., *Writing and Fighting the Civil War*, 25.

affirm themselves as soldiers and men. Even with all the adversity and disparagement the regiment had endured since their founding, they retained a reputation as formidable fighters. General Scott purportedly remarked that all he had to do was ring a fire bell "for some district on the other side of the rebels" and "half a million of the traitors could not keep the Fire Zouaves out of that district [for] five minutes."[85] In early July, a Minnesotan in camp with the New Yorkers wrote home: "The Zouaves are regarded with a great deal of confidence. All agree that they will fight like devils if they get a chance."[86]

Time seemed to be slipping away, even though it had been only a matter of months since leaving New York. Rev. Robert Lowry wrote regimental Chaplain Dodge from Brooklyn in mid-July, mistakenly believing that the Zouaves' enlistment was soon running out: "It will be a dry rain with them if they make a return march up Broadway without having had a real grand tug with the ice." Likening their disappointment to rushing to a conflagration, only to discover the fire already doused, Dodge said, "I hope, for their own sakes, they will have a chance to do a big thing with those infernal traitors before they get home."[87]

That "big thing" was coming very soon. And battle would, many assumed, determine once and for all if the Fire Zouaves could be good soldiers.

"Brag Regiment"

For weeks there had been increasing political pressure on President Lincoln to move "On To Richmond." In mid-July, Maj. Gen. Irvin McDowell devised a plan to attack Confederate troops amassing near Manassas Junction, some twenty-five miles southeast of Washington, DC, with his 35,000 troops. On Wednesday, July 17, the 11th New York, as part of Brig. Gen. Samuel Heintzelman's Third Division, set out for Fairfax Station, continuing on the "double-quick" toward Centerville. On July 18, two members ran off to participate in the skirmish at

---

[85] *The Buffalo Commercial* (Buffalo, NY), May 29, 1861.

[86] Edward G. Longacre, ed., "Indeed We Did Fight: A Soldier's Letters Describe the First Minnesota Regiment before and during the First Battle of Bull Run," *Minnesota History* Vol. 47, No. 2 (Summer 1980): 67.

[87] Robert Lowry to G. W. Dodge, July 12, 1861, published in the *Richmond Daily Dispatch*, September 4, 1861. Lowry's letter was found near the Sudley House after the Battle of Bull Run, no doubt lost after Dodge's capture. Lowry was minister of the Hanson Place Baptist Church in Brooklyn, New York.

Blackburn's Ford, scenting a "battle afar off" and unable to "control the temptation to step up and share the danger." Members of the 1st Massachusetts Volunteer Infantry took note of them fighting "with daring intrepidity, wholly on their own account, and conscious of no other authority beside their own."[88] Their impatience to fight, dismissive of the mores and necessities of military command, however, signaled what was to come. The regiment reached Centerville on July 19, "completely worn out."[89]

Waiting there, the tired and hungry troops had little clean water and no tents. Colonel Farnham was severely ill with typhoid fever, lying sick in an ambulance wagon.[90] An ominous still settled over the troops. On the evening of July 20, *The New York Times* editor Henry Jarvis Raymond described "one of the most beautiful nights that the imagination can conceive." He could hear music, including from the camp of the Fire Zouaves where, he wrote, "a party were singing the 'Star Spangled Banner.'"[91] This was in fact the slogan on their flag: "The Star Spangled Banner in triumph shall wave."

At 2:00 AM the regiments were aroused and readied for march, finally departing around 7:00 AM. As guns boomed in the distance, there was straggling, and queasy anticipation, but for most of the Fire Zouaves, it felt "something like what the ringing of a 'general alarm' had been in the days of fire-duty." They knew that they had "hard work before them."[92]

[88] *New York Daily Tribune*, July 23, 1861. This story is also recounted in Warren H. Cudworth, *First Regiment (Massachusetts Infantry), from the 25th of May to the 25th of May 1864: Including Brief References to the Operations of the Army of the Potomac* (Boston, MA: Walker, Fuller, 1866), 43–44. See also *The New York Times*, July 24, 1861; *Brooklyn Daily Eagle*, July 24, 1861.

[89] A. O. Alcock, "Journal of the Facts," *New York Atlas*, August 16, 1862, in Pohanka and Schroeder, eds., *With the 11th New York*, 183; See also General Orders, No. 17, July 16, 1861, OR, Ser. I, Vol. 2, 303–304.

[90] Morford, *Days of Shoddy*, 416; A few weeks earlier, Farnham had also fallen off his horse, badly bruising his leg. See *The New York Times*, July 2, 1861.

[91] *The New York Times*, July 24, 1861. According to Private Smith, on the evening before the battle, foragers provided beef to their brigade, "thus the only one, nearly that was supplied with fresh food that night and the ensuing morning." See John A. Smith, Letter to the Editor, July 25, 1861, *New York Sunday Mercury*, July 28, 1861, in Styple, ed. *Writing and Fighting the Civil War*, 32.

[92] Morford, *Days of Shoddy*, 417. Smith estimated that they started forward at 4:00 AM; Alcock said it was 5:30 AM, Knox recorded it to be 7:00 AM and Comings claimed it was as late as 11:00 AM; Knox's estimate seems to be the most accurate given the sequence to follow. See John A. Smith, Letter to the Editor, July 25, 1861, *New York Sunday Mercury*, in Styple, ed., *Writing and Fighting the Civil War*, 32; A. O. Alcock, "Journal of Facts," *New York Atlas*, August 16, 1862 in Pohanka and Schroeder, eds., *With the 11th*

Lieutenant Knox described the men in good spirits, moving "briskly forward through the woods, singing and laughing and eager for the fight."[93] At one point the Zouaves stripped themselves of their overcoats and blankets, some even threw off their shirts and caps, and resumed marching at a rapid pace. Private Metcalf remembered that there was little tactical precision in their movement: "Anyone who has seen a closely contested race between two fire engine companies down Grand Street can form a good idea of what double quick was with us." The "flying soldiers" hurried onward, occasionally halting, but then "away we went again at a double quick."[94]

Throughout the morning hours of July 21, in what became known as the First Battle of Bull Run, Union and Confederate troops fought in disjointed and frantic fashion, with the rebel army receding ground. By 11:30 AM, McDowell had prematurely declared "victory."[95] But the battle was far from over. Confederate reinforcements rushed by train from the Shenandoah Valley, and with their arrival, the entire momentum of the battle shifted. The 11th New York, ordered to support an artillery battery positioned on the Union's right flank, would meet those newly arrived troops head on. In the afternoon of July 21, the 11th New York was ordered to support artillery near Henry House Hill, but faltered and broke apart under heavy enemy fire (see Map 2.1).

Colonel Farnham led the regiment up Henry House Hill onto an open plane, feverish and weak, but determined to stay with his men. Gunfire suddenly crashed around them, "singing and whistling around our ears, making the air blue and sulphurous with smoke."[96] "On hearing the first

---

New York, 185–186; The. New York Times, July 26, 1861; and Comings, Personal Reminiscences, 8. Lt. Fred W. Shipman with the 38th New York Volunteer Infantry described the difficulties of the march with some men giving out "despairingly." See The Evening Star (Washington, DC), August 1, 1861.

[93] Knox's account, which was widely circulated in the press, appeared originally in The New York Times, July 26, 1861.

[94] Leonard Herbert Metcalf, "So Eager Were We All," American Heritage Vol. 16 (June 1965): 36–37. See also Morford, Days of Shoddy, 41; and Letter to the Editors, July 23, 1861, New York Leader (July 1861) accessed via museum.dmna.ny.gov. The letter to the Leader is credited to Pvt. John Johnson and "Marion of Engine 9," both of Company B. John Johnson (age twenty-four) mustered out with the company in June 1862, but it is unclear who "Marion" was based on the roster list. See AGNY, 1147; and State of New York, Third Annual Report of the Bureau of Military Record, 108.

[95] Davis, Battle at Bull Run, 184; John Hennessy, The First Battle of Manassas: An End to Innocence, July 18–21, 1861, Revised ed. (Mechanicsburg, PA: Stackpole Books, 2015), 69, 71.

[96] Metcalf, "So Eager Were We All," 37.

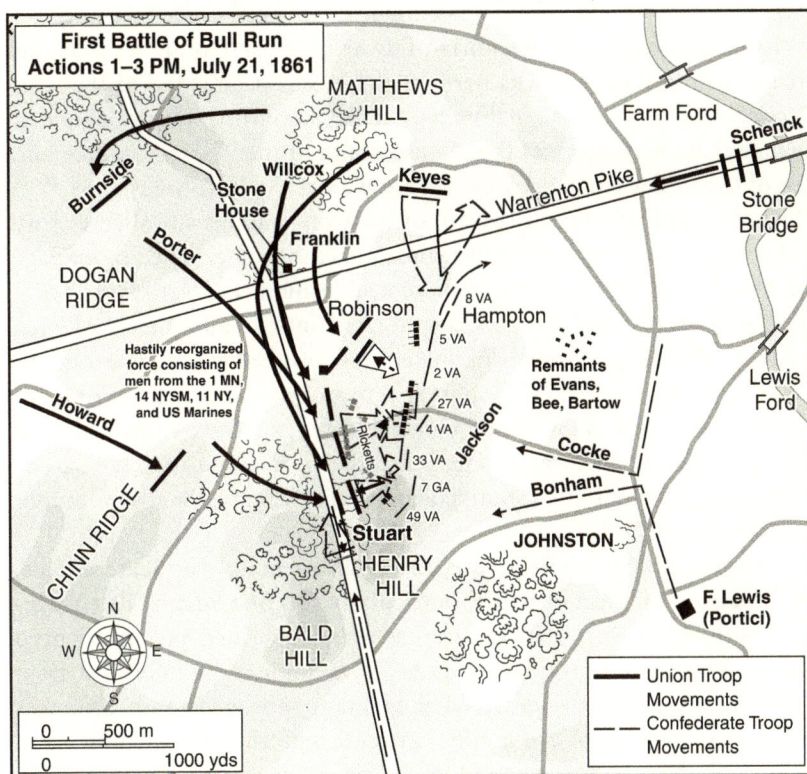

MAP 2.1 Map of the First Battle of Bull Run, July 21, 1861.

'whizz' of bullets," Captain Wildey "experienced a sensation similar to that felt years before when going into an old-time firemen's fight in front of the Astor House."[97] Shouts of "Remember Ellsworth!" and the Zouave "Tiger" cheer could be heard above the din.[98] The last order that Private Metcalf recalled was Colonel Farnham yelling: "*Down, every one of you.*"[99] With enemy fire coming from multiple directions, the regiment devolved into "a confused state, having no head to direct it, and every man was for himself."[100]

[97] Costello, *Our Firemen*, 726.
[98] Knox in *The New York Times*, July 26, 1861; and Letter to the Editors, July 23, 1861, *New York Leader* (July 1861), accessed via museum.dmna.ny.gov.
[99] Metcalf, "So Eager Were We All," 37.
[100] Comings, *Personal Reminiscences*, 9.

There are divergent descriptions of what happened to the Fire Zouaves over the next two hours. Historian Edward Longacre observes that this "battle within a battle" was perhaps the most documented of the war. "Yet no other action," he maintains, "remains so frustratingly opaque as the one that swirled across the plateau south of the Warrenton Pike and east of the Sudley Road between 2:00 and 4:00 PM on July 21, 1861."[101] McDowell had largely lost control of his army, and his so-called victory was slipping away. Brigade and regimental commanders tried to manage the troops, but that was done in piecemeal fashion. The 11th New York, like most other regiments, soon splintered into small clusters of men fighting, rallying, and some running entirely off the field. As one Zouave would later explain, they fought "by their own hook."[102] When the formal order for retreat finally came, Lieutenant Knox described it as "not particularly an orderly one, but rather a free and easy retrograde movement, which, if not a stampede or a rout, was at least a very unmilitary movement."[103]

Armed combat is, by its nature, deeply disorienting. The acute sounds, smells, tastes, and feel of battle, particularly this first large-scale engagement of the Civil War, was like nothing any of these men had experienced before. Historian Mark Smith notes that soldiers' inability to trust their own eyes was especially unsettling: maps were inaccurate, distances misjudged, and due to the motley array of uniforms, it was difficult to distinguish between friend and foe. But it was what many soldiers

[101] Edward G. Longacre, *The Early Morning of War: Bull Run, 1861* (Norman, OK: University of Oklahoma Press, 2014), 378.

[102] Knox in *The New York Times*, July 26, 1861; see also Letter to the Editors, July 23, 1861, *New York Leader*, (July 1861) accessed via museum.dmna.ny.gov; and Murray, *"They Fought like Tigers,"* 65–67; Longacre, *Early Morning of War*, 386. Murray argues that the 11th New York's excessive size, of over 1,000 men, made it difficult to lead in battle. However, according to contemporary reports, the 11th NY was not the largest unit, although it certainly was one of the largest regiments engaged that day. An article in the *Daily Richmond Examiner*, for example, counted 1,100 men in the 11th NY, but 1,563 in the 69th New York State Militia and 1,600 in the 28th New York Volunteer Infantry. Several other regiments numbered close to the standard 1,000 men. See *Daily Richmond Examiner*, August 9, 1861. Lt. Andrew Underhill wrote his brother from prison that the regiment was "broken and formed again three separate times" before the formal order to retreat. This letter is excerpted in Moore, ed., *Rebellion Record*, Vol. 2, "Rumors and Incidents," 18; and quoted in John W. Underhill, Letter to the Editor, September 3, 1861, *The New York Times*, September 8, 1861. Others supported Underhill's contention that portions of the regiment kept fighting in detail throughout the afternoon until the final retreat. See for example, Robert Garth Scott, *Forgotten Valor: The Memoirs, Journals & Civil War Letters of Orlando B. Willcox* (Kent, OH: Kent State Press, 1999), 289–293.

[103] Knox account in *The New York Times*, July 26, 1861.

perceived as deliberate "attempts to deceive the eye" which enraged them. Smith explains: "Visual deception was a tactic employed but condemned as cowardly, verging on unmanly."[104]

The Fire Zouaves were accused and accusers of such craven behavior. Members would later attest that, just as their regiment emerged on Henry House Hill in support of the Union batteries located there, Confederates disguised as Federals tricked them into approaching their position only to unleash a deadly fire into their ranks. The Fire Zouaves further alleged that Confederate cavalry displayed the US flag to "advance within almost a pistol shot," before "our men discovered their mistake."[105] South Carolina Col. J. B. Kershaw, however, singled out the Zouaves for feigning death or injury "when we charged over them," and then "treacherously turning upon us," to murder a Confederate soldier "in cold blood after he had surrendered."[106]

The day after the battle, a *New York Times* correspondent met 1st Lieutenant Knox with his company of about 125 men in Washington near the White House. "I tell you they were a sight to behold," the reporter wrote. "All of them wore the red skull cap, the red shirt, and regulation pants, and each carried his gun." With their heads shaved, faces darkened from the sun and battle, and bodies taunt, he judged their "eyes were keen and clear." They were "proud, boastful, full of excited and colored narrative, jolly good-natured and ready for more work." They wanted their story told, one of "personal adventure and regimental prowess, winding up invariably with a good round cursing of the General in command, and in earnest desire to have another chance at the 'bloody seceshers.'"[107]

Still, in letters home to family and friends, the Fire Zouaves struggled to describe their baptism of fire. For many, the most vivid memory of the fight was their severe thirst and fatigue. "We had a hard fight," Pvt. John Henry Walker assessed. "The bullets flew like hailstones around me, and I had to dodge cannon balls." His company was decimated; Walker calculated all that was left was about a third of his comrades. "I am," he

[104] Mark A. Smith, *The Smell of Battle, the Taste of Siege: A Sensory History of the Civil War* (New York: Oxford University Press, 2014), 52.
[105] John A. Smith, Letter to the Editor, July 25, 1861, *New York Sunday Mercury*, July 28, 1861 in Styple, ed., *Writing and Fighting the Civil War*, 33.
[106] J. B. Kershaw to M. L. Bonham, July 26, 1861, OR, Ser. I, Vol. 2: 526. See also Smith, *The Smell of Battle*, 52. A Fire Zouave recounted "feigning death" and disguising himself as a rebel in a story published in the *Evening Star* (Washington, DC), July 26, 1861.
[107] *The New York Times*, July 26, 1861.

attested, "tired out."[108] Sgt. Harry Lazarus would only say: "Our regiment suffered as severely as any." In trying to describe combat he wrote: "I find that fighting is rather warm work, especially when you hear the bullets whistling around you like hail-stones. I had the stock of my musket shot off in my hand; my cartridge-box was fairly riddled with bullets; although, strange to say, I escaped without a wound."[109] Another Fire Zouave confessed that at first he was "pretty shaky and could hardly load my gun." Regaining his composure, he found that he "did not mind anything that was going on around me. All I thought of was, firing as fast as possible, and killing as many as I could."[110]

Early reports maintained that the 11th New York performed well, but withstood terrible casualties, far worse than any other unit in numbers lost.[111] "The carnage of the late battle must have been dreadful, if we judge by the impression produced upon these Fire Zouaves," one newspaper remarked. "When men insensible to fear, become thoughtful and reticent, they have either encountered or anticipate the encounter, of something fearful."[112] Henry Jarvis Raymond, editor of *The New York Times*, who found himself caught up in the harried retreat, encountered Quartermaster Alexander Stetson in tears, bemoaning that "his regiment had been utterly cut to pieces."[113] Still, the *Evening Star* heralded them for performing "prodigies of valor."[114] A Kansas newspaper went so far as to compare "the charge of the Zouaves on the batteries of the rebels" to "the 'charge of the Light Brigade,' which Tennyson has immortalized in song," contending that the New Yorkers' gallantry surpassed any other example

---

[108] *New York Herald*, July 27, 1861. John Howard Walker, age twenty, Co. D, deserted September 19, 1861 from New York City. See AGNY, 1213.

[109] Harry Lazarus Letter, July 22, 1861, *New York Sunday Mercury*, July 28, 1861 in Styple, ed., *Writing and Fighting the Civil War*, 35. Henry (or Harry) Lazarus, twenty-eight years old (Co. G), was promoted to second lieutenant on March 1, 1862, but never commissioned; he mustered out in June 1862. See AGNY, 1155. Captain Wildey later recounted that the men were "thoroughly exhausted" and "suffering from thirst." See Costello, *Our Firemen*, 727.

[110] Wilber A. Apgar Letter, August 5, 1861, quoted in Murray, *"They Fought like Tigers,"* 60. This was most likely William Apgar, age twenty-three, Co. D, who deserted September 19, 1861. See AGNY, 1074.

[111] *New York Daily Tribune*, July 23, 1861; See also *Brooklyn Daily Eagle*, July 22, 1861; *The New York Times*, July 24, 1861. The *New York Leader* announced that the Fire Department should be proud of the regiment and that their "conduct was noble, brave, and fearfully heroic." See *New York Leader*, July 27, 1861.

[112] *North American and United States Gazette* (Philadelphia, PA), July 25, 1861.

[113] *The New York Times*, July 23, 1861.

[114] *Evening Star* (Washington, DC), July 23, 1861; See also *Brooklyn Daily Eagle*, July 26, 1861.

from the past. "Rank after rank were mowed down by the artillery of the enemy, column after column was decimated," the paper proclaimed, "but the enthusiasm of the Zoos-zoos was never quenched. – They fought until almost deserted by all others."[115]

Regimental officers, including Colonel Farnham, Major Leoser, and Captains Leverich and Wildey, were lauded for their cool courage and their fighting "bravely and manfully."[116] Lieutenant Colonel Creiger, in particular, seemed to be "everywhere and no braver spirit was on that field." Captain Murphy spotted "Old Creiger" riding along the lines, "coolly and collected as when walking up Broadway smoking a Havana," even after a cannon shot splattered the blood and intestines of one of his men on him.[117] Col. J. H. Hobart Ward of the 38th New York had nothing but "unqualified praise" for the regiment's field officers, extolling their "exertions in rallying and encouraging their men."[118] Post-battle accounts repeatedly cited Farnham's steely determination to lead the regiment into battle, notwithstanding his illness.[119] During the retreat, a spent shell grazed Colonel Farnham's head, knocking him to the ground, briefly insensible. Throughout he bore "himself like a brave man," refusing to "shirk from the hottest of the fire."[120] When accusations arose that Captain Murphy failed to accompany his company into the fray, one of his sergeants defended him, contending that Murphy "led his company until he fell from exhaustion on the field and was carried off." The sergeant declared: "too much praise cannot be awarded that officer of the brave and unflinching manner in which he acted during this time of action."[121]

The regiment also gained praise for their fearlessness when fighting alongside other units. A member of the 32nd New York Volunteer Infantry described them as armed with "butts of muskets, bayonets, fists, or anything handy. Some of the Fire Zouaves went hunting rebels on their

[115] *Freedman's Champion* (Atchison, KS), July 27, 1861.
[116] John A. Smith, Letter to the Editor, July 25, 1861, *New York Sunday Mercury*, July 28, 1861 in Styple, ed., *Writing and Fighting the Civil War*, 34. See also A. O. Alcock, "Journal of the Facts," *New York Atlas*, August 16, 1862, in Pohanka and Schroeder, *With the 11th New York*, 186–187.
[117] Michael C. Murphy Letter, July 30, 1861, *New York Atlas*, August 4, 1861, quoted in Pohanka and Schroeder, eds., *With the 11th New York*, 187, n.10.
[118] J. H. Hobart Ward to W. B. Franklin, July 29, 186, OR, Ser. I, Vol. 2: 411.
[119] See, for example, *New York Daily Tribune*, July 31, 1861.
[120] A. O. Alcock, "Journal of the Facts," *New York Atlas*, August 16, 1862, in Pohanka and Schroeder, *With the 11th New York*, 180–181.
[121] *New York Herald*, July 30, 1861. Murphy was also apparently injured by a spent ball. See Murray, *"They Fought like Tigers,"* 99.

own account, and kept tally of how many they bagged." "Some," he contended, "had as high as 15 or 20 notched on a stick."[122] A soldier from the 14th New York State Militia wrote two days after the battle: "I don't want to claim any more for our regiment than belongs to it, but I will say that they [the 14th] and the Zouaves charged in the face of the hottest fire of any regiments on that field, that is if I am any kind of judge."[123] "Never did men fight longer or with more determined courage," Capt. William Baird wrote, "than the 38th and the Fire Zouaves did in this battle, against overwhelming odds that we had to encounter."[124]

Other regiments that fought alongside the Fire Zouaves used the New Yorkers' reputed bravery to prove their own. A private from the 1st Minnesota defended his regiment, stating "we did not 'break and run into the bushes' before the proper order was communicated through the proper officers, and then simultaneously with the Fire Zouaves (who always receive so much praise) and the whole column." He deemed it "a base slander on the Minnesota First," to imply that they faltered when the entire regiment "fought side by side with the Zouaves, whose bravery is universally acknowledged."[125]

There was also macabre humor mixed in with tales about the New Yorkers' cheerful tenacity. Some Wisconsin soldiers encountered a wounded Fire Zouave with both hands shot off and bleeding, needing help to open a haversack. Assisting him, they watched as "he run off to the hospital as happy as a man could under the circumstances. – the Zoos Zoos were game to the last – plucky fellows all." Fire Zouaves would rather die in battle than risk falling "into the hands of the rebels for their death with all its torments would soon follow."[126]

Not surprisingly, some Union soldiers resented the Fire Zouaves, accusing the New Yorkers of getting too much credit. A soldier in the 1st Michigan, for example, maintained: "The story that all this fighting was done by the Zouaves is false"; his unit and that of the 69th New York "were mingled together, and all fought equally well."[127] The Michigander

---

[122] *Evening Star* (Washington, DC), July 30, 1861.

[123] *Brooklyn Daily Eagle*, July 29, 1861.

[124] William Baird, Letter to his Brother, July 23, 1861, in the *Geneva Daily Gazette* (Geneva, NY), August 2, 1861.

[125] "From Our Regular Correspondent," July 23, 1861, *Weekly Pioneer and Democrat* (St. Paul, MN), August 9, 1861.

[126] *Monroe Sentinel* (Monroe, WI), August 7, 1861.

[127] *Lansing State Republican* (Lansing, MI), August 14, 1861. A column in the *Christian Recorder* (Philadelphia, PA), on August 3, 1861, contended that the 1st Minnesota deserved "the palm of heroism" instead of the Fire Zouaves.

did not challenge those accounts that highlighted the Zouaves' bravery in the heat of battle; he merely wanted the heroism of his and other units similarly recognized.

Confederates were acutely aware of the Zouaves' famed reputation, referencing it in their own after-action reports. A soldier from the 33rd Virginia observed: "our comparatively undisciplined little regiment was contending against some of the best disciplined and most experienced men in Lincoln's army, to wit: the celebrated Fire Zouaves of New York, (the same that were so conspicuous in the capture of Alexandria, as the 'Pet Lambs,') the regulars of the army, and Michigan volunteers." He stated that when the Virginians broke "into utter confusion, and a 'free fight' ensued," "every man fought on his own hook, loading and firing at will. We were too hard for the Zouaves at this 'hunting' game, as most of our men were practiced hunters; and scores of the 'red shirts' suffered the penalty of their imprudence."[128] Pvt. Robert A. Glasgow of the 4th Virginia Volunteer Infantry told his father that his regiment charged on an enemy battery "supported by their brag regiment, the New York Zouaves."[129]

[128] "Services and Suffering of the 33rd Virginia Regiment," Letter to the Editors, July 31, 1861, *Richmond Enquirer*, August 6, 1861.

[129] Glasgow confused the 11th New York with the 14th New York State Militia (also known as the 14th Brooklyn Chasseurs) as later in the letter he referred to the "red breeches" running "off the field, leaving their men and guns strewed around." See Robert A. Glasgow to Father, July 22, 1861, in the *Lexington Gazette* (Lexington, VA), August 1, 1861. Another Confederate called the 11th NY a "much dreaded band of ruffians." See "Rebel Letter," July 23, 1861, to "Mother and Friends," printed in the *Boston Transcript*, August 16, 1861, reprinted in Moore, ed., *The Rebellion Record*, Vol 2, section: "Rumors and Incidents," 6. *The Charleston Mercury* published an "eyewitness account" of the battle with the gleeful declaration: "The Fire Zouaves who for months, have been the terror of women and children wherever they have gone, threw themselves upon their knees and pleaded for mercy. But mercy there was none. No quarters were shown, and only a scanty remnant of the famous Fire Zouave saved themselves by flight. So has the death of JACKSON been avenged at last!" See the *Charleston Mercury*, July 27, 1861. William H. Morgan from the 11th Virginia Infantry wrote in his postwar recollections that he saw dead Zouaves on the battlefield at Bull Run, although he too confused the 11th New York with the 14th New York State Militia. He recalled: "Conspicuous among the dead bodies could be seen the New York Zouaves with flashy uniforms and red fez with tassel, loose, red knee-pants and long stockings big stalwart fellows they were, with bronzed faces and necks, but now they lay dead upon the battlefield. And doubtless some, if not all of us, in the words of the 'good old Rebel,' 'wished we'd killed some more.'" See William H. Morgan, *Personal Reminiscences of the War of 1861–1865, In Camp – En Bivouac – On the March – On Picket – On the Skirmish Line – On the Battlefield – and in Prison* (Lynchburg, VA: J. P. Bell, 1911), 83.

The battle was chaotic; few denied that fact. But the Zouaves emerged from the fight with mixed reviews of their performance that day – from themselves, fellow Union soldiers, and the enemy.

"FEW SUCH ACTS OF HEROISM"

There were two particular incidents involving the Fire Zouaves that gained the most attention and helped, at first glance, to bolster their reputation for heroism. The first and best known was the charge of the so-called "Black Horse Cavalry." A number of poems and lithographs recounted the alleged assault including a dramatic image of the Fire Zouaves, many of them shirtless, wrestling with cavalrymen in the pages of *Harper's Weekly*.[130] The first-hand descriptions by two members of the regiment published alongside the illustration stressed their tenacious belligerence: "No quarter, no halting, no flinching now, marked the rapid and death-dealing blows of our men as they closed in upon the foe, in their madness and desperation." Over the clash of arms and fierce fighting were "the screams of the rebels, [and] the shout of 'Remember Ellsworth!'"[131] "Their achievements were many; but of all the greatest was the almost entire annihilation of the Black Rangers, a company of Virginia cavalry not easy to be excelled," a Philadelphia paper professed.[132]

In truth, about 150 horsemen from Col. J. E. B. Stuart's 1st Virginia Cavalry Regiment assailed the Zouaves and a portion of the 14th New York State Militia near the Sudley Road. The Fire Zouaves' red shirts, along with the scarlet pants worn by the 14th NYSM, initially confused the Confederate cavalrymen, unsure if their colorful dress was that of New Orleans Zouaves. But seeing the American flag, Virginian W. W. Blackford later remembered "we went like an arrow from

---

[130] "Charge of the Black Horse Cavalry upon the Fire Zouaves at the Battle of Bull Run," *Harper's Weekly*, August 10, 1861; See also poem by Edward Sprague Rand, Jr., "A Tale of the Battle of Bull Run," in the *Boston Evening Transcript*, July 30, 1861. There was an equally striking image of the Zouaves on the front page of *Frank Leslie's* with the caption: "Gallant and successful assault of the N.Y. Fire Zouaves on a Rebel Battery, which they take at the point of bayonet." See *Frank Leslie's Illustrated Newspaper*, August 3, 1861. An anonymous poem, "Bull Run by a Fire Zouave," described the attack by the "cursed Black Horse fellers," and included the stanza: "We didn't give up till we had to." See *New York Leader*, n.d., accessed via museum.dmna.ny.gov.

[131] One of these accounts was credited to a lieutenant in the regiment and another to a "private letter," in "The Fire Zouaves and the Black Horse Cavalry," *Harper's Weekly*, August 10, 1861; See also *New York Daily Tribune*, July 24, 1861.

[132] *North American and United States Gazette* (Philadelphia, PA), July 25, 1861.

FIGURE 2.3 "Charge of the Black Horse Cavalry upon the Fire Zouaves at the Battle of Bull Run." Image courtesy of *Harper's Weekly*, August 10, 1861.

a bow."[133] Lieutenant Knox described the regiment forming "hastily in line, kneeling, semi-kneeling and standing, that, Ellsworth fashion, they might receive their enemies with successive volleys."[134] The horsemen rushed toward them, and there followed desperate hand-to-hand fighting, with bowie knives and pistols "used with deadly effect."[135]

"What happened after that," Knox stated, "it is hard to detail." Artillery fire pounded at the men, Knox recalled, "for a long time, during which squad after squad was used up, man after man fell dead, or

[133] W. W. Blackford, *Wars Years with Jeb Stuart*. Reprint, 1945 (Baton Rouge: Louisiana State University Press, 1993), 29.

[134] See Knox's account in *The New York Times*, July 26, 1861.

[135] John A. Smith, Letter to the Editor, *New York Sunday Mercury*, July 28, 1861, in Styple, ed., *Writing and Fighting the Civil War*, 33. See also *New York Herald*, July 27 and 28, 1861; and the *Brooklyn Daily Eagle*, July 31, 1861. Metcalf wrote that initially the Confederate cavalry "were met by a volley from the regiment, and rode through us cutting right and left with their sabers but hitting no one." The Virginians rallied and two companies from the regiment, without orders, "rushed pell mell at them, running in their fury right up to the horses and bayoneting the riders when the bullet would happen to miss and drove them flying from the field in as short time as it takes me to tell it." See Metcalf, "So Eager Were We All," 38.

receiving a shot while on the ground, failed to rise at the next command."[136] An officer with the 38th New York Volunteer Infantry described the "furious charge," confirming that the Zouaves "emptied many a saddle, and sent the survivors to the right about in short order." Confederates staged another charge "by cavalry upon their right flank, and infantry in front," and this one fractured the regiment, sending them running "down the hill in disorder."[137] Stuart reported nine dead and eighteen horses killed in the fight – out of some 150 cavalrymen, this was not the annihilation the Zouaves and their supporters purported.[138] As historian Emory Thomas notes, "Stuart later claimed that his charge had completed the demoralization of the Zouaves and begun a general panic among all Federals. The Zouaves claimed that they had broken and scattered their foes." As Thomas observes: "Surely both claims were extravagant."[139]

A second story, only slightly less extravagant, was that of Capt. Jack Wildey heroically rescuing the flag of the 69th New York State Militia, a unit predominately made up of Irish immigrants. A letter written to the *Herald* described: "In the midst of the smoke of the battle field the stalwart form of 'Jack Wildey' could at all times be found at the head of his command, dealing death to the traitors, and fighting with a desperation that made them quail before him, giving hope and courage to his brave comrades." Wildey, in the lead, fought back at the rebels, killing three men including an officer whose sword he commandeered as a trophy. He then singlehandedly "recaptured the flag, and after marching with it four miles, he restored it to the gallant corps from whom it had been taken." The writer concluded: "The history of the world can produce but few such acts of heroism."[140] *The Irish-American* boasted the "lucky alliance" and

---

[136] Knox, in *The New York Times*, July 26, 1861; see also *Brooklyn Daily Eagle*, July 31, 1861.

[137] Fred W. Shipman quoted in the *Evening Star* (Washington, DC), August 1, 1861.

[138] J. E. B. Stuart to Joseph E. Johnston, July 26, 1861, OR, Ser. I, Vol. 2, 483. Blackford in a letter home estimated nine men killed, twenty-four wounded, and twenty horses killed. See William Willis Blackford to "Uncle John," August 6, 1861, accessed via bullrunnings.wordpress.com.

[139] Emory M. Thomas, *Bold Dragoon: The Life of J.E.B. Stuart* (New York: Harper and Row, 1986), 80. See also J. E. B. Stuart to Joseph E. Johnston, July 26, 1861, OR, Ser. I, Vol. 2, 483; and Longacre, *Early Morning of the War*, 392–395; For more on the irrational fear northern soldiers initially had of the southern cavalry, see Michael C. C. Adams, *Fighting for Defeat: Union Military Failure in the East, 1861–1865* (Lincoln, NE: University of Nebraska Press, 1992), 76–78.

[140] "M," "Honor the Brave," in the *New York Herald*, July 27, 1861. See also *The New York Times*, July 25, 1861; *New York Daily Tribune*, July 26, 1861, and poem

"gallant rivalry" between the Fire Zouaves and the 69th New York, stating that "three fourths of them [are] indisputably Celts, and many of whom, in the heat of conflict gravitated naturally towards the 69th, as they desired 'to be with a fighting regiment.'"[141]

There was, however, no exaggerating the regiment's losses. In the first twenty minutes of the fight, the 11th New York, with the 1st Minnesota, fighting alongside them, lost nearly forty men killed; the most deaths of any other Union regiment that day.[142] Final casualties tallied forty-eight killed; seventy-five wounded; sixty-five missing or captured; 188 total.[143] It was – and still is – common to cite a regiment's high casualty rate, any regiment, as proof of its bravery. *The Brooklyn Daily Eagle* observed the "immense sacrifice of life sustained by the Fire Zouaves" as well as another New York unit, in demonstrating "how dauntlessly both of them must have led the most dangerous positions, and urged their conflict with the enemy."[144]

These casualty numbers, as large as they were relative to other regiments, paled in comparison to the regiment's losses in the days and weeks

by W.S.V., "The Recaptured Flag," *New York Evening Post*, n.d. reprinted in Moore, ed., *The Rebellion Record*, Vol. 2, "Poetry and Incidents," 63. A later history of the New York firemen pronounced that Wildey and "a few of his men performed one of the most gallant deeds of the war," and "one of the most brilliant individual exploits of the great battle." See Costello, *Our Firemen*, 719, 726.

[141] *The Irish American* (New York, NY), August 3, 1861. Michael Corcoran, who commanded the 69th New York State Militia, later confirmed the basic details of this story, recalling that "some of the Fire Zouaves, who had been separated from their command," joined his men and while in the fight, some South Carolinians seized their flag from "the dying bearer." He wrote: "It was not long in their possession, however, for with a loud yell, an officer of the Fire Zouaves whose name I subsequently ascertained to be Wildey, dashed forward, and being a large, powerful man, rescued the glorious standard, and returned it to our color guard." Corcoran went on to claim that it was his Irishmen who fought the "famous Black Horse Cavalry" and "behaved with veteran coolness." See Michael Corcoran, *The Captivity of General Corcoran, the Only Authentic and Reliable Narrative of the Trial and Sufferings Endured, during His Twelve Months' Imprisonment in Richmond and Other Southern Cities, by Brig. General Michael Corcoran, the Hero of Bull Run* (Philadelphia, PA: Barclay, 1862), 24.

[142] Hennessey, *First Battle of Manassas*, 98.

[143] OR, Ser. 1, Vol. 2: 405. Another tally lists, killed: one officer; thirty-two men, wounded: one officer, seventy-five men; missing: two Officers, sixty-six men; Aggregate: 177. See OR Ser. 1, Vol. 51, pt. 1, 18. Among those captured were six officers, one captain, and five lieutenants. See Pohanka and Schroeder, eds., *With the 11th New York*, 187, n. 10. A secondary source counts 109 total in killed, wounded, and captured out of 945 engaged; with Companies D and F losing the most (twelve) and Company B the fewest (six). See "Orders of Battle," in Field, *Union Infantryman vs Confederate Infantryman*, 76.

[144] *Brooklyn Daily Eagle*, July 24, 1861.

that followed Bull Run. The day after the battle, Lieutenant Knox estimated only 400 men remained in the ranks, many of them gone, deserting and returning to New York City.[145] Private Smith predicted that it would take "at least month for our regiment to be fully recruited and ready to enter the field again."[146]

"CANNOT BE RELIED ON"

Alongside these stories of valor and sacrifice were darker ones of supposed atrocities, neglectful behavior, and abject cowardice. One Minnesota captain, who fell in with Major Leoser and a small group of Fire Zouaves, described encountering some wounded Confederates, "whom," he claimed, "the Zouaves wanted to kill but I ordered them off and called upon the Major to prevent them, telling him his regiment would be disgraced by such conduct – when he interfered."[147] There were exaggerated reports that the "black hearted rebels" committed atrocities, slashing throats and mauling wounded federals left on the field.[148] It was rumored, though, that the Confederates "held a special animosity" toward the Fire Zouaves.[149] One soldier purported that "the Zouaves were treated with Indian barbarity by the rebels, many being pinioned to trees and tormented with bayonets thrust at them." He professed that Confederates viciously sliced Captain Downey, wounded and left on the field, "into four quarters."[150] Private Smith admitted that some of these stories of "the barbarity of the rebels" were "perhaps exaggerated," but stated: "Certainly we

[145] *The New York Times*, July 26, 1861. The other regiment cited was the 69th New York State Militia.

[146] John A. Smith, Letter to the Editor, July 25, 1861, *New York Sunday Mercury*, July 28, 1861 in Styple, ed., *Writing and Fighting the Civil War*, 58.

[147] Alexander Wilkin, Letter to his father, July 23, 1861, Minnesota Historical Society, St. Paul, MN, accessed via bullrunnings.wordpress.com. Wilkin was captain in the 1st Minnesota Volunteer Infantry.

[148] Calvin S. DeWitt Letter to his sister, July 27, 1861, published in the *Elmira Weekly Advertiser* (Elmira, NY), August 10, 1861. DeWitt was a captain in the 38th New York Volunteer Infantry.

[149] *Hartford Daily Courant* (Hartford, CT), July 31, 1861. See also *New York Herald*, July 28, 1861; *National Republican* (Washington, DC), July 23, 1861.

[150] *New York Herald*, July 24, 1861. Downey was captured at Bull Run and later paroled. See AGNY, 1114. Other Fire Zouaves described witnessing Downey's killing. See for example the *New York Daily Tribune*, July 28, 1861; John Henry Walker, Letter, July 23, 1861, *New York Herald*, July 27, 1861. The *New York Leader* declared revenge for the Confederates mistreatment of the Fire Zouaves. See *New York Leader*, July 27, 1861.

were led to believe, before going into battle, and even on the retreat, that we need expect no mercy, and those who sank from exhaustion intending to deliver themselves up, lay down with but little hope of ever regaining their regiment or meeting their friends."[151] The *New Orleans Crescent* acknowledged that the Fire Zouaves were singled out for "retributive justice," due to the shootings in Alexandria.[152]

There were assertions, too, that Confederates deliberately left the bodies of Fire Zouaves unburied on the battlefield, and those of the 14th New York State Militia, whose uniform was so frequently mistaken for that of the Fire Zouaves.[153] Surgeon Charles W. Le Boutillier of the 1st Minnesota Infantry blamed Zouave officers, maintaining that they had deserted their wounded, leaving them on the field to suffer capture or die.[154] The *Richmond Examiner* echoed this allegation, describing a group of captured Fire Zouaves, "all wounded in the most horrible manner," and receiving no attention. "Their friends having run off and deserted them, they had lain on the field just where their injuries were received until picked by our troops, and our surgeons being more than busy attending to our own wounded, their cases were, of necessity, postponed till after their arrival in this city," the paper stated.[155]

---

[151] John A. Smith, Letter to the Editor, July 25, 1861, *New York Sunday Mercury*, July 28, 1861 in Styple, ed., *Writing and Fighting the Civil War*, 34. Harrison Comings, who spent the night in the woods, feared capture: "it had been said that if any of the Fire Zouaves should be taken[,] they would be made a puppet show of in Richmond." See Comings, *Personal Reminiscences*, 10.

[152] *New Orleans Daily Crescent* (New Orleans, LA), July 23, 1861.

[153] See, for example, *The Irish-American* (New York, NY), August 3, 1861. The 14th New York State Militia wore a French chasseur-inspired uniform, which as previously mentioned included red pants. See E. B. Fowler, "Colonel Fowler's Own Story," in C. V. Tevis, Comp., *The History of the Fighting Fourteenth: Published in Commemoration of the Fiftieth Anniversary of the Muster of the Regiment into the United States Service, May 23, 1861* (New York: Brooklyn Eagle Press, 1911), 213. The source of the rumor about the unburied Zouaves originated, it seems, from a member of the 71st New York Volunteer Infantry, Edward P. Doherty, who before escaping imprisonment returned to the battlefield in the company of a Virginia cavalry officer and stated: "I saw there numbers of our comrades unburied, principally in the uniform of the Fourteenth Brooklyn and Ellsworth's Zouaves. I asked the reason; the reply was they had not yet reached them." See "Statement of Edward P. Doherty," in *The New York Times*, August 6, 1861.

[154] "Surgeon Charles W. Le Boutillier, 1st Minnesota Infantry, On the Battle and Captivity," *St. Paul Daily Press* (St. Paul, MN), October 20, 1861, accessed via bullrunnings.wordpress.com.

[155] One of the wounded soldiers further told the paper: "that there were not ten Zouaves in the regiment of one hundred and fifty who did not rejoice when Ellsworth was killed; that he was one of the most brutal and tyrannical men that ever lived, that he never issued an

One of those injured Zouaves left on the field gave credence to both of these allegations. Private Metcalf remembered a comrade trying to carry him back to an ambulance, but "was stopped by the Colonel who told him to attend to the fighting instead of the wounded." "I have no doubt but that much of the disorder into which our regiment was thrown," the wounded Zouave reasoned, "was owing to the fact that those who were unhurt, instead of pressing on to the fight, would stop and carry their wounded friends out of the way." For firemen, "[t]hrown into all manner of danger," "soon learn to stand by each other in trouble, and the stern necessities of a battlefield even could not break them of it." He also recalled hearing Confederates vowing "Kill him, he's a Fire Zouave, kill him!" only to be restrained by a rebel captain who scolded: "Shame on you, men, would you hurt a wounded man?"[156] Alfred O. Alcock, the special fire correspondent for the *New York Leader*, who stayed on the field to tend the wounded, was captured. His wife Anne later had to defend him against accusations of disloyalty: "It was neither through carelessness nor accident that Mr. Arthur O. Alcock was taken a prisoner of war," she maintained, "but through his humanity in not deserting the dead and dying brother firemen and soldiers."[157]

William Howard Russell, reporting for the London *Times*, witnessed the chaotic retreat, and wrote a scathing description of the Fire Zouaves. Dismissive of much of the reports in the American press, Russell lamented: "A newspaper reporter is made the victim of some glorious myths by a frightened, intoxicated or needy warrior, and these are duly made immortal in type." "There was no annihilation of rebel horse by Zouaves, Fire or other," he stated. Instead, he asserted:

The Zouaves, as they are called, and the 11th New York, which were on the flank, fell into confusion not to be rallied and eventually retired from the field in disorder, to use the mildest term, with a contagious effect on their comrades, and with the loss of the guns, which they were supporting. Nothing would, or could, or did stop them. In vain they were reminded of their oaths to "avenge Ellsworth's death." Their flag was displayed to the winds – it has lost its attractions. They ran in all directions with a speed which their fortune favored.

order without accompanying it with an oath or a kick." See *Daily Richmond Examiner* quoted in *Nashville Union American* (Nashville, TN), July 28, 1861.

[156] Metcalf, "So Eager Were We All," 38; 40. Lewis H. Metcalf (Co. E) was shot in the leg (losing it to amputation) and imprisoned until January 1862 when he was paroled and then discharged for disability. He died in 1873 at the age of thirty-seven of a stroke. See AGNY, 1173; and *The Evening Republican* (Meadville, PA), April 21, 1873.

[157] See Anne Alcock, Letter to the Editor, *New York Leader*, October (19), 1861.

All of this Russell learned from "one who had more to do with them and had better opportunity of witnessing their conduct than I had."[158]

Official military reports added to these troubling allegations, singling out the Fire Zouaves' allegedly bad behavior on the field. Maj. William F. Barry, Chief of Artillery, wrote just two days after Bull Run: "The zouaves, catching sight of the cavalry a few moments before they were upon them, broke ranks to such a degree that the cavalry dashed through without doing them much harm." He described the 11th New York along with the 14th New York breaking and fleeing "in confusion to the rear, and in spite of the repeated and earnest efforts" by himself and other officers to stop them.[159] Gen. Andrew Porter was even more blunt: "The evanescent courage of the zouaves prompted them to fire perhaps a hundred shots, when they broke and fled, leaving the batteries open to a charge of the enemy's cavalry, which took place immediately." He bemoaned, "All further efforts were futile; the words, gestures, and threats of our officers were thrown away upon men who had lost all presence of mind and only longed for absence of body. Some of our noblest and best officers lost their lives in trying to rally them." Porter praised other regiments, including the 69th NYSM; and the, 38th, and 27th New York Volunteer Infantry, recognizing that some units like the US Marines and the 14th New York shattered, but then rallied and made a stand; he made no such allowance for the Fire Zouaves.[160] Their division commander Col. Samuel P. Heintzelman's report was also pretty damning. "Such a rout," the seasoned army veteran stated, "I never witnessed before. No efforts could induce a single regiment to form after the retreat was commenced." Like Porter, Heintzelman was quick to note that some regiments "behaved very well, and much excuse can be made for those who fled, as few of the enemy could at any time be seen." But ten days after the battle, he revealed, "more than three-fourths of the zouaves have disappeared."[161] Even Gen. Irvin McDowell made special mention of the Fire Zouaves' absconding the field, writing: "The officer commanding the

[158] "Russell's Second Letter of Bull Run," July 24, 186, in Moore, ed., *Rebellion Record*, Vol. 2, section "Documents," 67–68. The *Chicago Tribune* attacked Russell for his "errors and misstatements," but blamed them on "some Fire Zouave or a private of the Ohio Second, who left, terror stricken, in the early part of the fray." See "Comments on Mr. Russell's Letter," from the *Chicago Tribune* (n.d) reprinted in Moore, ed., *Rebellion Record*, Vol. 2, "Documents," 62.
[159] William F. Barry to James B. Fry, July 23, 1861, OR, Ser. I, Vol. 2, 347.
[160] Andrew Porter to James B. Fry, July 25, 1861, OR, Ser. I, Vol. 2, 385.
[161] Samuel P. Heintzelman to James B. Fry, July 31, 1861, OR, Ser. 1, Vol. 2: 404.

Eleventh New York (Zouaves) and Colonel Heintzelman say that the returns of that regiment cannot be relied on, as many there reported among the casualties have absented themselves since their return, and have gone to New York."[162]

Generated in the days and weeks after the battle, these overlapping narratives of the Fire Zouaves at Bull Run were often at odds with one another in their appraisal of how well the regiment performed on the battlefield.[163] The contrast was stark: the Fire Zouaves were stoic and determined, withstanding deadly attacks, fighting heroically with their bare hands at times, refusing to retreat until forced to do so; or they were cowardly and craven, rushing off the field and abandoning their comrades at the first shot of enemy fire. To be sure, each version sought to impose order and coherence on something inherently tumultuous: the first major engagement of the war. Soon, however, only one narrative of recklessness and failure would dominate.

---

[162] Irvin McDowell to E. D. Townsend, August 4, 1861, OR, Ser. 1, Vol. 2, 322. Many of these official reports were published (and commented on) in the northern and southern press. For example, see *New York Herald*, August 14, 1861; and the *Richmond Daily Dispatch*, August 16, 1861.

[163] Murray includes an appendix entitled "Did the Fire Zouaves Flee at the First Volley," and concludes that they made "good scapegoats." Murray, *"They Fought like Tigers,"* 114. However, as explained here and in the next chapter, there was much more to it than that.

3

"Soul Sick": Virginia and New York

"EXHAUSTED IN COURAGE"

The Union's humiliating defeat at Bull Run ushered in a deep soul-searching for many northerners. Political and military leaders, soldiers, the press, and everyday citizens grappled with notions of courage and cowardice in their evaluations of what went wrong and why. The *New York Herald* sought to contrast Northern and Southern bravery, derisively equating Confederate soldiers to "cunning" Indians who duped their foes and made war on innocent civilians, while describing Federal troops as civilized, humane white men.[1] More commonly, the Confederates' decisive win fueled stereotypical assumptions about Yankee weakness and timidity.[2] *The New York Times*, echoing Aristotle's distinctions between recklessness and courage, observed a few weeks after the battle: "The truly courageous man is he, who being sensible to fear, yet from faithfulness to duty and from self-respect conquers his fear and faces his enemy." *The Times* affirmed that the Union

---

[1] *New York Herald*, July 27, 1861. This editorial, titled "Northern and Southern Bravery Contrasted," was most likely penned by the *Herald*'s editor James Gordon Bennett, described by historian John C. Waugh as having "erratic opinions." See John C. Waugh, *Reelecting Lincoln: The Battle for the 1864 Presidency* (Cambridge, MA: De Capo Press, 2001), 138.

[2] For more on the negative impact of First Bull Run on northern morale, see Adams, *Fighting for Defeat*. Catherine Bateson explores how the 69th New York State Militia processed defeat and their own role in it to something more positive and affirmative in song. See Catherine V. Bateson, "'We Did Retreat but Were Not Beat': The Irish-American Experience at Bull Run as Told through Civil War Songs," in Timothy G. Heck and Walker D. Mills, eds. *Armies in Retreat: Chaos, Cohesion and Consequences* (Fort Leavenworth, KS: Army University Press, 2023), 327–352.

soldiers who failed that "hapless day" would learn from their experience and prove to be "better soldiers, as well as wiser men."[3]

Other assessments were far more dire. Frederick Law Olmstead wrote *New York Post* editor William Cullen Bryant that the retreat and its aftermath was "most disastrous." As newly appointed executive secretary of the Sanitary Commission, an organization founded to care for wounded and sick Union soldiers, Olmstead set out to interview the men themselves and determine what went wrong. After visiting each regiment, Olmstead and his team of investigators determined that "a large portion of our forces were stricken with the most terrible mental disease, under which all manliness was lost and the utmost cowardice, unreasonableness, and fiendish inhumanity were developed."[4] The causes of this malady were external: troops were poorly led and badly managed. Many entered battle without sufficient rest, food, or water.

But it was the Fire Zouaves whom Olmstead considered the "most distinct and notable example of demoralization after the battle." They had become "confessed cowards" and "certainly exhausted in courage, before the battle opened." Dauntless firemen and "whatever else they were," he wrote, "when they left New York, cowards they were not." He noted: "No one in Washington called them cowards during the fire at Willards' hotel." Their dejection was, he contended, due to preexisting conditions including the "bad terms on which the men had previously been with some of their officers," their "excessive fatigue and exhaustion before they came under fire," and their lack of pay. According to Olmstead, the Fire Zouaves were already "soul sick"; combat only exacerbated their illness.[5]

Olmstead was certainly right that after Bull Run, the 11th New York was in utter disarray. Members complained bitterly that they had "not been used well," asserting that they would rather be captured or shot than "remain and be treated as they are."[6] Hundreds had already left the ranks. About 250 Fire Zouaves encamped in Alexandria formed the surviving core of the original regiment. But of that number, more than two dozen

[3] *The New York Times*, August 14, 1861.

[4] Frederick Law Olmstead to William Cullen Bryant, July 31, 1861, in Jane Turner Censer, ed. *The Papers of Frederick Law Olmsted: Defending the Union: the Civil War and the U.S. Sanitary Commission, 1861–1863* (Baltimore, MD: Johns Hopkins University Press, 1986), Vol. IV: 133.

[5] Frederick Law Olmstead "Report on the Demoralization of the Volunteers," September 5, 1861, in Censer, ed., *Papers of Frederick Law Olmstead*, Vol. IV: 168–169; 174.

[6] *New York Daily Tribune*, August 3, 1861; *The Evening Star* (Washington, DC), July 26, 1861.

were in the guardhouse, awaiting court-martial trials on charges of desertion, and another twenty-five were hospitalized. The rest, some 500
soldiers, were scattered between Washington and New York City. At
one point, thirty Zouaves were evicted from a train for failing to possess
orders or tickets, which they protested with profanity and taunts.[7] A few
sought refuge in Philadelphia with fellow volunteer firemen; others
returned to their former fire companies in New York City, although one
foreman refused "any skulkers who leave their companions and the honor
of the New York Fire Department in danger behind them."[8] The
New York Leader was confident that all the absent Zouaves would return
to the regiment, insisting that those who left "with or without leave" were
wounded or "otherwise disabled from the effects of the late battle."
Perhaps, the paper speculated, the absentee soldiers did not trust hospital
physicians. "These men are now recovering rapidly," the paper insisted,
"and will doubtless hasten back as soon as possible."[9]

City officials and fire department representatives traveled southward to
assess the situation. In early August, John Baulch, a former New York
City councilman and assistant engineer in the New York Fire Department,
went to Alexandria to "learn the facts, and if possible[,] remedy the evils
existing with reference to the 1st Regiment Fire Zouaves." He found
confirmation of the regiment's demoralization. Men who deserted felt
justified because their officers had abandoned them and "they saw no
other way but to shift for themselves."[10] Another visitor to their camp,

---

[7] J. B. Gaddis, Letter to the Editor, August 12, 1861, *New York Herald*, August 13, 1861;
also printed in the *New York Daily Tribune*, August 14, 1861. Gaddis worked for the
railroad company. The *New York Daily Tribune* estimated that by the first week of
August, at least 300 of the Fire Zouaves had returned to New York City. See *New York
Daily Tribune*, August 5, 1861.

[8] "skulkers" from *New York Leader*, August 10, 1861; reference to Philadelphia from the
New York Daily Tribune, August 9, 1861. Harrison Comings went home to New York
with what he estimated to be about fifty other men. Comings was formally listed as
a deserter on August 1. He later re-enlisted in the 17th Connecticut Volunteer Infantry
and "served with conspicuous bravery." See *Malden City Press* (Malden, MA),
February 14, 1885, newspaper clippings from 11th New York Volunteer Infantry
Regimental Files, Manassas National Military Park, Manassas, VA. See also AGNY,
1098; *New York Herald*, August 3, 1861; *New York Daily Tribune*, August 6 and 9,
1861; and *New York Leader*, August 10, 1861.

[9] *New York Leader*, August 3, 1861.

[10] *New York Daily Tribune*, August 9, 1861. Other members of the fire department, David
Milliken, James Y. Watkins, and James Kelly, visited Washington to "do what they can for
the regiment." See *New York Daily Tribune*, August 3, 1861. Chief Engineer Decker, and
Alderman John H. Brady, were additional visitors. See *Evening Star* (Washington, DC),
July 26, 1861.

John W. Farmer, was "not surprised at so many taking French leave." Still, he was "satisfied that nearly all will return when they become convinced that they will be treated like men and not like dogs." If they had better care and leadership, Farmer predicted, "they will perform deeds that will astonish the world."[11]

It was not that the Fire Zouaves was the only unit in crisis after the Bull Run debacle. The 79th New York Volunteer Infantry, for example, was in near mutiny; several other regiments were also reeling from their losses. George Templeton Strong visited Washington and came away "depressed and despondent." He assessed that "men have lost faith in their officers, and no wonder, when so many officers set the example of running away." He bemoaned: "The splendid material of the Scotch Seventy-ninth and the Fire Zouaves has been wasted. Both regiments are disheartened and demoralized. Neither would stand fire for five minutes – they are almost in a state of mutiny, their men deserting and the sick list enlarging itself daily."[12]

The Fire Zouaves, a regiment that had garnered so much good and bad public attention in the months prior, now found that most of that notice was turning completely negative.[13] One of their advocates, H. M. Graham, urged Governor Morgan to issue a public letter of support to "set at rest" reports that the regiment had descended into a "wild and unregulated mob." The governor's office responded that it "would be a useless task to even attempt the correction of all the erroneous rumors afloat." Morgan's private secretary assured Graham: "Time will accomplish all in this direction; in the meantime the number is small who give any heed to the reckless gossip about the Fire Zouaves and others of our heroic soldiers in the field."[14] The governor could not have been more mistaken: the situation for the regiment was worsening by the day. It was

---

[11] John W. Farmer, Letter to the Editor, August 10, 1861, *New York Daily Tribune*, August 13, 1861; Farmer's letter was also reprinted in *The Irish American* (New York, NY), August 17, 1861. For more on troubles in other units, see *New York Daily Tribune*, August 16, 1861.

[12] Nevins and Thomas, eds. *Diary of George Templeton Strong*, August 2, 1861, 174.

[13] Kentucky lawyer and former Secretary of War Joseph Holt, for example, praised the Fire Zouaves, as well as the 69th New York State Militia and 1st Minnesota Volunteer Infantry for their "intrepid bearing" at Bull Run. See "Speech of Joseph Holt, to the Kentucky Troops under Gen. Rousseau at Camp 'Jo Holt,' in Indiana, Delivered July 31, 1861," in Moore, ed., *Rebellion Record*, Vol. 2," Documents," "Doc. 146," 453.

[14] H. M. Graham to Governor Edwin D. Morgan, July 31, 1861; and L. S. Doty to H. M. Graham, August 2, 1861, both letters published in *New York Daily Tribune*, August 6, 1861.

becoming nearly impossible for the Fire Zouaves and their supporters to regain control of their own narrative, no matter how hard they tried. With more criticisms mounting, their credibility was deteriorating.

Olmstead's overall bleak assessment of the regiment had a lot of truth to it: a number of things had gone wrong for the Fire Zouaves long before Bull Run. Ellsworth's impatience to raise the unit and rush them to Washington caused bureaucratic headaches, including delays in filing state militia rolls, which in turn caused problems in distributing pay and issuing officer commissions. Appointing so many former firemen as captains had proven disastrous, too.[15] There was also a persistent conspiracy circulating that the unit had never been officially mustered into federal service or was "illegally" done so by General McDowell, and this further complicated their lack of pay.[16] "J.H." wrote the editors of the *New York Herald* a few days after Bull Run to recount the dire conditions of a Fire Zouave's wife and three children, left with a certificate with promise for payment. "And I am told," the letter-writer stated, "that there is no remedy in the case of this regiment, other than by a special act of Congress."[17]

Col. Noah Farnham had tried to fix some of these problems himself, but his efforts to mainline the unit and rid it of its distinctive Zouave roots backfired, stirring resentment between officers and men. The "disaster at Bull Run" shattered any remnant of confidence the men had in their officers, making them "more difficult to manage."[18] The *New York Daily Tribune*, one of the regiment's stalwart defenders, blamed "demoralizing influences introduced into their ranks by politicians and outsiders," combined with the ongoing frustration with "the long delays and drawbacks on the part of certain governing officials of this State, who refused to recognize them as a legitimate portion of our army up to the day of battle."[19] "The men are willing to fight for their flag and their country," the *Tribune* insisted, "but they demand that they shall be treated like men."[20] John A. Smith, defended his regiment in a letter to the *Sunday Mercury*, stating that "one and all fought as bravely and manfully as the men could do." Still, Smith admitted that it would take

---

[15] *New York Daily Tribune*, July 28, 1861; see also *New York Herald*, August 2, 1861.
[16] "illegally" from Comings, *Personal Reminiscences*, 10.
[17] "J.H." Letter to the Editor, *New York Herald*, July 25, 1861. The regiment finally received their pay on July 31, 1861. See the *Semi-weekly Citizen* (Des Arc, AR), August 3, 1861.
[18] *New York Leader*, August 3, 1861.
[19] *New York Daily Tribune*, August 5, 1861.
[20] *New York Daily Tribune*, August 3, 1861.

"at least a month for our regiment to be fully recruited and ready to enter the field again."[21]

The loss of officers only added to the regiment's disintegration. Farnham was fighting for his life in a Washington hospital and Lt. Col. John Creiger was deathly ill with typhoid fever.[22] Capt. John Downey was imprisoned and 2nd Lt. Daniel Divver had been killed in the battle.[23] The first week of August, five captains and five lieutenants tendered their resignations.[24] Certainly, the 11th New York was not the only unit losing officers; many left their commands to seek opportunities in newly formed units. Others simply had had their fill of war after one battle. Less than a month after Bull Run, the *New York Daily Tribune* listed 225 officers from various northern regiments who resigned, estimating that only a small portion of this number were honorably discharged. "Who can wonder that we hear of insubordination or even mutiny among the men, when the officers desert their colors so rapidly?" the paper questioned.[25] For the 11th New York, the loss of so many officers was especially debilitating. On August 1, *The New York Times* characterized the Fire Zouaves as "so demoralized as to render them useless."[26]

Rumors soon began to circulate that the regiment would disband entirely.[27] Distraught by this possibility, Capt. John B. Leverich entreated

---

[21] John A. Smith, Letter to the Editor, July 25, 1861, *New York Sunday Mercury*, July 28, 1861, in Styple, ed., *Writing and Fighting the Civil War*, 34. Smith was soon promoted to 2nd lieutenant. in Co. C, but he resigned on October 11, 1861, to serve in the 47th New York Volunteer Infantry. See AGNY, 1201.

[22] *New York Herald*, August 6, 1861.

[23] Lt. Daniel Divver (Co. G) was an Irish immigrant and fireman and popular with his men. He was shot multiple times at Bull Run and carried off the field to a nearby wheelwright shop where he died. His body was apparently never recovered. See Costello, *Our Firemen*, 730.

[24] These resignations, occurring between August 1 and 5, 1861, included Capt. Michael C. Murphy, Co. C.; Capt. William H. Burns, Co. F; Capt. Michael A. Tagan, Co. G; Capt. William Hackett, Co. H.; 1st Lt. Edward B. Knox, Co. A; 1st Lt. Freeman Connor, Co. D; 1st Lt. Lucius F. Larrabee, Co. B; 1st Lt. E. M. Coates, Co. C; 1st Lt. Lewis [Louis] Fitzgerald, Co. C; and 2nd Lt. Cyrenus Harris, Co. B.

[25] *New York Daily Tribune*, August 19, 1861. Most of the names listed were from New York, but there were also officers from other states including Pennsylvania, Maine, New Jersey, and Wisconsin.

[26] *The New York Times*, August 1, 1861. In the Joint Committee on the Conduct of War proceedings later that year, the question arose over how many "incompetent" officers resigned after the battle. See *Report of the Joint Committee on the Conduct of the War in Three Parts* (Washington, DC: Government Printing Office, 1863), Part II: 62 (hereafter referred to as JCCW).

[27] *New York Leader*, August 3, 1861; see also *The Advance* (Ogdensburg, NY), August 2, 1861.

Col. Samuel P. Heintzelman that his Company E be spared: "They have behaved well since the fight of the 21st and were the only company that retreated in any kind of order, bringing with them every musket that they carried on the field, except those of the wounded and dead." He asked that Heintzelman vouch for his men and "save my company from any opprobrium that my befall the regiment on account of their disgraceful conduct."[28] Capt. Robert O. Tyler, in charge of supply depots at Alexandria, offered his endorsement, stating that the company had performed "their duties faithfully." "I cannot speak too highly of the company and its officers and should be sorry if any discredit should fall upon them for actions in which they had no share," Tyler asserted.[29] Brig. Gen. William B. Franklin conceded to Maj. Seth Williams that it would be "much to the interests of the service" that the Fire Zouaves should be "disbanded today," making an exception for Captain Leverich's company. Franklin maintained, however, that the "remainder [of the regiment] ought to be discharged at once & dishonorably."[30]

In the immediate aftermath of Bull Run, the Fire Zouaves appeared to be in a death spiral. Disaffection and desertion ran rampant, and things were going from bad to worse.

"THE ZOU-ZOU COLLAPSE"

In the midst of officer resignations, soldiers' desertions, and rumors of disbandment came the publication of the after-action reports from Bull Run in which several officers, including General McDowell, singled out the Fire

[28] John B. Leverich to Samuel P. Heintzelman, July 31, 1861, Samuel Peter Heintzelman Papers, Reel 9, Manuscript Division, Library of Congress, copy from Manassas National Military Park, Manassas, VA. Leverich, who figures prominently in Morford's *Days of Shoddy* as "Captain Jack," implied that there was "petty jealousy" among the other companies toward Co. E for "having a soft thing of it down at Alexandria." Morford describes Leverich telling the general in command of Alexandria that he would rather his entire company "be killed – at least killed a little, than have the name of shirkers when the rest of the regiment is going into active service." See Morford, *Days of Shoddy*, 413–414.

[29] Brig. Gen. William B. Franklin endorsed Tyler, adding that the company "has done good service, quite as good as that of any other Volunteer company." See Robert O. Tyler to Walworth Jenkins, August 6, 1861; and Franklin's endorsement on the back of letter, 11th New York Volunteer Infantry, Volunteer Organizations, Regimental Returns, RG 94, NARA.

[30] William B. Franklin to Seth Williams, August 9, 1861, 11th New York Volunteer Infantry, Volunteer Organizations, Regimental Returns, RG 94, NARA. Williams was A.A.G to George B. McClellan's Department of Ohio during summer of 1861.

Zouaves for their poor performance.[31] General Porter's devastating critique of their "effervescent courage" and Colonel Heintzelman's description of them breaking and fleeing "at the first fire" circulated widely.[32] The *New York Daily Tribune*, the same day it published Heintzelman's report, suggested that personal bravery was not the question: it was "subordination and practiced discipline" that distinguished the "regiments which behaved best upon the field" to those that did not.[33]

After the wide dissemination of these official reports, especially Heintzelman's, there was a marked turn in attitudes toward the regiment in the press. A narrative about the regiment was cementing in real time, with varying groups vying for control of it. There were the Fire Zouaves themselves, meeting, drafting resolutions, and issuing statements. And there were their commanders submitting official reports and castigating them for their poor behavior.

Word of the regiment's disintegration spread to Confederate newspapers, too, which took great satisfaction from hearing that Ellsworth's pet lambs were in crisis.[34] Referring to "the Zou-Zou Collapse," the New Orleans *Daily Picayune* summed up their implosion with relative accuracy: "Disorganization, disintegration, and demoralized followed hard upon the death of Ellsworth, and when under another commander, this vaunted band of rowdies were finally placed face to face with the enemy they boasted so much for their ability to vanquish, they scattered like scared sheep; and fled in disorders almost at the first fire." After the fight, the paper observed, "they came back a disheartened, turbulent and quarrelsome crew, and straightway fell into loud and querulous criminations, and recriminations and wrangling about their pay."[35]

And then there was the New York press, which essentially staged a war in print over the unit. Initially, these papers, both Republican and Democrat, had been supportive of Ellsworth and his firemen, and this had worked to their young colonel's advantage in recruiting and promoting the regiment. Ellsworth's shocking death had muted, at least

---

[31] See, for example, the *New York Daily Tribune*, August 9, 1861.

[32] *New York Daily Tribune*, August 12 and 14, 1861; *Brooklyn Daily Eagle*, August 12, 1861.

[33] *New York Daily Tribune*, August 11, 1861.

[34] Examples include *The Sugar Planter* (West Baton Rouge, LA), August 3, 1861; *Fayetteville Observer* (Fayetteville, NC), August 5, 1861; *Daily Register* (Raleigh, NC), August 3, 1861; *Semi-weekly Citizen* (Des Arc, Arkansas), August 3, 1861; see also *Richmond Daily Dispatch*, August 3, 5, and 17, 1861. See Chapter 4 for coverage in Texas papers, too.

[35] *The Daily Picayune* (New Orleans, LA), August 31, 1861.

temporarily, many of the stories about their unruliness in camp and bad behavior. Now, however, there was a marked shift in that coverage, with major papers squaring off in their views of the regiment not entirely along partisan lines. In the first few weeks after the battle, the Democratic-leaning *New York Herald* was supportive of the Fire Zouaves, dismissing negative reporting as "monstrously exaggerated," predicting that "when we are furnished with the official details in full, it will in all probability prove to have been much less calamitous than we even now suppose," and The paper cited the "heroic charge of the Fire Zouaves upon the rebel cavalry" as proof of the "pluck and stamina of our men."[36] Horace Greeley's Republican *New York Tribune* was also steadfast, recalling "the whole bright record of the volunteer fireman's career – a career as free from base motive or any meanness as that of many of the world's highest heroes, and only sullied, as the sun is by its spots, by his occasional excesses." At Bull Run, the *Tribune* affirmed that the regiment "went up to cannon's mouth as they use to go up to crackling walls of houses. There was really no fear in them, and the flower of the Chivalry went to seed before their burning blast. They cared for no odds, they thought of no orders, but they remember their little Colonel and wrote his epitaph in sacred soil with blood-stained bayonets."[37]

The *New York Leader*, the mouthpiece for the city's fire department, tried to take a more judicious view, contending that the men themselves were not to blame for their failures. New units of Fire Zouaves were looking to form, and the paper attested that "if properly-trained under competent U. S. Army officers, no better fighting men can be found anywhere." "Let us, however," the paper added, "caution the organizers of these new regiments from falling into some of the errors of the original corps." Discipline "in its strictest sense" had to be administered, and all "silly slang talk, all lounging disposition, all restlessness, should be left off when the uniform goes on." In retrospect, the paper judged that the regiment had been overindulged and enabled by weak leadership. Furthermore, the loss of Ellsworth was "a severe drawback to the regiment's thriving existence." After Bull Run, members deserted, some willfully ignorant of military law, others entirely disenchanted with the army. The *Leader* was hopeful "the original Fire Zouaves may yet become as noted for strict discipline as they are in actual conflict."[38]

[36] *New York Herald*, August 2, 1861.
[37] *New York Daily Tribune*, August 7, 1861.
[38] *New York Leader*, August 1, 1861.

In contrast, the *Brooklyn Daily Eagle* and the *New York World*, both Democratic publications, were blunt in their criticisms. The *New York World* traced the "cause of the panic on the battlefield" to the Fire Zouaves, who "broke and ran on the first fire and whose bad example was followed by the New York Fourteenth and other regiments, who communicated the panic to the rest of the army."[39]

The conservative Republican *New York Times* was even more strident in rejecting the "quasi-martyrdom of the Fire Zouaves."[40] In a series of searing editorials, the *Times'* Henry Jarvis Raymond dismissed excuses for their demoralization. "The truth is," he surmised, "the Fire Zouaves lacked one essential quality of good soldiers – subordination." Their natural recklessness was their fatal flaw, even though there were individual exceptions.[41] He countered "romantic tales of their own bravery, told by members of the Ellsworth Zouaves" with excerpts from Colonel Heintzelman's official report. "In simple truth, the Fire Zouaves were just about the worst men in the Army, the most reckless in their behavior, the least amenable to discipline, the most discontented and complaining, the first to run from the field, and the loudest braggarts after they had left it," the editor declared.[42] Going even further in another piece, the paper indicted the entire regiment for blatant cowardice, insisting that it was important to distinguish between their disgraceful failure and "those noble and gallant regiments" who "stood their ground." Redemption could only come if individual men re-enlisted in a new regiment with "a resolute determination to redeem their characters, and wipe out the shame of the past by better behavior hereafter."[43] The very logic Ellsworth and others had used in creating the regiment was turned on its head: firemen made the worst soldiers, not the best.

Defending his position on behalf of his newspaper, Raymond maintained: "We have expressed our opinion fully and emphatically in regard to the conduct of this regiment, not from any special hostility to them, but solely from regard to the honor of the country." Quoting the derogatory reports from Heintzelman and Porter, he contended that it was unfair to other regiments which did their duty at Bull Run to lavish attention on the "undeserving" and "indiscriminately upon renegades and cowards." The

[39] *New York World*, n. d., excerpted in *Brooklyn Daily Eagle*, August 15, 1861.
[40] *The New York Times*, August 8, 1861.
[41] *The New York Times*, August 8, 1861.
[42] *The New York Times*, August 11, 1861.
[43] *The New York Times*, August 11, 1861.

Fire Zouaves, the *Times* charged, "broke at the first fire, and fled the field."[44]

The *Tribune*'s editor, Greeley, reacted defensively to these attacks, suggesting that such criticism undermined the entire Union war effort. "Even if the editor of The Times had seen with his own eyes cowardice and inefficiency among the Zouaves," the *Tribune* argued, "which does not seem to have been the case, it would ill become him to add to the natural discouragement of a reverse by their exposure." Quoting directly from the *Times*, Greeley took aim at his rival newspaper's accusations that: "the Fire Zouaves were just about the worst men in the army, the most reckless in their behavior, the least amenable to discipline, the most discontented and complaining, the first to run from the field, and the loudest braggarts after they had left it." Such allegations, Greeley contended, "are the more remarkable because *The Times* seems to appreciate fully the wisdom of cheerfulness just at this juncture, of crediting the returned soldiers with honorable patriotism and zeal, and of inspiring them to renew their sacrifices on the altar of their country." Greeley went on to liken the *Times'* disparagement of the Fire Zouaves to that of the rebels, citing Confederates who called them gorillas and "men without character" who "can't be made either gentlemen or soldiers." "We are as ready," the *Tribune*'s editor declared, "as *The Times* to admit that the Fire Zouaves, like all recruits, need better drill and discipline. But we cannot, and possibly the Zouaves who are yet in embryo in New-York cannot, agree that there is an 'End of Them' because they are below the standard of the 'crack regiments.'"[45] The implication, Greeley asserted, was that disparaging the Fire Zouaves, as the Confederate press did, was the equivalent of giving "'aid and comfort to the enemy.'" He deduced that the number of casualties was proof enough to counter any charges of cowardice.[46]

Condemnations against the individual editors became increasingly strident. Raymond's *The New York Times* accused the *New York Daily News'* editor Benjamin Wood of funding "the traveling expenses of those among them who wished to desert" and besmirched Horace Greeley's *New York Tribune* for "its natural sympathy with those who are loud-mouthed and vociferous in advance of danger, and who run howling with

[44] *The New York Times*, August 16, 1861.
[45] *New York Daily Tribune*, August 12, 1861.
[46] *New York Daily Tribune*, August 15, 1861.

fear the moment they come upon it."[47] The *Brooklyn Daily Eagle* accused the *Tribune* of "fear-exhorted adulation" of the regiment. "The Zouaves behaved badly," the paper conceded, "but they did not deserve such punishment as to be slavered over with the saliva of the Tribune cowardly bloodhounds."[48] And Wood, who was accused of pro-Confederate sympathies and later had his paper censured, attacked the "New York Journals of the War" for being "mere panderers to popular passion and partisan interests." "They pushed our troops into the jaws of death. They are alone responsible, for the terrible reverse of the 21st of July, for the blood of our soldiers shed at Bull Run, and the subsequent demoralization of the army," he declared.[49]

Things got so heated that on August 31, members of the regiment assaulted a group of compositors employed by the *Times* when they exited a restaurant. The Fire Zouaves "declared that they took this mode of revenging themselves in part for the remarks that have been made in the columns of the Times on their conduct at and after the battle of Bull Run."[50] *Times* editor Raymond defended himself as "the only person" responsible for these criticisms, remarking that "if the injured reputation of the regiment requires that some one should be stealthily attacked and beaten on their account," he was "the proper victim."[51]

The impassioned debate found within the pages of these newspapers continued to center on definitions of soldiers' courage and cowardice. In the aftermath of the debacle at Bull Run, northerners asked, could an entire army be cowardly? A whole regiment? Or was it simply due to a few bad seeds? What would happen if officers behaved cowardly? Did that mean the troops that they commanded were absolved? If firemen were assumed to be brave men, how could they be cowardly soldiers? Was cowardice somehow a malady, as Olmstead suggested, cured by improved conditions and competent leadership? Was the answer better training? A "well known" and "held in high esteem" gentleman who praised the *Times* for its criticisms of the Fire Zouaves thought so. "The Fire Zouaves in vast numbers, showed exceeding bravery individually," the anonymous

[47] *The New York Times,* August 13, 1861.
[48] *Brooklyn Daily Eagle,* August 15, 1861.
[49] *New York Daily News,* August 26, 1861.
[50] *The New York Times,* September 2, 1861; also excerpted in the *Richmond Daily Dispatch,* September 7, 1861. The *Chicago Tribune* explained that the attackers sought revenge "on the editors of the Times for remarks" "not at all complimentary to the 'pet lambs.'" See *Chicago Tribune,* September 5, 1861.
[51] *The New York Times,* September 2, 1861.

commentator maintained, "but as soldiers, they unquestionably were cowards. Discipline! Discipline! Discipline! Without it we are lost!"[52]

The Fire Zouaves were furious at any insinuation that they were cowards, whether individually or as a unit. Pvt. Ed Logan wrote directly to the *Times* demanding a retraction of their accusations. "Do this, therefore, manfully, and you will confer a lasting favor on a much abused and ill-understood body of men, who, when the test comes will always be found ready and willing to fight and die under their country's flag," he admonished. The paper responded that they would be "happy to oblige Mr. Logan by complying with his request,–but as we have no power to alter the official reports, on which alone we have based our remarks on the Fire Zouaves, we are compelled to let them stand." They agreed to publishing Logan's note, though, "omitting merely some superfluous epithets."[53]

Israel Underhill, the father of captured 1st Lt. Andrew M. Underhill (Co. G), penned a letter to the editor of the *New York Daily Tribune* defending his son and pointing to the regiment's losses as irrefutable proof of the Fire Zouaves' courage. He asked: "If, therefore, it be true that they fled from the battle, how could so many have been killed, wounded, and made prisoners, if the main body of the army was between them and the enemy?" Underhill, though, did cast aspersions on the company's captain, Michael Tagan, whom he accused of chronic absences from camp and dereliction of duty. "On arriving at the battlefield the same captain was taken with paralysis and carried to the rear, and is now safe home, enjoying the good state of health, while his lieutenant is a prisoner in the hands of the thieving Rebels in Richmond, and God only knows what his fate may be," Underhill complained.[54] A few weeks later, John Underhill shared a letter from his imprisoned brother, who was fully aware of the attacks on his men, to insist that the Fire Zouaves "did behave better than

---

[52] Letter to the Editor, August 14, 1861, *The New York Times*, August 16, 1861.
[53] *The New York Times*, August 18, 1861. Logan deserted the regiment a few weeks later. See Roster, AGNY, 1158.
[54] Israel Underhill, Letter to the Editor, August 15, 1861, *New York Daily Tribune*, August 18, 1861. Michael A. Tagan, age twenty-seven, was captain of Co. G, and resigned on August 1, 1861. Underhill, a twenty-three-year-old former bookkeeper from Brooklyn, was eventually exchanged, reassigned to Co. A, and not mustered out of service until August 1862. See AGNY, 1207; 1211; and Eighth Census of the United States, 1860: Population Schedule, Brooklyn Ward 4, District 2, Kings, NY, Records of the Bureau of the Census, RG 29, NARA; accessed via ancestry.com. During his imprisonment, Underhill suffered from a "severe attack of typhoid fever," but eventually recovered. See Corcoran, *The Captivity*, 68.

has been generally reported." "Our regiment," the lieutenant averred, "(had they been the veterans that you read about in the history of Napoleon, &c.,) might have held that hill, but it would have been held in a short time by their *dead bodies only.*"[55]

Despite the Fire Zouaves' objections, the press was increasingly antagonist toward them. And accusations of cowardice were gaining ground.

"TREATED WITH BAD FAITH"

Meantime, genuine attempts were underway to try to salvage the unit. On August 12, 1861, Brigadier General McDowell ordered the regiment to return to New York for reorganization under the direction of the city's Union Defense Committee.[56] Two days later, nearly 400 Fire Zouaves officially arrived home in New York City.[57] A good number had come back already, but they returned to the ranks to "obtain credit for not

---

[55] Andrew Underhill's letter repeated the claim that, although the regiment broke three times during the battle, it did not entirely flee the field until late in the fight. See Andrew M. Underhill to John W. Underhill, September 1, 1861, excerpted in John W. Underhill, Letter to the Editor, September 3, 1861, *The New York Times*, September 8, 1861. For correspondence regarding efforts to exchange Underhill, see John E. Wool to Benjamin Huger, February 4, 1862, OR, Ser. II, Vol. 3: 236; and John E. Wool to Lorenzo. Thomas, May 30, 1862, OR, Ser. II, Vol 3: 609. It is unclear when Underhill was finally released.

[56] "General Orders No. 31" "Extract," August 12, 1861, 11th New York Volunteer Infantry, Volunteer Organizations, Regimental Returns, RG 94, NARA. The Union Defense Committee was formed in April 1861 to "represent the citizens in the collection of funds, and the transaction of such other business in the movements of the Government as the public interest may require." Its members included prominent New Yorkers John A. Dix, John Jacob Astor, Jr., and Hamilton Fish, as well as the city's mayor, comptroller, and president of the Board of Aldermen. The Union Defense Committee "were understood to have as special reference to providing means for creating and sustaining a military force, to be used in the public service of the country." The Committee raised money, secured supplies, and appropriated funds to soldiers' families. By July 31, 1861, the Committee had contributed $726,000 in aid (including clothing, equipment, outfit, and rations) to the 11th New York; by comparison, it contributed more than $67,000 to the "Mozart Regiment," the 40th New York Volunteer Infantry Regiment. See "New York City in the Civil War," museum.dmna.ny.gov; and *Reports and Documents of the Union Defense Committee of the Citizens of New York. Board of Alderman, September 9, 1861. Document No. 18.* (New York: Edmund Jones, Printers of the Corporation, 1861), 35, 55.

[57] Estimates vary, with an initial expectation that 500 members would appear, but that number lessened when the regiment arrived. See *The New York Times*, August 14 and 15, 1861; *Brooklyn Daily Eagle*, August 14 and 15, 1861; *New York Herald*, August 15, 1861; *New York Daily Tribune*, August 15, 1861; *New York Sun*, August 15, 1861. Four carriages with more than a dozen wounded soldiers followed those able to march. See Sheldon, *The Story of the Volunteer Fire Department*, 314–315.

deserting."[58] The men's appearance was, in the words of one account, "motley": "some had knapsacks, some not; some had red fez, others blue; some had Zouave caps, while others were adorned with felt hats, or ordinary civilian caps."[59] Chief Decker and fellow firemen greeted them warmly, but as the Zouaves marched through the streets, the *New York World* described, there was but "a few feeble cheers, bestowed upon them in pity by personal friends."[60] The *New York Sun* strained in claiming that their "reception was as enthusiastic as that of any regiment yet returned, and it was evident that by the public they were not regarded as either cowards or demoralized."[61]

Their muted homecoming differed dramatically from their boisterous departure less than four months earlier. Prosper M. Wetmore, the executive secretary of the Union Defense Committee, briefly addressed the men, reminding them of their storied beginnings and opportunity for a second chance. He told them that he "could not consider any of them as deserters and hoped that they would now prove their honor." Having obtained a "favor" from the Secretary of War to allow the regiment to come home and recruit, Wetmore was confident that they would soon regain their full strength as a regiment. They stacked their arms and dispersed, ordered to reappear five days later or risk being charged with desertion.[62] Optimistic about their reorganization, the ever-supportive *New York Tribune* predicted that soon the regiment would return to "their splendid fighting qualities, which the lamented Ellsworth was so fond of eulogizing, and prevent a recurrence of the demoralization under which it now suffers."[63]

A few days before their formal homecoming, a group of Fire Zouaves had taken it upon themselves to organize a meeting to voice their ire about the attacks on them, but also "to get an expression of the feeling of the members of the regiment now in this city and elsewhere (with or without leave of absence), as to the propriety of returning to the regiment."[64] One

[58] *The New York Times*, August 15, 1861.

[59] *The New York Times*, August 15, 1861.

[60] *New York World*, n.d., quoted in the *Richmond Daily Dispatch*, August 19, 1861.

[61] *New York Sun*, August 15, 1861. The *Tribune* alternatively claimed that "an immense throng of friends" greeted the regiment, giving them "the most enthusiastic demonstrations of welcome." See *New York Daily Tribune*, August 15, 1861.

[62] *New York Sun*, August 15, 1861; see also *New York Herald*, August 15, 1861; *The New York Times*, August 15, 1861.

[63] *New York Daily Tribune*, August 15, 1861.

[64] *New York Herald*, August 11, 1861. The representatives met at the Phoenix Hose Company on August 10, and planned to meet again on August 12, but with the regiment formally returning to the city, that date was moved to the evening of August 14.

member from each company had been tasked with drafting resolutions to challenge "statements published against the regiment, and to give full explanations to the public of the treatment they have been subject to since leaving the city."[65] To them, there was a lot of blame to go around.

Then, later the same evening of their homecoming, a number of the Fire Zouaves recongregated, this time at Humboldt Hall. The mood was contentious from the start, and "several times a personal acrimony seemed very near breaking out into a row." Members mounted an especially animated repudiation that "they are deserters."[66] 1st Sgt. John W. Dunn chaired the meeting, but it took some time to bring any semblance of order.[67] Eventually, a series of resolutions unanimously passed, enumerating the perceived wrongs wrought against the regiment and explanations for their current state of demoralization. With reporters there from the very newspapers that had disparaged them, the men angrily blasted the New York press for labeling them "vagabonds and demoralized deserters," and their commanding officers who "falsely charged us with dereliction of duty and cowardice, which, if true, would be sufficient to call down the condemnation of the entire republic." The Fire Zouaves asserted that they had willingly left their families, occupations, and the fire department to serve, and yet "we suffered more than almost any other regiment in the service through want of a regular supply of provisions, water, baggage, wagons, and innumerable other necessities." They avowed their eagerness to return to battle and defend "the glorious Stars and Stripes – that flag we all love so dearly."[68]

Some of their complaints were familiar: that they did not receive enough of the promised Sharp's rifles, Colt revolvers, and bowie knives; that they were pressured to serve "for the war" by threats of arrest; and that their rations were paltry and spoiled, and they had yet to be paid. They "refused the United States uniform, having enlisted as Zouaves." They were especially resentful toward Colonel Farnham for abandoning

---

Representatives included 1st Lt. W. R. Chambers as pro tem, Pvt. Henry Mott as secretary, and seven additional men, all privates or NCOs. Only two of these nine men would still be with the regiment when it formally mustered out in June 1862. The other seven either deserted or were discharged for disability, including Henry Mott, who deserted on September 19, 1861. See *New York Herald*, August 11, 1861; and AGNY.

[65] *New York Herald*, August 13, 1861; see also *New York Daily Tribune*, August 14, 1861.

[66] *New York Daily Tribune*, August 16, 1861.

[67] Sgt. John W. Dunn, age twenty-four, (Co. G) later deserted on January 1, 1862. See AGNY, 1115.

[68] *New York Herald*, August 15, 1861; see also *New York Daily Tribune*, August 16, 1861; *The New York Times*, August 15, 1861.

the Zouave Drill and dismissingly calling it "played out." They further accused their colonel of forcing the original Chicago Zouave officers out of the regiment in order to replace them with his comrades from the 7th New York State Militia, men "who had nothing to do with the Fire Zouaves" preventing promotions for the original volunteers.[69] The rest of the officers, they charged were "afraid of the worst men" and unwilling to discipline them.[70]

The Fire Zouaves further detailed injustices traced to the battle itself, complaining that they were rushed into combat without their canteens, and suffered severely from want of fresh water. Their own officers, Lieutenant Colonel Creiger for one, had encouraged them to flee the battle and go home, because "everything was going to the devil generally; and the best thing they could do would be to take care of themselves."[71] They forcefully objected to the publication of official reports, including Colonel Heintzelman's, which they deemed misleading and distorted. In some cases, the Fire Zouaves also insisted that officers credited other units "with duty performed by us alone."[72] *The New York Times* summarized, "the regiment has been treated with bad faith; fed like dogs; deprived of the credit of what they did on the field of battle; stigmatized as deserters for doing as their officers told them and kept out of their pay for an unreasonable length of time."[73]

The following week, the Fire Zouaves tried to reform themselves into a viable regiment again. On Monday, August 19, at 8:00 AM several hundred filled Humboldt Hall; some were in uniform, but many donned civilian dress, though most of them wore their Zouave fez caps.[74] Several members loitered outside the entrance; a good number refused to come at all, unconvinced that their grievances would be heard. After taking roll call with more than 600 members present, Major Leoser dismissed them, ordering their return the next day at 9:00 AM to prepare for new quarters. The regiment "scattered" again, "discussing their prospects for pay, active duty, their treatment by the Government, &c."[75]

[69] *The New York Times*, August 15, 1861; and *New York Daily Tribune*, August 16, 1861. The *Tribune* described the original Chicago Zouaves including Lieutenants Larrabee, Yates, and Stryker, as "disgusted."

[70] *New York Herald*, August 15, 1861.

[71] *New York Daily Tribune*, August 16, 1861; see also *New York Herald*, August 15, 1861.

[72] *New York Daily Tribune*, August 16, 1861.

[73] *The New York Times*, August 15, 1861.

[74] The *New York Times*, August 20, 1861; *New York Daily Tribune*, August 21, 1861; *New York Daily News*, August 20, 1861.

[75] *The New York Times*, August 20, 1861; see also *Brooklyn Daily Eagle*, August 20, 1861; and *New York Daily Tribune*, August 21, 1861; *New York Daily News*, August 20, 1861.

The next day, August 20, the regiment reconvened in the City Assembly Rooms. Many streamed in late and wore civilian clothes. The police had to help clear the hall and control the crowd that had assembled outside.[76] This time when roll was taken by company, 513 men were present and 269 absent; nearly 100 men had failed to return. Capt. Edward Byrnes' Company B had the highest number of men present (sixty-six), with twenty-five absent, while Company H under acting Capt. Patrick A. Gillon counted only thirty-five present and forty-one absent.[77] In the streets, reporters interviewed a few members who refused to fall into line and were vowing that "they would have nothing more to do with the regiment until they were paid."[78] One soldier from Co. G groused that "the whole thing has been a 'dead beat,' or swindle on the men; that they never got the arms or uniforms promised; that they never elected their officers," and that most of their officers "deceived and neglected the men, advised them to go home, run away from the field of battle and done everything to disorganize the regiment."[79]

Major Leoser sent the men home to retrieve all government-issued equipment, including guns, advising them that anyone who did not return at 2:00 PM "would be arrested as deserters and rigidly dealt with."[80] A few hours later, 300 or 400 of the 500 men returned from the morning, and the police again assisted with trying to keep good order. For nearly two hours, officers struggled to form the soldiers into line and march them down Broadway Avenue to the Battery where they were to set up temporary quarters. Once they finally started moving, incalcitrant members lined the sidewalk, "jeering as their comrades passed."[81]

So far there was little evidence that the regiment could be successfully reorganized; in fact, there was proof that it was already too late. Each time the regiment convened, fewer and fewer men materialized. It had shed 200 members since its homecoming, in addition to the losses sustained at Bull Run and officer resignations. The regiment's demoralization was palpable, a fact that they city's press, even those sympathetic to it, widely

---

[76] *New York Daily Tribune*, August 21, 1861.

[77] *New York Daily News*, August 21, 1861; *New York Daily Tribune*, August 21, 1861; see also *The New York Times*, August 21, 1861.

[78] *New York Daily Tribune*, August 21, 1861.

[79] *The New York Times*, August 21, 1861.

[80] *The New York Times*, August 21, 1861.

[81] *The New York Times*, August 21, 1861; *New York Daily News*, August 21, 1861. *The Daily News* estimated 400 returned in the afternoon, while *The New York Times* stated the number was closer to 300.

telegraphed. It began to seem like a death watch, witnessing the slow demise of the regiment. The day after their dual meetings to reorganize, *The New York Times* blasted the regiment's officers as "utterly incompetent," urging the unit to disband. "They have unquestionably good fighting material among them," the paper acknowledged, "but it will be worse than wasted without proper discipline."[82]

"Aggravated by the Shame"

With the Fire Zouaves splintered and angrily defensive of their reputation, their colonel lay dying in a Washington hospital. Rumors spread that Farnham was out of his mind, but there were also early reports that he was rapidly improving. "The illness of Col. Farnham," one account claimed, "has been greatly aggravated by the shame he feels for the demoralization of his command."[83] Initially, his battle wound seemed superficial; a spent ball had grazed the side of his head, knocked him off his horse, and left him insensible. The wound healed, but he began to exhibit signs of "irritation of the brain." For successive days he lingered, becoming partially paralyzed, irritable, and delirious, and eventually comatose.[84]

Farnham died on August 14, the very day that his regiment returned to New York and more than three weeks after the battle. An autopsy revealed an abscess in his brain near the bullet wound.[85] Some blamed Farnham's prior sickness for his death and the failure of his officers to keep him out of the battle, but Medical Inspector F. H. Hamilton, who personally examined him, avowed that "his previous condition I do not think had much, if anything, to do with his death, which, in my opinion, and in the opinions of many other surgeons who saw him, was due directly to the apparently slight wound which he received during the fight." Hamilton admitted that prior to the battle Farnham was "unfit to perform duties at the time the battle took place; but, being a gallant officer, he was determined to lead his regiment to the charge."[86] "The Zouaves," the

---

[82] *The New York Times*, August 22, 1861.

[83] *New York Leader*, August 3, 1861.

[84] There were rumors, too, that Farnham had to be admitted to the insane asylum, but this was untrue. See *New York Daily Tribune*, July 31, 1861.

[85] *The Medical and Surgical History of the War of the Rebellion (1861–65)*, 6 Vols. (Washington, DC: Government Printing Office, 1875), Vol II, Pt. 1: 109–110.

[86] *The Medical and Surgical History*, Vol II, Pt. 1: 110; see also *Evening Star* (Washington, DC), July 30, 1861.

Brooklyn Daily Eagle observed, "are exceedingly unfortunate in their officers."[87]

News of Farnham's death reached New York just as the Fire Zouaves formally arrived home.[88] Alongside printed columns recounting the regiment's many grievances were eulogies to their commander and descriptions of his funeral. The city's firemen passed resolutions expressing their "gratitude of the whole department" for Farnham's "disinterested zeal and unwearied executions to maintain its efficiency and discipline, and that we unitedly bear testimony to the unsullied character, the exalted integrity and upright bearing that characterized his whole career as a fellow member." Referring to the "slanderous assault" on him and his regiment, the firemen affirmed that "the truth will place both beyond the reach of malignant jealousy, and preserve their reputation for valour untarnished."[89]

The Fire Department further adopted a set of resolutions to bear "testimony to the exalted character of Colonel Farnham his pure life, his great integrity, his unfaltering courage, his devotion to his country and her flag, his Christian virtues, and his possession of all these characteristics which make the honest man." Using the conventional definition of courage, the firemen declared that "his noble conduct on the battle-field" needed "no better record than the bullet which he received from the enemy. He died for his country and in her service, with his armor on."[90] There was a marked disconnect between these tributes to Farnham and the Fire Zouaves' loudly expressed grievances. Within their complaints were pointed criticisms of Farnham, his abandonment of Ellsworth's Zouave drill, the Zouave uniform, and his attempt to populate the officer ranks with his former comrades from the 7th NYSM. And yet the published tributes maintained that his men adored him and "would have gone through any amount of hardship or hard fighting with Colonel Farnham at their head."[91]

Farnham's death, and the mixed reactions to it, further underscored the fragile condition of the regiment. There were festering problems within and without that seemed impossible to resolve.

---

[87] *Brooklyn Daily Eagle*, August 15, 1861.
[88] *New York Daily Tribune*, August 15, 1861.
[89] *New York Herald*, August 17, 1861.
[90] Sheldon, *The Story of the Volunteer Fire Department*, 315.
[91] *New York Herald*, August 18, 1861.

"MORE LIKE DEMONS THAN LIKE MEN"

Nevertheless, the 11th New York, or what was left of it, settled into temporary quarters at the Battery waiting for a new assignment and fresh recruits. That first night nearly every member "evaded the sentries, climbed the gates and disappeared."[92] The few who complied with orders began complaining about staying in camp, insisting they would be "ready when wanted" to return to the front.[93] The editor of the *New York Leader*, John Clancy, visited their camp and was troubled by their lackadaisical attitude. There was little semblance of proper military protocols or behavior. Men were idle or lounging around, smoking, eating cakes, and drinking lemonade. It was not, Clancy believed, that these men, or firemen by nature, were incapable of being good soldiers. Instead, he determined, as others had begun to assess, that the root of their problems stemmed from their beginnings: the rushed nature in which they were raised, and the many allowances offered for their swagger and irreverence. The notoriety they gained in Washington and constant complaining and slipping away from camp; their refusal to wear standard-issue uniforms, and finally, in battle, "breaking themselves up, as a regiment," were signs of their failings. "In all these things," Clancy surmised, "they have acted like everything but soldiers." The only solution was to start over with new officers, more consistent training, and the prohibition of "swaggering, lounging about, [and] slang talk," all of which was "unbecoming and ridiculous in a soldier."[94]

For the Zouaves, as it was for most Americans early in the conflict, there was no distinction between good soldiering and good character, and they continued to react defensively to any such slights. A few days after they arrived at the Battery, the Fire Zouaves got into a "striking argument" with the 68th New York Volunteer Infantry Regiment, the Cameron Rifles, a unit consisting of mostly German immigrants, over the "relative valor of the two organizations." When a policeman tried to intervene, he was stabbed with a bayonet. Two members of the Cameron Rifles were shot, one mortally.[95]

[92] *New York Daily Tribune*, August 22, 1861. See also *New York Albion* n.d., excerpted in *The Raleigh Register* (Raleigh, NC), September 4, 1861; and the *Richmond Daily Dispatch*, August 29, 1861.
[93] *New York Daily News*, August 22, 1861. See also *Brooklyn Daily Eagle*, August 22, 1861.
[94] *New York Leader*, August 24, 1861.
[95] *New York Herald*, August 25, 1861. The Cameron Rifles, named after Secretary of War Simon Cameron, was officially designated the 68th NY Infantry and was on its way to Washington, DC. See Joseph Tyler Butts, ed. *A Gallant Captain of the Civil War: Being*

Clearly, this location was not going to work. Major Leoser then requested a new encampment, ideally on an island without easy access to the city and "where he can keep his men in good order and enforce strict discipline."[96] On August 28, the regiment traveled by steamer to Bedloe's Island (presently Liberty Island) to "undergo a little discipline," where their sleeping accommodations and rations improved.[97] The *New York Herald* reported, "it seems impossible to get the full corps together." Several Fire Zouaves wanted to go to a Hibernian festival to benefit the families of the 69th NYSM, with whom they had fought at Bull Run, and thus refused to appear.[98] On the very day of their departure, fourteen Fire Zouaves were arrested for desertion, and many more than that were absent without leave.[99]

Their stay at Bedloe's Island proved short. Less than a week after they arrived there, the Fire Zouaves were sent to a Camp of Instruction in Scarsdale, to make way for Confederate prisoners captured at Fort Hatteras. It was feared "that if they remain on the Island, some trouble will arise between them and the prisoners."[100] Things did not improve in Scarsdale, either. In fact, they worsened. Reports quickly emerged that other troops stationed near the 11th New York "were obliged to sleep upon their arms in apprehension of a disturbance." A double guard was instituted, and "every means" was "adopted to prevent any serious disturbance."[101]

Word of their bad behavior continued to spread. The *Chicago Daily Tribune* snidely reported that "Ellsworth's Fire Zouaves," "once the 'pride' of New Yorkers," had now "sunk beneath contempt, and is now a stench in the nostrils of all people." Since their arrival at Scarsdale, the

---

the Record of the Extraordinary Adventures of Frederick Otto, Barron Von Fritsch, Comp. from His War Record in Washington and His Private Papers (New York: F. Tennyson Neely, 1902), 18–19.

[96] *New York Daily News*, August 22, 1861. See also *New York Daily News*, August 23, 1861.

[97] *Brooklyn Daily Eagle*, August 28, 1861; *New York Daily News*, August 31, 1861. See also *Brooklyn Daily Eagle*, August 23, 1861; *New York Herald*, August 28, 1861.

[98] *New York Herald*, August 29 and 30, 1861.

[99] *New York Daily News*, August 30, 1861. The *Daily News* estimated 200 Fire Zouaves left for Bedloe's Island, but except for a handful of officers, only a few wore uniforms. See *New York Daily News*, August 27, 1861. One week later, thirty-four men were listed as deserting the regiment on September 8, with twenty-four of them from Co. A; 9 from Co. C; and 1 from Co. G. See AGNY.

[100] *Brooklyn Daily Eagle*, September 5, 1861; see also *New York Daily News*, September 5, 1861.

[101] *New York Daily News*, September 13, 1861.

paper maintained "they have behaved more like demons than like men."[102] Second Lt. James Cameron protested that these alleged "outrages" were "committed by scoundrels attached to the other regiments quartered here, who claim to be Fire Zouaves," but the damage was done.[103]

Efforts began in earnest to start over. On September 13, 1861, the War Department issued special orders to immediately muster the 11th New York out of service, "with the exception of such officers, non-commissioned officers, musicians and privates as may be retained upon the recommendation of the Colonel."[104] Those left would move again, this time hundreds of miles south to Fort Monroe, Virginia, where they would "be under proper discipline," as Governor Morgan pronounced.[105] Regimental Surgeon Charles Gray spoke out in support of his regiment, blaming their "bad name" on "a few blackguards" who "no longer belong to us." He argued that the "men whose names remain on our roll have nothing to be ashamed of." They had "been badly treated in a few cases," and have "(on account of the incompetency of their officers) not received pay for the last two, and in many cases, for the last five months"; yet, he insisted there were more than "five hundred of the original Zouaves, all of whom have the interests of the Fire Department at stake, will, on the day of embarkation, proceed to the seat of war."[106]

Still, there remained an "unruly portion" of the unit.[107] As they prepared to leave, a group of Fire Zouaves harassed members of the "Engineer Regiment" who had moved into their former camp at the Battery, and physically assaulted civilians passing by, including one man whom they mistakenly believed was a reporter for *The New York Times*.

[102] *Chicago Daily Tribune*, September 17, 1861. See also *New York Herald*, September 17, 1861.

[103] James Cameron, Letter to the Editor, September 13, 1861, *New York Leader*, September 14, 1861.

[104] Lorenzo Thomas, "Special Orders No. 247," September 13, 1861, 11th New York Volunteer Infantry, Volunteer Organizations, Regimental Returns, RG 94, NARA. Orders for their transfer appeared in *The New York Times*, September 18, 1861; *New York Herald*, September 18, 1861; and the *Evening Star* (Washington, DC), September 19, 1861.

[105] E. D. Morgan to Simon Cameron, September 17, 1861, OR, Ser. III, Vol. 1: 524; see also *New York Daily News*, September 14, 1861. Morgan dispatched the 11th NY to Fort Monroe after receiving a call from Washington to send "all the regiments you can." The Secretary of War issued this same plea to several northern governors. See the correspondence between Morgan and Cameron on this matter in OR, Ser. III, Vol. 1: 510, 515, 522, 524.

[106] Charles Gray, Letter to the Editor, n.d., *New York Herald*, September 19, 1861.

[107] *The Brooklyn Daily Eagle*, September 21, 1861.

In these assaults, the Engineer Regiment loaded their guns and threatened to shoot. Turning instead on the civilians, the Fire Zouaves wrapped their victims in canvas tents, threw them about, and kicked and punched them. They also fought each other, resulting in "a few bloody noses and scratched heads." Colonel Leoser finally arrived in person and ordered the soldiers to the pier for departure. "At this a few went down to the boat," the *Times* reported, but "the remainder straggled off in different directions."[108] That single day, more than eighty Fire Zouaves were arrested for desertion.[109]

The rest of the regiment, some 200 or 300 "manly" "good men," arrived at Fort Monroe on September 23, 1861.[110] William G. Watkins, who had recently joined, was hopeful, describing the 11th New York to be "in good health and fast recovering their former discipline and esprit de corps." They were to receive new uniforms and arms and commence drilling to get "on a war footing, and thus," the *New York Leader* pronounced, "give them an opportunity to recover any laurels they may have lost since the Bull Run disaster."[111]

Even the regiment's sharpest critics were optimistic that this "much abused regiment" could be redeemed. The *New York Herald* was encouraged by these attempts at regeneration, applauding the "expulsion of the regiment's 'black sheep,'" and contending that "the personal and individual bravery of the Fire Zouaves has never been debated." The paper instead blamed their failures on incompetent officers.[112] *The Brooklyn Daily Eagle* similarly predicted that the "stigma" which had cast a shadow on the regiment since Bull Run "is now being cleared away by

[108] *The New York Times*, September 20, 1861. This regiment was later designated the 50th New York Regiment of Engineers.

[109] *The New York Times* reported that "no less than sixty were captured in various parts of the City." See also *The New York Times*, September 22, 1861; and the *New York Herald*, September 22, 1861. Based on information gleaned from the AGNY roster, eighty-four soldiers deserted on September 19, 1861; this is in addition to thirty-five who deserted the first week of September.

[110] "good men" from *New York Leader*, September 28, 1861; in an article from same paper and date the number was estimated to be 197 men; see also *Brooklyn Daily Eagle*, September 23, 1861. "manly" from *The New York Times*, September 24, 1861. *The New York Times* further called the few men who boarded the boat "the most orderly and tractable," describing the "most unruly" members trying to intimidate their comrades from leaving. See *The New York Times*, September 21, 1861.

[111] *New York Leader*, September 28, 1861. Watkins enrolled on September 1, but resigned on November 27, 1861. According to the Adjutant General's report, he never formally received his commission as first lieutenant. See AGNY, 1216.

[112] *New York Herald*, September 19, 1861.

the expulsion of about seventy-five disreputable members, who have from the first, been the cause of all the trouble; and the whole body, composed in the main part of respectable men, have been made to suffer from their misdeeds." Ellsworth's Zouave drill and uniform, which had proven ill adapted and ill-suited for war, were both gone for good, too. The regiment, the paper anticipated, would soon "wipe out the disagreeable reminiscences" of their past and entirely start anew.[113] As the Fire Zouaves began what was supposed to be their recovery at Fort Monroe, word came that their original flags, the ones presented to them in front of boisterous crowds five months earlier, were "found in a pile of rubbish" in Alexandria.[114]

Their colors in the trash was a bit too symbolic for the current state of the regiment. So much of their distinctive identity as Fire Zouaves had been stripped and metaphorically thrown away. Certainly, some of this was due to the standard uniformity of the military and the realities of war, but it was also due to the unique circumstances of this unit and faulty expectations of what made a good soldier.

"CAGED UP"

Meanwhile, more than forty Fire Zouaves captured at Bull Run were "caged up" in a converted tobacco factory in Richmond. Capt. John Downey, whom many of his men swore was dead and cut in quarters, was very much alive. He wrote his wife Anne soon after his capture to assure her that he and the other prisoners, including those wounded, "are treated as well as we could expect, though a good deal stared at and gaped at just at first."[115] Indeed, curiosity seekers gawked at them "as if they

---

[113] *Brooklyn Daily Eagle*, September 19, 1861.
[114] *New York Leader*, September 28, 1861. Discovered by members of the 17th New York Volunteer Infantry, the colors were returned to the mayor's office. See *New York Leader*, (October 1861); *The New York Times*, September 18 and 26, 1861; *Brooklyn Daily Eagle*, September 24, 1861.
[115] John Downey to Anne Downey, August 3, 1861, in *The New York Times*, August 19, 1861. See also "Mr. Julius Bing's Adventures," Washington, August 1, 1861, *New York Daily Tribune*, n.d., reprinted in Moore, ed., *Rebellion Record*, Vol. 2, "Documents," 19. See also Charles W. Sanders Jr., *While in the Hands of the Enemy: Military Prisons of the Civil War* (Baton Rouge, LA: Louisiana State University Press, 2005), 42; William H. Jeffery, *Richmond Prisons, 1861–62, Compiled from the Original Records Kept by the Confederate Government. Journals Kept by Union Prisoners of War together with the Name, Rank, Company, Regiment and State of the Four Thousand Who Were Confined There.* (St. Johnsbury, VT: Caledonia County, 1893), 8.

FIGURE 3.1 Regimental flag of the 11th New York Volunteer Infantry. Artist rendition by Bradley Smith.

were wild beasts."[116] It was not just the Fire Zouaves who attracted Richmonders' attention; New York Congressman Alfred Ely and Colonel Corcoran from the 69th New York were also imprisoned with them.[117] The Fire Zouaves, though, drew especially negative mention in many of the contemporary accounts. One reporter from the *Richmond Enquirer*, for example, who visited the wounded prisoners soon after Bull Run, claimed that everyone except the Fire Zouaves regretted "taking up arms against the people." The Fire Zouaves, however, he deemed "incorrigible." "They seem," he wrote, "perfectly oblivious to every sentiment of

---

[116] *The New York Times*, August 5, 1861. See also Charles Lanman, ed., *Journal of Alfred Ely, A Prisoner of War in Richmond* (New York: D. Appleton, 1862), 29, 32. Capt. John Downey counted 640 prisoners from varying regiments confined in Richmond with him and his comrades. See John Downey to Anne Downey, July 28, 1861, printed in *New York Herald*, August 11, 1861; The *Richmond Enquirer* estimated 585 "Hessian prisoners" arrived soon after the battle, and made special note that thirty of them were "Ellsworth's Fire Zouaves." See *Richmond Enquirer*, July 24, 1861, reprinted in Moore, ed., *Rebellion Record*, Vol. 2, "Rumors and Incidents," 6. A letter by an unidentified Zouave published in the *New York Tribune* counted forty-four total officers and men. See "(Extract from a private letter from a Fire Zouave now a prisoner of war.)" to "Dear Brother," Richmond, Va., August 16, 1861, reprinted in Moore, ed., *Rebellion Record*, Vol. 2, "Rumors and Incidents," 18. Alcock listed forty-six Fire Zouaves captured and with him in Richmond including himself, two of whom perished and twelve who were in the hospital. See A. O. Alcock to "M," August 11, 1861, *New York Atlas*, August 18, 1861.

[117] Ely described the steady stream of curiosity seekers getting so bad that he implored prison officials to limit visitor passes. See Lanman, ed. *Journal of Alfred Ely*, 62.

FIGURE 3.2 Captured Fire Zouaves at Castle Pickney, South Carolina. Image courtesy of the Library of Congress, Prints and Photographs Division, Washington, DC.

honor, gratitude, or decency. They have nothing but the human form and faculty of speech to distinguish them from Gorillas."[118] In fact, captured Fire Zouaves were growing dispirited, too. Alcock observed soberly: "not one of those here would have volunteered, had he supposed that when, by the fortune of war, we became prisoners, we would be left to our fate and no exchange recognized."[119] Early on, prisoners drafted and signed a petition requesting President Lincoln to release them. Lincoln, though, failed to respond.[120]

Confederates struggling with the unexpected number of prisoners crowding facilities in Richmond arranged in September for 150 of them

[118] *Richmond Enquirer*, July 27, 1861, excerpted in the *New York Daily Tribune*, August 6, 1861. See also Lanman, ed., *Journal of Alfred Ely*, 57–58; also 77.

[119] A. O. Alcock to "M," August 11, 1861, *New York Atlas*, August 18, 1861. In another letter, Alcock expressed his frustration with the delayed release and his bitter animosity toward Colonel Farhnam, stating that he had "suffered grievous wrongs at that man's hands," without specifying what those wrongs were. See A. O. Alcock to "M," August 27, 1861, *New York Atlas*, October 13, 1861.

[120] New York Congressman Alfred Ely, imprisoned with the Zouaves, drafted the petition. Ely's prison messmates in Richmond included Captain Downey and Colonel Corcoran. See Lanman, ed., *Journal of Alfred Ely*, 25; 41; Corcoran, *The Captivity*, 29. See also William B. Hesseltine, *Civil War Prisons: A Study in War Psychology*. Reprint, 1930. Forward by William Blair (Columbus: Ohio State University Press, 1998), 10–11; Sanders Jr., *While in the Hands of the Enemy*, 79.

to travel further south to Charleston, South Carolina. Included in this group were twenty-four Fire Zouaves.[121] *The Daily Richmond Examiner* maintained that those selected for transfer had demonstrated "the most insolent and insubordinate dispositions," but when they arrived in the city three days later, the *Charleston Mercury* commented that "their deportment" was "generally as orderly as could be desired."[122] Congressman Ely, who stayed in Richmond, later contended that he never learned the "real motives" behind the move, but speculated that worries of escapes probably prompted the decision.[123]

After a week confined in the city jail, and "crowded like cattle in pens," the transferred prisoners entered Castle Pickney, where they were, according to one captive, in "a better atmosphere."[124] They were far more secluded without idle visitors coming to stare at them. Here, the Charleston Zouaves Cadets – ironically a unit inspired by Ellsworth's original Chicago Zouaves – guarded them.[125] Similar to what they had done in Richmond, prisoners formed "The Castle Pinckney Brotherhood" to "improve our minds, pass away our time and amuse ourselves."[126] Overall, conditions were markedly better than in Richmond, and a friendly comradery developed between guards and prisoners. The 11th New York's Chaplain Dodge, along with Chaplain Hiram Eddy from the 2nd Connecticut, held church services and administered communion to comfort the men.[127]

[121] Of those two dozen were Private Alcock, Captain Downey, Chaplain Dodge, and Lieutenant Underhill. For the complete list, see Jeffery, *Journals Kept*, 193–196.
[122] *Daily Richmond Examiner*, September 11, 1861; *Charleston Mercury*, September 14, 1861. The *Mercury* further counted thirty-four officers and 120 men. Those selected to move south were primarily from the 11th New York, 79th New York, 69th New York, and 8th Michigan and included Colonel Willcox from the 1st Michigan and Colonel Corcoran from the 69th NYSM. See also Lonnie R. Speer, *Portals of Hell: Military Prisons of the Civil War* (Lincoln, NE: University of Nebraska Press, 2005), 25–26; Hesseltine, *Civil War Prisons*, 62; *Brooklyn Daily Eagle*, September 23, 1861.
[123] Lanman, ed., *Journal of Alfred Ely*, 106–112.
[124] Scott, *Forgotten Valor*, 311; See also Corcoran, *The Captivity*, 46.
[125] For more on the Charleston Zouave Cadets, see Arthur M. Willcox and Warren Ripley, *The Civil War at Charleston* (Charleston, SC: The News and Courier and the Evening Post, 1983), 3; *The New York Times*, September 25, 1861; and Speer, *Portals of Hell*, 26–27.
[126] Corcoran, *The Captivity*, 66.
[127] Alcock described relatively kind treatment and "courtesy and commiseration" from the Charleston Zouaves. See A. O. Alcock, Letter to the Editor, October 17, 1861, *New York Atlas*, November 24, 1861. Alcock's positive reports fueled allegations that he was disloyal to the Union. See *New York Atlas*, January 5, 1862.

Even so, the Zouaves stood out. Fellow prisoner Orlando Willcox, whose contempt for the regiment had only grown since the fiasco in Alexandria, unfavorably compared Dodge to Eddy, observing: "Chaplain Eddy was a big, noble-hearted specimen of 'muscular Christianity,'" but, Willcox claimed, "he had to give his weaker brother Dodge an occasional shake down when the latter complained of things that could not be helped." Such despondency, Willcox observed, "was but a step to illness and the graveyard."[128] At one point the prison commandant, Capt. C. E. Chichester, personally paid a photographer to take pictures inside the pen. These images by George S. Cook offer a rare glimpse of prison life during the early part of the war, but they also show members of the 11th New York distinctive from the other POWs. The New Yorkers, donning their red shirts, fez caps, and silver firemen badges, posed defiantly under a sign: "Hotel Zouave."[129]

Castle Pickney proved ill-suited for long-term imprisonment, so by the end of October, the captives moved back to the city jail, where they were again "closely confined."[130] This was where, Willcox recalled, their "greatest suffering" occurred. With the weather turning cooler, they had little to wear and "clamored," Willcox wrote, "our friends and even to the Northern government to send us clothing and blanket."[131] When a fire swept the city in December, prisoners struggled to break free, only to be blocked by guards and reimprisoned.[132]

With weeks turning to months, there was little to encourage the men that release was imminent. Enduring captivity brought unexpected challenges mentally as much as physically. Colonel Corcoran, imprisoned alongside the Fire Zouaves, later reflected that "dying for one's country is glorious when it is accompanied by features that strip it of its terror, yet languishing in the dungeons of your country's enemy, almost within hearing of the booming guns of the struggling armies, is a most awful fate."[133] This feeling of helplessness was emasculating to soldiers

---

[128] Scott, *Forgotten Valor*, 311. Ely also mentioned Dodge holding divine services in Richmond before the move to Charleston. See Lanman, ed., *Journal of Alfred Ely*, 36; 92.

[129] Richard B. McCaslin, *Portraits of Conflict: A Photographic History of South Carolina in the Civil War* (Little Rock, AR: University of Arkansas Press, 1995), 13–14; Speer, *Portals of Hell*, 28–29. The photos can be found via the Library of Congress's website: www.loc.gov. On the LOC site, however, the images are erroneously dated August 1861; the Zouaves did not arrive at Castle Pickney until September 1861.

[130] Corcoran, *The Captivity*, 70.

[131] Scott, *Forgotten Valor*, 311–312.

[132] Corcoran, *The Captivity*, 74, 85.

[133] Corcoran, *The Captivity*, 27–28.

expected to fight and prove their manly worth in combat, not stay caged up in a dank prison cell.[134] Pvt. Alex MacArthur from Co. I wrote a friend in November and described being "confined in the common jail at Charleston, with thieves and murderers." MacArthur was recovering from "a very severe attack of the fever," worried that they had been imprisoned so long. Still, he was hopeful that "our Congress will do something for us this winter. If they don't[,] we will have to remain here for the war."[135] He expressed similar sentiments in a letter to his brother Archie, hoping Congress would intervene, adding: "The men are all plucky, and we would rather stay here ten years than let up one atom, or even take the oath for them. We are still for the Union now, and the Union forever."[136] Eventually, prisoners were divided again, some going to a jail in Columbia, South Carolina, and others even further south to Tuscaloosa, Alabama. Most of the Fire Zouave POWs would not be released until May or June 1862.[137]

Imprisoned and far from New York, the captured Zouaves attracted a good deal of negative attention from their captors and fellow prisoners. Nonetheless, during their many months in successive prisons, they strove to retain some semblance of their defiant identity.

"VIRTUALLY DISBANDED ITSELF"

The rest of the unit, including new recruits and a portion of the original volunteers, settled into "Camp Butler" in Newport News, under the command of Gen. Joseph K. Mansfield as part of the Department of Virginia.[138] A correspondent from the *New York Herald* visiting them in late September reported that the ranks were "filling up slowly." He noted, however, that some of the Fire Zouaves had raided a boat stocked with beer, but assured readers that "no great damage was done."[139]

---

[134] I discuss this contrast between incarceration and combat, and the feelings of helplessness common among POWs in Gordon, *A Broken Regiment*, 150–151.

[135] Alexander McArthur to "Friend Carroll," November 20, 1861, *New York Herald*, December 24, 1861. Alexander McArthur, Age 23, Co. I, survived imprisonment and later mustered out of the regiment in May 1862. See AGNY, 1163.

[136] Alexander McArthur to Archie McArthur, November 18, 1861, *New York Daily Tribune*, December 5, 1861.

[137] *New York Leader*, May 24, 1862; See also *New York Tribune*, December 5, 1861; Hesseltine, *Civil War Prisons*, 63; Jeffery, *Journals Kept*, 193–196.

[138] OR, Ser. I, Vol. 9: 15; OR Ser. I, Vol. 11, Pt. 3: 54.

[139] *New York Herald*, October 6, 1861.

Colonel Leoser, restless for new orders, worried that the regiment might never go to the front again.[140] He also complained that a military board had not properly examined his newly commissioned officers as stipulated by a law passed by Congress the summer prior.[141] Sometime in September, Leoser wrote what in retrospect reads like the unit's obituary. Alongside the monthly company rolls, he penned: "The Eleventh Regiment New York Volunteers (Colonel Elmer Ellsworth) otherwise known as the First Regiment of Fire Zouaves virtually disbanded itself at and from the Battle of Bull's Run." Attempts to reorganize failed, Leoser complained, after "several efforts and many contradictory orders." He candidly described the unit "yet in a fragmentary" and "disorganized condition."[142]

In October 1861, the regiment suffered yet another humiliation. A detail of about fifty men, including a number of Fire Zouaves, had gone out from Newport News to gather firewood. According to Confederates, the party of Union soldiers was trying to pull down a house, some four miles from rebel lines, when a cavalry unit charged on them.[143] "The Zouaves were armed," another account described, "but had neglected to establish any sentinels to give an alarm in case the enemy should be in the vicinity." The Federals, entirely surrounded and outnumbered, were captured, including twelve Fire Zouaves.[144] The ever-defensive *New York Leader* claimed that this story was "all moonshine," but the state's postwar adjutant general's roster lists twelve soldiers taken prisoner on October 12, 1861.[145]

One Fire Zouave took stock of the regiment as 1861 drew to a close. He described dull conditions in their camp, only broken up by the incessant

---

[140] Charles McKnight Leoser to [no one identified], October 3, 1861, 11th New York Volunteer Infantry, Volunteer Organizations, Regimental Returns, RG 94, NARA.

[141] Charles McKnight Leoser to H. Stevens, November 4, 1861, 11th New York Volunteer Infantry, Volunteer Organizations, Regimental Returns, RG 94, NARA; see endorsement on back, as well. For more on the utility of such boards, see Stanley L. Swart, "The Military Examination Board in the Civil War: A Case Study," *Civil War History*, Vol. 16, No. 3 (September, 1970), 227–245.

[142] This same text appears for each company and the field and staff officer rolls, too. See Charles McK.Leoser, [n.d], 11th New York Volunteer Infantry, Volunteer Organizations, Regimental Returns, RG 94, NARA.

[143] *New York Herald*, October 15, 1861.

[144] *The Philadelphia Inquirer*, n.d., excepted in *Richmond Daily Dispatch*, October 24, 1861.

[145] *New York Leader*, October 19, 1861. Among those captured was Richard Gleason, whom some accounts allege was later killed by a guard at Libby Prison "for looking out a window." It appears, though, that he survived the war. See Costello, *Our Firemen*, 720; Jeffery, *Journals Kept*, 22; AGNY, 1129.

drilling. The regiment, he determined, "though not full, is improving very much in discipline." Painful memories of Bull Run were starting to recede for some members of the unit, but the debacle was not completely forgotten. "It is still the great topic of conversation around the camp and guard fires," he noted, "and it is laughable to hear the reminiscences of that fight."[146]

End-of-the-year returns put in stark terms the regiment's decline. All told, of the original 1,128 officers and men mustered into service, twenty-five officers had resigned and three were prisoners of war, and three, including Ellsworth and Farnham, were dead. Four hundred men in the ranks had deserted, and thirty-five were counted as killed in action. Eighty-five were discharged for disability and three were discharged for "civil disability." Seventy-four Fire Zouaves were prisoners of war, and only 480 men were left. Broken down by companies, Co. I had the most desertions (sixty-seven) and Co. E. had the fewest (twenty-six). In sum, from April to December 1861, more than half the regiment was gone, notably 400 due to desertion.[147]

The Fire Zouaves' disbandment was slow but steady, even without formal orders to do so. It was a dramatic change from the height of their strength and support less than a year earlier.

"NOT AT ALL RELIABLE"

With the Fire Zouaves in disarray and their future unclear, Congress launched a formal investigation into the Battle of Bull Run with the creation of the Joint Committee on the Conduct of War. The JCCW, headed by Republican Ohio Senator Benjamin Wade, included a mix of Democrats and Republicans: Representative Moses Odell, from Brooklyn, New York, was one of two Democrats on the committee – with Tennessee Senator Andrew Johnson the second.[148] The Committee's role was largely investigative; it had no real power to legislate, yet it remained in existence

---

[146] "Occasional," Letter to the Editor, December 16, 1861, *New York Sunday Mercury*, December 22, 1861, in Styple, ed., *Writing and Fighting the Civil War*, 58–59. The letter writer's identity is unknown.

[147] See "Enlisted Men Deserted," & "Consolidated annual return of Casualties, 11th Reg't N.Y. Vols.," in Volunteer Organizations, Regimental Returns, RG 94, NARA. The identity of two of the three men "Discharged by Civil Authority" is unclear; George Stevens is listed in the AGNY roster as discharged "by civil authority." See AGNY, 1204.

[148] Congressman Odell was a booster for his hometown 14th New York State Militia, but there is little evidence in these proceedings that he expressed prejudices against the Fire

throughout the conflict, making recommendations and issuing its judg-
ments on federal military operations.[149] Historians have criticized the
JCCW and its pretense of bi-partisanship. It succeeded, in the words of
Brian Holden Reid, in making "a nuisance of itself by searching for
scapegoats."[150] For the Fire Zouaves, already scapegoats in the sphere of
public opinion, this proved to be another opportunity for a new authority
to besmirch their already tattered reputation.

The JCCW began taking sworn testimony in late December 1861,
continuing into the summer of 1862. During the hearings, all proceedings
were conducted in secret in the Capitol basement, with witnesses forbid-
den from speaking to the press.[151] Committee members questioned thirty-
eight individuals, including Generals Irvin McDowell and Robert
Patterson, as well as division and brigade commanders – all commissioned
officers and no enlisted men – about what caused the "disaster at Bull
Run."[152] The Committee was not interested in "particulars," or extended
details, but they did want witnesses to answer as "military men."[153]
Nonetheless, members were skeptical of professional officers, voicing
the prevailing belief that the mostly volunteer army's "courage and
moral purity would suffice for training and discipline."[154]

In response, officers blamed the rawness of the troops, their fatigue
from marching, and overall tiredness the day of the battle as reasons for

Zouaves. A featured article on Odell in *Harper's Weekly* noted his caring for sick and
wounded soldiers after the Battle of Bull Run, "especially those of the gallant 14th
(Brooklyn) regiment, many of them young men who had grown up under his eye in
business and the Sunday-school of the Sands Street Methodist Church, of which he has
been for many years the efficient and beloved superintendent." See *Harper's* Weekly,
June 14, 1862. Other members of the JCCW were: Senator Zachariah Chandler (R-MI);
Representative John Covode (R-PA); Representative George Washington Julian (R-IN);
and Representative Daniel Gooch (R-MA).

[149] Bruce Tap, *Over Lincoln's Shoulder: The Committee on the Conduct of the War*
(Lawrence, KS: University Press of Kansas, 1998), 34. The Committee was also investi-
gating the Union defeat at Ball's Bluff in October 1861.

[150] Brian Holden Reid, "Historians and the Joint Committee on the Conduct of the War,"
Civil War History Vol. 38, No. 4 (December 1992), 337.

[151] Tap, *Over Lincoln's Shoulder*, 35. See also "Joint Committee on the Conduct of the
War," www.senate.gov.

[152] JCCW, Pt. II: 3; see also 511 for a list of witnesses. Notably, no officers from the 11th
New York were invited to testify.

[153] Congressmen repeatedly qualified their questions with this phrase. See, for example,
JCCW, Pt. II: 106; 187.

[154] Tap, *Over Lincoln's Shoulder*, 44–45. See also Carol Reardon, *With a Sword in One
Hand and Jomini in the Other: The Problem of Military Thought in the Civil War North*
(Chapel Hill, NC: University of North Carolina Press, 2012), 64.

the Union defeat.[155] General McDowell himself attributed his inability to execute his battle plans to the greenness of his army and difficulties of maneuvering them.[156] Brig. Gen. Daniel Tyler, who was second in command to General McDowell, assessed an overall "want of discipline and instruction in the troops" and "a great want of instruction and professional knowledge" among officers, especially at the regimental and company level.[157] If there was one person most vilified by the investigation, it was Gen. Robert Patterson, who allowed CSA Gen. Joseph Johnston to slip away from his position in the Shenandoah Valley and reach Manassas in time to decisively turn the battle in favor of the Confederates.

As the testimony mounted, there was increasing focus on the afternoon of July 21, and the actions of the Fire Zouaves on Henry House Hill. Despite officers' insistence that the entire army was green and raw, and that their lack of training unavoidably contributed to defeat, several homed in on the Zouaves' poor performance as pivotal to the events of the day. Gen. Samuel P. Heintzelman, the regiment's former division commander, reiterated what he had said in his initial report of the battle: that he ordered the Zouaves to support the batteries on the hill, but after exchanging fire with the Confederates, "both parties broke and run [sic]." When asked if the 11th New York later rallied, Heintzelman answered: "Not as a regiment. Many of the officers and men joined other regiments, or fought on their own hook."[158] William F. Barry, who had served as Chief of Artillery at the battle, then promoted to brigadier-general by the time of the hearings, was also pointedly critical of the 11th New York. When asked by Congressman Gooch (R-MA) what "condition" the Fire Zouaves were in at the time he ordered them to assist the artillery batteries, Barry responded that he initially perceived them to be "an efficient regiment." "I thought so," he explained. But he admitted that he "knew very little of them, except by newspaper reports. I knew what New York firemen were, and I supposed there was fight and pluck in them. I was struck with the manner they marched forward, very handsomely in line of battle." He was, he said, "very much disappointed and surprised when they broke."[159]

[155] See for example, JCCW, Pt. II: 181–82.
[156] JCCW, Pt. II: 38.
[157] JCCW, Pt. II: 198.
[158] JCCW, Pt. II: 30–31
[159] JCCW, Pt. II: 143.

Perhaps the most damning testimony against the Fire Zouaves came from Capt. Charles Griffin, who commanded Battery D, 5th US Artillery. Griffin, whom Major Barry had assured would be reinforced by the Fire Zouaves, recounted his prediction that "they would not support us." His memory of the regiment in the moments leading to their collapse was devastating:

The Zouaves were about twenty yards to the rear of us; they were sitting down. I begged them to come up and give a volley and then try the bayonet. They did not run at first, but stood as if panic-stricken. I do not believe they fired fifty shots, certainly not over one hundred. And after they had received three, perhaps four volleys from this regiment of confederates [sic], they broke and ran.

Griffin recalled confronting Barry on the field about the major's confidence that the Zouaves would support the batteries. Barry could only admit: "I was mistaken." Griffin, who was a West Point graduate and regular army officer, found enough blame to go around; he traced the breakdown on Henry House Hill to several factors including the superior numbers of the enemy, mistakes in identifying Confederate troops, and the exhaustion of the volunteers.[160] In repeated questioning, the captain conceded that even if the Fire Zouaves had held firm, a single infantry regiment was no doubt wholly insufficient to sustain his guns. Yet when New York Congressman Moses Odell pressed Griffin why he was so sure of the regiment's undependability, he responded: "I had seen them on the field in a state of disorganization, and I did not think they had the moral courage to fight." "I do not think," he testified, "that any troops that will go through the country in a disorganized state, thieving and robbing, are brave men. They were all running around the field in any way. They were in no kind of order." Chairman Ben Wade proposed: "You do not believe in the maxim, 'The worse the man the better the soldier'?" The captain was unmoved: "No, sir; I do not. I believe in the maxim that he who is universally cruel to a fallen foe is a coward."[161]

Other officers piled on to these condemnations. Gen. Andrew Porter, like Griffin a fellow West Pointer and professional army officer, described volunteer units "constantly breaking," then reforming and continuing to fight; yet in regard to the Fire Zouaves, he judged them "not at all reliable." Had they "been reliable, and could have kept up their work," he mused, they would have successfully protected the artillery batteries on

[160] JCCW, Pt. II: 169–171.
[161] JCCW, Pt. II: 174.

the hill.[162] Interestingly, Porter did not mention the 11th New York by name, only saying there was "another regiment there," on Henry House Hill, and that he did not "remember distinctly which it was." It is not clear if he honestly failed to remember the Fire Zouaves, which seems unlikely given their notoriety, or that he did not want to single them out in these hearings. He further maintained that the artillery batteries would have been fine had there been "good" and "steady" support. "I know," he said, "one regiment of the old regulars would have held it."[163]

Col. William W. Averell (who was Porter's assistant adjutant general at the battle) disparaged the Zouaves, but also the US Marines, testifying that their officers struggled to keep them in ranks, "but the destruction of the battery was so complete that the marines and zouaves seemed to be struck with such astonishment, such consternation, that they could not do anything." After ineffectively shooting their rifles, they "began to break and run down the hill, and nothing could stop them, and then the enemy rushed right over there like a lowering cloud – right over the hill."[164] Averell pointed to this moment as the "turning point of the affair" and "start of the panic."[165] Republican Congressman Gooch asked Lt. Horatio Reed, chief of a line of caissons in Griffin's Battery: "Did the panic on the field commence immediately after the capture of those batteries?" Reed answered matter-of-factly: "Well, sir, the Ellsworth zouaves were ordered to support us, but they ran away before that."[166] Gen. James B. Ricketts (who was an artillery captain at the time of the battle) recounted seeing the Fire Zouaves "in confusion" and tried to encourage them forward by saying "something cheering to them."[167] When asked more pointedly by Congressman George Julian (R-IN): "What kind of support did you receive from the Fire Zouaves?" Ricketts answered: "Well, sir, these Fire Zouaves came up to the ground, but they soon got into confusion and left." Democrat Odell wanted to know if the Zouaves' failure was due to "want of proper directions from their officers." Ricketts was careful in his answer: "I should judge, from the manner in which the men stood there, and from

---

[162] JCCW, Pt. II: 211.

[163] JCCW, Pt. II: 213.

[164] JCCW, Pt. II: 216.

[165] JCCW, Pt. II: 217.

[166] JCCW, Pt. II: 220–221.

[167] JCCW, Pt. II: 243. Ricketts was wounded multiple times at Bull Run, captured, and eventually released from prison in January 1862. He appeared before the Committee on April 3, 1862.

their not being properly in line, that it was from want of officers; either that their officers were ignorant of their duty at that time, or that they were not there. I cannot say how that was." "Our men really behaved very gallantly," Ricketts assured the congressmen, "up to a certain time."[168]

In its summary of the battle's failure, the Committee pointed to the capture of the artillery guns on Henry House Hill as the day's decisive turning point before complete panic set in. It "appears," the report concluded, that these batteries were "exposed" and "not sufficiently supported."[169] The JCCW submitted its final report to Congress in April 1863 and it became public soon after.[170] The dominant narrative was solidifying: the 11th New York was an unreliable regiment long before the battle started, arriving on the battlefield in a "disorganized state."[171]

The JCCW investigation laid bare several preconceived assumptions about effective soldiering. Civilian congressmen were skeptical of professional officers; while the officers were dismissive of volunteers. The Fire Zouaves became fodder for both sides; perceived not as brave, plucky fighters, but instead, from top to bottom, craven cowards.

"THE LAST OF THE FIRE ZOUAVES"

Nevertheless, the 11th New York tried to stay alive and refill its depleted ranks with new recruits.[172] In January, Lt. Patrick Gillon wrote to the state's adjutant general's office arguing: "If we were to recruit for the 11th reg't I think we could get a great many more recruits than we could for the

---

[168] JCCW, Pt. II: 246. Ricketts was also a regular army officer and West Point graduate. A tension running through these professional officers' testimony, including Griffin, Porter, and Ricketts, was their distrust and often blatant disapproval of volunteer troops and the lack of qualified officers leading them. Still, the Fire Zouaves faced greater disapprobation than most all other units. Odell also asked Ricketts if the 14th New York State Militia supported the artillery and Ricketts was noncommittal that he did not know, and they were often confused for Fire Zouaves. See JCCW, Pt. II: 246.

[169] JCCW, Pt. II: 4.

[170] *The New York Times* published most of the testimony on April 10, 1863.

[171] My discussion of the JCCW report is based on my earlier essay, Lesley J. Gordon, "'These Zouaves will never support us': Cowardice, Congress and the First Battle of Bull Run." In *Congress and the People's Contest: The Conduct of the Civil War*, ed. by Donald Kennon and Paul Finkleman (Athens, OH: Ohio University Press, 2018), 59–80; used with permission from Ohio University Press.

[172] News of their recruiting efforts included a column in *The New York Times*, January 1, 1862. George Coffin, for example, age twenty, enlisted in Co. H. on December 16, 1861, in Buffalo, New York, but five weeks later, he deserted. See AGNY, 1097.

service at large."[173] Around the same time, one Fire Zouave described the regiment "still in their tents, with little hopes of again doing service as a regiment." POWs were starting to return, but enlisting new volunteers seemed "next to impossible."[174] After receiving orders from the War Department "to fill up the 11th Regiment of New York Volunteers to the maximum standard prescribed by law," Colonel Leoser pleaded to any former members to return, offering "full amnesty for all past offences in the way of alleged desertion, and the payment of back dues."[175] Leoser also requested the recall of several soldiers already sent home to recruit, including Lieutenant Gillen, "for the reason that they have not obtained one recruit as yet, and I have every reason to believe are neglecting their business, in sufficient measure to justify their return to their Regiment."[176]

On February 27, 1862, recruiters hosted a meeting in a New York City hotel with hundreds in attendance, to encourage "old members of the First Fire Zouave to return to the regiment." Speakers, including some of the regiment's original boosters, the Union Defense Committee, and fire department officials, made impassioned pleas to the men to come back and demonstrate their patriotism. Prosper Wetmore, the secretary of the Union Defense Committee – the same man who had addressed them when they came home in August – assured the audience that the 11th New York "was now in a first state of discipline, and commanded by a highly efficient officer, Col. Leoser, who had graduated at West Point." He repeated the offer that all "who returned to the regiment would have their pay, during

---

[173] P. A. Gillen to J. T. Sprague, January 24, 1862; See also Special Order No. 47, February 17, 1862, both in 11th New York Volunteer Infantry, Volunteer Organizations, Regimental Returns, RG 94, NARA. Three men from each company were assigned to recruit, one commissioned, one non-commissioned, and one private, for a total of thirty soldiers. Leoser suggested changes to the list the next day. See Charles McKnight Leoser to William D. Whipple, February 18, 1862, 11th New York Volunteer Infantry, Volunteer Organizations, Regimental Returns, RG 94, NARA.

[174] *New York Leader*, January 25, 1862.

[175] Lorenzo Thomas to John E. Wool, February 6, 1862, 11th New York Volunteer Infantry, Volunteer Organizations, Regimental Returns, RG 94, NARA. See also *New York Leader*, February 22, 1862.

[176] Charles McKnight Leoser to J. T. Sprague, February 19, 1862, 11th New York Volunteer Infantry, Volunteer Organizations, Regimental Returns, RG 94, NARA. Gillen was included in the special order on February 17, but it appears he had been detailed to recruit in December. Gillen and the additional men Leoser wanted pulled from recruiting were ordered to do so a few weeks later, but at least at their formal mustering out, Gillen was absent without leave. See Special Orders No. 61, March 3, 1862; and Orders No. 107, March 8, 1862, 11th New York Volunteer Infantry, Volunteer Organizations, Regimental Returns, RG 94, NARA; and AGNY, 1128.

the time they have been absent, given them, and no charge of desertion, brought against them." Two soldiers in attendance who had been captured at Bull Run and recently released from prison offered the same message: rejoin, restore your honor, and restore the 11th New York to its prior grandeur. Nine men signed up that night to return.[177] The *New York Leader* urged more to follow but cautioned that "[s]ome are not wanted." "We allude to the cowardly crew who," the paper maintained, "fearing that they might be again called upon to fight, created dissension among the members, and left in the trouble for this city. These men had better stay away, as they were worth nothing in the army, and the charge of rations would be wasted."[178]

Former Capt. John Leverich, who had despaired over the disbanding of the unit several months earlier, offered his opinion, too. He had resigned in October, but now he wanted his old regiment back. Penning an extended piece in the *New York Leader*, Leverich blasted his former fellow officers for their incompetence and inexperience. He harshly condemned Ellsworth for rushing them out of the city "against orders" and keeping the regiment harried until their arrival in Alexandria. "Some of the officers were apparently on the 'make,'" he alleged, "while others amused themselves by getting drunk and carousing; and had it not been for Colonel Farnham they, and the regiment with them, would have been disgraced before they left." They went to battle "[b]efore they were ready," Leverich acknowledged, resulting in a loss of confidence in the entire unit. Now, Leverich insisted, things were better. There was ample food and supplies and good quarters: "They look like regular soldiers, and their officers are held responsible for inattention to the wants of their men, or neglect of their own duty." Less than two weeks later, Leverich regained his commission as captain.[179]

Efforts continued into the spring to return the "Old Members" back to the regiment. These men, Lt. Col. Joseph McFarland informed New York's Adjutant General Major Sprague, were "absent in this City without leave," yet were "willing to rejoin the regiment voluntarily." McFarland wanted to allow them to return without the threat of arrest,

---

[177] *The New York Times*, February 28, 1862; see also *New York Herald*, February 27, 1862.
[178] *New York Leader*, March 1, 1862.
[179] *New York Leader*, March 15, 1862; AGNY, 1157. At least one of the Fire Zouaves' new captains, James L. Waugh, had commanded the "Tompkins Blues," another of the city's volunteer militia units. *The New York Times* praised him for his "military instincts and experience." See *The New York Times*, April 22, 1862.

which apparently the War Department allowed.[180] By May 1862, the regiment had grown to more than 600 men including returning POWs and new recruits.[181]

It was evident, though, that the Fire Zouaves faced disheartening prospects. Except for witnessing the famed clash between the CSS *Virginia* and the USS *Monitor* at Hampton Roads in March 1862, where they helped to man rifle pits on shore, there was little break in their monotonous routine.[182] Complaining that they had been serving merely as "hospital nurses, gravediggers and longshoremen" since they had arrived at Newport News, the soldiers wanted to "participate in the movements now in progress."[183] Colonel Leoser requested permission for the regiment to join the expedition to capture Norfolk, but it was denied. "This," a later history recounted, "seemed to throw a damper upon the entire organization, as it was evidently the intention of the authorities to keep the men engaged in garrison duty, while all the fighting was to be done, all the chances for promotion taken, by the more fortunate members of other commands."[184]

Charles Leoser, the young West Pointer who had been detached from the regular army to join Ellsworth as acting adjutant in May 1861, had been steadfastly loyal to the regiment even after the post-Bull Run difficulties. But now he had had enough. He tendered his resignation, as did a good number of other commissioned officers, leaving the men feeling "disheartened."[185] A few weeks later, recruiting had halted entirely, and

[180] Joseph E. McFarland to John T. Sprague, April 8, 1862: Muster Rolls, Returns and Regimental Papers, RG 94, NARA. McFarland enrolled as a 1st lieutenant in Co. H. on May 25, 1861; commissioned as captain in August 1861; and then promoted to lieutenant-colonel in March 1862. He mustered out on June 2, 1862. See AGNY, 1167; and *New York Leader*, March 22, 1862.

[181] *New York Evening Post*, n.d., excerpted in the *North American and United States Gazette* (Philadelphia, PA), May 20, 1862. Another source estimated that there were about 500 officers and men in the regiment by the time of its mustering out on June 2, 1862. See *Union and Dakotaian* (Yankton, SD), June 10, 1862.

[182] Costello, *Our Firemen*, 720; Two Fire Zouaves from Company E, Pvt. John Bracken, and Pvt. Charles A. McManus, helped "working the batteries" aboard the USS *Cumberland* and were wounded in the fight. See *New York Leader*, March 22, 1862; and AGNY, 1083, 1170.

[183] *New York Evening Post*, n.d., excerpted in the *North American and United States Gazette* (Philadelphia, PA), May 20, 1861.

[184] Costello, *Our Firemen*, 720.

[185] *The New York Times*, May 4, 1862. Eight commissioned officers resigned between March 5 and April 20, 1862, including Leoser's younger brother, Christopher, who was a captain. Some of these men had not formally received their commissions, at least according to the post war adjutant general's report. See also "Christopher Leoser,"

a series of orders were issued for the regiment to return to New York for a formal mustering out of service.[186]

The unit, or what was left of it, arrived home on May 19, 1862. The 11th New York, the *New York Evening Post* wrote, would "become permanently extinct."[187] The *Boston Daily Advertiser*, in an article entitled "The Last of the Fire Zouaves," pronounced that the regiment, though "heralded by an extraordinary reputation for fighting," in the end "never proved a valuable addition to the army." The paper concluded: "The history of this regiment will show, we suspect, that 'bruisers' may serve very well for street fighting, but are not the best material for soldiers."[188] The staunchly supportive *New York Leader* conceded: "No body of men left the city with such flattering opinions and so many friends; but now, after one year's service, they come back almost unnoticed."[189]

Prevented from returning to the front, the regiment had no chance to quiet the doubters and redeem their reputation once and for all. Slowly but surely, the unit had collapsed under the weight of recrimination and doubt.

"THE STIGMA LEFT BEHIND"

While the 11th New York's final homecoming may have been largely ignored, they did not disappear entirely from public notice, at least not yet. Col. Orlando Willcox, exchanged and released from prison, gave a speech in his hometown of Detroit on August 27, 1862, saying he wanted "to place Michigan right" in accounts about Bull Run. He lauded

---

findagrave.com. The *New York Evening Post* reported: "adjutant, quartermaster, four captains, and some lieutenants also resigned at that time, and it was understood, for similar reasons, and the privates who were anxious to proceed at once, made known their unwillingness to remain in the service." See *New York Evening Post* [n.d.], reprinted in the *North American and United States Gazette* (Philadelphia, PA), May 20, 1862; See also Costello, *Our Firemen*, 720-722.

[186] See Special Orders No. 58, April 28, 1862; Special Orders No. 62, May 2, 1862; Special Orders No. 72, May 16, 1862; Special Orders No. 74, May 18, 1862, 11th New York Volunteer Infantry, Volunteer Organizations, Regimental Returns, RG 94, NARA. It seems unlikely that, as some accounts attest, the men were "asked whether they would prefer to continue in service or be disbanded. The vote in favor of the latter was almost unanimous." See *Union and Dakotaian* (Yankton, SD), June 10, 1862.

[187] *New York Evening Post* [n.d.], reprinted in the *North American and United States Gazette* (Philadelphia, PA), May 20, 1862.

[188] *Boston Daily Advertiser*, May 21, 1862.

[189] *New York Leader*, June 7, 1862.

his 1st Michigan regiment for standing "up under fire like the bravest veteran troops," but he echoed allegations by other commanders that the Zouaves fled "at the first fire of the enemy."[190] In his official report, dated a few days later, Willcox was even more harsh, assessing that the Zouaves fell back "bewildered and broken." He allowed that those who reformed with him, about one hundred in his estimation, "did good service, under my own eyes, in the woods and detachments of them joined other regiments in the fight."[191]

The Zouaves also took center stage in Henry Morford's *Days of Shoddy: A Novel of the Great Rebellion*, a harsh indictment of the Union's war effort that included a thinly veiled critique of the Fire Zouaves. In an advertisement in *The New York Times*, the list of "The People Talked About" in the novel included all three colonels from the 11th New York, as well as its ten original captains, and "the Zouave war-correspondent" A. O. Alcock.[192] The novel's main character "Burtnett Haviland" joins the regiment and experiences its many humiliations. Morford blamed Ellsworth and the original attempt to transform firemen into soldiers. Firemen, he contended, were courageous, but also inherently clannish, rebellious, and untrainable. Morford castigated Ellsworth as "bravely insubordinate himself and therefore the last man in the world to teach subordination to a regiment of peculiarly independent character."[193]

There was one final attempt to resurrect the 11th New York Infantry Regiment with fresh recruits in the summer of 1863. But when the draft riots swept the city in July, the 11th NY's Col. Henry F. O'Brian "was seized by the mob and brutally murdered." "The organization," a postwar history noted, "seemed fated." On October 1, 1863, all the current

---

[190] Orlando B. Willcox Speech, August 27, 1862, in *New York Herald*, August 30, 1862.

[191] Orlando B. Willcox to Lorenzo Thomas, September 3, 1862. OR, Ser. I, Vol. 2: 408–409. In another account included in his published memoirs, Willcox described the Fire Zouaves "swept back as by a tornado" during the fight. See Scott, *Forgotten Valor*, 291–92.

[192] *The New York Times*, December 12, 1863.

[193] Morford, *Days of Shoddy*, 287; see also 273 and 362. The novel proved a vehicle for Capt. "Jack" Leverich, a key character in the book, to express his personal grievances against many officers, including Ellsworth. Historian J. Matthew Gallman labels *Days of Shoddy* a "home front" novel, which "tackles, 'shoddy' and the corruption surrounding war contracting," yet a good portion of the book centers on the Fire Zouaves military record – much of it accurate and verifiable from other contemporary sources. See J. Matthew Gallman, *Defining Duty during the Civil War: Personal Choice, Popular Culture, and the Union Homefront* (Chapel Hill, NC: University of North Carolina Press, 2015), 18–19.

members of the 11th New York transferred to the 17th New York Volunteer Infantry to serve out their time.[194] In 1866, the annual report of the New York's Chief of the Bureau of Military Record included a brief history of the unit, repeating the familiar explanation that Ellsworth's tragic demise marked the beginning of the end for the regiment. Successive efforts to revitalize the 11th New York were futile, the report stated, with "the spirit of the organization" essentially "in the grave with Ellsworth and Farnham."[195]

To date, no complete unit history of the 11th New York exists. While an outpouring of regimental histories appeared after the war, first written by the veterans themselves, and then later by amateur and professional historians, former members of the 1st Fire Zouaves stayed mostly quiet. Charles Leoser, who continued in active service with the 2nd US Cavalry until October 1865, refused to criticize the Fire Zouaves. In one account, he maintained that if he had had to raise "a regiment to-morrow, he would prefer, had he his choice of material, to recruit it from the old firemen of New York." He further believed that "if they made any failures during their brief regimental existence, it was due to the mistakes of the officers, and not to any lack of bravery on the part of the rank and file."[196]

Stories of the unit instead folded into celebratory histories of the New York City Volunteer Fire Department and Ellsworth himself. In 1874, a monument to Ellsworth was erected at his gravesite in his hometown of Mechanicville, using some of the funds donated to the regiment after they saved the Willard's Hotel from fire.[197] In Chicago, there were efforts to commemorate Ellsworth's original Zouave Cadets, which included men who went on to serve in the 11th New York, including George H. Fergus, Frank E. Yates, and E. M. Coates.[198] There were also Grand Army of the Republic posts named after Ellsworth, as well as Noah Farnham, the latter composed mainly of members of the original Fire Zouaves. In 1884, these veterans met along with the Independence Fire Company, No. 1 of

[194] State of New York, *Third Annual Report of the Chief of the Bureau of Military Record*, 109. For more on Col. Henry F. O'Brian and his violent death during the riots, see "Irish Colonels: Henry F. O'Brian, 11th New York Infantry," irishamericancivilwar.com.

[195] New York State, *Third Annual Report of the Chief of the Bureau of Military Record*, 108–109.

[196] Costello, *Our Firemen*, 723; see also 729.

[197] *The New York Times*, May 28, 1874. See also *Chicago Daily Tribune*, July 16, 1872. Nearly forty years later, House Representative John R. Farr sought to appropriate $25,000 to erect a second monument to Ellsworth in Washington, DC, that never materialized. See *Chicago Daily Tribune*, June 2, 1912.

[198] *Chicago Daily Tribune*, July 2, 1910; also August 14, 1910.

Bayonne, NJ, to participate in exhibition drills and "a sham fight and sham fire."[199] Historian Patrick Schroeder, in his preface to an edited volume of Arthur O'Neil Alcock's letters, wondered if "the stigma left behind" from accusations of cowardice and failure at Bull Run "may be a reason why no book was assembled to fully recount their service."[200]

In the end, the tribulations the regiment faced seemed baked in from the start. The shocking death of their colonel demoralized them and quashed, it seems, any chance that they might fulfill the high expectations put upon them to perform valiantly in combat. There were other Zouave regiments and other regiments of firemen, and many earned venerated reputations as elite fighters.[201] Several members of the original unit went on to prove themselves as effective soldiers, too. It is also true that other Union regiments that had faltered at Bull Run recovered and went on to become reliable veterans. But not the Fire Zouaves. Their bravado and in Dickens' words "affect[ed] recklessness" as firemen, exaggerated by their Zouave attire and affiliation, served them poorly when faced with the loss of leadership and limited training. Prejudices toward them, as Irish immigrants, as firemen, as Ellsworth's "pet lambs," all conspired against them. They had few advocates once Ellsworth was gone.

Ellsworth's Fire Zouaves were raised in the heady early days of the war when soldiering seemed like a springtime lark. As New York City firemen, they garnered enormous public attention, some good but a lot of it negative. Very soon, however, it was clear that their seemingly natural courage and manliness were not enough to be effective and disciplined soldiers. Ellsworth tried to rush them to battle and prove the naysayers wrong, but his own rashness led to his demise. Allegations of cowardice in combat proved the death knell for the regiment; it never recovered.

Nearly forty years after the Civil War ended, on the eve of America's war with Spain, an Arizona newspaper editor pondered what made good fighting units, using the failed example of the Fire Zouaves as a cautionary tale. This regiment, the writer affirmed, was raised from "the known fighting stock of the country." Nonetheless, he wrote, "The Fire

[199] *The New York Times*, August 8, 1884; see also November 15, 1903.
[200] Schroeder, "Preface," to Pohanka and Schroeder, eds., *With the 11th New York*, 17.
[201] The 2nd Fire Zouaves, officially designated the 73rd New York Infantry Regiment, fought well, most notably at Gettysburg. *See* Costello, *Our Firemen*, 730–732. Other examples of Zouave units were the 5th New York Volunteer Infantry (Duryee's Zouaves), and the 114th Pennsylvania Volunteer Infantry. In the Confederacy, the Louisiana Tigers were also formidable troops. Most Zouave units modified their uniforms and their tactics as the war progressed.

Zouaves were mustered out of the service in disgrace because of their insubordination." He added that individually, they were "fine fighters," "but collectively they were worthless on the field of battle." "The man who is spoiling for a fight," he concluded, "never makes a good soldier."[202]

---

[202] *The Oasis* (Nogales, AZ), March 12, 1898. The editor also cited Billy Wilson's Zouaves (the 6th New York Volunteer Infantry) as equally unreliable soldiers, citing instead regiments made up of humble clerks, farmers, and mechanics as preferable soldiers.

PART II

THE 2ND TEXAS INFANTRY REGIMENT

4

"The Display of Soldiery": Texas

"THOUSANDS OF BRAVE MEN"

More than 1,500 miles from New York, Texas newspapers closely followed the history and fate of the "celebrated" Fire Zouaves including their forma-tion, Ellsworth's death in Alexandria, and their debacle at Bull Run.[1] Using precious column space, these broadsheets reprinted salacious allegations of the Zouaves' brutality and lawlessness, reveling in their downfall.[2] The Houston *Weekly Telegraph*'s special correspondent in Richmond even took time out from his updates on the new Confederate government to tell readers that the "oft repeated boast of Southern men, that the fighting qualifications and courage of the South was as much superior to that of the North, is being continually verified." Conflating the "terrible" Zouaves' bad behavior with all Union soldiers, the correspondent concluded: "The Northern soldier won't fight."[3] This same correspondent later visited

---

[1] "celebrated" from *The Weekly Telegraph* (Houston, TX), July 31, 1861; see also *The Civilian and Gazette* (Galveston, TX), July 30, 1861. Some of these reports were reprints from New York papers; others included the paper's own editorial commentary. On the regiment's formation see *The Civilian and Gazette*, April 23, 1861; *The Weekly Telegraph*, April 23 and 30, 1861; on Ellsworth's death, see *Civilian and Gazette*, June 4, 1861; *The Weekly Telegraph*, June 5 and 12, 1861.

[2] See, for example, *The Weekly Telegraph* (Houston, TX), August 7 and 14, 1861; and September 4, 1861. Heintzelman's damning official report and Russell's harsh critiques of the Fire Zouaves' failed performance at Bull Run also appeared in Texas papers. See for example *The Civilian and Gazette* (Galveston, TX), September 3, 10, 11, 1861; and *Galveston Weekly News* (Galveston, TX), September 10, 1861.

[3] "Special Correspondent," Letter to the Editor, July 1, 1861, *The Weekly Telegraph* (Houston, TX), July 31, 1861. The unnamed correspondent referenced the Fire Zouaves' acting out in Alexandria but also referred to the "terrible(!) Zouaves" scattering "like sheep before the bayonets of the gallant North Carolinians" at the battle of Big Bethel.

captured prisoners in Richmond. Among their number were Fire Zouaves, and the journalist judged them the most "repulsive set of men" he had ever encountered. "I saw," the correspondent sarcastically explained, "a number of the crack company[.] [T]hey expected to carry everything before them, but as they say themselves, they found they were no-where, and those that are prisoners, under no circumstances could they be induced to try another engagement with us."[4] There was even mention of the Fire Zouaves' humiliating capture near Fort Monroe.[5] Stories of the New Yorkers' failings confirmed to Confederates the North's abject cowardice and brutality.

As the 11th New York was collapsing for the world to see, a new regiment of soldiers in Texas was coalescing. This unit, the 2nd Texas Infantry Regiment, was expected to fight bravely; but they too would face devastating accusations of cowardice, casting a dark shadow over them. Their fate was different from the Zouaves, although they too experienced a slow but decidedly unheroic anticlimax to their military service. Both regiments went to war caught up in the jingoistic bombast of war-making, and both found the reality of combat fell far short of that heady rhetoric. For the Texans, however, the cost of failure somehow seemed higher.

The 2nd Texas Infantry Regiment's origins can be traced to the first wave of southern secession. On February 23, 1861, Texas formally ratified its ordinance to secede from the Union; it was the last southern state to do so before the surrender of Fort Sumter and formal outbreak of war. Texas, on the far western edge of the Confederacy, was deeply tied to slavery and white supremacy. Its delegates said as much in their ordinance of secession, stating bluntly that "the governments of the various States, and of the confederacy itself, were established exclusively by the white race, for themselves and their posterity" and that African Americans "were rightfully held and regarded as an inferior and dependent race."[6]

These were probably Duryee's Zouaves or the 5th New York Volunteer Infantry, which faced the 1st North Carolina Infantry at that Confederate victory.

[4] W.A.C. to E. H. Cushing, September 18, 1861, in *The Weekly Telegraph* (Houston, TX), October 9, 1861. It would make sense if this was same special correspondent mentioned above.

[5] See *The Weekly Telegraph* (Houston, TX), October 30, 1861. For more on the jaundiced view most Confederates had of Union soldiers, not just the Fire Zouaves, see George C. Rable, *Damn Yankees!: Demonization and Defiance in the Confederate South* (Baton Rouge, LA: Louisiana State University Press, 2015).

[6] "A Declaration of Causes Which Impel the state of Texas to Secede from the Federal Union," February 2, 1861, from Ernest William Winkler, ed. *Journal of the Secession*

Establishing Texas for the "white race" had been a key tenet of its revolution against centralized Mexican rule some twenty-five years prior. In 1836, white Texans helped lead a successful rebellion against Mexico, seeking to ensure protection of slavery and the production of cotton. The Texas Revolution fueled stories of legendary fights and heroic victories against overwhelming odds, with talk of "liberty" and "freedom" meant solely for white men. For a brief time, Texas was an independent republic, but in 1845 it became annexed to the United States. With statehood came US federal protection of enslavers' human property and expansion of slavery westward. Most Texans, therefore, did not question the decision to side with the Confederacy in 1861.[7]

Still, there were some outspoken dissenters to secession, including Texas' own governor at the time, Sam Houston. Houston had a storied career as a soldier, notably in his victory over the Mexican Army at the Battle of San Jacinto, which secured Texan independence. By 1861, Houston had become a wealthy slaveholder, but he deemed secession foolish and shortsighted and believed that this move would in fact signal the end of slavery, not its continuation.[8] When he refused to take an oath of allegiance to the Confederacy, "[a]n infuriated Texas legislature discharged him of his duties."[9] On April 19, 1861, he defended his Unionist position from a hotel balcony in Galveston, predicting that southern rebellion would cause "the sacrifice of countless millions of treasure, and hundreds of

---

Convention of Texas 1861 (Austin, TX: Texas Library and Historical Commission, 1912), 61–65, Texas State Library, www.tsl.texas.gov.

[7] Like other slave states, the majority of Texas' white population did not own slaves and only a slim majority could be classified as large slave owners. Nonetheless, protection of the institution and fears of slave rebellion were prime motivators for secession and military enlistment. See Charles David Grear, *Why Texans Fought in the Civil War* (College Station: Texas A & M University Press, 2010), 13–18. For more on the Texas Revolution, Texas Republic, and Anglo-Texans' desires for annexation, see Sam W. Haynes, *Unsettled Land: From Revolution to Republic, the Struggle for Texas* (New York: Basic Books, 2022).

[8] According to the 1860 federal census and slave schedule, Sam Houston's real estate was valued at $50,000 and his personal estate at $10,000. He owned six enslaved males and six enslaved females, ranging in age from fifty-five to two years old. See Eighth Census of the United States, 1860: Population Schedule, Austin, Travis County, Texas; and Slave Schedule, City of Austin, Travis County, Texas, Records of the Bureau of the Census, RG 29, NARA; accessed via ancestry.com. Houston's biographers insist that he was a reluctant supporter of slavery and that he and his wife Margaret were kind enslavers. See for example Frank Krystyniak, "Houston, the Emancipator," www.shsu.edu; see also Madge Thornall, Roberts, *Star of Destiny: The Private Life of Sam and Margaret Houston* (Denton, TX: University of North Texas Press, 1993), 319–320.

[9] "Sam Houston," Biography.com.

thousands of precious lives," with only "a bare possibility, [to] win Southern independence, if God be not against you; but I doubt it." In the end, he feared that the North would "overwhelm the South with ignoble defeat."[10]

Houston's warnings fell on deaf ears. On April 17, 1861, his lieutenant-governor, Edward Clark, replaced Houston, and issued a "Proclamation to the People of the State of Texas," "calling at once for Three Thousand Volunteers, to be drilled, equipped and held in readiness the most perfect, to meet any requisition from this Department." He divided the state into districts and subdistricts to aid in recruiting and organizing these volunteers. He stipulated for the creation of infantry units, rather than cavalry, which was the branch of military service Texans preferred. Time was of the essence: the governor wanted these companies mustered in immediately and readying themselves for active service. "The well known chivalry and patriotism" of his fellow Texans, Clark maintained in his proclamation, "render me confident in the belief that the instant they are aware of the requestion for their service, thousands of brave men will spring into the field, armed and equipped, and eager with the determination of defending the rights and honor of the country."[11]

Volunteer militia companies in counties across Texas quickly answered the governor's call. The "military spirit," the press declared, was high.[12] In Houston and Galveston, companies prepared for the state's defense. Soon after Clark's proclamation, Henry "Hal" G. Runnels informed the governor that he had sixty men ready "to go wherever emergency may require be it to the Frontier of Texas or any portion of the Confederate States of

[10] Houston quoted in Thomas North, *Five Years in Texas: What You Did Not Hear during the War from January 1861–January 1866. A Narrative of His Travel Experiences, and Observations in Texas and Mexico* (Cincinnati, OH: Elm Street Printing, 1871), 94. According to the editors of the *Writings of Sam Houston*, a "verbatim report of this speech has not been found." They credited this to "newspapers of this time" "afraid of losing popularity if they printed Houston's speeches." See Amelia W. Williams and Eugene C. Barker, eds., *The Writings of Sam Houston, 1813–1863*, 8 Vols. (Austin, TX: The University of Texas Press, 1938–42), Vol. 8: 301n1. Galveston's *Civilian and Gazette* described the speech but did not quote it, stating that "we regret that we have neither time or space for a more extended report of his remarks; but so far as our city readers are concerned, this would be needless, as the attendance was very general, and the speech was listened to with the most respectful attention throughout." See *The Civilian and Gazette* (Galveston, TX), April 23, 1861. He spoke in Houston a few days later, too. See *The Weekly Telegraph* (Houston, TX), April 30, 1861.
[11] Edward Clark, "Proclamation. to the People of the State of Texas," April 17, 1861, *The Civilian & Gazette* (Galveston, TX), April 30, 1861.
[12] References to "the military spirit" in the press include *The Civilian and Gazette* (Galveston, TX), April 30, 1861 and May 28, 1861; *The Weekly Telegraph* (Houston, TX), June 26, 1861; also April 23, 1861.

America." Runnels' "San Jacinto Guards," however, he explained, "being nearly all country raised Texas boys [they] will not serve as Infantry unless we have to leave the state."[13] A few weeks later, Runnels again wrote Clark, declaring that his company was ready "to march at an hours [sic] notice." "My company," he bragged, "is composed of men raised in Texas as the very bone and sinew of the country and when they volunteered to leave their friends, their homes and their families, they meant [to] <u>fight</u> and were ready if necessary to lay down their lives in defence of their country."[14] They would, he assured Clark, "move right on to Richmond, Va or Washington City at five minutes notice, to either of those places."[15] Governor Clark welcomed these new troops and their enthusiasm to serve, but had to explain not only that he had no arms or pay to provide them, but that he could not "receive any but Infantry for Confederate Service."[16]

Still, men rushed to enlist. The "Confederate Guards" raised by William Timmons in Harris County quickly won plaudits from the *Telegraph*, which reported that their "drill is highly spoken of, and the officers, gentlemen fully competent are indefatigable in their endeavors to render the Confederate Guards a company that may be safely relied on in any emergency."[17] In Galveston, city companies were also forming, making steady "progress towards efficiency."[18]

The frenzied martialism of disunion and war was palatable in Texas, as it was across the country, but it would take a bit longer for the 2nd Texas to fuse into a cohesive regiment.

"BE A GOOD SOLDIER"

During these early weeks of war, a familiar query arose: what did it mean to be a good and effective soldier? This question, which had hung heavy over the fate of the Fire Zouaves, was debated extensively in Texas

---

[13] Hal G. Runnels to Edward Clark, April 23, 1861, Folder 22, Box 2014/099-1, Edward Clark Papers, Dolph Briscoe Center for American History, The University of Texas at Austin, TX (hereafter referred to as DBC).

[14] Hal G. Runnels to Edward Clark, May 10, 1861, Folder 44, Box 2014/099-2, Edward Clark Papers, DBC.

[15] Hal G. Runnels to Edward Clark, May 12, 1861, Folder 46, Box 2014/099-2, Edward Clark Papers, DBC.

[16] Edward Clark to Hal Runnels, April 30, 1861, Folder 22, Box 2014/099-1, Edward Clark Papers, DBC.

[17] *The Weekly Telegraph* (Houston, TX), May 14, 1861.

[18] *The Civilian and Gazette* (Galveston, TX), May 28, 1861. For more on the necessity of drill, see *The Weekly Telegraph* (Houston, TX), May 7, 1861.

editorials and public speeches. There were discussions over which drill
manual to follow, how to shoot a rifle, and what soldiers should wear in
inclement weather.[19] An unidentified "Old Soldier" wrote a series of
letters to the *Weekly Telegraph* concerned about how to instill "proper
drill and discipline" and ensure "efficient soldiers." He maintained
"Volunteers are too often called out [in] hasty, confused, pell-mell manner, half made up and unfit for the march or campaign. In camp, they
would be instructed in guard mounting, fatigue duty and relieving sentinels." Such preparation would help soldiers "learn how to take care of
their health, and avoid the diseases produced by a sudden transition from
civil life to that of a soldier's."[20] Additional posts were more specific,
advising volunteers to obtain good coverings for the changeable weather,
and to keep their "entire person clean." "Remember that in a campaign
more men die from sickness than by the bullet," he advised.[21] "Old

[19] For examples see *The Weekly Telegraph* (Houston, TX), August 28, 1861; and *The
Civilian and Gazette* (Galveston, TX), August 27, 1861 and September 3, 1861. The
preferred manual in the state, and published in "cheap pocket form" by Willard
Richardson, the publisher of the *Galveston News*, was "Gillham's Manual." Gilham's
text originated in Virginia after John Brown's raid and the then Governor John Wise's
demand for better-prepared state militias and volunteers to suppress any future slave
uprisings. Interestingly, Gilham's manual appeared at the same time as Ellsworth's rise to
fame with his Chicago Zouaves and his own drill book; but Virginia entrusted Gilham to
develop a system best suited for their slave state. Georgia adopted Gilham, as did the
Washington Artillery Battalion in New Orleans; and it was recommended for use in
Mississippi. In Texas, it was promoted for wide use to ensure consistent training and
was formally adopted by the state in June. See William Gilham, *Manual of Instruction for
the Volunteers and Militia of the State of Texas; Taken from Gilham's Manual of
Instruction for the Volunteers and Militia of the United States* (Galveston, TX:
Richardson, 1861) and the *Galveston News*, June 15 and 18, 1861. Governor Clark
pronounced its adoption in "General Orders No. 4," June 10, 1861, published in the
Galveston Weekly News, June 25, 1861. Heinrich Wickeland, a German-born civil
engineer, wrote to the *Weekly Telegraph* dismissing the usefulness of the manual, stating
that "*is a whole generation behind the time.*" See H. Wickeland, Letter to the Editor, n.d.
The Weekly Telegraph (Houston, TX), June 12, 1861, emphasis from original. Heinrich
Wickeland (1833–1864) was a German immigrant, educated as civil engineer, who later
served in Waul's Legion but died of yellow fever in Galveston in September 1864. See
Heinrich Wickeland Compiled Military Service Record, War Department Collection of
Confederate Records, RG 109, NARA, hereafter referred to as CMSR; also see
Anonymous, "Wickeland, Heinrich," The Handbook of Texas Online, www.tshaon
line.org.
[20] "An Old Soldier," Letter to the Editor, n. d., *The Weekly Telegraph* (Houston, TX),
May 7, 1861.
[21] "An Old Soldier," Letter to the Editor, n. d., *The Weekly Telegraph* (Houston, TX),
May 14, 1861. This letter also appeared in the *The Civilian and Gazette* (Galveston, TX),
May 14, 1861.

Soldier" further urged Texas to establish formal "camps of instruction" throughout the state to prepare "our citizen soldiers" "for a war of invasion of the most alarming and destructive character." He dismissed concerns over costs, arguing that the "The moral effect produced by camps of instruction would far outweigh any consideration of outlay in money necessary for their establishment."[22]

On May 10, 1861, in Independence, Texas, Sam Houston, certainly an old soldier himself, weighed in on the same question. Despite his initial hesitancy to support secession and the new Confederacy, he now urged unity and resilience. But "above all," he counseled his fellow Texans, "there must be discipline and subordination to law and order." He fore-saw: "Without this, armies will be raised in vain, and carnage will be wasted in hopeless enterprises. The South, chivalric, brave, and impetuous as it is, must add to these attributes of success through discipline, or disaster will come upon the country." Houston believed that Northerners were "by their nature and occupation" naturally subordinate and "capable of great endurance and a high state of discipline." "The South," he observed "claims superiority over them in point of fearless courage." But it was discipline and obedience, Houston argued, that "always makes a good soldier."[23]

Weeks later, as companies continued to fill, Texas Governor Edward Clark issued a proclamation to establish formal camps of instruction for the "heroic volunteers," declaring: "There is not upon earth a people, whom nature has endowed with more courage, whom experience has more thoroughly skilled in the use of arms and inured to the hardships of the campaign, than Texans. The State may be proud indeed, of her strong and valiant sons." Still, he urged them that in order "to give efficiency to valor – direction to their skill, and to render them irresistible in war," they needed training. They are to meet," Clark predicated, "a well disciplined, perfectly armed, Anglo-Saxon soldiery, and must be drilled to a thorough familiarity with every movement of the

---

[22] "An Old Soldier," Letter, n.d., *The Weekly Telegraph* (Houston, TX), May 29, 1861. "An Old Soldier" wrote again in October to urge "a levy, en masse, of all the citizens." See "An Old Soldier," Letter to the Editor, n.d., *The Weekly Telegraph* (Houston, TX), October 9, 1861. Kathryn Shively explores how Civil War soldiers in the eastern theater engaged in this sort of self-care during the war. See Kathryn Shively Meier, *Nature's Civil War: Common Soldiers and the Environment in 1862 Virginia* (Chapel Hill, NC: University of North Carolina Press, 2013).

[23] "Sam Houston Speech at Independence, Texas, May 10, 1861," in Williams and Barker, eds., *Writings of Sam Houston*, Vol. 8: 304–305; also published in *The Weekly Telegraph* (Houston, TX), May 22, 1861.

battlefield."[24] Their enemy was not, Clark reiterated in racialized language a few weeks later, "the wily and lurking Indian, [and] not the weak and listless Mexican."[25] Houston and Clark agreed that it would take more than the presumed natural courage of Anglo-Texans to prevail in combat; they had to have discipline and training.

Editor Edward H. Cushing added to this debate in the pages of his newspaper *The Weekly Telegraph*. During these early months of war, Cushing repeatedly warned his readers that Texas Confederates needed to be compliant and relinquish their individual autonomy. "When a soldier is in his place in battle," he bluntly stated, "it is his duty to obey orders, and it is his captain's duty to shoot him down if he disobeys."[26] Cushing's devotion to the Confederacy was unwavering, despite his New England roots. He was born in Vermont and educated at Dartmouth. But his decade-long residence in Texas converted him to become "an aggressive slavocrat" and "profound Confederate patriot."[27] Cushing pleaded with white Texans to serve willingly, submit to military discipline, and go wherever the state or CSA required. In a column entitled "A Soldier's Duty," Cushing maintained that the "best soldiers," and "those who will be most honored when the war is over, are those who do their duty best in whatever position they may be placed, whether it be a private in the rear guard, or a leader of a forlorn hope." Recognizing the frenzied desire to rush to combat, Cushing was confident that "every brave man will have full opportunity to show his courage."[28]

Not all of Cushing's readers agreed. One contended that white male Texans needed nothing more than their natural courage to defend Galveston: there was no reason for "*captains*," nor "*camp drills to defend their shores*." "They will cover it," the letter writer attested, "with a living

[24] "Proclamation by the Governor of Texas," June 8, 1861, *Galveston Weekly News*, June 18, 1861.
[25] General Orders No. 4, June 10, 1861, *Galveston Weekly News*, June 25, 1861. On August 26, 1861, Clark repeated his concern about the "well disciplined enemy" in another public call for volunteers to fill the requisition issued by Richmond. See *The Civilian and Gazette* (Galveston, TX), September 3, 1861.
[26] *The Weekly Telegraph* (Houston, TX), July 3, 1861.
[27] Emory M. Thomas, "Rebel Nationalism: E. H. Cushing and the Confederate Experience," *The Southwestern Historical Quarterly* Vol. 73, No. 3 (January 1970): 347; 349. In addition, Cushing, who believed the slave South needed to diversify its economy to succeed and lessen its dependency on the North and Europe, used the *Telegraph* to bolster Texan Confederate morale and warn of a long, difficult conflict. See Thomas, "Rebel Nationalism," 350.
[28] *The Weekly Telegraph* (Houston, TX), July 3, 1861.

mass of moral and physical courage that is without parallel."²⁹ Cushing doubled down in a lengthy response, dismissing out of hand this "errone-ous idea," and predicting disaster should tens of thousands of "unorgan-ized, undisciplined, and *undrilled* men" face "even *five hundred* disciplined troops." "We say this," he maintained, "in no derogation to their courage – without meaning to cast the slightest slur on their valor – but it is the truth, plain and unvarnished and we would to God that every Texian was convinced of it." Cushing, like Clark, Houston, and the "Old Soldier" writing letters to the press, recognized that this was a different war with a different foe: "In short, *no troops are efficient, be their courage as indomitable as you will, unless they are thoroughly drilled.*"³⁰ "It was not enough," Cushing emphasized again and again to his readers, "that there should be individual bravery."³¹

These exhortations were contradictory and confusing: Texan, native-born white men were presumed chivalric and motivated by high ideals; men who would fight nobly, even without pay to protect their homes, land, and enslaved peoples.³² Many believed Confederate Texans would, as *Weekly News* Editor Willard Richardson proclaimed, "fight as in the days of yore, when one Texan expected to have to meet several invaders, Indians and Mexicans."³³

But powerful and influential politicians and editors were also stressing the necessity of preparation in order to be effectual "*soldiers*" and "not

---

²⁹ Letter to the Editor, September 25, 1861, *The Weekly Telegraph* (Houston, TX), October 9, 1861. Emphasis from the original.

³⁰ *The Weekly Telegraph* (Houston, TX), October 9, 1861.

³¹ *The Weekly Telegraph* (Houston, TX), October 16, 1861. Examples of soldiers amplifying these calls for discipline include an unnamed officer who allegedly lectured his volunteers: "all your zeal and patriotism, will be of no avail in the day of battle without a thorough knowledge of company drill"; and another soldier who was confident "that Texas gentlemen will prove themselves not only brave men and patriots, but *good and obedient soldiers.*" See *Weekly Galveston News*, June 15, 1861; and *The Weekly Telegraph* (Houston, TX), June 26, 1861. Emphasis from original.

³² In July, Governor Clark contended "that our chivalric soldiers will bear cheerfully with the delay in remunerating them for their services." Drawing a contrast to the negative perception of their northern enemy, he maintained that Texas soldiers "are not hirelings; they rush to arms for the defense of their families, friends and liberties." See Edward Clark, Special Orders No. 18, July 25, 1861, OR, Ser. 1, Vol., 4, 95–96. Charles Grear contends that Texans, unlike other Confederates, had "multiple local attachments." See Grear, *Why Texans Fought*, 5.

³³ *Galveston Weekly News*, October 8, 1861. Richardson, who like editors Cave and Cushing was born in the North, arrived in Texas in 1837, taking over the Galveston *News*. He soon transformed it into the "wealthiest, most important newspaper of ante-bellum Texas." See Randolph Lewis, "Richardson, Willard," Handbook of Texas Online,

a *mob*."[34] The enemy, meanwhile, was portrayed as somehow both craven and controlled; driven only by pay, yet also a cool and determined "Anglo-Saxon soldiery." The Fire Zouaves' ignoble rise and fall, charted in detail in the Texas press, seemed a perfect example of northern soldiers' cowardice.[35] How could both be true? White Texan men were brave and fearless, martialized by a heritage of armed conflict, but not yet ready to defeat the Yankee army? One letter writer to the *Telegraph* reasoned that after the debacle of Bull Run, "the scum and dregs of Northern society" would be replaced by a "better class" and "a different sort of men to fight."[36]

As citizens debated Texan's fitness for battle, army officials continued to organize companies across the state. In June 1861, Texas received a formal requestion for twenty infantry companies to raise, arm, and muster into service in the Confederate States Army, but President Jefferson Davis would appoint the field and staff officers, allowing men in the ranks to elect company officers.[37] The persistent challenge was that most Texans still preferred the cavalry; their visions of military glory only involved riding on horseback. The infantry was perceived as less glamorous, more dangerous, and more pedestrian (literally). There was, as Governor Clark pronounced it, "a repugnance to infantry service.'"[38]

---

www.tshaonline.org. See also Hébert's proclamation "To the Men of Texas," October 7, 1861, in *Galveston Weekly News*, October 8, 1861. In December 1861, William P. Doran, the special correspondent for the *Telegraph*, spotted Richardson in "the ranks" of the troops stationed in Galveston. See "Sioux" Letter to the Editor, December 13, 1861, *The Weekly Telegraph* (Houston, TX), December 18, 1861.

[34] *The Weekly Telegraph* (Houston, TX), December 4, 1861. Emphasis from original.

[35] Examples of the Texas press continuing to reference the Union debacle at Manassas include the *Galveston Weekly News*, December 3, 1861.

[36] "Allan," Letter to the Editor, n.d. *The Weekly Telegraph* (Houston, TX), August 7, 1861. Texas itself had a good number of immigrants. Grear estimates 7 percent of the Texas population in 1860 was foreign-born, with the majority hailing from Germany, but also Irish, French, English, and "a mix of people from eastern Europe." See Grear, *Why Texans Fought*, 39. For more on immigrants and their significance in the war, see Susannah J. Ural, ed., *Civil War Citizens: Race, Ethnicity and Identity in America's Bloodiest Conflict* (New York: New York University Press, 2010); also Ella Lonn, *Foreigners in the Confederacy* (Chapel Hill, NC: University of North Carolina Press, 1940).

[37] Samuel Cooper to Earl Van Dorn, June 12, 1861, OR, Ser. 1, Vol. 4, 91–92.

[38] Clark quoted in C. W. Raines, ed., *Six Decades in Texas: Or Memoirs of Francis Richard Lubbock, Governor of Texas in War Time, 1861–63. A Personal Experience in Business, War and Politics* (Austin, TX: B. C. Jones, 1900), 330–331; see also Allan C. Ashcroft, *Texas in the Civil War: A Résumé History* (Austin, TX: Texas Civil War Centennial Commission, 1962), 10; and X. B. Debray to T. A. Washington, July 27, 1861, OR, Ser. 1, Vol. 4: 94. Lubbock reiterated Texans' preference for the cavalry in a letter to Richmond in February 1862, complaining that it "is utterly impossible to recruit Infantry." See

Tensions also rose between state officials and Richmond authorities on the duration of service and where these new volunteers would go; nor was there any money to arm or supply them.[39]

Preparing Texas soldiers for combat was no less difficult than it was in New York City. There was the emotional jingoism of war-making, which often contrasted sharply with the mundane reality of military service. And mixed in between were persistent questions about what made good soldiers.

"COOLNESS AND COURAGE"

As Texas mobilized for war, Lincoln declared a blockade of the southern coastline, including Texas. Galveston, on the east end of Galveston Island, was the state's second largest city and a vital port for the import and export of cotton and slaves. Thomas North, who visited Texas in 1861, called Galveston the "New York of Texas."[40] To defend it, Capt. John C. Moore, was dispatched to the city. Moore was a native Tennessean, West Point graduate, and veteran of the Seminole Wars who had resigned from the army in 1855 to work as a civil engineer and teach. In February 1861, he quit his professorship at Shelby College in Kentucky to accept a commission as a captain of artillery in the newly created Confederate regular army.[41] Moore arrived in Galveston to find it, as

Francis R. Lubbock to J. P. Benjamin, February 14, 1862, Letterpress book, Outgoing Correspondence, November 1861–April 1862, Governor Francis Richard Lubbock Records, Texas State Library and Archives Commission, Austin, TX. Hereafter referred to as TSLAC.

[39] Edward Clark, Special Orders No. 18, July 25, 1861, OR, Ser. 1, Vol. 4, 95–96.

[40] Thomas North, *Five Years in Texas; What You Did Not Hear during the War from January 1861–January 1866. A Narrative of His Travels, Experiences, and Observations in Texas and Mexico* (Cincinnati, OH: Elm Street Printing Co, 1871), 57. See also Edward T. Cotham, Jr., *Battle on the Bay: The Civil War Struggle for Galveston* (Austin, TX: University of Texas Press, 1998), 1; 3–4; and Ralph A. Wooster, *Civil War Texas: A History and a Guide* (Austin, TX: Texas State Historical Association, 1999), 15. Lincoln ordered the blockade of southern ports on April 19, 1861. For the full text of the Proclamation, see Roy P. Basler, ed., *The Collected Works of Abraham Lincoln*, 8. Vols. (New Brunswick, NJ: Rutgers University Press, 1953): Vol. 4: 339–340.

[41] Bradley Palmer, "Moore, John Creed," in Eldon Stephen Branda, ed., *The Handbook of Texas: A Supplement*, Vol. III (Austin, TX: Texas State Historical Association, 1976), 609. See also, Charles I. Evans, "The Second Texas Infantry," in Dudley G., Wooten, ed. *A Comprehensive History of Texas, 1685–1897*, 2 Vols. (Dallas, TX: William G. Scarff, 1898), Vol. 2: 605–606. Charles Grear misleadingly labels Moore a "recruiting colonel" dispatched to Texas to raise a regiment with the preordained purpose of taking them east of the Mississippi, "where," according to Grear, "he had his own desire to defend Kentucky

FIGURE 4.1 John C. Moore. Image courtesy of the Alabama Department of Archives and History, Montgomery, AL.

one inhabitant described, "crowded with troops" and "in a terrible state of excitement."[42]

Moore quickly got to work, manning the defenses of the city, building a coastal battery with local enslaved laborers, and in the words of Francis Lubbock, doing "much to inspire confidence."[43] Moore requested that the newly created "citizens committee," made up of the city's wealthiest residents, "procure for him a cash advance of $10,000" to purchase necessary military supplies, in addition to any funds he could obtain from Richmond.[44] He further called on the "patriotism of the people of

and Tennessee." There is, however, no evidence of this at all – instead Moore was simply following orders from Richmond. See Grear, *Why Texans Fought*, 51. Grear appears to have borrowed the term "recruiting colonels" from Ashcraft, *Texas in the Civil War*, 10.

[42] John Johnson letter, April 25, 1861, quoted in James Schmidt, *Galveston and the Civil War: An Island City in the Maelstrom* (Cheltenham: History Press, 2012), 26–27.

[43] Lubbock quoted in Raines, ed. *Six Decades in Texas*, 317. The use of enslaved laborers caused some debate in the German immigrant community where there was concern that white men should be employed on the battery rather than enslaved men. See *Union* (Galveston, TX), May 9, 1861. This and all other quotes from this newspaper are translated from the original German.

[44] *The Civilian and Gazette* (Galveston, TX), July 2, 1861.

Texas," and sought supplies for his growing command including "beef, flour, pork, coffee, sugar, rice, soap, candles, vinegar, salt, corn and hay," offering to pay with Confederate bonds or treasury notes.[45]

In early July 1861, the steamer USS *South Carolina*, a trade vessel refitted for war, arrived in Galveston Harbor to enforce the federal blockade. Moore later remembered that the sight of the ship "threw the people of the city into a temporary state of violent convulsions. Then followed a wild rushing to and from, the tops of buildings and many upper story windows were filled with anxious gazers discussing the terrible consequences they expected soon to follow."[46] When Moore sent an officer under a flag of truce to ask why the boat had dropped anchor, the ship's captain. James Alden explained that he was simply enforcing the blockade, and would do so "to the best of my ability."[47] According to Moore, Alden added that he "hoped he would not be obliged to resort to violent measures during his sojourn."[48] Alden and his crew commenced capturing vessels, a total of eleven schooners, some he deemed "worthless."[49] Tensions escalated when a pilot schooner, the USS *Dart*, brushed close to the city's batteries under Moore's command. Confederates fired, landing two shots through the *Dart*'s mainsail. Alden responded in turn, ordering the *South Carolina* to steam close to shore. A steady exchange of fire commenced between the artillery on land and the ship at sea.

Crowds rushed to the beach to watch the fire fight, and one man, Frank Sylva, a Portuguese immigrant, was "cut to pieces" and died; others were injured.[50] *The Civilian and Gazette*, whose editor Eber Worthington Cave

---

[45] *The Weekly Telegraph* (Houston, TX), August 28, 1861; also *The Civilian and Gazette* (Galveston, TX), August 27, 1861 and September 3, 1861.

[46] Moore quoted in Ben C. Stuart, "Some True Tales of Sixty-One," *Galveston Daily News* (Galveston, TX), July 2, 1911.

[47] James Alden, to William Mervine, July 18, 1861, ORN, Ser. 1, Vol. 16, 576–577; see also John C. Moore to James Alden, July 2, 1862, ORN, Ser. 1, Vol. 16, 577.

[48] Moore quoted in Ben C. Stuart, "Some True Tales of Sixty-One," *Galveston Daily News* (Galveston, TX), July 2, 1911.

[49] James Alden, to William Mervine, July 8, 1861, ORN, Ser. 1, Vol. 16, 576–577.

[50] Ben C. Stuart, "Some True Tales of Sixty-One," *Galveston Daily News* (Galveston, TX), July 2, 1911; and "C," Letter to the Editor, August 3, 1861, *The Weekly Telegraph* (Houston, TX), August 7, 1861. "C" was mostly likely Eber Worthington Cave, editor of *The Civilian and Gazette*. For more details on the bombardment see also *Nashville Union American* (Nashville, TN), August 16, 1861. Cave further praised the "Houston boys" who "worked the guns like men." See *The Weekly Telegraph* (Houston, TX), August 7, 1861. Thirty-year-old Cave, born in Philadelphia, had come to Texas in 1853 and steadily amassed a good deal of influence and power, serving as Texas Secretary of State during Houston's presidency. For more on Cave, see Linda S. Hudson, "Cave, Eber Worthington," Handbook of Texas Online, www.tshaonline.org.

was helping to man the city's defenses, angrily blasted President Lincoln and his US forces for defying "all the rules of civilized warfare," and "the flag of neutral nations then flying," in seeking "to murder our women and elderly."[51]

An international incident threatened to erupt when several foreign consuls signed a letter of "solemn protest" accusing Captain Alden of committing "acts of inhumanity unrecognized in modern warfare and meriting the condemnation of Christian and civilized nations." They demanded to know why there was no warning before the navy guns unleashed on the city, killing the "unoffending" Sylva and wounding other "peacefully disposed persons."[52] Alden pushed back on the complaint, telling the foreign consuls that they were misinformed and accusing Confederates of being the aggressors.[53] Moore offered his own response to the consuls, mocking Alden for his "bad shot" and insisting that he had personally "warned him against coming within the range of our guns." According to Moore, Alden "answered he would be careful not to do so" and that "he desired to have no difficulty with the people of Galveston."[54]

The "Galveston Bombardment" merited enough national attention to be featured in *Frank Leslie's* and *The New York Times*, among other northern publications.[55] For Texans, the engagement showed their resolve and superiority as fighters, despite the continued Union threat to the city. Moore's defiance of the US Navy earned praise from local authorities. "Too much credit cannot be given to Col. Moore," *The Civilian and Gazette* declared, "for the coolness and courage with which he conducted the engagement."[56] George Newton penned a poem

[51] Cave's editorial from the *Civilian Extra* (Galveston, TX) was also reprinted in the *Dallas Daily Herald* (Dallas, TX), August 14, 1861. A longer account of the incident with excerpts from the *Galveston News* appeared in the *Nashville Union American* (Nashville, TN), August 16, 1861.

[52] "Protest of Foreign Consular Officers" to James Alden, August 5, 1861, ORN, Ser. 1, Vol. 16, 605–606; see also *The Civilian and Gazette* (Galveston, TX), August 13, 1861.

[53] James Alden to Arthur Lynn, J. C. Kuhn, F. W. Steil, and others, August 6, 1861, ORN, Ser. 1, Vol. 16, 606–607.

[54] John C. Moore to Messers. Lynn, Jockusch, Frederick and others, August 7, 1861, published in *The Weekly Telegraph* (Houston, TX), August 14, 1861.

[55] "The Galveston Bombardment" was the headline in *The New York Times* on September 8, 1861, which reprinted Alden's report and his exchange with the foreign consuls. *Frank Leslie's Illustrated Newspaper* included an image of the USS *South Carolina* "shelling the batteries at Galveston," and a defense of Alden, on October 12, 1861.

[56] Article originally from the *Civilian Extra* (Galveston, TX), then republished in *The Weekly Telegraph* (Houston, TX), August 7, 1861. See also the *Dallas Daily Herald*

celebrating Moore's success, likening it to Confederate victories at Fort Sumter and Manassas where the "Yankee cowards run hog or die."[57]

One week after the bombardment, Brig. Gen. Earl Van Dorn, commander of the Department of Texas, selected Moore as colonel of the first formally organized infantry regiment in the state.[58] It seems likely that Moore's performance in Galveston attracted Van Dorn's and other military officials' favorable attention. As he looked to raise his regiment, Moore retained command of the Military District of Galveston and sought to keep control of that district. In November he complained to Brig. Gen. Paul O. Hébert that naval commander W. W. Hunter was undermining his authority, "communicating with the blockading frigate without my being informed of the nature of such Communications."[59] Hébert's assistant adjutant general, Samuel B. Davis, replied that Hunter "has been placed on special duty," to oversee the navel defenses of the ports as well as any assigned vessels. Hunter was, Davis assured Moore, "subject to the orders of military superiors in this military district."[60] Moore later bemoaned taking "charge of the defences of that city without any assistance," often paying out of his own pocket to obtain necessary supplies. When he failed to file quarterly paperwork on time, he responded defensively to Quartermaster Abraham C. Meyers: "If you or the President only knew the amount of labor performed and trouble encountered, I feel assured I would be pardoned for my seeming neglect of duty."[61]

The 11th New York's rushed beginnings were far different than those of this new Texas regiment. But there was at least one similarity from the start: both regiments had colonels sensitive to slights and their positions of power.

(Dallas, TX), August 14, 1861; and *Nashville Union American* (Nashville, TN), August 16, 1861.

[57] George Newton, "Run Hog or Die," *The Weekly Telegraph* (Houston, TX), December 11, 1861.

[58] Earl Van Dorn to L. P. Walker, August 10, 1861, OR, Ser. 1, Vol. 4: 97; see also John C. Moore to Ashbel Smith, August 19, 1861, Folder 1: "Letters 1861," Box 2G224, Ashbel Smith Papers, DBC. Some of the companies that made up the new regiment began arriving in Galveston in August. See Ashbel Smith to P. O. Hébert, Nov 6, 1861, Folder 1: "Letters 1861," Box 2G224, Ashbel Smith Papers, DBC; and John C. Moore to Ashbel Smith, August 19, 1861, Folder 1:" Letters 1861," Box 2G224, Ashbel Smith Papers, DBC. See also *The Weekly Telegraph* (Houston, TX), August 7 and 14, 1861.

[59] John C. Moore to Samuel B. Davis, November 4, 1861, Moore Papers, DBC. A duplicate of this letter can be found in John C. Moore, CMSR, War Department Collection of Confederate Records, RG 109, NARA fold3.com.

[60] Samuel B. Davis to John C. Moore, November 4, 1861, OR, Ser. 1, Vol. 4, 131.

[61] John C. Moore to Abraham C. Myers, January 19, 1862, John C. Moore, CMSR, War Department Collection of Confederate Records, RG 109, NARA, fold3.com.

"OUR LEADING MEN ARE ALL ENLISTED"

Moore began consolidating companies from Houston and Galveston and surrounding counties. These included the "Bayland Guards," which would be formally designated as Co. C, as well as the "San Jacinto Guards" (Co. A), "The Confederate Guards" (Co. B), and "The Confederate Grays," also known as the "Gentry Volunteers" (Co. D), from Harris County; "The Burleson Guards" (Co. G) and "The Lexington Grays" (Co. H) from Burleson County; "The Gonzales Invincibles" (Co. I), from Gonzales and Wilson counties; and "The Texana Guards" (Co. K) from Jackson County. There was an additional company from Robertson and Brazos counties (Co. E), and one from Galveston (Co. F), "The German Island City Company," consisting almost entirely of German immigrants.[62]

In September 1861, all ten companies were mustered into service "for the war" and officially designated the First Texas Infantry Regiment.[63] "But a few days afterwards," Charles Evans, who enlisted as a private in Co. G., recalled, "intelligence was received that the number of the regiment had been changed to the Second." Texas companies that had already arrived in Richmond and organized under command of Senator now Col. Louis Wigfall "claimed the right" that his regiment "be called the First Texas." Evans remembered his comrades' bitter disappointment, contending that as the first regiment formally organized in Texas, they were "justly entitled to that designation."[64]

This sense of entitlement is not surprising given the fact that the regiment consisted of powerful and wealthy men from top to bottom. Second in command was Lt. Col. William P. Rogers, who encapsulated the

---

[62] *Union* (Galveston, TX), February 23, 1861. The company was also referred to as the "Island City Company" and "German Island City Fighters." See *Union* (Galveston, TX), April 30, 1861; May 1, 1861; Ralph A. Wooster, *Lone Star Regiments in Gray* (Austin, TX: Eakin Press, 2002), 88; and the *The Civilian and Gazette* (Galveston, TX), May 28, 1861.

[63] See for example Ralph Smith, CMSR, War Department Collection of Confederate Records, RG 109, NARA, accessed via fold3.com, which indicates he enlisted "for the war" in October 1861.

[64] Evans, "The Second Texas Infantry," 576. As late as November 1861, Capt. John W. Hood took his oath of office to the Confederate Army, referencing his command as the "1st Reg. Texas Infy." See John W. Hood, CMSR, War Department Collection of Confederate Records, RG 109, NARA, accessed via fold3.com. Moore was still referred to as colonel of the "First Regiment of Texas Volunteers," in "Orders No. 19," October 2, 1861, OR, Ser. 1, Vol. 4, 113. The regiment was also called "Moore's Regiment," the "Galveston Regiment," or "Van Dorn's Regiment." See for example, *The Weekly Telegraph* (Houston, TX), September 4, 1861.

values and outlook of the slaveholding elite. A cousin to Sam Houston's wife Margaret, Rogers grew up on a sprawling plantation near Aberdeen, in Monroe County, Mississippi.[65] On the urging of his father, Rogers attended medical school in Kentucky, but later turned to law, and served as a captain in Jefferson Davis' 1st Mississippi Rifles regiment in the Mexican-American War. During that conflict, he confided in his diary that he had grown tired of a soldier's life and frustrated with leading volunteers. He also chafed under Davis' command, feeling underappreciated, describing his own "coolness" in leading his company as compared to the hot "fury" of a fellow officer. At one point, with battle imminent, he wrote that he would "distinguish himself or die."[66] His antipathy toward Davis (which seemed mutual) never really dissipated.[67]

After the war, Rogers gained appointment as US consul to Veracruz. In 1851 he moved with his growing family to Texas and continued practicing law, becoming, according to one source, "one of the finest criminal lawyers in the state."[68] He also amassed considerable wealth in slaves and land.[69] During the secession crisis, Rogers served as a delegate to the state convention, and signed Texas' ordinance of secession. Days before the surrender at Fort Sumter, he had written his old nemesis, now President

---

[65] William's father Timothy Lincoln Rogers (1791–1844) was born in Georgia, a veteran of the War of 1812, and died in Aberdeen, Monroe County, MS. In 1840, Timothy owned nearly fifty slaves. See Sixth Census of the United States, 1840: Population Schedule, Monroe County, MS, Records of the Bureau of the Census, RG 29, NARA; accessed via ancestry.com.

[66] Eleanor Damon Pace, ed. "The Diary and Letters of William P. Rogers, 1846–1862," *Southwestern Historical Quarterly* Vol. 37, No. 4 (April 1929): 263–265; 270; 273. It should be noted that the editor of these published Rogers' letters made some errors in her transcription and identification of names and places. In the case of any discrepancies, I relied on copies of the originals housed at the DBC. The fellow officer Rogers referenced was Lt. Col. Alexander Keith McClung, an infamous duelist, nicknamed the "Black Knight of the South." For more on Rogers' relationship to Davis during the Mexican-American War, see Joseph E. Chance, *Jefferson Davis's Mexican War Regiment* (Jackson, MS: University Press of Mississippi, 1991).

[67] Joseph E. Chance, "William Peleg Rogers: A Short Biography," 3, unpublished copy in 2nd Texas Infantry Regimental Files, Shiloh National Military Park, Corinth Civil War Interpretive Center, Corinth, Mississippi; hereafter referred to as CCWIC.

[68] Marcus J. Wright, *Texas in the War, 1861–1865*. Edited by Harold Simpson (Hillsboro, TX: Junior College Press, 1965), 100.

[69] In 1860, Rogers had personal and real estate wealth valued at $40,000, and he owned fifteen men, women, and children, ranging in ages from nine to forty-two. See Eighth Census of the United States, 1860: Population and Slave Schedule, Harris County, TX; Records of the Bureau of the Census, RG 29, NARA; accessed via ancestry.com.

Davis, for the authority to raise his own regiment.[70] For now, Rogers gained appointment as head of the "Houston Brigade," tasked with helping to defend the coast. By early July 1861, the brigade counted 450 men and was "eager to march to any point, whether it be Virginia, Arkansas or Mexico, to which the Government of the C.S. may order them."[71] At some point, Rogers was under serious consideration to lead one of the regiments leaving for Virginia, but his wife Martha was adamantly opposed to his going so far away. Instead, he accepted a commission in the 2nd Texas.[72]

Like Rogers, Dr. Ashbel Smith had an abundance of power and prestige. Unlike his fellow officer, however, Smith was not native to the South: he was born in Connecticut in 1805, earned his medical degree at Yale University in 1828, and practiced medicine in Paris and North Carolina. In 1837 he migrated to the new Texas Republic, serving in various prominent military and government positions. He became surgeon general for the Texas army, diplomat to England and France, and secretary of state. During the war with Mexico, he served as a surgeon and in 1848, was appointed to the United States Military Academy's Board of Visitors. As he rose to prominence, Smith gained wealth in land and slaves, purchasing Evergreen Plantation on a bay near Cedar Bayou in 1847 for some $5,000.[73]

[70] William P. Rogers to Jefferson Davis, April 12, 1861, in Lynda Lasswell Crist, ed. *The Papers of Jefferson Davis*, 14 Vols. (Baton Rouge, LA: Louisiana State University Press, 1971–2015), Vol. 7: 102.

[71] *The Weekly Telegraph* (Houston, TX), July 3, 1861. Initially, it seems this brigade was part of the Texas militia and meant to consist of men "unattached to volunteer companies." But soon it counted several additional volunteer companies including Timmons' Confederate Guard, and Williams' Gentry Volunteers. See *The Weekly Telegraph* (Houston, TX), May 29 and June 26, 1861.

[72] Biographical details from T. Michael Parrish, "Rogers, William Peleg" Handbook of Texas Online, www.tshaonline.org; see also Wright, *Texas in the War*, 99–100; Chance, *The Second Texas*, 13–14; and Wooster, *Civil War Texas*, 1–2. Later in the fall of 1861, there was continued speculation that Rogers would gain a colonelcy and have his own regiment to command. See D. M. Whaley to E. H. Cushing, September 15, 1861 in *The Weekly Telegraph* (Houston, TX), October 9, 1861; see also October 16, 1861.

[73] "Evergreen Plantation," The Handbook of Texas, www.tshaonline.org. According to the 1850 federal census, Smith owned thirty-two enslaved people; in 1860, he owned twenty enslaved people, with real estate worth $100,000 and personal wealth $35,000. See Seventh Census of the United States, 1850: Population and Slave Schedule, Harris County, TX; and Eighth Census of the United States, 1860: Population Schedule, Harris County, TX; and Slave Schedule, Precinct 8, Harris County, TX, Records of the Bureau of the Census, RG 29, NARA; accessed via ancestry.com.

Although later celebrated as "perhaps the most learned man in the state," and "one of the most accomplished Texans of the nineteenth century," Smith was also described as eccentric, even cruel.[74] His embrace of white supremacy and slavery was unequivocal. In 1848, he gave a speech in Galveston celebrating the nation's victories in the war with Mexico. This conflict was, he declared, "part of the mission, of the destiny allotted to the Anglo Saxon race on the continent. It is our destiny, our mission to civilize, to Americanize this continent."[75]

Over the spring and summer, Ashbel Smith had organized the "Bayland Guards," drilling them on the grounds of his plantation. At their first meeting, Smith counted fifty enlistees, deeming them: "A finer looking set of men, physically, I have never seen." He wrote to Cushing at the *Weekly Telegraph*: "It would have done you good to see the six-footers, and also the broad shoulders, and the bold and intelligent countenances. All was animated, thoughtful, cheerful and determined."[76] A few days later, Smith counted sixty-five men enrolled and put the word out that he wanted to form a battalion and find a larger encampment near Houston.[77] On April 27, a group of "ladies" bestowed Smith's company with a "beautiful banner," exhorting them to "conquer or die and to never forsake those colors or let them trail before the enemy." An observer described the scene, asking: "Will such men be conquered? Will such

---

[74] Flavia Fleischman, *Old River Country: A History of West Chambers County* (Fort Worth, TX: Worth Bindery, 1976), 48; Wright, *Texas in the War*, 100. There is convincing evidence that Smith was an absent and callous slave-owner who allowed his overseer to brutalize his slaves; see Candice D. Lyons, "Rage and Resistance at Ashbel Smith's Evergreen Plantation," notevenpast.org. Most other accounts of Smith are uncritical, including his most recent biographer, who strains to recognize his faults by labeling him a "slave-owning humanitarian." See Elizabeth Silverthorne, *Ashbel Smith of Texas: Pioneer, Patriot and Statesman, 1805–1886* (College Station: Texas A & M University Press, 1982), 233. For more biographical details on Smith, see also Wright, *Texas in the War*, 100. A decidedly dated and biased study of Texas and slavery is Abigail Curlee, "A Study of Texas Slave Plantations, 1822–1865," PhD Dissertation, University of Texas, Austin, TX, 1932.

[75] Ashbel Smith, *An Address Delivered in the City of Galveston on the 22d of February, 1848, The Anniversary of the Birth Day of Washington and the Battle of Buena Vista* (Galveston, TX: News Office, 1848), 11.

[76] Ashbel Smith to E. H. Cushing, April 24, 1861, *The Weekly Telegraph* (Houston, TX), April 30, 1861. See also W. J. Mills to Ashbel Smith, November 7, 1861, Folder 1: Letters 1861, Ashbel Smith Papers, DBC. Mills, who self-identified as an orderly sergeant, reported that the company was "fully officered" by April 27, 1861. However, his name does not appear on any of the regimental rosters or CMSRs – he may not have formally enlisted in the company once it mustered into service as the 2nd Texas.

[77] Ashbel Smith to E. H. Cushing, April 27, 1861, *The Weekly Telegraph* (Houston, TX), May 7, 1861.

men suffer the invader of our rights to despoil their hearthstones, to murder and violate their wives and daughters? No never! never! never! so help us God." Captain Smith and his Bayland Guards looked invincible. "We are now on a complete war footing, ready to do or dare to slay or be slain," the onlooker pronounced, disparaging Lincoln and his "cowardly cut throat minions."[78] *The Weekly Telegraph* predicted: "Let us also say that we believe Capt. Smith will show all the gallantry and courage on the field which have characterized him elsewhere."[79] The state's adjutant general, William Byrd, praised Smith for his "excellent company," adding: "The fire of the old Texan state burns in your breast."[80]

Almost all the other company officers were wealthy land and slave-owners, and many, like the majority of white Texans, were recent migrants to the state.[81] Eight out of ten of the captains were from the upper or border south, including Tennessee, Virginia, Kentucky, and North Carolina; two were born in the north – New York and Connecticut. Several, like Smith, had military experience in the Texas Revolution, the Mexican-American War, or prewar militia companies. Most were in their mid-thirties and well established with families and civilian professions. Capt. Hal G. Runnels (Co. A) was a Mexican-American War veteran, son of Mississippi Governor Hiram Runnels, and cousin to Hardin R. Runnels, the fifth governor of Texas.[82] Capt. William Chance Timmons (Co. B) was

---

[78] W.H.B., Letter to the Editor, April 28, 1861, *The Weekly Telegraph* (Houston, TX), May 7, 1861. W.H.B. seems to be William H. Bryan, who later enlisted in the Bayland Guards (Co. C of the 2nd Texas) in August. He was killed at Corinth on October 4, 1862. Bryan's family resided near Smith's plantation and his father John L. Bryan owned fifteen enslaved people with $18,000 in real estate and $16,000 personal estate worth. See, Eighth Census of the United States, 1860: Population and Slave Schedule, Precinct 6, Harris County, TX, Records of the Bureau of the Census, RG 29, NARA; accessed via ancestry.com.

[79] *The Weekly Telegraph* (Houston, TX), June 26, 1861.

[80] William Byrd to Ashbel Smith, July 12, 1861, Folder 1: "Letters 1861," Box 2G224, Ashbel Smith Papers, DBC.

[81] Charles Grear estimates that by the late 1850s, nearly 80 percent of the white population in Texas were "southern born," with a small portion of them owning slaves. See Grear, *Why Texans Fought*, 12. Still, as discussed below, the officer ranks of the 2nd Texas were nearly all filled with slave-owners. Joseph Glatthaar finds slaveowners well represented in Robert E. Lee's Army of Northern Virginia, too. See Glatthaar, *General Lee's Army*. Susannah Ural's study of Hood's Texas Brigade offers a nuanced portrait of Confederate soldiers' unwavering support of slavery and southern independence. See Ural, *Hood's Texas Brigade*, 2–6. The fate of the Texas regiments in the eastern theater was notably different than that of the 2nd Texas.

[82] According to the 1860 US Federal Census, Runnels, listed as a "contractor," owned seven enslaved people, with real estate valued at $24,420, and personal estate valued at $19,729. See Eighth Census of the United States, 1860: Population and Slave Schedule, Precinct 10,

a Houston clerk, born in New York, who had resided in New Orleans for many years, and served in the Washington Artillery before coming to Texas.[83] Capt. Edward F. Williams (Co. D), a native of South Carolina, was a restaurant owner from Houston.[84] Capt. Belvidere Brooks (Co. E), a native of North Carolina, was a doctor and merchant.[85] Capt. John Wyatt Hood (Co. G), born in Virginia, was a Burleson County merchant.[86] Capt. Noble Lafayette McGinnis (Co. H), also from Burleson County, was a farmer, born in Tennessee.[87] Capt. Clarke Owen (Co. K), the oldest of the ten captains, was born in 1808 in Shelby County, Kentucky, fought in the Texas Revolution, participated in the failed "Mier Expedition" in 1842, and served in the Texas legislature.[88] George Washington Lafayette Fly, age

Harris County, TX, Records of the Bureau of the Census, RG 29, NARA; accessed via ancestry.com.

[83] Timmons had also sought a commission in the regular Confederate Army, which never materialized. See Samuel B. Davis to D. F. Kennen, March 8, 1862, in William C. Timmons, CMSR, War Department Collection of Confederate Records, RG 109, NARA; accessed via fold3.com. See also Eighth Census of the United States, 1860: Population Schedule, Houston, Ward No. 3, Harris County, TX, Records of the Bureau of the Census, RG 29, NARA; accessed via ancestry.com. See also Timmons' biography found at findagrave.com.

[84] In 1860, Williams owned six slaves, with real estate valued at $15,000 and personal estate valued at $12,000. In 1850, Williams was listed as a restaurant owner and in 1870, a "saloon keeper," but had no occupation listed in 1860. See Seventh Census of the United States, 1850: Population Schedule, Houston, Harris County, TX; and Eighth Census of the United States, 1860: Population and Slave Schedule, Houston Ward 2, Harris County, TX; and Ninth Census of the United States, 1870: Population Schedule, Houston Ward 1, Harris County, TX, Records of the Bureau of the Census, RG 29, NARA; accessed via ancestry.com.

[85] In 1860, Brooks' real estate was valued at $500 and personal estate valued at $8,000; he owned one ten-year-old boy. His wife Nancy was thirty-two years old, and he had two young sons: Joseph (age five) and Belvidere (eleven months). See Eighth Census of the United States, 1860: Population and Slave Schedule, Robertson County, Records of the Bureau of the Census, RG 29, NARA, accessed via ancestry.com.

[86] Hood owned one enslaved fifty-year-old woman. See Eighth Census of the United States, 1860: Population and Slave Schedule, Burleson County, TX, Records of the Bureau of the Census, RG 29, NARA, accessed via ancestry.com; See also "John Wyatt Hood," findagrave.com.

[87] In 1860, McGinnis had real estate valued at $2,500 and personal estate valued at $2,900; he also owned a single black man, age twenty-five. See Eighth Census of the United States, 1860: Population and Slave Schedule, Burleson County, TX, Records of the Bureau of the Census, RG 29, NARA; accessed via ancestry.com. See also "Noble Lafayette McGinnis," findagrave.com.

[88] Ernest R. Lindley, Comp., *Biographical Directory of the Texan Conventions and Congresses, 1832–1845 of Texas*, (Austin, TX: Book Exchange, 1941), 147. According to census records, Owen was a "Farmer & Stock Raiser," with real estate valued at $54,367; and his personal estate valued at $71,600. He and his wife had six children, and he owned twenty-three enslaved people, ages two to fifty-five; eleven females and

twenty-six, was the youngest company captain in the regiment (Co. I); still, his family's wealth and influence was considerable. Fly's father William had moved to Texas in 1853 and quickly established himself as a large slave- and land-owner in Gonzales County. By 1860, George listed himself as a "planter" alongside his widowed mother, who owned nearly fifty slaves.[89]

The "Island City Company" (Co. F) was led by forty-year-old John Herman Nicolaus Müller, a native of Germany and Galveston merchant who had immigrated to Texas sometime in the 1840s, serving as a clerk in the Quartermaster Department during the Mexican-American War.[90] Although historians have recognized that many German Texans dissented from supporting secession and the Confederacy, Müller was decidedly pro-secession and pro-Confederacy, elected as a delegate to the secession convention.[91] The German-language newspaper *Union* praised Müller as having "a reputation as an outstanding member of commercial circles" and "one of the few Germans in Texas who was active in the promotion of secession."[92] In February 1861, Müller began organizing his company,

twelve males. See Eighth Census of the United States, 1860: Population and Slave Schedule, Jackson County, TX, Records of the Bureau of the Census, RG 29, NARA; accessed via ancestry.com. Owen, like Sam Houston opposed secession, but still raised troops. See Stephen L. Hardin, "Clark L. Owen," Handbook of Texas Online, www.tsh aonline.org. See also W. Lamar Fly, "George Washington Layfette Fly" in 2nd Texas Infantry, Regimental Files, CCWIC.

[89] Fly also attended the University of Mississippi's newly opened law school. By 1860, Fly owned eleven enslaved people; his mother owned forty-seven. Nearby were several other family members who also owned land and slaves. See Eighth Census of the United States, 1860: Population and Slave Schedule: Gonzales County, TX, Records of the Bureau of the Census, RG 29, NARA; accessed via ancestry.com.

[90] The 1860 census lists Müller as a merchant, living with his wife Mary and two young children in Austin County, Texas. His real estate was then valued at $500, and he apparently owned no slaves. See Eighth Census of the United States, 1860: Population Schedule, Cat Springs, New Ulm, and Industry, Austin, TX, Records of the Bureau of the Census, RG 29, NARA; accessed via ancestry.com; and John Müller, CMSR War Department Collection of Confederate Records, RG 109, NARA; accessed via fold3.com. His CMSR indicates his Mexican-American service as a clerk; but the *Union* newspaper claimed he migrated after the war in 1849. See *Union* (Galveston, TX), March 12, 1861.

[91] For more on the divided loyalty of German immigrants in the state, see Grear, *Why Texans Fought*, 136–144; 148.

[92] *Union* (Galveston, TX), March 12, 1861; and February 9, 1861. Ferdinand Flake, the editor of this German-language newspaper, was staunchly pro-Union (hence the name of his paper), but like Sam Houston, became pro-Confederate and helped Müller raise men for his company. See *Union*, April 16, 1861; and Randolph Lewis, "Flake, Ferdinand," Handbook of Texas Online, www.tshaonline.org.

and by early March, he had nearly seventy men enlisted, and was "fully organized."[93]

There were other officers and men in the ranks as well with considerable military experience, wealth, and political influence including French-born Xavier Blanchard Debray, who, according to some sources, graduated from the French Military Academy at St. Cyr, France. Debray emigrated to the United States in 1848, and came to Texas in 1852, and for a time ran a Spanish-language newspaper and worked in the General Land office as an interpreter and translator. In the summer of 1861, he served as an aide-de-camp to Governor Edward Clark, and gained appointment to major of the 2nd Texas in September.[94] Regimental surgeon Dr. Henry P. Howard was a career army doctor who had served in Mexican-American War.[95] First Lt. William D. Goff (Co. I), a thirty-nine-year-old Tennessee native and school teacher from Gonzales County, had served as a three-month volunteer in the Mexican-American War.[96] Samuel and Charles Jones (Co. C) were sons of Anson Jones, former president of the Texas Republic who committed suicide in 1858 after a failed bid to become US Senator.[97]

[93] *Union*, March 2, 1861; see also March 5, 1861. In addition, Governor Clark designated Müller as one of the enrolling officers for the Galveston subdistrict in April 1861. See Edward Clark, "Proclamation. To the People of the State of Texas," April 17, 1861, published in the *Weekly Civilian & Gazette* (Galveston, TX), April 30, 1861.

[94] Debray's tenure with the regiment was short; in December he was elected colonel in a cavalry battalion and later became colonel of the 26th Texas cavalry. See Anne J. Bailey and Bruce Allardice, "Debray, Xavier Blanchard," Handbook of Texas Online, www.tshaonline.org; Xavier B. Debray, CMSR, War Department Collection of Confederate Records, RG 109, NARA, accessed via fold3.com; See also "Xavier Blanchard DeBray," findagrave.com; Xavier Blanchard Debray, *A Sketch of the History of Debray's (26th) Regiment of Texas Cavalry*, Reprint, 1884 (Waco, TX: Waco Village, 1961); and Walter Prescott Webb, ed., *The Handbook of Texas* 2 Vols. (Austin, TX: Texas State Historical Association, 1952), Vol. 1: 477.

[95] Howard was also from the "famous Howard family of Maryland." See Howard obituary in *San Antonio Light* (San Antonio, TX), November 21, 1913, excerpted in "Henry Peyton Howard," findagrave.com.

[96] In 1860, Goff had five children and no slaves. He later became captain of Co. K. See Eighth Census of the United States, 1860: Population Schedule, Gonzales County, TX, Records of the Bureau of the Census, RG 29, NARA; accessed via ancestry.com; "William D. Goff," findagrave.com; and William D. Goff, CMSR, War Department Collection of Confederate Records, RG 109, NARA; accessed via fold3.com.

[97] *The Citizen* (Columbus, TX), August 31, 1861. The Jones brothers apparently viewed Ashbel Smith as a father-figure, so it is not surprising they would enlist in his company. Charles, eighteen years old, was corporal; Samuel, twenty years old, was a private. See Charles Elliot Jones, CMSR War Department Collection of Confederate Records, RG 109, NARA, accessed via fold3.com; and "Charles Elliot Jones," findagrave.com.

Maurice K. Simons was another well-connected and prominent Texan in the unit. Simons migrated from Canada to Texas with his family in 1835 and served as a beef contractor and messenger to Gen. Zachery Taylor during the Mexican-American War, losing his leg in an ambush in April 1847. He recovered and became a successful merchant in Jackson County. In 1860, the thirty-six-year-old Simons resided in Jackson County with his wife Elizabeth and their infant daughter. The family enslaved one man (Green, age nineteen), a young boy (Canada, age four), and a woman called "Aunt Mily." Green accompanied Simons when he left for Houston to formally enroll in Confederate service. Historian Joseph Chance imagines that Simons "showed concern for" Green "as one friend to another, exceeding the bonds of a master-slave relationship."[98] Chance's inferences are unsubstantiated, and misleading given the harsh reality of enslavement. We only have Simons' words and actions, and very limited information about Green at all; his eventual fate, like so many enslaved people, is unknown. We do know, though, that Simons bringing an enslaved man with him as his "body servant" was a sign of his prestige as a commissioned officer and membership in the slaveholding elite.[99]

When Simons and his company arrived in Houston to be formally mustered into Confederate service, the recruiting officer balked at enrolling him given his disability. His men refused to take the oath of allegiance unless Simons was permitted to join them; Simons was duly sworn in as 2nd lieutenant.[100] Charles Evans later remembered Simons as "the most unusual spectacle of a man on a crutch serving in the infantry."[101]

---

[98] Chance, *Second Texas*, 16.

[99] For more on Confederate soldiers like Simons bringing enslaved men as "body servants" to the front, and the controversy over so-called (and entirely fictional) "Black Confederates," see Kevin M. Levin, *Searching for Black Confederates: The Civil War's Most Persistent Myth* (Chapel Hill, NC: University of North Carolina Press, 2019).

[100] Biographical information on Simons from Douglas Lee Braudaway, "A Texan Records the Civil War Siege of Vicksburg Mississippi: The Journal of Maj. Maurice Kavanaugh Simons, 1863," *The Journal of Southwest History* Vol. 105, No. 1 (July 2001): 95; Eighth Census of the United States, 1860: Slave Schedule, Jackson County, TX, Records of the Bureau of the Census, RG 29, NARA; accessed via ancestry.com; Julie Lynn Brandt, "The Civil War Diary of Elizabeth Hatcher Simons: Life and Hardship in Texana, Texas," (MA Thesis. Texas A&M University – Kingsville, 1999), 11–18. According to Brandt, Simons purchased Aunt Mily in 1855, though she does not seem to appear in the 1860 slave schedule. See Brandt, "Civil War Diary," 30, n31. Rogers met Simons during the Mexican-American War and was stunned to discover Simons had not died from his wound. Rogers mentioned "our Butcher" being shot in his diary on April 28, 1847. See Pace, ed., "Diary and Letters of William P. Rogers," 284.

[101] Evans, "The Second Texas Infantry," 581. Such a sight became less unusual as the Civil War progressed and more soldiers became amputees. For more on Confederate amputees

FIGURE 4.2 Sam Houston, Jr. Image courtesy the Sam Houston Memorial Museum & Republic of Texas Presidential Library, Huntsville, TX.

Perhaps the soldier with the most famous family name in the regiment, though, was eighteen–year-old Sam Houston, Jr., the eldest son of the outspoken former governor. His parents expected much from him, providing young Sam the kind of education common among slaveholding elite white males.[102] They hired private tutors and sent him to a preparatory school at Baylor University as well as Bastrop Military

and the challenges they faced both during the war and after, see Brian Craig Miller, *Empty Sleeves: Amputation in the Civil War South* (Athens: University of Georgia Press, 2015).

[102] Peter Carmichael and Timothy Williams both explore the expectations, attitudes, and intellectual world of this generation of young white southern male elites on the eve of war. See Peter S. Carmichael, *The Last Generation: Young Virginians in Peace, War and Reunion* (Chapel Hill, NC: University of North Carolina Press, 2005); Timothy J. Williams, *Intellectual Manhood: University, Self and Society in the Antebellum South* (Chapel Hill, NC: University of North Carolina Press, 2015).

Academy – the latter education was meant to teach him self-discipline.[103] Described as "tall and good looking," Sam was the "favorite of his parents, who indulged him and found him sometimes difficult to control."[104]

When Civil War erupted, however, neither of his parents wanted Sam Jr. to enlist in the Confederate army. In late May 1861, Houston Sr. conceded that it was "every man's duty to defend his country." He cautioned his son, though, to wait, "be content," and stay ready to defend his home state.[105] On July 23, 1861, two days after the Confederate victory at Manassas, Houston again counseled his son that his "first allegiance" was to Texas. He warned: "let nothing cause you in a moment of ardor to assume any obligation to any other power whatever without my consent."[106]

Sam Jr., though, had already made his decision without his parent's approval. On August 13, he enlisted as a private in Ashbel Smith's Bayland Guards.[107] Upon his arrival in Galveston with the rest of his company, he wrote his mother to assure her that the port was the "healthiest place in Texas now." "The people are very well prepared and troops are coming in everyday," he insisted, promising her that he was dutifully reading his Bible, confident the war "will not last long." Houston included a sketch he had made of the USS *South Carolina*, judging that she was "peaceable indeed, and I think she has enough to do here for some time," but that "she does not intend to land troops for some time at any rate."[108]

---

[103] It is not clear how long Houston attended Bastrop Military Academy, but in May 1860 he wrote his father from Bastrop and complained that he had little discretionary time to himself, which was probably what his parents wanted. See Sam Houston, Jr. to Sam Houston, May 5, 1860, Sam Houston Family Papers, Southwest Collection, Special Collections Library, Texas Tech University, Lubbock, TX (hereafter referred to as TTU). For more on the academy, see Nancy Young, "Texas Military Academy," in Handbook of Texas Online, tshaonline.org.

[104] William Seale, *Sam Houston's Wife: A Biography of Margaret Lea Houston* (Norman, OK: University of Oklahoma Press, 1970), 195; also 214.

[105] Sam Houston to Sam Houston, Jr., May 22, 1861 in Williams and Baker, eds. *The Writings of Sam Houston*, Vol. 8: 306.

[106] Sam Houston to Sam Houston, Jr., July 23, 1861, Williams and Baker, eds., *Writings of Sam Houston*, Vol. 8: 309.

[107] Sam Houston Jr., CMSR, War Department Collection of Confederate Records, RG 109, NARA, accessed via fold3.com. Houston's biographer Marquis James claims: "The boy asked for his father's forgiveness and received it." See Marquis James, *The Raven: A Biography of Sam Houston* (New York: Blue Ribbon Books, 1929), 418.

[108] Sam Houston Jr. to Margaret Houston, August 26, 1861, Sam Houston Family Papers, Special Collections Library, Southwest Collection, TTU. See also Madge Thornall Roberts, ed., *The Personal Correspondence of Sam Houston* 4 Vols. (Denton, Tex. University of North Texas Press, 1996–2001), Vol. 4: 387–388.

By late June 1861, Houston's *Weekly Telegraph* was able to declare that "Our leading men are all enlisted," and certainly it looked that way for the 2nd Texas.[109] Yet, there remained ongoing problems with supplying new regiments, even those with such powerful men, particularly when it came to arms and clothing. The Confederacy still had no weapons to provide; nor did the state.[110] Earlier in the summer, editor E. W. Cave from *The Civilian and Gazette* had urged Texans to "arm themselves, as best they can! Bring every rifle, musket, shot-gun, pistol, sword and knife, in the country into requestion."[111] Members of Capt. Müller's Galveston company did just this, carrying guns dating to the Texas Revolution. In June 1861, when the company participated in what was supposed to be a "mock battle," they were horrified to discover that some of these old rifles were still loaded with live rounds.[112]

The lack of adequate supplies and weapons was bad enough that X. B. Debray informed Governor Clark in mid-August that Ashbel Smith's company, with no provisions and no arms, "can scarcely be held

---

[109] *The Weekly Telegraph* (Houston, TX), June 26, 1861.

[110] Securing sufficient weaponry for the new volunteers began in April and proved a chronic problem. In early April 1861, William P. Rogers wrote Governor Clark from Houston describing "a great anxiety that our companies should be armed." See William P. Rogers to Edward Clark, April 6, 1861, Box 2014/099–1, Folder 4, Edward Clark Papers, DBC. A few months later, Texas Adjutant General William Byrd informed Ashbel Smith that the governor "regrets that he is unable at present to furnish them to your company but is making every [effort] to procure arms and ammunition from other states." See William Byrd to Ashbel Smith, July 12, 1861, Folder 1: "Letters 1861," Box 2G224, Ashbel Smith Papers, DBC. Confederate Secretary of War L. P. Walker notified Samuel Maxey, who wanted to form a regiment in Texas, that an infantry regiment would only be accepted "if fully armed," explaining that the Confederacy could not "promise to furnish arms to a Regiment of unarmed troops." See L. P. Walker to S. B. Maxey, August 31, 1861, Letters Sent, CSA War Department, Confederate States of America Records, Library of Congress, Washington, DC; hereafter referred to as LC. Hal Runnels complained to Governor Clark in April that his new company had no arms and that "there are no arms of any description to be had in Galveston Houston," but Clark told him the state had nothing to provide. See Hal G. Runnels to Edward Clark, April 23, 1861; and Edward Clark to Hal G. Runnels, April 30, 1861, Box 2014/099–1, Folder 22, Edward Clark Papers, DBC.

[111] *The Civilian and Gazette Weekly* (Galveston, TX), July 30, 1861.

[112] The result of this "mock battle" was comic and terrifying. The worst injury appeared to be to Henry Berlocher, whose rifle went off unexpectedly, firing through his hand and mutilating it badly enough that he risked amputation. See *Union* (Galveston, TX), June 6, 1861. It is not clear, however, if Berlocher lost his hand; he recovered well enough to remain in service and be mustered into the 2nd Texas as a corporal. Berlocher was later mortally wounded at Corinth, dying on November 25, 1862. See Henry Berlocher, CMSR, War Department Collection of Confederate Records, RG 109, NARA, accessed via fold3.com.

together." Debray personally paid for a barrel of bacon just to "try to assist in keeping up the organization."[113] Later that fall, Moore was reduced to pleading with other counties to forward to him any "oversupply of powder or lead, or other munitions of war."[114] Weeks later, Moore lacked muster and pay rolls and had no tents, suggesting his men construct them themselves.[115] One local resident, A. R. Peel, was so dismayed to learn that the troops in Galveston, including the 2nd Regiment, had no blankets, Peel donated three from home, "with the promise to send more soon."[116]

Hébert was finding it more difficult to attract volunteers, too, despite claims that "the war spirit at that time was at a fever heat."[117] In November, he complained that along with his inability to properly arm his troops, fewer Texans were willing to enlist "for the war."[118] Nor was the 2nd Texas fully manned, prompting Moore to ask that one of his lieutenants "be placed on duty as a recruiting officer." "I would like," he told Hébert's assistant adjutant general Samuel B. Davis, "to have my companies filled."[119]

On the surface, the 2nd Texas seemed filled with influential men with impressive credentials. There were problems, however, from the start with supplies and manpower, which would only become more troublesome with time.

[113] X. B. Debray to Edward Clark, August 14, 1861, Box 2014/099-4, Folder 90, Edward Clark Papers, DBC.

[114] *Galveston Weekly News*, October 8, 1861.

[115] John C. Moore to Samuel B. Davis, December 18, 186 and John C. Moore to Samuel B. Davis, December 19, 1861, John C. Moore, CMSR, War Department Collection of Confederate Records, RG 109, NARA, accessed via fold3.com.

[116] A. R. Peel to E. H. Cushing, September 27, 1861, *The Weekly Telegraph* (Houston, TX), October 2, 1861.

[117] Oran M. Roberts, "Texas," in Clement A. Evans, ed. *Confederate Military History*. 12 Vols. (Atlanta, GA: Confederate Publishing, 1899), Vol. 9: 68.

[118] P. O. Hébert to J. P. Benjamin, November 15, 1861, OR, Ser. 1, Vol. 4, 139–140. In another letter to Benjamin, Hébert complained: "To tell you how totally unprepared, confused and defenseless I found this department, and to describe fully the difficulties under which I have labored, and do still, from lack of means, guns, arms ammunition, and proper military organization, would be tedious, and employ too much of your valuable time." See P. O. Hébert to J. P. Benjamin, October 31, 1861, OR, Ser. 1, Vol. 4, 130–131; also P. O. Hébert to J. P. Benjamin, October 24, 1861, OR, Ser. 1, Vol. 4: 127.

[119] John C. Moore to Samuel B. Davis, December 11, 1861, John C. Moore, CMSR, War Department Collection of Confederate Records, RG 109, NARA, accessed via fold3.com. The lieutenant appears to have been 1st Lt. Richard S. Henry (Co. A). It is unclear if Moore's request was granted.

"CHAFING AT THE DELAY"

Moore set about training the men he had with daily drills, dress parades, and battalion maneuvers. Unlike Elmer Ellsworth and his hurried preparation of the Fire Zouaves, Moore had the luxury of time, and he took advantage of it. It may have been his West Point education and prewar experiences, but Moore understood that instructing volunteers, no matter how seemingly brave and devoted they were, was no easy task. His efforts appeared successful at first, and he was pleased with their progress. One onlooker recalled that the men "presented a charming appearance" with their commander "justly proud of them, and fond of exhibiting their superior drill and 'dress' to the public, and particularly to old military men."[120] In October, during a flag ceremony where they accepted a silken banner made by "two of the ladies of Galveston," another observer assured the *Telegraph* that the 2nd Texas had "already the exterior of a veteran column" General Hébert reviewed the men and was highly pleased, the letter-writer attested, "with the display of soldiery."[121] Later in the fall, the *Galveston News* cheered the regiment, along with other units posted on the island, for their "soldierly bearing."[122]

Men in the ranks, though, had mixed views of their new commander and military life. Pvt. Ralph Smith (Co. K) found Colonel Moore "a brave and gallant officer but not a Christian, for he was red-headed, red-bearded, red faced, and extremely high tempered." Smith believed he had "joined a regiment of devils."[123] Twenty-year-old Pvt. Charles I. Evans (Co. G), whose family was one of the richest and largest slave-owners in Burleson County, remembered: "During the first four months, the regiment was quartered in cotton compresses and warehouses in the

---

[120] North, *Five Years in Texas*, 95. See also *Galveston Weekly News*, October 22, 1861.

[121] "A Soldier," Letter to the Editor, October 25, 1861, *The Weekly Telegraph* (Houston, TX) November 6, 1861. See also *Galveston Weekly News*, October 22, 1861. Charles Evans appears to have confused the dates of the flag presentation, conflating several separate events together on the same day. He claimed that it was the "day before its departure" from Texas that "the ladies presented the regiment with a beautiful silk battle-flag, which was received with the usual flow of oratory." See Evans, "The Second Texas Infantry," 577; also Chance, *The Second Texas*, 18.

[122] *Galveston Weekly News*, November 26, 1861.

[123] Ralph J. Smith, "To the Daughters of the Confederacy. An Insight into the Character of a Volunteer Soldier," in *Reminiscences of the Civil War and Other Sketches*. 1911 reprint (Waco, TX: W. M. Morrison, 1962), 39; see also Chance, *Second Texas*, 15. Twenty-three-year-old Smith, a native of Louisiana, enlisted "for the war," in Co. K on October 12, 1861. See Ralph J. Smith, CMSR, War Department Collection of Confederate Records, RG 109, NARA, accessed via fold3.com.

city of Galveston, and six hours every day, except Sunday, were spent in the most arduous drilling." There was a good deal of griping about "the strict discipline and hard drilling, and much chafing at the delay which retarded the advance of the regiment to the front, where active service was to be seen." "The men," Evans recalled, "were anxious to go forward to the scenes of conflict and participate in the glorious achievements which they confidently believed awaited them; and much fear expressed that the war would be over, the Yankees whipped, and the independence of the Southern Confederacy established before they could have an opportunity of firing a gun in the glorious cause."[124]

William P. Doran, who wrote regular columns for the *Telegraph* under the pseudonym "Sioux," and later enlisted in the unit, assured readers that "Col. Moore is in command of the Island and seems thoroughly to understand his business." Doran added: "Everything goes on like clock-work. Capts. Runnels and Timmons, of Houston, have well drilled companies; and, in fact, all the companies are men Texas may ever feel proud of."[125] Disputing accounts of the lack of supplies, Doran reported that the "troops here have plenty of provisions, and the boys enjoy themselves." But, he added: "Many of the troops stationed here are anxious to go to Kentucky, to assist in expelling the invaders."[126]

[124] Evans, "The Second Texas Infantry," 577. Charles Evans was born in Mississippi and moved with his family to Burleson County, Texas. According to the 1860 census, his father, Thomas Evans, had real estate valued at $60,000 and personal estate valued at more than $81,000, owning seventy slaves, aged one to seventy-three. See Eighth Census of the United States, 1860: Population and Slave Schedule, Burleson County, TX, Records of the Bureau of the Census, RG 29, NARA; accessed via ancestry.com

[125] "Sioux" Letter to the Editor, November 4, 1861, *The Weekly Telegraph* (Houston, TX), November 13, 1861. Editors Cushing and Richardson arranged for Doran to accompany the 2nd Texas when it left the state; but eventually he had to enlist, according to his autobiography, because if he had not, he would be banned from traveling with the army. He was later discharged for disability on June 15, 1862. In a postwar interview, he stated that he was "forced to enlist as a private in Company A," putting "on the uniform and was a soldier bold." See *Galveston Daily News* (Galveston, TX), May 24, 1895; also William P. Doran CMSR, War Department Collection of Confederate Records, RG 109, NARA, accessed via fold3.com; and William P. Doran, "Autobiography of Major William P. Doran (Sioux) Confederate Soldier in the Battles of Galveston, Shiloh, Vicksburg, Mansfield, Pleasant Hill, and Forty Skirmishes along Red River in 1864," typescript, n. d., TSLAC.

[126] "Sioux" Letter to the Editor, November 16, 1861, *The Weekly Telegraph* (Houston, TX), November 27, 1861. By the fall of 1861, both sides, including Union Gen. U.S. Grant in Paducah, had begun concentrating troops in Kentucky, soon ending the state's attempt to stay neutral in the war.

In early November 1861, Lt. Maurice K. Simons wrote his wife Elizabeth that the regiment was "pretty busy," with drills, dress parades, inspection, and a review by General Hébert. He noted that: "The health of the troops is generally improved in the last few days. Some of our men have been complaining so long that it is hard to convince them that they are not sick." When Simons' wife inquired how their enslaved man Green was fairing, Maurice wrote: "Well Green is not much attached to this kind of life, I assure you. He says that he would rather be at home with Miss Bettie and the baby." Simons added, without any recognition of what it might have been like for Green to be in the midst of training rebel troops to fight for his ongoing enslavement, "He is quite attentive to me and enjoys seeing the troops drill very much."[127]

Meantime, Union threats to the coast persisted as summer turned to fall. State and local officials continued to beg Richmond for help to bolster their defenses. P. O. Hébert, who had replaced Earl Van Dorn in August as commander of the Department of Texas, saw little hope of keeping Galveston safe. He still issued a rousing address titled "To the Men of Texas," calling on the familiar narrative of proud Anglo-Texans winning their independence – a variation of the Revolutionary War mantra Confederates adopted everywhere.[128] "Let every man," Hébert declared, "then clean his old musket, shot gun, or rifle; run his bullets, fill his powder horn, sharpen his knife, and see that his revolver is ready to his hand, as in the trying yet glorious days, when Mexico was your foe." Referencing a false rumor that Sam Houston had died, Hébert asserted, "The Hero of San Jacinto has just breathed his last. In his name, and the names of his illustrious brother soldiers, I call upon you, men of Texas, to arm and be prepared."[129]

Newly elected Texas governor Francis Lubbock pleaded with his fellow citizens to help provide for the troops, affirming that the men would "sustain the reputation of their State as the home of a chivalrous and warlike people." Unlike his predecessor, Lubbock repeated familiar

[127] Maurice K. Simons to Elizabeth Simons, November 3, 1861, in "The Maurice Kavanaugh Simons Diary," 27–30, Simons Family Collection, The South Texas Archives & Special Collections, James C. Jernigan Library, Texas A & M University-Kingsville, Kingsville, Texas.

[128] For more on Confederates repurposing Revolutionary War rhetoric and symbolism for themselves, see Anne Sarah Rubin, *A Shattered Nation: The Rise and Fall of the Confederacy, 1861–1868* (Chapel Hill, NC: University of North Carolina Press, 2005).

[129] P. O. Hébert Address "To the Men of Texas," October 7, 1861, OR, Ser. 1, Vol. 4, 115–116. also published in *The Civilian and Gazette* (Galveston, TX), October 8, 1861.

tropes about their northern foe, calling them a "base and hireling soldierly" as well as "base Hessians of a corrupt and fanatical government" who would shamefully "flee panic stricken before our army of citizens."[130]

Bombastic promises of victory would continue, but for the 2nd Texas they could do little but wait and watch for their chance to prove their valor.

"SOLDIERLY APPEARANCE"

By December 1861, the regiment moved to a camp a few miles west of Houston.[131] Moore described their location near White Oak Bayou with "a fine running stream," "an abundance of fuel and high dry land for camp," and "good grounds for drill."[132] To onlookers, the regiment displayed "an excellent appearance": "well drilled, and doubtless ready to do some responsible fighting."[133] Doran, the correspondent for the *Telegraph*, published a rousing account of "our brave boys," near town, but warned: "If we have any cowards among us, let us know who they are; and when the banners of victory wave, and the blessings of peace come they may receive all the merit they deserve."[134]

While encamped near Houston, the city's namesake Sam Houston was a frequent visitor. One day Moore invited him to review the soldiers and put them through "some military evolutions." Houston, donning his old uniform and sword from the Texas Revolution, relished the

---

[130] Francis R. Lubbock, Inaugural Speech, November 7, 861, in Raines, *Six Decades in Texas*, 333–336; also printed in *Galveston Weekly News*, November 26, 1861. Lubbock repeated much of this rhetoric in his proclamation calling for fifteen more regiments in February 1862.

[131] Galveston fell to Union forces in October 1862, but Confederates retook the city in January 1863. Moore became commander of the Military District of Houston in January 1862, having been relieved of his command at Galveston. See Special Orders No. 227, December 7, 1861, OR, Ser. 1, Vol. 4, 155; and Special Orders, No. 8, January 3, 1862, OR, Ser. 1, Vol. 4, 169. Ralph Smith claimed that the regiment moved to Houston in October. See Smith, *Reminiscences*, 1.

[132] John C. Moore to Samuel B. Davis, December 13, 1861, in John C. Moore, CMSR, War Department Collection of Confederate Records, RG 109, NARA, accessed via fold3.com.

[133] *The Weekly Telegraph* (Houston, TX), December 11, 1861. Cushing's *Telegraph* singled out William Timmons' "The Confederate Guards" for their "steady and soldierly bearing," but added: "we do not mean to disparage any other company."

[134] "Sioux," Letter to the Editor, December 13, 1861, *The Weekly Telegraph* (Houston, TX), December 18, 1861.

opportunity. As he belted out orders, he asked if two of his political rivals, Williamson S. Oldham, "Judge Campbell" or Campbell's son, were present. The soldiers responded excitedly "No," and that Campbell and Oldham were "not found at the front, nor even at the rear"; Campbell's son, the soldiers scoffed, had "gone to Paris to school." When Houston then asked if his son had enlisted, "the regiment and citizens together responded, in thunder tones, 'Yes!' and then united in a triple round of three times three and a tiger for the old hero."[135]

Another day, both Governor Lubbock and Houston happened to be in camp at the same time. Lubbock, according to one account, "made a brief speech, in his usual felicitous style, urging the soldiers to guard well the honor of the State and do their duty manfully in the field." Houston then stepped up to address the men, recalling his initial resistance to secession but affirming that now "all his feelings and interests were bound up in the success of our cause." He told the soldiers that his age and old wounds made him incapable of serving anymore, yet he "offered up his only son old enough to fight" for the Confederate cause. Houston further "complimented the men of their soldierly appearance and urged them to fight bravely for their liberties."[136]

On another occasion, Moore's regiment welcomed Col. William Henry Parson's 12th Texas Cavalry to the city, with a formal review, marching, speeches, and a reception "by a number of our most beautiful young ladies." The high point was to be a "sham battle, the result of which was to be the capture of Col. Parson's regiment, their rescue and subsequent entertainment by sundry of our citizens." But an outpouring of cold rain spoiled the event, "causing general scattering of civilians, and finally a gloomy departure of the military."[137]

---

[135] North, *Five Years in Texas*, 97–98. I have been unable to identify who "Judge Campbell" was; Oldham served as Confederate senator from Texas February 1862–March 1865. A postwar version of this story substituted Louis Wigfall's name with Campbell's and alleged that it was Ashbel Smith who requested Houston to serve as "drill-master." See *Southern Intelligencer* (Austin, TX), October 25, 1866; see also Chance, *Second Texas Infantry*, 5. Houston visited the unit while they were in Galveston, too, taking meals with the men and sleeping in the colonel's tent. See Marquis, *The Raven*, 418; and Seale, *Sam Houston's Wife*, 216.

[136] *The Weekly Telegraph* (Houston, TX), March 12, 1862; see also Raines, ed., *Six Decades in Texas*, 380–381.

[137] *The Weekly Telegraph* (Houston, TX), December 18, 1861.

Soon another event lifted their spirits. In January, the 2nd Texas hosted a "regimental souiree [*sic*]" for the "ladies of Houston."[138] A few days later, the *Weekly Telegraph* proclaimed the "military ball" a "decided success," adding that it was "one of the most brilliant affairs ever witnessed in the city. The large hall was filled with the gay throng and everything was as merry as though grim visaged war was not all about us."[139]

Ralph Smith recalled those early days in uniform filled with "glorious anticipation." There were rousing speeches and beautiful young women who came to camp to admire their brave new warriors. The men felt invincible. The "possibility of such a thing as defeat never for a moment entered the mind of a member of our inexperienced corps. Day after day we were dined, wined, and flattered. Night after night we floated upon a sea of glory. The ladies petted and lionized us; preachers prayed with and for us, declaring that the lord was on our side, so we need have no fears."[140]

Despite festive dances, important visitors, inspiring speeches, and declarations of divine protection, all was not a "sea of glory." Like other new soldiers crowded into camps and vulnerable to disease, many members of the regiment fell ill that winter of 1861–1862. And they were increasingly "tired of inaction." Rather than sham battles and balls, they wanted "to practice shooting at invaders."[141] In December, the death of Benjamin Franklin Terry, colonel of the 8th Texas Cavalry (also known as Terry's Texas Rangers), at the Battle of Rowlett's Station in Kentucky was a jarring reminder of war's horrors. The regiment accompanied Terry's body as its military escort when it arrived in Houston, and Moore acting as marshal, led the funeral procession. Effusive tributes to Terry followed,

---

[138] *The Weekly Telegraph* (Houston, TX), January 8, 1862. The paper proclaimed: "The well known gallantry of the officers and men of this fine regiment is ample guarantee of the success of the affair."

[139] *The Weekly Telegraph* (Houston, TX), January 15, 1862. See also *The Civilian and Gazette* (Galveston, TX), January 21, 1862.

[140] Smith, *Reminiscences*, 1.

[141] "Sioux," Letter to the Editor, January 10, 1862, in *The Tri-Weekly Telegraph* (Houston, TX), January 13, 1862. Pvt. Preston Casey was one of the soldiers absent and sick within a month of his enlistment in September 1861 with a "sore leg." In March 1862, when the 2nd Texas was en route to Corinth, Casey wrote Captain Smith asking for help to obtain his pay, complaining that he had no money and was "almost without clothes." See Preston Casey to Ashbel Smith, March 27, 1862, in Folder "Letters 1862," Box 2G224, Ashbel Smith Papers, DBC. Casey was eventually discharged from the regiment in April 1862, but recovered enough to enlist in a Ragsdale's Battalion Cavalry and survive the war. See Preston Casey, CMSR, War Department Collection of Confederate Records, RG 109, NARA, accessed via fold3.com.

celebrating him as "the embodiment of southern valor" despite his "strict and almost stern" demeanor.[142] Lt. Col. William P. Rogers issued an order to the regiment celebrating the slain "gallant officer," adding that: "In an army like ours, where gallantry belongs to all, it is unnecessary to speak of this element in the character of the deceased, although [it was] possessed by him in an eminent degree."[143]

Newly promoted Maj. Hal G. Runnels, who was Terry's cousin, wrote letters to President Davis and Louis Wigfall, bemoaning not only Terry's death but his frustration with the regiment's inactivity. He also requested a three-month leave to join Terry's unit in Kentucky and redress their colonel's death. The 2nd Texas would prefer to go to Kentucky, too, he added, "where there is a chance of active service." Davis considered Runnels' request if a regiment could "be spared" or transferred, but nothing came of it.[144] To Wigfall, Runnels said he had initially declined the opportunity to serve in Terry's regiment, "preferring to fight the enemy at home if Texas needed my services." But now after months of inaction, he was "very anxious to get into an active field." He reiterated that the 2nd Texas was also ready to go: "Our Regiment," he told Wigfall, "is well drilled and will compare favorably with any in the service. The officers and men are all anxious for active service."[145]

Runnels' appeal for a leave of absence was declined too, but several other Texas officers made similar requests over the next three months. Regimental Surgeon Henry P. Howard took a leave of twenty days to visit

[142] Except from *Bowling Green Courier* (Bowling Green, KY), n.d., republished in *The Weekly Telegraph* (Houston, TX) January 8, 1862. Hardee praised Terry as "one of its bravest officers." See Special Order No. 64, printed in the *The Weekly Telegraph* (Houston, TX), February 15, 1862.

[143] Rogers' Order was issued on December 26, 1861, and published in *The Tri-Weekly Telegraph* (Houston, TX), December 30, 1861. See also Rein, *Six Decades in Texas*, 377–378. The regiment acted as ceremonial military escort for the funeral processions of Col. Thomas S. Lubbock, who had succeeded Terry but died of typhoid fever, Judge John Hemphill (a member of the Provisional Confederate Congress); and Col. Hugh McLeod from the 1st Texas Infantry Regiment. See *The Weekly Telegraph* (Houston, TX), January 29, 1862; and *Dallas Daily Herald*, February 5, 1862.

[144] Hal G. Runnels to Jefferson Davis, January 3, 1862; and editor's notes in Crist, ed., *Papers of Jefferson Davis* Vol. 8: 5. Runnels was promoted to major on December 7, 1861, and appointed Provost Marshall at Galveston on December 9, 1861. See Hal Runnels, CMSR, War Department Collection of Confederate Records, RG 109, NARA, accessed via fold3.com. When Debray left to command a cavalry unit, Captain Runnels replaced him, with William Christian elected the new captain in Runnels' company. See Evans, "The Second Texas Infantry," 576–577.

[145] Hal G. Runnels to Louis T. Wigfall, January 10, 1862, Hal Runnels, CMSR, War Department Collection of Confederate Records, RG 109, NARA, accessed via fold3.com.

his family and "to attend to some private business at San Antonio."[146] Capt. John W. Hood sought a leave of absence due to "urgent business," and 1st Lt. William D. Goff wanted a furlough to visit his family, whom, he stated, "are in need of attention from me."[147] Capt. Clark Owen said he needed twenty days "to visit my home and arrange matters of business which are of much importance to me." Owen had been ill with a fever but remained in camp; now he had word that his "Overseer has acted badly and quit my service," requiring him to go home and sort things out for himself.[148] Capt. Belvidere Brooks was also sick, gaining a furlough in January due to illness; but then he formally submitted his resignation on February 17, 1862, although it was never approved.[149] Second Lt. Joseph C. Rowland, who was nearly seventy years old, was finding soldier life overly taxing, despite the unit's idleness. He too penned his resignation in January 1862, asking to go home "where I can be kept out of the weather." His request was duly granted.[150]

Lt. Col. William P. Rogers was having health issues as well, writing in February that an unspecified "wound" rendered him "unable to report for duty." Frustrated and anxious to get back to the regiment, he noted that "it is the first time in the history of my military life that I was ever unable to respond to orders." If it was a battle wound, Rogers reasoned, "it would not try my patience as it has, but I bow to the truth of the old adage, '*Quisque suos patimur Mane*" – translated from Virgil: Each of us

[146] Henry P. Howard to Samuel B. Davis, Jan 8, 1862, Henry P. Howard, CMSR, War Department Collection of Confederate Records, RG 109, NARA, accessed via fold3.com.

[147] John W. Hood to Samuel B. Davis, January 11, 1862, John W. Hood, CMSR, War Department Collection of Confederate Records, RG 109, NARA, accessed via fold3.com. Hood also received orders from Hébert to recruit while on furlough. See William D. Goff to Samuel B. Davis, January 13, 1862, William D. Goff, CMSR, War Department Collection of Confederate Records, RG 109, NARA, accessed via fold3.com.

[148] Clark L. Owen to Samuel B. Davis, February 18, 1862, Clark L. Owen, CMSR War Department Collection of Confederate Records, RG 109, NARA, accessed via fold3.com. Colonel Moore approved Owen's request on Feb 19, 1862.

[149] Belvidere Brooks, CMSR War Department Collection of Confederate Records, RG 109, NARA, accessed via fold3.com.

[150] Joseph C. Rowland to Samuel B. Davis, January 23, 1862, and J. C. Rowland to Samuel Cooper, January 23, 1862, both in J.C. Rowland, CMSR, War Department Collection of Confederate Records, RG 109, NARA, accessed via fold3.com. Rowland is listed in the 1860 census as a wealthy "farmer" and slaveowner. He ended up living a very long life, dying in 1881 at the age of ninety-five. Eighth Census of the United States, 1860: Population and Slave Schedule, Burleson County, TX, Records of the Bureau of the Census, RG 29, NARA; accessed via ancestry.com; and "Joseph Rowland," findagrave.com

bears his own hell."[151] His furlough was granted on March 11 for thirty days.[152]

Lt. Jerome I. McGinnis, the brother of Capt. Noble L. McGinnis, was indeed suffering, but with a more discreet problem: he was diagnosed with gonorrhea and asked for twenty days reprieve due to his "ill health." The next day, Hébert granted him thirty days.[153] Jerome's brother Noble was also absent from the regiment about the same time, with orders from Moore "to proceed up the country and organize one or more companies to serve for the war."[154]

Capt. Ashbel Smith seriously considered leaving the regiment, too. In a long, rambling letter to Governor Lubbock, he expressed his disappointment in the "sluggishness of the last few months." Anticipating both conscription and the impressment of enslaved people, Smith stated, "We are a brave people and eminently adapted from individual character and from our institutions to become warlike people, but we aren't yet a warlike people." To become fully "warlike" he urged drill and "habits of military obedience which can be acquired only by practice." Viewing enslaved people as "our weakness or our strength," he advocated their mobilization to produce food and clothing for the military and "products for export."[155]

---

[151] William P. Rogers to Samuel B. Davis, Feb. 17, 1862, William P. Rogers, CMSR, War Department Collection of Confederate Records, RG 109, NARA, accessed via fold3.com. Virgil, *Aeneid*, Book VI, line 743, translated via artandpopularculture.com; another translation is "Each of us suffers his own spirit." See also William P, Rogers to Samuel B. Davis, February 7, 1862, William P. Rogers, CMSR, War Department Collection of Confederate Records, RG 109, NARA, accessed via fold3.com. Rogers, it seems, had asked Smith to help him in extending his furlough, also thanking Smith for bandaging his wound. He was granted a twenty-day furlough but then rushed to rejoin the regiment once it left the state. See William P. Rogers to Ashbel Smith, March 11, 1862, Folder 2 "Letters: 1862," Box 2G224, Ashbel Smith Papers, DBC; and William P. Rogers to Martha Rogers, March 28, 1862, in Letters and Papers of Colonel W. P. Rogers, 1848–1862, DBC. In addition to talk of Roger commanding a Texas regiment in Virginia, there was speculation that Rogers would be commissioned colonel in one of the newly raised regiments in the fall, but nothing came of it. See D. M. Whaley to E. H. Cushing, September 15, 1861, *The Weekly Telegraph* (Houston, TX), October 9, 1861.

[152] Special Orders No. 298, March 11, 1862, in William P. Rogers, CMSR, War Department Collection of Confederate Records, RG 109, NARA, accessed via fold3.com.

[153] Jerome I. McGinnis to Samuel B. Davis, Feb 17, 1862; and Special Orders No. 180, February 18, 1862, in J. I. McGinnis, CMSR, War Department Collection of Confederate Records, RG 109, NARA, accessed via fold3.com.

[154] John C. Moore to Samuel B. Davis, February 23, 1862, Noble McGinnis, CMSR, War Department Collection of Confederate Records, RG 109, NARA, accessed via fold3.com.

[155] Ashbel Smith to Francis Lubbock, February 1, 1862, Folder 2: "Letters: 1862," Box 2G224, Ashbel Smith Papers, DBC. In April 1862, the Confederacy enacted the

Staying with the 2nd Texas, though, seemed hopeless. It was not that Smith was unhappy with his company or the regiment. He wrote: "My relations with the officers of my Regiment are all of the most friendly character; with the great majority of the men of my company my relations are affectionate with all they are very friendly." Smith would resign nonetheless, he told the governor, because he needed "a larger field where my experience may turn to a greater advantage of our state and of the Confederacy." "Can you place me?" he asked. "Don't the state want me? Can you give a Regiment or anything better?"[156]

While these officers pondered leaving the regiment, temporarily or permanently, at least one private, twenty-year-old John R. Glass (Co. B), was challenged for even trying. Due to a childhood bout of scarlet fever, Glass suffered intermittent deafness in one ear. Standing close to six-pound cannons, his deafness returned, so much so that "he could not hold a common conversation."[157] His captain, William Timmons, however, was suspicious of Glass' complaint, refusing "to sign his discharge on the grounds that he publicly stated that *he was tired of the service*, he has regularly done & is now doing duty and if his hearing is defective, it in no way interferes with his duties at present."[158] Two months later, Glass, after submitting sworn depositions from his father and a doctor, and offering to acquire a "good substitute," finally gained a disability discharge.[159] Martha Barnard, the grandmother of musician William Grant, sought her grandson's discharge "by reason of minority, he being only seventeen years old, next November." Her entreaty was never approved, and Grant remained in the ranks until he deserted two years later.[160]

first draft in American history and Union impressment followed in March, 1863. Smith's support for conscription proved conflicted as discussed in Chapter 6.

[156] Ashbel Smith to Francis Lubbock, February 1, 1862, Folder 2: "Letters: 1862," Box 2G224, Ashbel Smith Papers, DBC.

[157] Testimony of Edward Daly, January 8, 1862, John R. Glass, CMSR, War Department Collection of Confederate Records, RG 109, NARA, accessed via fold3.com.

[158] William C. Timmons to Samuel B. Davis, January 14, 1862, William C. Timmons, CMSR, War Department Collection of Confederate Records, RG 109, NARA, accessed via fold3.com.

[159] Glass' discharge was finally authorized by Hébert on March 10, 1862. See W. H. Glass sworn deposition, January 9, 1862; Dr. William Howard, surgeon certificate, February 27, 1862, John R. Glass, CMSR, War Department Collection of Confederate Records, RG 109, NARA, accessed via fold3.com.

[160] Martha Barnard to Samuel B. Davis, March 14, 1862, Folder 2 "Letters: 1862," Box 2G224, Ashbel Smith Papers, DBC; see also William Grant, CMSR, War Department Collection of Confederate Records, RG 109, NARA, accessed via fold3 .com; and Eighth Census of the United States, 1860: Population Schedule, Galveston

There were also efforts afoot to get Sam Houston, Jr. reassigned. His father wrote his old rival Williamson Oldham, whom he had previously derided when drilling the regiment, to make his case that Sam Jr. deserved a commission. He described his son as "a very good soldier, his habits are good, and he is ardently devoted to the cause in which he is engaged, as well as to the life of a soldier." Sam Jr. had been offered, Houston explained, a brevet lieutenancy, "if he would consent to be transferred and stationed in Galveston, but he proffered the glory of an active, and immediate campaign." Instead, Houston asked Oldham, now a Confederate senator: "If you can procure for him a Lieutenancy, or any promotion that you may think proper, you will confer upon me an enduring obligation, and I trust and believe, he will never disgrace his *patron.*"[161] Ashbel Smith had already successfully petitioned Brig. Gen. P.O. Hébert to promote Houston as "Instructor of Tactics" and remain attached to his company. But Sam Jr. refused this too, preferring to stay in the ranks as a private.[162]

The 2nd Texas' soldierly appearance was wearing thin. These many weeks of inaction increased the chances of sickness and demoralization and some, with privilege and opportunity, sought ways to leave the regiment rather than wait for the chance to lead it into glorious combat.

"LET COWARDS SHRINK AMID THE STORM!"

Across Texas, war fever was cooling as winter turned to spring. Governor Lubbock had issued a new requisition for fifteen regiments in late February 1862, repeating much of the same rhetoric from his prior proclamations, but threatening conscription if he could not meet the state quota. "I will not insult the chivalry and military fame of the brave Texans, by doubting for a moment that sufficient number of volunteers will be tendered to meet the present call," Lubbock stated. He pleaded to his white male citizens: "Your mothers, daughters, sisters, wives, and little children all appeal to you as you love them, your country, their honor and your honor to stand as a breastwork between them."[163]

Ward 2, TX, Records of the Bureau of the Census, RG 29, NARA; accessed via ancestry .com.

[161] Sam Houston to Williamson S. Oldham, April 5, 1862, Williams and Baker, eds., *Writings of Sam Houston,* Vol. 8: 315.

[162] Ashbel Smith to P. O. Hébert, March 10, 1862, Sam Houston, Jr., CMSR, War Department Collection of Confederate Records, RG 109, NARA, accessed via fold3.com; see also Roberts, *Star of Destiny,* 313.

[163] "Proclamation by the Governor, to the People of the State of Texas," February 26, 1862, published in *The Weekly Telegraph* (Houston, TX), March 5, 1862. See also Francis

One of these white women, identifying herself as a "Southern Mother," was mortified to see in the streets of Houston "enough lounging stay-at-home young men to form a regiment." Attacking their masculinity and seeking to shame them to enlist, she exclaimed: "Great God, can it be that any young man who has ever drawn the breath of liberty, can be so stupefied, so cowardly – so base – so lost to every feeling of manhood pride, sensibility, respectability and ambition!" Amplifying Lubbock's proclamation, she urged them to enlist and "shake of[f] this selfish sloth."[164]

In *The Weekly Telegraph*, Edward H. Cushing, who had been publishing repeated pleas for enlistments, tried to assure his readers that already "Texas is winning a name for gallantry and bravery in this war, second to that of no State or people that ever lived." Still more soldiers were needed, specifically Anglo-Texans who were, he ascribed, "the unconquerable kind." Much like the early descriptions of the Fire Zouaves, such men were assumed to possess naturally a "wild spirit that will dash boldly into the face of danger, and win victory by their very boldness."[165] Nonetheless, Cushing worried about their lack of preparation: "Will you go," he asked, "as efficient soldiers or will you go as rabble, which however brave, is incapable of good upon the battle field?"[166]

Gen. P. G. T. Beauregard, newly appointed as commander of the Army of the Mississippi, addressed his soldiers with similar rhetoric: "Our mothers and wives, our sisters and children, expect us to do our duty

R. Lubbock to Judah P. Benjamin, March 7, 1862, Governor Francis Richard Lubbock Records, Letterpress Book, Outgoing Correspondence November 1861to April 1862, TSLAC, via Texas Digital Archives, tsl.access.preservica.com. In his letter to Richmond, Lubbock again complained about the lack of supplies and arms for the troops.

[164] "A Southern Mother," Letter to the Editor, n.d. *The Weekly Telegraph* (Houston, TX), March 5, 1862. Drew Gilpin Faust argues that elite white southern women enthusiastically urged their men to enlist, but then, dissatisfied with the war's demands on them, soured on the Confederacy and added to the general malaise and demoralization as the conflict dragged on. See Drew Gilpin Faust, *Mothers of Invention: Women of the Slaveholding South in the American Civil War* (Chapel Hill, NC: University of North Carolina Press, 1996); Other historians who have explored the important interconnection between white women, the morale of Confederate soldiers, and Confederate nationalism include George C. Rable, *Civil Wars: Women and the Crisis of Southern Nationalism* (Champaign, IL: University of Illinois Press, 1989); LeeAnn Whites, *Gender Matters: Civil War, Reconstruction, and the Making of the New South* (New York: Palgrave Macmillan, 2005); and Stephanie McCurry, *Confederate Reckoning: Power and Politics in the Civil War South* (Cambridge, MA: Harvard University Press, 2010).

[165] *The Weekly Telegraph* (Houston, TX), March 5, 1862.

[166] *The Weekly Telegraph* (Houston, TX), March 12, 1862.

even to the sacrifice of our lives." But he wanted no cowards in the ranks. "Should any one in this army," he admonished, "be unequal to the task before us, let him transfer his arms and equipment at once to braver, firmer hands, and return to his home."[167]

In the pages of *The Weekly Telegraph*, seventeen-year-old Mollie E. Moore (apparently no relation to Colonel Moore) penned a foreboding and angry poem entitled "An Appeal to Texans yet Idle," where she admonished white men to "Rise! Rise! Aloft the battle-flag" or face terrible scorn.

> Shall Texan tongues forget to speak
>   When breaks the bloody strife?
> Let *cowards* shrink amid the storm!
>   Will Texan freemen quail?
> Will Texans bow before the foe?
>   Will Texan rifles fail?
> No, never! Other years have shown
>   That Texans never yield;

After conjuring images of blood-soaked battlefields where "bright streams crimson flow!" she returned to the subject of cowardice:

> But freemen must meet the battle-shock.
>   Let cowards shrink and cower,
> While death-devoted Texan bands
>   Go forth to meet the hour,
> Rise! Texans! Rise! The battle cry
>   Awakes e'en earth's cold sod;
> It thunders on our startled ears,
>   And sends back "Blood for blood."
> Arm! Texans! Arm! the Southern stars
>   Are glowing into life.[168]

[167] P. G. T. Beauregard to "Soldiers," March 5, 1862, OR, Ser. 1, Vol. 10, pt. 2, 297.

[168] Mollie E. Moore, "An Appeal to Texans yet Idle," March 4, 1862, *The Weekly Telegraph* (Houston, TX), March 12, 1862. According to the 1860 census, Moore was sixteen, listed as a "poetess," and daughter of Dr. John Moore from Garden Valley, Smith County, Texas. See Eighth Census of the United States, 1860: Population Schedule: Garden Valley, TX, Records of the Bureau of the Census, RG 29, NARA; accessed via ancestry.com. Moore's brothers served in Texas units and as did her husband, Thomas Edward Davis. The Tyler, Texas United Daughters of the Confederacy Chapter is named after her. In a biography posted on the chapter's website it states: "Mollie's family sacrificed much for the Confederacy." See "Mary (Mollie) Evelyn Moore," www.mollie mooredavis.org; and C. W. Wilkinson, "Davis, Mollie Evelyn Moore," Handbook of Texas Online, www.tshaonline.org.

Would the 2nd Texas "shrink and cower," or rise up and meet young Mollie Moore's demand for bloody violence? Would they sacrifice their lives as their political and military leaders demanded them to do? During these early days of the regiment's existence, it was not entirely clear. These white male Texans, like the Fire Zouaves from New York, were expected to perform bravely. It was hard to imagine they would not. They certainly had the outward trappings of a courageous regiment with competent and experienced officers leading them. But already several men had left or, like Ashbel Smith and Hal Runnels, wanted a new command. Lt. Daniel P. Gallagher had found some of the 2nd Texas' new recruits "not very well instructed in regard to their duty."[169]

In early March 1862, the regiment received orders to "meet the invaders of Arkansas."[170] Finally, after weeks and months of waiting, everything was moving quickly; furloughs and discharges would be delayed or prohibited entirely; there was no time left to instruct new recruits or seek new commissions.[171] Sam Houston addressed the regiment just before they left, assuring them that "he was not ashamed to have his name" associated with them and that he was confident they would "reflect credit upon the State and add lustre to any name that might be connected with it; and he knew that he would hear only good reports of it." He "bade it be strong and valiant, remembering that his eyes and prayers should follow it, and he committed his beloved son to its fate."[172]

With these final words of goodbye, Moore scrambled to reassemble everyone, decamping from Houston on March 12, 1862, on an arduous journey by rail, train, steamboat, and foot.[173] Numbering more than

[169] Daniel P. Gallagher to Ashbel Smith, March 11, 1862, Folder 2 "Letters: 1862," Box 2G224, Ashbel Smith Papers, DBC.
[170] *The Civilian & Gazette* (Galveston, TX), March 18, 1862. Colonel Moore referenced preparing his regiment to march in a letter to the state Adjutant General's office requesting Capt. Edward DF. Williams' return to the unit from court-martial duty. See John C. Moore to Samuel B. Davis, March 4, 1862, in John C. Moore, CMSR, War Department Collection of Confederate Records, RG 109, NARA, accessed via fold3.com. See also Edward DF. Williams, CMSR.
[171] On March 24, 1862, the Confederate War Department revoked "all leaves of absences and furloughs, from whatever source obtained," unless excused on "surgeon's disability." See "General Orders, No. 16.," March 24, 1862, OR, Ser. 1, Vol. 10, pt. 2, 394. Hébert reaffirmed this order with his own on April 18, 1862. See General Orders, No. 18, published in *The Tri-Weekly Telegraph* (Houston, TX), April 21, 1862.
[172] Evans, "The Second Texas Infantry," 577–578.
[173] There are some discrepancies in the sources as to what day the 2nd Texas left Houston. Some cite March 11; others March 12. See Evans, "The Second Texas Infantry," 578; Silverthorne, *Ashbel Smith of Texas*, 149.

1,000 men, the regiment could not all travel together, but had to separate into two sections.[174] Once the 2nd Texas reached Wise Bluff on the Neches River, they began their first land march toward Alexandria, Louisiana.

At this point, any doubts or questions about the regiment's future seemed to vanish, at least temporarily. A "big crowd of friends of the boys and men" cheered them in Houston as they boarded train cars.[175] And for the soldiers, "a thousand hearts beat happily" with the prospect of battle.[176] William P. Doran writing for the *Telegraph* reported: "Our regiment withstood the march better than many expected of them." He maintained: "None but Texians could have pushed through in the same space of time we have." Their journey to Alexandria, Louisiana, was met by "kindly greetings," and "fair ladies" who "strew our pathway with the flowers of spring." "The boys," he wrote, "are as enthusiastic as ever." It was not yet clear what their final destination was, but even those "who are on the sick list talk of nothing but 'Let's press onward.'" Doran was confident that whatever fate had in store for the 2nd Texas, "the name and fame of the Texian character will still be maintained." Quoting a verse from an unidentified poem, Doran anticipated that even "in the shock of battle perhaps a few of us may fall," yet our friends

> Might better weep o'er honor's tomb
> Than greet a coward's safe return.[177]

The stakes were high and the scene was set. Battle was imminent and all expectations were for the 2nd Texas to perform well. Certainly, no one dared to think that there was any chance they would, in Mollie Moore's words, "shrink before the storm."

---

[174] Charles Evans estimated the strength of his regiment to be "about thirteen hundred strong" upon their departure from Texas. See Evans, "The Second Texas Infantry," 578.

[175] Almeron Fields Amerman, "Memoirs," [1902], 5, Typescript copy, Regimental Files, 2nd Texas Infantry Regiment, Shiloh National Military Park, Shiloh, Tennessee, heretofore referred to as SNMP. Ralph Smith, though, claimed that the "citizens of Houston were glad when we left" after members of the regiment mocked the eulogy given for Thomas F. Lubbock when acting as escorts for his funeral. See Smith, "To the Daughters of the Confederacy," in Smith, *Reminiscences*, 20.

[176] Smith, *Reminiscences*, 1.

[177] "Sioux," Letter to the Editor, March 27, 1862, *The Tri-Weekly Telegraph* (Houston, TX), April 4, 1862. Doran was aboard one of the two steamers transporting the regiment across the Red River. Doran called Union troops "cowardly hessians" and the conflict a "war to filch from the Southern people the homesteads where they were reared" and a "war to emancipate the negroes of the South."

5

"A Pack of Cowards": Tennessee and Mississippi

"DISCIPLINED VALOR"

The regiment's destination, however, was not Arkansas; instead, once the 2nd Texas reached Helena, they were ordered to Memphis and then on to Corinth, Mississippi, where Confederates were amassing troops. They arrived in Corinth on the evening of April 1, 1862, having traveled nearly 700 miles from home.[1] Despite the long journey, the Texans remained excited about the prospect of battle. William P. Doran reported from Memphis: "Many are suffering with bad colds; but all are in the best of spirits and anxious to meet the foe." Doran shared their confidence that "they will do their duty." "They have not come so far as this," he stated, "to play soldiers any longer."[2]

And yet, even as the 2nd Texas journeyed further east to what appeared to be certain battle, there were signs of trouble. Three captains were still seeking a way out. Aboard the CSS *Magnolia*, Capt. Ashbel Smith, writing "amid the confusion of a steamboat cabin," felt the need to dispatch a letter to General Hébert contending that he, as well as Captains

---

[1] It was a bit of a circuitous route with the regiment first heading toward Napoleon, Arkansas, but then diverted to Helena due to high water on the Mississippi River, landing in Memphis, and finally pushing on to Corinth. See "Sioux," Letter to the Editor, March 31, 1862, *The Tri-Weekly Telegraph* (Houston, TX), April 16, 1862. Charles Grear again implies that all of this was done against the wishes of the 2nd Texas' soldiers and was somehow schemed by Moore. Certainly, there was confusion and anticipation in the ranks about where they were heading, but there is no evidence that Colonel Moore did anything except follow orders. The Confederates were concentrating troops for an attack in Tennessee and the 2nd Texas, like other units in the Army of the Mississippi, were anxious for battle. See Grear, *Why Texans Fought*, 51–52.

[2] "Sioux" Letter to the Editor, March 31, 1862, *Tri-Weekly Telegraph*, April 16, 1862.

McGinnis and Müller, were entitled to command one of the newly created state regiments. It had been a year, Smith reasoned, and they had each gained considerable experience and demonstrated their competence as officers; they had even conducted "our respective companies over a long land route," even though they were still in transit as he wrote. The state needed "the best services of every man" to command and they considered themselves just that. Smith thought Colonel Moore would support them, but he conceded that it had "not seemed proper to me to ask for any written memorandum concerning us." Hébert could not commission anyone to command a regiment, something Smith acknowledged; nonetheless he wrote Hébert "to beg most respectfully to commend the consideration of our appointments" and if were not possible to have separate regiments, he asked "to be assigned to the command as field officers of a single regiment." Either way, these three men wanted out of the 2nd Texas.[3]

There was trouble, too, with another captain, Edward D.F. Williams from Co. D. Just prior to the regiment leaving Texas, Williams was on detached service for court-martial duty in Houston; but when the 2nd Texas left the state, he was notably absent, blaming a host of reasons, including illness and delays in communication. Receiving orders to "gather men belonging to the Regiment," Williams allegedly used his own money to pay their transportation and bounties and set out to rejoin the regiment. Learning, though, that he had been dropped from the rolls as a deserter and replaced as captain, Williams went home to Harris County. He ran for local election as sheriff, but continued to write letters that stretched over two years seeking to clear his name and return to active duty with his company, which he maintained he had raised "at my own expense." He also was briefly under arrest in December 1861, although the charges are unclear. He never did return to duty.[4]

This unsettled situation with the regiment's officers was concerning. These were officers wanting to leave, or refusing to return, just as it was clear the regiment was hurrying to confront the Federals. It is not clear if

[3] Ashbel Smith to P. O. Hébert, March 28, 1862, Ashbel Smith, CMSR, War Department Collection of Confederate Records, RG 109, NARA, accessed via fold3.com.

[4] Edward F. Williams to Charles M. Mason, August 20, 1862; Edward F. Williams to P. O. Hébert, October 6, 1862; Edward D.F. Williams to Ashbel Smith, August 31, 1863, in Edward F. Williams, CMSR, War Department Collection of Confederate Records, RG 109, NARA, accessed via fold3.com; and Edward F. Williams to Ashbel Smith, March 8, 1864, Folder "1864"; Box 2G224, Ashbel Smith Papers, DBC. Responding in February 1864, Ashbel Smith was somewhat sympathetic to Williams' predicament but wrote that it would be inappropriate to restore him to the captaincy after two years away from the regiment and the "privations of severe campaigns" it had endured.

men in the ranks sensed that so many of their officers did not want to be leading them – if they did, it would have to have given them pause.

Their lieutenant colonel was, however, rushing to be at their side. William P. Rogers had been granted a 30-day furlough the day before the 2nd Texas left the state, and probably could have remained home due to his poor health. But he was not going to miss the chance to resume command. Traveling with his teenage son Halbert, Rogers wrote his wife Martha from Alexandria, Louisiana, estimating that they were some twenty hours behind the regiment. He had secured a boat to take them the next morning "in pursuit."[5]

In the meantime, the 2nd Texas received new uniforms. Originally, due to the chronic supply problems, they wore standard blue Federal uniforms taken from US Army posts when Texas seceded. But now, with active campaigning commenced, Colonel Moore worried that "Federal blue" was not "a life-prolonging color" for Confederate troops. He dispatched Capt. Thomas J. Poole to New Orleans to obtain gray ones.[6] As Moore later recounted, when "the packages were opened, we found the so-called uniforms as white as washed wool could make them." Hurriedly prepared and shipped, they lacked any markings to indicate size, so it was "hit or miss as to fit." Soldiers reacted with humor, some of it quite dark, comparing them to burial shrouds.[7]

[5] William P. Rogers to Martha Rogers, March 28, 1862, Rogers Collection, DBC; see also Pace, ed., "Diary and Letters of William P. Rogers," 285–286. Joshua Halbert Rogers was sixteen years old and although Rogers alleged that his son later joined the regiment, there is no evidence that Halbert formally enrolled. Despite the revocation of furloughs on March 24, it seems Rogers could have stayed home since he had his surgeon's corroboration.

[6] Poole had traveled to New Orleans to obtain the uniforms and other supplies but had some issues with obtaining a bond to back the purchase. He eventually caught up with the regiment on April 7, just as the Battle of Shiloh was ending, finding, in his words, "that nearly all the supplies invoiced to me at New Orleans and not transferred by me, had been issued to the command upon the eve of the Battle of Shiloh, by order of the Colonel, and generally in an irregular manner, from want of sufficient time to make a proper issue." He added: "Such a course was imperative from the necessities of the Regt. and more particularly with regard to uniforms, being required to replace those they had, which were the same as those of the enemy." See Thomas J. Poole to (Samuel B. Davis), June 16, 1862, typescript copy in 2nd Texas Infantry Regiment Regimental Files, SNMP; original in Thomas J. Poole, CMSR, War Department Collection of Confederate Records, RG 109, NARA, accessed via fold3.com.

[7] John C. Moore, "Some Confederate War Incidents," *Confederate Veteran*, Vol. 12, no. 3 (March 1904): 116. See also Amerman, "Memoirs," 7, SNMP. Apparently, other Confederate units had undyed wool (white) uniforms too; but they were still unusual. For reference to "white woolen kersey cloth from the Huntsville Penitentiary cloth," see discussion of "Texas white fatigue uniforms," on CivilWarTalk.com.

The 2nd Texas had become part of Gen. Albert Sidney Johnston's newly configured Army of the Mississippi.[8] With Confederate defeats at Forts Henry and Donelson, and Federals moving deep into Tennessee, Johnston was a man under considerable duress to secure a victory. When a group of Tennessee congressmen angrily demanded Johnston's removal after his abandonment of Nashville, Jefferson Davis, an old friend and loyal supporter of the general, stood firm, responding: "Gentlemen, I know Sidney Johnston well. If he is not a general, we had better give up the war for we have no general."[9]

Johnston, who was a native Kentuckian and West Point graduate, had a long affiliation with Texas. He had fought in both the Texas Revolution and the Mexican-American War, and served as the Texas Republic's Secretary of War under President Mirabeau B. Lamar. In between his stints in the US and Texas Army, he resided in the state, owning a large plantation, "China Grove," in Brazoria County.[10] After his resignation from the US Army, Johnston gained commission as a full general, making him the second-highest-ranking general in the Confederate army.

But now, from Johnston's headquarters in Corinth, where he was gathering his army, the pressure was undeniable: he had to have a victory. On April 3, two days after the 2nd Texas arrived in Corinth, Johnston issued a formal address to his troops, telling them to be ready to "offer battle to the invaders of your country." His speech, circulated among the soldiers and subsequently printed in newspapers, reinforced many of the same themes members of the 2nd Texas had heard repeatedly over the past year. Contrasting their "resolution and disciplined valor" to "the agrarian mercenaries who have been sent to despoil you of your liberties, your prosperity and your honor," he urged them to remember the white women and children dependent on them; indeed, the entire

---

[8] The 2nd Texas was now part of Brig. Gen. John K. Jackson's Third Brigade, Brig. Gen. Jones M. Wither's Second Division, and Maj. Gen. Braxton Bragg's Second Corps. Other units in their brigade included the 17th, 18th, and 19th Alabama Infantry regiments, the Arkansas Battalion, and Girardey's Battery from Georgia. For the Confederate Army's organization at Shiloh, see Larry J. Daniel, *Shiloh: The Battle that Changed the Civil War* (New York: Simon and Schuster, 1997), 320–321; also Chance, *The Second Texas Infantry*, 24.

[9] Davis quoted in William Preston Johnston, *The Life of General Albert Sidney Johnston Embracing His Services in the Armies of the United States, the Republic of Texas, and the Confederate States* (New York: D. Appleton, 1878), 496.

[10] Biographical details from Johnston, *The Life of General Albert Sidney Johnston*, and Jeanette H. Flachmeier, "Johnston, Albert Sidney," Handbook of Texas Online, www.tshaonline.org.

Confederacy relied, he emphasized, on their success. "You are expected," Johnston admonished, to "show yourselves worthy of your race, and your lineage; worthy of the women of the South, whose noble devotion in this war has never been exceeded in any time." It would be with these "incentives to brave deeds and in the trust that God is with us" that would lead them into battle, "fully assured of ultimate and glorious success."[11] These were inspiring words, and they left a positive impact on the men. One Mississippi soldier called it the "best written and most thrilling address I have ever seen."[12]

Johnston's term "disciplined valor" is revealing. As a professional army officer with years of experience fighting and leading troops, he had to appreciate the value of training. Still, his gendered and racialist rhetoric, contrasting his southern soldiers with the so-called mercenaries of the north, was deliberate. He combined the worries of some pundits about their readiness for battle with assumptions about their natural courage: his troops would fight bravely in battle with both discipline *and* valor because of who they were and their Confederate "cause" of defending slavery and white supremacy. And he no doubt was speaking for himself – with his own reputation and career on the line, he had to prove his own disciplined valor.[13]

Of course, vows of military success were one thing: putting those declarations into an effective military strategy proved more challenging. Johnston's plan was to advance his troops, some 44,000 in number,

[11] Albert Sidney Johnston's address to "Soldiers of the Army of the Mississippi, April 3, 1862, OR, Ser. 1, vol. 10, pt. 2, 389. Johnston's address was also printed in the *Houston Telegraph Extra*, April 10, 1862, and is included in his son's postwar biography with a few notable differences, including the deletion of the word "race." See Johnston, *The Life of General Albert Sidney Johnston*, 566. Union troops captured a copy of Johnston's address leading Gen. Thomas J. Wood to comment on it in his official report of Shiloh: "The address, made on the eve of the march to the encounter, shows that the commander-in-chief sought to inflame the zeal and courage of his troops by the most incendiary appeal, as well as proves how momentous was the conflict through which our troops have so fortunately and honorably passed." See Thomas J. Wood to J. B. Fry, April 10, 1862, OR, Ser. 1, Vol. 10, pt. 1, 379.

[12] Quoted in Timothy B. Smith, *Shiloh: Conquer or Perish* (Lawrence, KS: University Press of Kansas, 2014), 73.

[13] The stereotype that the white southern man was naturally a warrior, and the north was full of pasty-faced, weak cowards had deep roots, much of it due to the violence of slavery and anxieties about industrialization. These preconceptions also fed expectations that the Confederates were destined for victory, especially after the Union defeat at Bull Run. See John Hope Franklin, *The Militant South: 1800–1861* (Cambridge, MA: Harvard University Press, 1956); William R. Taylor, *Cavalier and Yankee: The Old South and American National Character* (New York: George Braziller, 1961); Adams, *Fighting for Defeat*; and Greenberg, *Honor & Slavery*.

twenty-two miles northeast of Corinth to confront Maj. Gen. Ulysses S. Grant's Army of the Tennessee, estimated to be around 42,000 in strength, encamped along the Tennessee River at Pittsburg Landing.[14] Timing was crucial as Johnston sought to hit Grant hard before any Federal reinforcements could arrive. His men were "urgently enjoined to be observant of the orders of their superiors in the hour of battle;" and for their officers to "endeavor to hold them in hand and prevent the waste of ammunition by heedless aimless fire." Close combat was anticipated with "much and effective work" to "be done with the bayonet."[15] Johnston projected turning "the left flank of the enemy so as to cut off his line of retreat to the Tennessee River and throw him back on Owl Creek, where he will be obliged to surrender."[16]

These orders, issued by Beauregard and conceived by his Adjutant Thomas Jordan, were in the words of historians Mark Grimsley and Steven E. Woodworth, "a marvel of ineptitude."[17] Apparently inspired by Napoleon's battle plan for Waterloo, the complicated scheme failed to take into account the conditions on the ground, and perhaps most importantly the limited routes between Corinth and Pittsburg Landing. Nor was there much consideration for the greenness of the troops, and the inherent chaos of battle. Braxton Bragg complained that not only had few of his regiments "ever made a day's march," but that a "very large proportion of the rank and file had never performed a day's labor."[18]

Forward movement commenced on April 3, and despite the "high spirits" of the troops, it was soon clear that things were not going to go by design.[19] Soaking rains, which had been unrelenting the past several days, persisted, making the dirt roads muddy and difficult to traverse.

[14] Earl Hess estimates that these numbers are inflated. Instead, he surmises that both armies had around 30,000 troops before Federal reinforcements arrived. See Earl J. Hess, *Braxton Bragg: The Most Hated Man of the Confederacy* (Chapel Hill, NC: University of North Carolina Press, 2016), 32.

[15] Special Orders, No. 8, April 3, 1862, OR, Ser. 1, Vol. 10, pt. 1, 392–395.

[16] "Memorandum for the Commanders of the Corps and of the Reserve," April 3, 1862, OR, Ser. 1, Vol. 10, pt. 1, 397.

[17] Mark Grimsley and Steven E. Woodworth, *Shiloh: A Battlefield Guide* (Lincoln, NE: University of Nebraska Press, 2006), 23.

[18] Braxton Bragg to Thomas Jordan, April 30, 1862, OR, Ser. 1, Vol. 10, pt.1, 463. See also Smith, *Shiloh* 33; 62.

[19] "high spirits" from Braxton Bragg to Thomas Jordan, April 30, 1862, OR, Ser. 1, Vol. 10, pt.1, 464. Beauregard similarly wrote that the men were "in admirable spirits" on the eve of battle. See P. G. T. Beauregard to Samuel Cooper, April 11, 1862, OR, Ser. 1, Vol. 10, pt. 1,385.

And with so many troops traveling at the same time, there were stops and starts, with soldiers, horses, wagons, and all the machinery of a large army clogging the narrow thoroughfares. On the morning of April 4, Bragg informed Generals Johnston and Beauregard that terrible road conditions combined with the "badly managed" transportation of his men impeded his corps from staying on schedule.[20]

After months of anticipation, the 2nd Texas knew battle was imminent. But from their poor-fitting uniforms, discontented officers, and the inclement weather, there were undeniable signs of storms on the horizon.

"THE THICKEST OF THE FIGHT"

Revised plans were to attack on April 5, but the rain kept coming and so did the delays. After spending two straight days "floundering through the slush," the 2nd Texas camped the night of April 5 "in a muddy corn field," intermittently "drowsing and freezing, hungry and soaking."[21] They had already devoured all of the rations issued to them at Corinth, and threw away their blankets and overcoats; many were barefoot, too, their shoes giving out from weeks of strenuous marching.[22] Close enough to the enemy lines, Pvt. Almeron Fields Amerman described hearing "the Yankee bands and bugles very plainly." "That night," he remembered, "it rained for keeps."[23]

---

[20] Braxton Bragg to Albert Sidney Johnston and P. G. T. Beauregard, April 4, 1862, OR, Ser. 1, Vol. 10, pt. 2, 391; see also Braxton Bragg to Thomas Jordan, April 30, 1862, OR, Ser. 1, Vol. 10, pt.1, 463–464; and P. G. T. Beauregard to Samuel Cooper, April 11, 1862, OR, Ser. 1, Vol. 10, pt. 1, 385–386.

[21] Smith, *Reminiscences*, 2–3. Several officers remarked on the troops' exhaustion before the battle. See, for example, John K. Jackson to (J. B. Cummings), April 26, 1862, OR, Ser. 1, Vol. 10, pt. 1, 553; Braxton Bragg to Thomas Jordan, April 30, 1862, OR, Ser. 1, Vol. 10, pt.1, 464.

[22] Smith, *Reminiscences*, 2–3; "Sioux," Letter to the Editor, April 18, 1862, *The Tri-Weekly Telegraph* (Houston, TX), May 9, 1862; Evans, "The Second Texas Infantry," 578; and Chance, *Second Texas*, 25. Bragg and his officers spent the night trying to provide "for a portion of the troops then suffering from their improvidence." He wrote that they had been issued five days rations, but had consumed it all, complaining: "This is one of the evils of raw troops, imperfectly organized and badly commanded; a tribute, it seems, we must continue to pay to universal suffrage, the bane of our military organization." See Braxton Bragg to Thomas Jordan, April 30, 1862, OR, Ser. 1, Vol. 10, pt. 1, 464. On March 26, Moore issued two days' rations to his regiment, including cooked meat and "Burnt & Ground" coffee. He noted that there was "no way of cooking on the boats" as they journeyed toward Corinth. So, already the regiment was on a limited diet. See John C. Moore to Ashbel Smith, March 26, 1862, in Folder "1862," Box 2G224, Ashbel Smith Papers, DBC.

[23] Amerman, *Memoirs*, 7, SNMP.

Before daybreak on April 6, the Confederates were "in motion," and as later characterized by General Beauregard, "all were animated evidently by a promising spirit."[24] The skies had cleared, and the Texans, as part of Bragg's Second Corps, Jones M. Withers Second Division, and John K. Jackson's Third Brigade, advanced rapidly on the Union left flank.[25] Following Johnston's original battle plan, the three corps tried to align themselves behind one another, seeking, in the words of Earl Hess, to cover "the entire front of the army, one behind the other." This was an "unusual formation" and a complicated one. Hess explains: "The more normal method was to assign each corps a separate sector of the total frontage so that one man could command all successive lines in that area." Instead, once the fight began, controlling troops became exceedingly difficult, and the result was "a much more confusing, chaotic, and ill-coordinated affair than most Civil War battles tended to be."[26]

For the 2nd Texas, like the 11th New York, the sensory experience of their first battle was jarring, and difficult to comprehend. "All I remember for the first few minutes after," Ralph Smith later wrote, "was a terrible noise great smoke, incessant rattling of small arms, infernal confusion and then I realized that the whole line of the enemy was in disorderly retreat."[27] Another member of the regiment described the adrenaline of running through the woods and coming upon the enemy camps. The shocking and bloody violence was surreal. "It was my first battle," the soldier reflected, "and I blush not to say a thrill went through me as my file leader, not four feet in advance, fell in his tracks, with the whole top of his head blown completely off by a six pound cannon ball." His "heart throbbed almost to bursting." Then they were "in the thickest of the fight in a moment." The Texan recalled: "The rattle of musketry, the booming of cannon, and the roar of those great shells from the gunboats, bursting over our heads was deafening, and hardly left time to notice the terrible sights on every side; men without heads, arms, legs – lifeless – and covered with blood, lay on every side; and none could tell when his turn would end."[28] Doran, the journalist-turned-soldier, asked

---

[24] P. G. T. Beauregard to Samuel Cooper, April 11, 1862, OR, Ser. 1, Vol. 10, pt. 1, 386.

[25] John K. Jackson to (J. B. Cummings), April 26, 1862, OR, Ser. 1, Vol. 10, pt. 1, 553–554.

[26] Hess, *Braxton Bragg*, 33.

[27] Smith, *Reminiscences*, 3.

[28] "Member of Colonel Moore's Regiment," letter to "a friend," and "citizen of Galveston," April 9, 1862, excerpted in *The Civilian & Gazette* (Galveston, TX), April 27, 1862. The unnamed soldier wrote from Corinth and details from the letter appear to indicate that he was in Co. B.

pointedly: "Reader, did you ever see a battle? Did you ever see two powerful armies, each furnished with the most improved implements for each others [*sic*] destruction, approach each other? If not, then you can form no idea what a battle is; there you see a whole line of humanity, eagerly eyeing the other. The order to fire is given, and the ground is covered with the dying, dead, and wounded."[29] Pvt. J. Henry Cravey thought of his family at home and prayed to God to "be my helper and lead me thru saft." The image was seared in his mind of blood "flowen down the sides of the hilles like water."[30]

Upon encountering hastily abandoned enemy camps, men broke ranks and ransacked their contents. There seemed to be "every article that a soldier could desire, from the commonest article to that of costly luxuries." These included personal letters, photographs, alcohol, coffee, tobacco, furniture, and even "steel plated vests."[31] Sam Houston, Jr. remembered: "I severely scalded my hand in fishing from a camp kettle, a piece of beef weighing some three pounds."[32] This interruption, though, wasted precious time, and exacerbated issues of control and command.

[29] "Sioux," Letter to the Editor, April 18, 1862, *The Tri-Weekly Telegraph* (Houston, TX), May 9, 1862.

[30] John Henry Cravey "Reminiscences," typescript copy, n.d., Historical Research Center, Texas Heritage Museum, Hill College, Hillsboro, TX. Spelling retained from original. Hereafter referred to as THM. Cravey, a native Georgian, is listed as "driving stock" in the 1860 US Federal Census. See Eighth Census of the United States, 1860: Population Schedule, Precinct 7, Harris County, TX, Records of the Bureau of the Census, RG 29, NARA; accessed via ancestry.com. His younger brother William also served in the regiment.

[31] "Sparta," Letter to the Editor, April 10, 1862, *Daily Picayune* (New Orleans, LA), reprinted in *The Tri-Weekly Telegraph* (Houston, TX), April 25, 1862. Sparta is described as a "special correspondent" but he may have been a Confederate soldier. Mention of a "steel plated vest" is significant as Colonel Rogers obtained one at some point, and may well have gotten his from Federal troops at Shiloh. Another reference to the "enemy" wearing "steel-plated vest" is in the *Houston Telegraph Extra*, April 19, 1862. Beauregard sent Mayor John T. Monroe of New Orleans one of these "new fangled bullet proof vests worn by the Yankees" along with a "copper ball" as "specimens of Federal ingenuity" and asked that they be placed on public display in the Lyceum Library at City Hall "where citizens can have an opportunity of examining them." See *The Daily True Delta* (New Orleans, LA), April 17, 1862, excerpted in *The Weekly Telegraph* (Houston, TX), April 21, 1862. Another description of the abandoned camps is included in the letter of an unnamed soldier in Co. B, 2nd Texas to a "friend," and "citizen of Galveston," April 9, 1862, excerpted in *The Civilian & Gazette* (Galveston, TX), April 27, 1862.

[32] According to Houston, among the items taken were "a magnificent dressing case," a "silver mounted revolver," and a hand mirror. He also wrote that firing by enemy sharpshooters did not dissuade their plunder, even after some men fell wounded. When a member of the regiment began distributing whiskey he stole from a hospital tent, Houston wrote, "our major smashed the jug and offered the cheering assurance that the

Beauregard later admonished those soldiers, including members of the 2nd Texas, who "abandoned their colors early in the first day to pillage the captured encampments."[33]

Fighting raged on throughout the day. U.S. Grant, who was loathe to admit he had been surprised by the morning assault, rushed to bolster his lines and hurry reinforcements. He recounted that "the battle soon waxed warm on the left and center, varying at times to all parts of the line."[34] It was exhausting and relentless combat. When Gen. Albert Sidney Johnston appeared atop his horse, rallying his troops, the effect was palpable. One soldier remembered him specifically calling out for the 2nd Texas: "'Where is that Texas Regiment?' asked General Johnston, and on our gallant Colonel answering, 'Here they are.'" He then ordered the 2nd Texas to "charge the enemy and drive them 'out of the camp.'" After three attempts, and ammunition running low, Moore called for them to advance with bayonets; the Texans obliged, rushing forward with a yell, and scattering the Union soldiers into disarray.[35]

next galoot who brought whiskey into the ranks would be bodaciously shot!" See Sam Houston Jr., "Shiloh Shadows. Number Two," (1886), 2–4, DBC.

[33] P. G. T. Beauregard to Samuel Cooper, April 11, 1862, OR, Ser. 1, Vol. 10, pt. 1,391; Although Beauregard did not single out the 2nd Texas by name, there were published letters openly admitting that the Texans partook in the raiding, even sending back mementos that they had stolen. Beauregard's entire report appeared in *The Tri-Weekly Telegraph* (Houston, TX), May 28, 1862, adding to the steady stream of negative insinuations against them. The special correspondent to the *Daily Picayune* admitted, "It must be confessed that the capture of these tents tended to demoralize our men very much, as hundreds left the ranks to pillage the enemy's camps." See "Sparta," Letter to the Editor, April 10, 1862, *Daily Picayune* (New Orleans, LA), reprinted in *The Tri-weekly Telegraph* (Houston, TX), April 25, 1862.

[34] U. S. Grant to N. E. Mclaine, April 9, 1862, OR, Ser. 1, Vol. 10, pt. 1,109. Timothy Smith argues that "on the tactical level, however, Federals were not as surprised as later newspapers described." Smith, *Shiloh*, 92–93.

[35] "Confederate," Letter to the Editor, June 28, 1862, *The Tri-Weekly Telegraph* (Houston, TX), July 16, 1862; also "Sioux," Letter to the Editor, April 18, 1862, *The Tri-Weekly Telegraph*, May 9, 1862. In his official report, General Jackson referenced: "One of my regiments, retiring for want of ammunition was rallied and sent back into the contest, with orders to use the bayonet." See John K. Jackson to (J. B. Cummings) April 26, 1862, OR, Ser. 1, Vol. 10, pt. 1, 555. James Lee McDonough, citing Jackson's report, lists the 2nd Texas, 17th Alabama and 19th Alabama as low on ammunition and having to use their bayonets to fight. See James Lee McDonough, *Shiloh: In Hell before Night* (Knoxville, TN: University of Tennessee Press, 1977), 177. However, in a postwar account of Shiloh, Moore contends that the 2nd Texas were in fact not out of ammunition at all, but waited in a ravine for hours with no orders. See John C. Moore, "Shiloh Issues Again," *Confederate Veteran*, Vol. X (July 1902): 317. Johnston did not single out only the 2nd Texas in his attempts to rally the men. Col. Joseph Wheeler commanding the 19th Alabama stated: "General A. S. Johnston ordered the regiment, with his own lips, to

Lieutenant Colonel Rogers, who had hastened to reunite with the regiment, arrived on the field early on April 6. At first, he could not find them, and briefly joined the staff of Brig. Gen. John Breckenridge. A few hours later, he learned the unit's location, and discovered they had not yet entered the fray. He later wrote: "The boys greeted me with a shout and (in) ten minutes we advanced upon the enemy." Rogers remained with his men as they charged forward, leading at least one of the frontal assaults himself, "carrying," he stated, "our battle flag."[36]

After that first day of battle, General Beauregard declared a "complete victory," and that his men were "driving the enemy from every position."[37] Casualties were high on both sides, including the loss of Albert Sidney Johnston, who had bled to death after a bullet nicked an artery behind his knee, the general initially unaware that he had even been shot. The "substantial fruits of a complete victory," Beauregard tallied, included: "nearly all of his field artillery; about 30 flags, colors and standards; over 3,000 prisoners, including a division commander (General Prentiss) and several brigade commanders; thousands of small-arms; an immense supply of subsistence, forage, and munitions of war, and a large amount of means of transportation."[38]

In reality, this was hardly a "complete victory" for the Confederates. As the daylight began to wane, Bragg had ordered his corps to "sweep everything forward" and drive fleeing Union troops with their backs against the Tennessee River.[39] And then, suddenly, it seemed to many, those orders were countermanded, and the men ordered to fall back to the

---

charge the camps of the Fifty-ninth Illinois Regiment, to do which it was necessary to pass down a deep ravine and mount a steep hill on the other side." See Joseph Wheeler to J. B. Cummings, April 12, 1862, OR, Ser. 1, Vol. 10, pt. 1, 558. William P. Doran in a postwar account stated that the 2nd Texas cheered Johnston as they passed by his headquarters in Corinth on the way to the front, but Johnston quieted them "as the noise would betray the location of the Confederate army." Doran does not mention seeing Johnston during the battle except spotting him with another officer, "galloping forward carrying orders." See William P. Doran, "A Tribute to the Memory of the Late Col. T. M. Jack," *Galveston Daily News*, August 29, 1880. Evans recalled charging with a "Texas yell" and scattering the Federal troops. See Evans, "The Second Texas Infantry," 579.

[36] William P. Rogers to Martha Rogers, April 18, 1862, in Pace, ed., "Diary and Letters of William P. Rogers," 286–287; "our battle flag" from William P. Rogers to Martha Rogers, May 1, 1862, Rogers Collection, DBC.

[37] P. G. T. Beauregard to Samuel Cooper, April 6, (1862), OR, Ser. 1, Vol. 10, pt. 1, 384.

[38] P. G. T. Beauregard to Samuel Cooper, April 11, 1862, OR, Ser. 1, Vol. 10, pt. 1, 386.

[39] Jones M. Withers to George G. Garner, June 20, 1862, OR, Ser. 1, Vol. 10, pt. 1, 534. See also Braxton Bragg to Thomas Jordan, April 30, 1862, OR, Ser. 1, Vol. 10, pt. 1, 466–467.

positions they had held hours earlier. Fire from Union gunboats on the river was reaching the ranks, and Beauregard, sick and prostrate but now commanding the whole army, determined his men had done enough for the day. "Thus ended the fight on Sunday," Brig. Gen. J. M. Withers wrote, "and thus was this command disorganized, an evil sorely felt during the next day."[40] The "whole army," Braxton Bragg judged, "was very much shattered."[41]

As darkness fell, confusion among the ranks worsened. Shooting from the Union gunboats was incessant, as were the cries and moans of wounded and dying men. It rained again, but this time with hail and "furious thunderstorms."[42] The 2nd Texas was at first protected from the gunboats by their position in a ravine, but Private Houston remembered: "we were marched hither and thither, through the darkness; continually becoming tangled with other commands, until one felt himself threatened with the forfeiture of his own identity."[43] Moore dispatched 1st Lt. Daniel Gallagher to scour up more ammunition for the regiment, but he never returned.[44] Eventually, the 2nd Texas settled to encamp for the night, as Rogers described, "without tents or food except such as we took from the Yankees."[45] By morning, the men were already "worn out by the previous day's fight and all night watch."[46] And their brigade was in

[40] Jones M. Withers to George G. Garner, June 20, 1862, OR, Ser. 1, Vol. 10, pt. 1, 534.

[41] Braxton Bragg to Thomas Jordan, April 30, 1862, OR, Ser. 1, Vol. 10, pt. 1, 467.

[42] "Sparta," Letter to the Editor, April 10, 1862, *Daily Picayune* (New Orleans, LA), reprinted in *The Tri-Weekly Telegraph* (Houston, TX), April 25, 1862.

[43] Houston, Jr., "Shiloh Shadows, No. 2," 6, DBC.

[44] John C. Moore to J. B. Cummings, to April 19, 1862, OR, Ser. I, Vol. 10, pt. 1, 562. Gallagher (sometimes spelled "Gallaher") was taken prisoner, sent first to Camp Chase, Ohio, and eventually to Johnson's Island, Ohio. He is misidentified in one of the rolls as having been captured at Fort Donelson. Gallagher rejoined the regiment and was with them at Vicksburg where he was paroled. See Selected Records of the War Department Relating to Confederate Prisoners of War, 1861–1865, War Department Collection of Confederate Records, RG 109, NARA, accessed via ancestry.com (March 22, 2022). See also "Sioux," Letter to the Editor, June 10, 1862, *The Tri-Weekly Telegraph* (Houston, TX), July 4, 1862.

[45] William P. Rogers to Martha Rogers, April 18, 1862, in Pace, ed., "Diary and Letters of William P. Rogers," 286. See also Jones M. Withers to George G. Garner, June 20, 1862, OR, Ser. 1, Vol. 10, pt. 1, 534. Exactly where the 2nd Texas camped that night is not clear, with Chance alleging that they rested in an abandoned enemy camp. NPS Historian Stacy Allen, however, states: "Quite frankly, there is no documentary confirmation to support Joseph E. Chance's interpretation that the 2nd Texas bivouacked in the camps of the 41st Illinois and 3rd Iowa after the first day of fighting concluded at Shiloh." See Stacy Allen to Gregory C. Beckham, August 24, 2017, 2nd Texas Infantry, Regimental Files, SNMP.

[46] "Member of Colonel Moore's Regiment," letter to "a friend," and "citizen of Galveston," April 9, 1862, excerpted in *The Civilian & Gazette* (Galveston, TX), April 27, 1862.

disarray, too, with only the 19th Alabama Infantry nearby and their brigade commander nowhere to be found. Brig. Gen. John K. Jackson later faced accusations of cowardice for abandoning his command; he maintained, though, that he lost track of his men in the darkness of the night.[47]

April 6, 1862, marked the 2nd Texas' baptism of fire. They performed as well as could be expected for green troops, despite the violent maelstrom of combat. Their frenzied raid of Union camps gave pause to their commanders and their exhaustion was severe. But another day of battle, most assumed, would seal a Confederate victory.

"SULLEN DESPERATION"

On the "cloudy, murky" morning of April 7, it was the Federals' turn to initiate the attack.[48] Infused with fresh reinforcements, Grant advanced slowly, and soon the fighting turned hot up and down the lines. By early afternoon, Union troops had pushed Confederates across the very same ground they had yielded twenty-four hours earlier.

Colonel Moore was now in command of a newly configured brigade which included his Texans, along with the 19th and 21st Alabama Infantry regiments. Lieutenant Colonel Rogers took the helm of the 2nd Texas, along with Major Runnels. That morning orders came to resume the fight, but to be mindful that close by were John C. Breckenridge's troops in reserve and ready to provide support. Maj. Gen. William Hardee, taking "personal direction of the brigade," warned the men repeatedly not to fire on what he believed to be friendly troops; but as the brigade edged closer, it suddenly became clear that these were not Breckenridge's men; they were Union soldiers. It was, as Moore later stated, "a truly sad mistake."[49]

---

[47] See John K. Jackson to (J. B. Cummings), April 26, 1862, OR, Ser. 1, Vol. 10, pt. 1, 555. Examples of the accusations against Jackson include an undated history of the 19th Alabama Infantry which states: "On the Shiloh field the brigadier-general of that brigade did not display the courage requisite, but went to the rear, and for a time could not be found." See Undated Clipping, 19th Alabama Infantry Regiment, Folder 1, Part 1, Confederate Regimental History Files, Alabama Department of Archives and History; hereafter referred to as ADAH. These typescript regimental histories are not dated and there is no author, but they seem to date to the twentieth century.

[48] "cloudy, murky," from "Special Correspondence of the Picayune," "Sparta," Letter to the Editor, April 10, 1862, *Daily Picayune* (New Orleans, LA), reprinted in *The Tri-Weekly Telegraph* (Houston, TX), April 25, 1862.

[49] "21st Alabama Infantry Regiment," Folder 3, Confederate Regimental Histories, ADAH. With Moore leading this newly created brigade, Rogers was in direct command of the 2nd Texas for the rest of the battle. See William P. Rogers to Martha Rogers, April 18, 1862, in

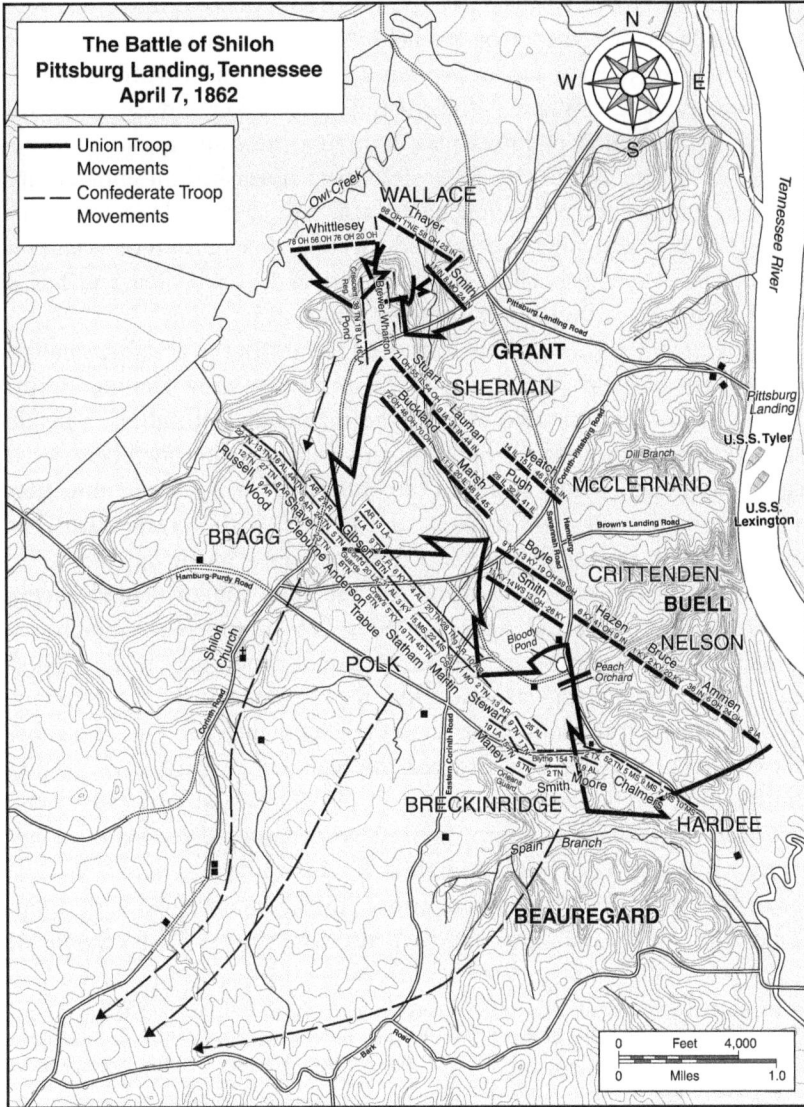

MAP 5.1 Map of the second day of the Battle of Shiloh, April 7, 1862.

Sam Houston, Jr. maintained that he and his comrades "were too little versed in warfare to realize our isolated condition and went blithely on;

Pace, ed., "Diary and Letters of William P. Rogers," 286–287; also John C. Moore to J. B. Cummings, to April 19, 1862, OR, Ser. 1, Vol. 10, pt. 1, 563.

for Sunday's victory had given us unbounded confidence in ourselves." An eerie silence seemed to envelop the field. "I do not remember that on our way across the open space, a command was given or a word spoken," Houston recalled. "'Where is the enemy' I kept asking myself, and suppose that every man in ranks was revolving the same question in his mind," he wrote. Suddenly, Federal soldiers unleashed an enfilade fire on the brigade, sending it reeling backward. "[O]ur line," Houston recollected, "seemed actually to wither and curl up; while in front of us and on both our flanks, the very earth swarmed with Federals."[50] The 2nd Texas broke, its members fleeing in full-blown panic.

Desperately, Hardee and his staff tried to reform the brigade, singling out the Texans and pleading with them to stay their ground. Capt. William Clare was "unable to rally the regiment or to induce a single man to return to the field."[51] Spotting an officer and some members of the regiment hiding behind a tree, Clare rebuked them, threatening that Hardee would "call them a 'pack of cowards,'" They responded that "they did not care a damn what" the general "might call them."[52] Ralph Smith, who was shot in the leg and soon caught behind enemy lines and captured, defended his comrades: "I was not in a position to see how fast the boys moved to the rear but understood they made a good record for speed, which was wise under the circumstances."[53] Lieutenant Colonel Rogers frantically "reformed the alignment" and "made a short talk of encouragement, and ordered the regiment to advance." Despite Hardee and Clare's later pronouncements, Rogers was able to lead at least a portion of his men back into the fray, who "pursued the flying enemy nearly half a mile" but were ultimately "repulsed."[54]

For the rest of the Confederate army, "the fight continued with sullen desperation for several hours and with alternate success."[55] By 2:00 PM,

[50] Houston remembered identifying the enemy troops by the insignia on their hats as the 3rd Iowa Volunteer Infantry Regiment, but he may have mistaken them for the 2nd Iowa Volunteer Infantry Regiment, which was closer to his regiment's location. See Houston, Jr., "Shiloh Shadows," No. 2, 8–9, DBC.
[51] Clare was shot in the foot trying to rally the 2nd Texas. See William Clare to Samuel Cooper, October 29, 1862, OR, Ser. 1, Vol. 10, pt. 1, 572–573; and James Phelan to James A. Seddon, (April 1863), in William Clare, CMSR, War Department Collection of Confederate Records, RG 109, NARA, accessed via fold3.
[52] William J. Hardee to Samuel Cooper, October 29, 1862, OR, Ser. 1, Vol. 10, pt. 1, 571–572.
[53] Smith, "To the Daughters of the Confederacy," in *Reminiscences*, 21.
[54] Evans, "The Second Texas Infantry," 580. See also Chance, *Second Texas*, 37. According to the CMSR, at least fifty members of the 2nd Texas are listed as having lost their rifles at Shiloh. It may well be that in the panicked retreat, some Texans threw away their guns.
[55] Jones M. Withers to George G. Garner, June 20, 1862, OR, Ser. 1, Vol. 10, pt. 1, 534.

Beauregard issued orders to withdraw, deeming his men exhausted and outnumbered.[56] Grant reported the southern troops retreating in "good order," but noted that the "enemy suffered terribly from demoralization and desertion."[57]

Grant was right; Confederate troops were demoralized. Lt. Col. William D. Chadick from the 26th Alabama Infantry Regiment, for example, bluntly stated that by April 7: "Attacks of sickness, extreme exhaustion, and in some cases a want of moral courage had reduced our number to less than 150 men." His soldiers, depleted and fatigued, "were exceedingly dispirited, though they obeyed every order, and the most of them did the best they could."[58] Brig. Gen. J. K. Jackson, who found himself on April 7 essentially "without a command," tried to round up stragglers and return them to the fight. But he found it "very difficult to make men reform after they have lost their pride sufficiently to obtain their consent to flee."[59] The next day, Bragg informed Beauregard in no uncertain terms that the condition of his men was "horrible." In two

---

[56] P. G. T. Beauregard to Samuel Cooper, April 11, 1862, OR, Ser. 1, Vol. 10, pt. 1, 387.

[57] U.S. Grant to N. E. Mclaine, April 9, 1862, OR, Ser. 1, Vol. 10, pt. 1, 109–110. Grant's report was later published in *The Tri-Weekly Telegraph* (Houston, TX), on May 23, 1862, with the paper stressing that the Confederates *"retreated in good order"* (emphasis from original) despite the debilitating loss. Bragg, who was sharply critical of the decision to withdraw on the night of April 6, and what he perceived to be the poor condition of his men, also called the retreat to Corinth an "orderly movement." See Braxton Bragg to Thomas Jordan, April 30, 1862, OR, Ser. 1, Vol. 10, pt. 1, 468. See also Jones M. Withers to George G. Garner, June 20, 1862, OR, Ser. 1, Vol. 10, pt. 1, 535; and "Sparta," Letter to the Editor, April 10, 1862, *Daily Picayune* (New Orleans, LA), reprinted in *The Tri-weekly Telegraph* (Houston, TX), April 25, 1862.

[58] William D. Chadick, to C. D. Anderson, April 12, 1862, OR, Ser. 1, Vol. 10, pt. 1, 546. The 26th Alabama was also in Wither's Second Division.

[59] John K. Jackson to (J. B. Cummings), April 26, 1862, OR, Ser. 1, Vol. 10, pt. 1, 555. Other examples of accusations of individual cowardice include Lt. E. J. Rogers of the 18th Alabama Infantry, whom Col. Eli S. Shorter described as having "abandoned his company twice and wholly disappeared from the field." See Eli S. Shorter to J. B. Cummings, April 9, 1862, OR, Ser. 1, Vol. 10, pt. 1, 557. Rogers resigned his commission on April 15, 1862. See E. J. Rogers, CMSR, War Department Collection of Confederate Records, RG 109, NARA, accessed via fold3.com. An officer in the 21st Alabama singled out Pvt. Edwin M. Treat for showing "the white feather at the very commencement of the fight" and disappearing from the fray. See James M. Williams to Lizzie Williams, April 10, 1862, in John Kent Folmar, ed., *From that Terrible Field: Civil War Letters of James M. Williams, 21st Alabama Infantry Volunteers* (Tuscaloosa, AL: University of Alabama Press, 1981), 54. Williams castigated other Confederates in another letter to his wife on April 17, describing men fading from the ranks until the fighting ended. See James M. Williams to Lizzie Williams, April 17, 1862, in Folmar, ed., *From that Terrible Field*, 57. Lt. Col. Job R. Parker accused his own color bearer of "shamefully" deserting his regiment, the 48th Ohio Infantry, during the battle. See J. R. Parker, "Report of

separate telegrams, one in the morning and another later in the afternoon on April 8, Bragg described his corps as: "utterly disorganized and demoralized;" and "exhausted, dispirited and work with no zeal." As for himself and his staff, they, too, were "utterly exhausted."[60]

To be sure, there had been widespread disaffection on the Union side, as well, especially on that first day of the battle. In their after-action reports, Union officers did not mince words in describing skulkers who absconded from the field and the "throng of disorganized and demoralized troops" desperately trying to escape across the river to safety.[61] Brig. Gen. Stephen Hurlbut blasted the "officers and men" of the 13th Ohio Battery whom, he alleged, "with a common impulse of disgraceful cowardice, abandoned the entire battery, horses, caissons, and guns, and fled, and I saw them no more until Tuesday." Pushed back to the river by the oncoming Confederates, he wrote: "Many officers and men unknown to me, and whom I never desire to know, fled in confusion through the line."[62] The sight of soldiers recoiling and begging for mercy also disgusted Brig. Gen. William Nelson, who arrived on the scene late in the day on April 6. His efforts to rally them failed: "They were insensible to shame or sarcasm – for I tried both on them – and indignant at such poltroonery, I asked permission to open fire upon the knaves."[63] The Confederate press took great satisfaction from these accounts of craven Yankees. "The Northern papers are filled with details of the battle of Shiloh," the *Houston Telegraph* crowed. "The charge of cowardice is very freely

---

Lieut. Col. Job R. Parker, Forty-eighth Ohio Infantry," April 9, 1862, OR, Ser. 1, Vol. 10, pt. 1 270.

[60] Braxton Bragg to P. G. T. Beauregard, 7:30 AM and 2:00 PM, April 8, 1862, OR, Ser. 1, Vol. 10, pt. 2, 398–399.

[61] "throng of disorganized and demoralized troops" from Don Carlos Buell to N. H. McLean, April 15, 1862, OR, Ser. 1, Vol. 10, pt. 1,292; See "Col. Jacob Ammen's Diary of March to and Battle of Pittsburg Landing, Tenn. [Extracts.]," April 6–7, 1862, OR, Ser. 1, Vol. 10, pt. 1, 333.

[62] Stephen A. Hurlbut to John A. Rawlins, April 12, 1862, OR, Ser. 1, Vol. 10, pt. 1, 203; 204. Hulbert also noticed "two Texas regiments" advancing on his men and Hurlbut in turn, directing artillery fire on "the 'Lone Star' flags" (204). The two Texas regiments were most likely the 2nd Texas and the 9th Texas Infantry Regiment. The 9th Texas was part of J. Patton Anderson's Brigade, Ruggles Division in Bragg's 2nd Corps. For more on the 9th Texas, see Tim Bell, "Ninth Texas Infantry," "Handbook of Texas Online," www.tshaonline.org.

[63] William Nelson to (J. B. Fry), April 10, 1862, OR, Ser. 1, Vol. 10, pt. 1, 323–324. For a closer look at the uneven performance by the "raw recruits" on both sides, see Frank and Reaves, *Seeing the Elephant*.

made against both generals and troops and that several of the regiments foully disgraced themselves."[64]

But it was the Confederates who suffered the debilitating defeat. And despite Beauregard's insistence that "this army is more confident of ultimate success than before its encounter with the enemy," even he had to concede the disappointing performance of some of his troops. It was not fair, Beauregard contended, to "the brave men under me, as a contrast to the behavior of most of the army who fought so heroically." He ended his official report of Shiloh by stating that "some officers, non-commissioned offices and men, abandoned their colors early in the first day to pillage the captured encampments; others returned shamefully from the field on both days, while the thunder of cannon and the roar and rattle of musketry told them that their brothers were being slaughtered by the fresh legions of the enemy." "I have ordered," he pronounced, "the names of the most conspicuous upon this roll of laggards and cowards to be published in orders."[65]

The second day of Shiloh proved disastrous for the Confederate army, especially for the 2nd Texas. Confused and distraught, most of the regiment panicked and fled from the field, despite frantic efforts to shame them back into action.

---

[64] *Houston Telegraph Extra*, April 29, 1862. A former member of the 12th Iowa Volunteer Infantry Regiment, Joseph Rich, suggested that there were probably the same number of stragglers on both sides, but because a large number of Union soldiers were "crowding the Landing and 'cowering' under the river bluffs," their skulking appeared more pronounced than that of the Confederates, who were spread out over "miles of territory." See Joseph W. Rich, *The Battle of Shiloh* (Iowa City: The State Historical Society of Iowa, 1911), 59.

[65] P. G. T. Beauregard to Samuel Cooper, April 11, 1862, OR, Ser. 1, Vol. 10, pt. 1, 388; 391. Another Confederate unit singled out publicly in these published reports was the 52nd Tennessee Infantry Regiment. Brig. Gen. James R. Chalmers sharply criticized them as having "broke and fled in most shameful confusion" on April 6. After frantic attempts to rally them, "this regiment was ordered out of the lines, where it remained during the balance of the engagement, with the exception of two companies" which "fought gallantly in the ranks of the Fifth Mississippi Regiment." See James R. Chalmers to (J. B. Cummings), April 12, 1862, OR, Ser. 1, Vol. 10, pt. 1, 549. The 52nd Tennessee, or remnants of it, was aligned to the right of the 2nd Texas at various times during the two-day battle. Measles swept its ranks soon after the regiment's formation in January 1862, sickening nearly one third of its members, which may well have played a role in its poor performance at Shiloh. After the battle, the 52nd briefly merged with the 51st Tennessee and then later separated out as the "52nd Consolidated Regiment." The unit went on to fight in the battles of Perryville, Murfreesboro, and Chickamauga and eventually, according to one source, "redeemed itself nobly." See "Regimental Sketches," www.tngenweb.org; also Soldiers and Sailors Database, www.nps.gov; and Benjamin J. Lea to Daniel Ruggles, February 26, 1862, OR, Ser. I, Vol. 7, 910.

"SEVERE DISCIPLINE"

Public recognition of the "laggards and cowards" reignited debates about the relationship between soldierly discipline and manly bravery. If Confederate troops at Shiloh were inherently courageous, and even according to Grant "the flower of Southern Army," then how to explain the breakdown in control and organization on both days – as evidenced by the raiding of Union camps on April 6 and the disintegration of commands on April 7?[66] Braxton Bragg blamed "the want of proper organization and discipline" for many of the failings at Shiloh, a battle he believed "would have changed the entire complexion of the war."[67] Maj. Franklin H. Clack, who commanded a home guard battalion from New Orleans, agreed, and in his report he blasted the poorly prepared volunteers and called for the "strong, immediate necessity for the strictest, most severe discipline." It was only the "daring courage exhibited by a large portion of our force that enabled us to sustain ourselves" and not suffer complete annihilation. Clack believed, though, that such "daring courage" was not enough: there had to be training and preparation: "Be assured, general, that we never can cope successfully with our foe unless we discipline our force, and that the discipline necessary to perfect our military organization can never be obtained under the volunteer system."[68]

Beauregard, too, felt the need to remind his own army of the importance of discipline, issuing an address on April 8, the day after the defeat. The "gallantry with which" his men "assaulted the enemy, and the persevering courage with which they maintained an incessant conflict against superior numbers" were "not attained by individual prowess alone," he maintained. Instead, Beauregard credited their "subordination and careful training," instilled by their "their division, brigade and regimental commanders, who first disciplined them in camp and then led them judiciously and gallantly in battle."[69]

---

[66] In his congratulatory address, Grant praised his own men as "brave and gallant soldiers." See U.S. Grant, General Orders No. 34, April 8, 1862, OR, Ser. 1, Vol. 10, pt. 1, 111–112.

[67] Braxton Bragg to Thomas Jordan, April 30, 1862, OR, Ser. 1, Vol. 10, pt. 1, 469.

[68] Franklin H. Clack to Patton Anderson, April 10, 1862, OR, Ser. 1, Vol. 10, pt. 1, 512. Clack commanded the "Confederate Guards Response Battalion," meant to protect New Orleans but called into action at Shiloh.

[69] P. G. T. Beauregard, General Orders No. 6, April 8, 1862, OR, Ser. 1, Vol. 10, pt. 1, 297. About a week later, Beauregard returned to the familiar rhetoric of soldierly bravery, citing the enemy's superiority in arms and numbers for their defeat, rather than any failings on the part of his army or himself. These same excuses would reappear in postwar Lost Cause propaganda. See P. G. T. Beauregard's address to "Soldiers of the Army of the

Inherent here was a renewed acknowledgment that individual bravery was not always sufficient and could even be debilitating, if as in Aristotle's definition an excess of courage became recklessness. On one hand, Beauregard heralded the "sublime courage" of the slain Johnston, telling his men that the general's "signal example of heroism and patriotism, if imitated would make this army invincible."[70] On the other hand, when some implied that it was Johnston's "rash exposure of his person" which helped cause the Confederate defeat, his aid Maj. D. M. Hayden felt the need to defend his commander: "He [Johnston] fell where heroes like to fall, in the arms of victory, on the battle field."[71]

Gen. William T. Sherman, whose division suffered the effects of the early Confederate attack on the first day of battle, noted a difference between "individual fears" and group cohesion. His troops were like nearly all the regiments that day, "perfectly new," only just receiving their guns, and never having faced enemy fire before. They, thus, "knew nothing of the value of combination and organization. When individual fears seized them the first impulse was to get away. To expect of them the coolness and steadiness of older troops would be wrong."[72]

Discussions over bravery and cowardice mattered, not just for the effectiveness of Beauregard's army and for the reputation of individual regiments like the 2nd Texas, but for the Confederacy writ large. Soon

West," April 16, 1862, OR, Ser. 1, Vol. 10, pt. 1, 397; also published in *The Civilian and Gazette* (Galveston, TX), April 27, 1862.

[70] P. G. T. Beauregard's to "Soldiers," April 10, 1862, OR, Ser 1, Vol. 10, pt. 2, 408–409. This address appeared in the *Houston Telegraph* on April 19, 1862; and in *The Tri-Weekly Telegraph* (Houston, TX) on April 21, 1862.

[71] This excerpt came from Hayden's diary made public when published in *The Weekly Telegraph* (Houston, TX), May 14, 1862.

[72] William T. Sherman to John A. Rawlins, April 10, 1862, OR, Ser. 1, Vol. 10, pt. 1, 252. It is noteworthy that one of the most common compliments used by officers on both sides in describing their troops at Shiloh was that they behaved "like veterans." A review of the official reports from Shiloh finds numerous examples of this. See, for example, Daniel Ruggles to George G. Garner, April 25, 1862, OR, Ser. 1, Vol. 10, pt. 1, 473; A. J. Vaughan, Jr. to R. M. Russell, April 10, 1862, OR, Ser. 1, Vol. 10, pt. 1, 426; and John W. Foster to J. C. Veatch, April 11, 1862, OR, Ser. 1, Vol. 10, Pt. 1, 232; and J. G. Lauman to Stephen A. Hurlbut, April 9, 1862, OR, Ser. 1, Vol. 10, Pt. 1, 234; Maj. Gen. Leonidas Polk even equated a direct connection between "the inspiration of the cause which animates" the Confederate troops and their fighting "with the steadiness and gallantry of well-trained troops." See Leonidas Polk to Samuel Cooper, (September 1862), OR, Ser. 1, Vol. 10, pt. 1, 411. British historian John Keegan similarly describes the battlefield as "a place of terror," but that the inner dynamics within the army help to harness and control fear so that individual soldiers do not behave cowardly. See *The Face of Battle* (New York: Viking Press, 1976), 71.

after Shiloh, the Confederate Congress passed legislation for the first national draft in American history. Jefferson Davis authorized the Conscription Act on April 16, 1862, requiring all white men between the ages of eighteen and thirty-five to serve; for men already in the ranks, their service would be extended two more years. The implementation of this law, including the allowance for substitutes and later, the exemption of planters who owned twenty or more slaves, was difficult to enforce. But most Confederates realized it was necessary: they needed more troops and the loss of men, not only due to combat, but especially disease, was increasing.[73] And soldiers who had volunteered for one year in the aftermath of Fort Sumter were about to see their enlistments end. Texas Governor Lubbock urged his fellow citizens to willingly enlist and thus be allowed "to choose their own service and officers." "Let every citizen become a soldier," he declared, "and be on the alert, willing to march at a moment's warning in defence of his country and her liberties."[74]

Making every white male citizen a willing volunteer *and* an efficient soldier was not necessarily a sure thing. On the day that Confederate conscription became law, editor Cushing published an impassioned critique of it, asking his readers a series of rhetorical questions about the "irresistible" bravery of southern troops and whether they really were "physically any stronger or naturally braver" than the enemy. He answered forcefully that the "Southern soldier volunteers for the love of the cause, and fights for the love of the cause." Thus, it did not matter, he avowed, if they were paid or properly fed or clothed. "Our soldiers fight, not because they are compelled to, but because their heart is in the cause they fight for."[75] Cushing's ringing endorsement of the willing volunteer ran counter to his ongoing worry about training. But it did fit with other

[73] In early October 1862 a letter-writer identified as "Ranger" claimed that the "spirit of the people" was "against conscription." See "Ranger," Letter to the Editor, October 6, 1862, *The Tri-Weekly Telegraph* (Houston, TX), October 15, 1862. For more on the Confederate draft, see Albert B. Moore, *Conscription and Conflict in the Confederacy* (New York: Macmillan, 1924); and more recently, John M. Sacher, *Confederate Conscription and the Struggle for Southern Soldiers* (Baton Rouge, LA: Louisiana State University Press, 2021). Sacher notes mixed reactions to Confederate conscription, arguing that most Confederates supported the draft although they sharply criticized its implementation. He further acknowledges that it proved difficult to enforce and balance with the very real needs on the homefront.

[74] Francis R. Lubbock, "Proclamation by the Governor to the People of State of Texas," May 7, 1862, *The Tri-Weekly Telegraph* (Houston, TX), May 14, 1862.

[75] *The Tri-Weekly Telegraph* (Houston, TX), April 16, 1862.

jingoistic rhetoric that, ultimately, the naturally courageous southern white man could and would defeat their inferior foe.

In the aftermath of bloody Shiloh, it was clear that every Confederate soldier was not valorous; and many, if not most, cared quite a bit about pay, rations, and their uniforms. Nor did the 2nd Texas behave "like veterans" in their first battle, as everyone assumed they would; instead, there were troubling signs that they were the "laggards and cowards" that Beauregard castigated in his report.

"SO SUDDEN WAS THE SHOCK"

Their corps, division, and brigade commanders, however, made no direct reference to the 2nd Texas performing badly in their official reports. Beauregard never said anything publicly either, at least it would seem not in print. Instead, two of their officers, namely Colonel Moore and Major Runnells, were both praised for their gallantry.[76] Mention of the shameful charges made against the regiment did appear in Moore's reports of the battle – plural, as he submitted three separate explanations of the 2nd Texas' performance at Shiloh over the course of six days. Moore opened his first report dated April 19, the lengthiest of the three, by stating plainly: "In justice to my regiment permit me to say that no other regiment entered the fight on that day under more unfavorable circumstances than the Second Texas." He then recounted their long journey from Texas and the final "long and exhausting march" to Corinth. By the time the battle commenced, Moore ascertained that his men had consumed all of their provisions, and many were barefoot, their shoes having worn completely out. And "yet," he professed, "the men moved forward with light hearts and buoyant sprits without a murmur of complaint." He went on to detail the regiment's actions on April 6, the successive charges, and advances until late into the day. In assessing their conduct, Moore then rather oddly switched to the first-person plural, stating: "We think we may be permitted to say that the regiment had already done noble work, yet this last and closing action of the day may be remembered with pride by the officers and men of the Second Texas Infantry." He praised Lieutenant Colonel Rogers and Major Runnels for executing their duty, adding, "we doubt not their coolness and courage attracted the attention of the general commanding." He continued: "The company officers, so far as we could observe, with one exception – Lieutenant Foster, now under

---

[76] Jones M. Withers to George G. Garner, June 20, 1862, OR, Ser. 1, Vol. 10, pt. 1, 533; 536.

arrest – performed their respective parts bravely." Then mid-sentence, Moore switched back to the first-person singular, and declared, "so much so, indeed, that it seems to me if I should mention favorably only a portion of them, I would be doing injustice to the others." He closed by admitting that the report was longer than he had intended.[77]

Still, most of Moore's focus was on the first day, where there is little question that the 2nd Texas performed well. The only allusion he made to the second day was his taking command of a brigade and leaving Rogers and Runnels to lead the regiment in his place. He referred to Lieutenant Foster's arrest but failed to mention that he, too, was under arrest, if only briefly, soon after the battle ended.[78]

Moore's second report, addressed again to the assistant adjutant general of Wither's division and dated two days later, was more direct in dealing with the second day's actions. Reiterating that he was "only nominally in command of an irregular organization" that day and that he still lacked complete reports from "other commanders," he sketched out the advance personally led by General Hardee and his staff on the morning of April 7 where it was incorrectly believed that the "large force" aligned "in our front and to the right, but in thick woods" were "our friends, and the caution again and again, given not to fire, as they were Breckinridge's men." As they drew closer to these soldiers, it quickly became clear that they were not reinforcements at all, but the enemy, which "had a deadly cross-fire on our left wing," and "from the shelter of the woods, now poured into the whole line a most murderous fire." Moore admitted, "So sudden was the shock and so unexpected was the character of our supposed friends, that the whole line soon gave way from right to left in utter confusion. The regiments became so scattered and

---

[77] John C. Moore to J. B. Cummings, to April 19, 1862, OR, Ser. I, Vol. 10, pt. 1, 560–563. Moore also attached a casualty list from the first day of battle, but it is missing from the published OR.

[78] There is no indication that 2nd Lt. James E. Foster (Co. D) was ever formally charged with anything based on his behavior at Shiloh, yet, as detailed in Chapter Six, Foster's wife apparently wrote Rogers asking him to help clear her husband's name. Foster was later promoted to captain and served alongside Colonel Rogers in the Battle of Corinth, where he was wounded. James E. Foster was born in 1830 in Pennsylvania and later died in Houston at the age of 55. Biographical information on Foster from ancestry.com. Mention of Moore's arrest is in a few places including in Rogers' letter to his wife on April 18 when he stated: "The Col. was unjustly arrested and is now released." See William P. Rogers to Martha Rogers, April 18, 1862, in Pace, ed., "Diary and Letters of William P. Rogers," 286. See also *The Weekly Telegraph* (Houston, TX), April 30, 1862, for mention by an unnamed soldier that Moore was under arrest for "representing our unfitness for the march."

mixed that all efforts to reform them became fruitless." Not unlike the Fire Zouaves at Bull Run, Moore insisted that many of his men regrouped to fight in small squads or join other commands.[79]

Then on April 25, Colonel Moore took up his pen for the third time to detail what happened to the 2nd Texas at Shiloh, addressing this report to Braxton Bragg, his corps commander. "Having heard," Moore explained, "that the Second Regiment Texas Infantry, of which I am proud to have the honor of being colonel, has been spoken of as having acted badly on the field of battle on the morning of the 7th instant, I feel it my duty, in justice to the regiment, to make the following special report for the information of the general commanding the Second Corps, Army of the Mississippi." Moore repeated his account of Hardee giving direct orders to advance, then the alarming discovery that the troops believed to be Confederates were in fact enemy soldiers. Moore wanted to set the record straight not just for his men, but himself. Bragg had recommended him for promotion, and he understood that the commander might now be doubting his endorsement given these shameful allegations. Had he been responsible for the advance, and had he failed to send skirmishers to scout the position, "then," Moore acknowledged, "I might justly be held responsible for the result; but such was not the case." In fact, it was Hardee and his staff who failed, even when officers in the 2nd Texas realized the mistake. Moore recounted that "in one instance, after a private returned the fire of the enemy, a staff officer rode up and drew his pistol, threating to blow off the man's head if he fired again." The regiment instead faced "the most galling cross-fire," causing the men to retreat "in great confusion." In sum, the colonel concluded: "I doubt not that our failure to drive back the enemy at this time and place may be attributed wholly to the mistake regarding the character of the force in front, the multiplicity of commands, and the consequent confusion of the men not knowing whom to obey."[80]

It took him several attempts, but by that third report, Moore admitted that something had gone very wrong for his regiment at the Battle of Shiloh. He blamed higher ups for the failure, not the men, their officers, and certainly not himself.

[79] John C. Moore to (J. B. Cummings), April 21, 1862, OR, Ser. 1, Vol. 10, pt. 1, 556–557.

[80] John C. Moore to D. E. Huger, April 25, 1862, OR, Ser. 1, Vol. 10, pt. 1, 563–564. Moore addressed this to Captain Huger, who was the Assistant Adjutant-General to Withers' Division, which followed the proper chain of command, but he clearly meant this for Bragg's perusal.

"NONE OF THE GLORIES OF THE WAR"

News of these embarrassing allegations eventually made their way back to Texas. First, though, there was word of the regiment's casualties, and they were considerable.[81] The chaos on the second day of the fight meant there were members of the unit who disappeared from the ranks and their fate was unclear for some time. "I cannot say how many we have lost in our regiment, as they have not all got together yet," a member of Co. H. wrote home a few days after the battle. Among the officers killed were Clark L. Owen and Belvidere Brooks, who had both been sick and sought furloughs just before the regiment left Texas. Brooks, who had been waiting for his resignation to be approved, was killed on Sunday morning by skirmishers, before the regiment had even "fired a gun." Owen was shot "in the bowels," and declared "incurable" by surgeons trying to treat him.[82] Lt. John H. Feeney and Sgt-Maj. A. T. Paull were also killed; and Capt. Ashbel Smith was wounded in the arm but alive and recovering in Memphis. In the ranks, Cpl. Charles Edward Jones, one of the sons of ex-President Anson Jones, was shot in the chest and captured; he would later die of his wounds.[83] Preliminary reports were that Pvt. Sam Houston, Jr. was "shot through the head"

---

[81] Jackson's brigade, which included the 2nd Texas, listed losses of 865 killed; 365 wounded; and 213 missing, a much higher ratio than the other two brigades in their division. Brig. Gen. Jones M. Withers cited these staggering numbers as "sad evidence of the manner in which the command discharged its duty," again implying, as was a common sentiment, that high losses equated bravery and exposure to danger rather than incompetence. See Jones M. Withers to George G. Garner, June 20, 1862, OR, Ser. 1, Vol. 10, pt. 1, 535. Another example is Col. J. C. Tappan from the 13th Arkansas Infantry, who reasoned in his official report: "The loss of my regiment, in the two days fighting, was heavy, showing that we were in places where the danger was greatest." See J. C. Tappan to "Captain Green," April 12, 1862, OR, Ser. 1, Vol. 10, pt. 1, 430.

[82] "fired a gun" from Hal G. Runnels to E. H. Cushing, April 12, 1862, *The Weekly Telegraph* (Houston, TX), April 30, 1862; also in *The Tri-Weekly Telegraph* (Houston, TX), April 25, 1862; "in the bowels" and "incurable," from "Galveston," Letter to the Editor, April 14, 1862, *The Civilian and Gazette* (Galveston, TX), April 27, 1862. See also *The Tri-Weekly Telegraph* (Houston, TX), April 23, 1862. Owen's CMSR states that he was "shot in breast." See Clark L. Owen, CMSR, War Department Collection of Confederate Records, RG 109, NARA, accessed via fold3.com.

[83] Jones died in May 1862 in a hospital in Dennison, Ohio. See Charles Elliot Jones, CMSR, War Department Collection of Confederate Records, RG 109, NARA, accessed via fold3.com; and "Charles Elliot Jones," findagrave.com. Evans identified Pvt. James Forney (Co. B) as the first man killed in the regiment "before it had fired a gun." See Evans, "The Second Texas Infantry," 579. For more reports of casualties see *The Civilian and Gazette* (Galveston, TX), April 27, 1862.

and left for dead.[84] Estimates of the total killed, wounded, missing, or captured ranged from 20 percent to 30 percent or more.[85]

Major Runnels, in an extended letter to *The Weekly Telegraph*'s editor E. H. Cushing, painted a grim picture of the regiment one week removed from their first battle. The wounded and sick were scattered about in various makeshift hospitals or in camps with insufficient care and medicines. Runnels, who was himself ill, added: "I do not complain for myself, but speak for the brave men who are suffering from wounds received in defence of our common rights, and for whom my heart bleeds." "When we arrived here," Runnels stated, "our regiment was comparatively healthy, and was given up to be the finest in the army. It numbered near 900. Now, however, I don't think we can count on 400 for duty, and the whole number does not much exceed 700."[86]

Lt. Col. William P. Rogers wrote home, too, in letters unpublished in the local papers. Echoing the concerns of Runnels, he told his wife Martha that sickness in camp was running rampant and that he was sending their son Halbert home to his mother's plantation in Mississippi for a few weeks to keep him safe. Compared to Runnells' assessment, Rogers was more optimistic. He admitted that the regiment's "exposure during the battle was very great and our sick list in the Reg. is over 400 this morning," losing "many of our best and noblest." Still, he was confident that the regiment would recover quickly, and "the bloody 2nd" would "be ready to fight again."[87]

---

[84] "Extracts from a letter from a member of Capt. McGinnis's company, Moore's regiment," April 10' 1862, in *The Tri-Weekly Telegraph* (Houston, TX), April 28, 1862.

[85] Evans estimated 33 percent casualties, and of that number 10 percent killed, but it is not clear what he based this on. See Evans, "The Second Texas Infantry," 580. Other estimates of the regiment's casualties, include: "Member of Colonel Moore's Regiment," letter to "a friend," and "citizen of Galveston," April 9, 1862, excerpted in *The Civilian & Gazette* (Galveston, TX), April 27, 1862; and "G. W. C," Letter to the Editor, April 12, 1862, *The Tri-Weekly Telegraph* (Houston, TX), April, 23, 1862. G. W. C. was most likely George Washington Carter (1826–1901), a native Virginian, minister, and participant in the state's secession convention, who later recruited three cavalry regiments in Texas and was commissioned colonel; see Anne J. Bailey and Bruce Allardice, "Carter, George Washington," Handbook of Texas Online, www.tshaonline; and "Galveston," Letter to the Editor, April 13, 1862, *The Civilian and Gazette* (Galveston, TX), April 27, 1862.

[86] Hal G. Runnels to E. H. Cushing, April 12, 1862, *The Weekly Telegraph* (Houston, TX), April 30, 1862; also in *The Tri-Weekly Telegraph* (Houston, TX), April 25, 1862. Runnels provided more details about the officers slain, attesting that Captain Brooks and Lieutenant Feeney had premonitions that they would die the night before.

[87] William P. Rogers to Martha Rogers, April 18, 1862, in Pace, ed., "Diary and Letters of William P. Rogers," 286. Regimental surgeon Dr. Benjamin F. Eades reported "the great

Other soldiers' letters were a similar mix of optimism and gloom. There was plenty of bravado, too, despite the defeat. Letters home were meant to reassure and inform family and friends, but soldiers frequently reflected on the significance of the awful carnage. To be sure, letters published in newspapers were often deliberately culled to stress positive news. One soldier took stock and declared that Shiloh was "a glorious victory," even though he believed the regiment's "experience in war came rather sooner than we all expected" – a surprising admission given the impatience expressed by many of his comrades to go to battle. Nonetheless, he was "satisfied, and would most gladly hail an order for our regiment to return to Texas." After "seeing my friends and comrades falling by my side and the bullets, like hail," he was thankful to be alive. He added: "Our regiment gained golden opinions, and every where along the line as we went on the battle ground and returned, could be heard, 'Go it, my bullies,' 'There go the boys,' 'Hurrah for Texas,' etc. The 'Yankees' have a holy horror of Texians, and our yell when we rushed to the charge, would scatter them more than the bullets." "But," he continued, "the suffering I saw will never be forgotten, should I live a thousand years."[88] Another Texan was surprised to see the enemy run away." "I thought," he stated, "the Yankees were better fighters than they are. I can assure you that every time our regiment got at them they run." He determined that the northern troops simply "could not stand the cold steel."[89] Yet another soldier lamented that with Johnston's death, "the Texians haven't got a friend amongst the Generals and all the hard word is put upon them." "The 2nd Texas, was highly complimented on the field of battle, and wherever their yell was heard, the Federals broke, but still," he admitted, "they are not made of iron."[90]

number of cases of Diarrhea and Dysentery constantly occurring in the Command" in his requisition for "Medical and Hospital Supplies" for May 16–June 16, 1862. See Benjamin F. Eads, CMSR, accessed via fold3.com. Later that summer, Rogers wrote to his sister Helen that "disease is so fatal in my Reg" that one to two soldiers were dying a week. See William P. Rogers to Helen Gordon, August 21, 1862, Rogers Collection, DBC. See also Evans, "The Second Texas Infantry," 581. The 2nd Texas was not alone; sickness was high among nearly all Confederate troops in the weeks following Shiloh. See Timothy B. Smith, *Corinth 1862: Siege, Battle, Occupation* (Lawrence, KS: University Press of Kansas, 2012), 33–34.
[88] "Member of Colonel Moore's Regiment," letter to "a friend," and "citizen of Galveston," April 9, 1862, excerpted in *The Civilian & Gazette* (Galveston, TX), April 27, 1862.
[89] "Excepts from a member of Capt. McGinnis's company, Moore's regiment, dated April 10, 1862," *Tri-Weekly Telegraph* (Houston, TX), April 28, 1862.
[90] This quote comes from an unidentified soldier in the regiment included with "Extracts from Letters from Members of Moore's Regiment," April 11, 1862, in *The Weekly Telegraph* (Houston, TX), April 30, 1862.

Many of these letters exaggerated the number of prisoners taken, with some stating the regiment helped capture Union Brig. Gen. Benjamin Prentiss – which was inaccurate. They boasted, too, about raiding the abandoned enemy camps. Pvt. Henry P. Roberts, the twenty-year-old son of Houston doctor and president of the Texas and New Orleans Railroad Ingham Stephen Roberts, bragged in his letter home, written on "yankee paper," that "he shot a yankee and got his coat, knapsack, port-folio, etc."[91] Twelve-year-old drummer boy Harvey "Clark" Downs sent home to Texas "a large lot of Federal pictures, taken in the Federal camps at Corinth. Some of them are amusing enough."[92]

Little of this was amusing to the friends and families of slain, wounded, and missing soldiers. Clara Jane Sparks Cavitt wrote her brother Elijah, anxious for any news about their younger brother William. She found herself imagining the worst: "Poor William I feel for him when the Yankee bullets are falling around him thick as hail an[d] perhaps ere this the po[o]r boy is lying dead on the cold battle ground but I will hope for better things." Other families she knew in Robertson County were equally distraught. There was, she described, "a great deal of anxiety and distress here" and "every person has some of their family in the Service and a good many have already been killed." It was especially concerning to learn that Captain Brooks was dead. "I had great confidence in him as a man and his men loved him as captain and he told me that he would at all times do all he could for William that he

---

[91] Undated "private letter" from Henry P. Roberts excerpted in *The Tri-Weekly Telegraph* (Houston, TX), April 23, 186. Roberts' CMSR reveals multiple charges against him including going AWOL and "gross neglect of duty" for trying to steal clothing from a boat in Galveston. See Henry P. Roberts, CMSR, War Department Collection of Confederate Records, RG 109, NARA, accessed via fold3.com. According to the 1860 census, Henry's father, Ingham Stephen Roberts, a native of New York, was the president of the Texas & New Orleans Railroad, and worth $2,000 in personal estate and owned five people including three children ages six, four, and one. See Eighth Census of the United States, 1860: Population and Slave Schedule, Houston Ward 4, Harris County, TX, Records of the Bureau of the Census, RG 29, NARA; accessed via ancestry.com. Another comment on the "yankee paper" stolen from the camps appeared in *The Weekly Telegraph*, musing that if Confederate soldiers used the stationery, they might be mistaken for Unionists. See *The Weekly Telegraph* (Houston, TX), April 30, 1862.

[92] *The Weekly Telegraph* (Houston, TX), April 30, 1862; also *The Tri-Weekly Telegraph* (Houston, TX), April 28, 1862. Downs became ill not long after Shiloh and was eventually discharged. His brother Ambrose W. Downs in Co. D was also sick after Shiloh for several weeks. See Harvey C. Downs and Ambrose W. Downs, CMSR, War Department Collection of Confederate Records, RG 109, NARA, accessed via fold3.com

knew he was young and he would advise him to the best of his ability and I knew he would," she despaired.[93]

Sam Houston Jr.'s family was in the dark for several weeks about his fate, too. Early reports were that he was captured and maybe even dead. One soldier recounted seeing "the young hero" "dangerously wounded," and helping him to rest by a tree. "This was the last seen of him, and it is supposed he was carried off by the enemy."[94] Lieutenant Colonel Rogers wrote his wife Martha that he feared Houston was dead, but added that he was "a noble, gallant boy and went through the Sunday fight with great courage."[95] While recuperating from a painful wound to his right arm, Ashbel Smith tried to reassure Sam's father that there was a good chance that the young soldier would make his way back safely to the regiment or if captured would be "decently treated." In recounting the battle, Smith wrote that Sam Jr. "fought like a hero and with the coolness of a veteran." "He was," he avowed, "in the front rank, and I saw him repeatedly having loaded his gun step forward a pace lay his gun to his shoulder throw his eye long the barrel till the sight covered the enemy and then having discharged the piece, he would drop back and reload." Smith admitted to trying to keep the private protected, knowing how anxious Sam's mother was about him. When the captain "occasionally cautioned him with a friendly threat to tell his mother of his so exposing himself – Sam replied with a pleasant smile and cheery word."[96]

Houston was in fact alive; he had been wounded in the groin on April 7, and left semi-conscious on the ground, when a Union chaplain tending to the wounded found him. Rather miraculously, the Bible that his mother had given him, which he had tucked in his breast pocket, stopped a bullet from entering his body the day prior. But the second day he was not so

[93] Clara Jane Sparks Cavitt to Elijah Sparks May 11, 1862, Sparks Family Papers, Box 1, 1856–July 1863, Huntington Library; original punctuation and spelling retained. Although Sparks' CMSR lists him as twenty-one, other sources indicate that Sparks was sixteen years old when he enlisted in October 1861 in Co. E. See William C. Sparks, CMSR, War Department Collection of Confederate Records, RG 109, NARA, accessed via fold3.com; and Seventh Census of the United States, 1850: Population Schedule, Brazos, Burleson and Brazos County, TX, Records of the Bureau of the Census, RG 29, NARA; accessed via ancestry.com. Sparks survived the war and died in 1921. See "William Crain Sparks," findagrave.com
[94] *The Civilian and Gazette* (Galveston, TX), April 27, 1862.
[95] William P. Rogers to Martha Rogers, April 18, 1862, in Pace, ed., "Diary and Letters of William P. Rogers," 287.
[96] Ashbel Smith to Sam Houston, April 16, 1862, excerpted in Chance, *The Second Texas Infantry*, 39.

lucky.[97] His mother, overwhelmed by worry, sat alone at a window, reading her own Bible for hours at a time, waiting to hear word of her son's fate.[98]

Kate Cumming, a Scottish-born Alabamian who had traveled to Corinth to help nurse injured soldiers, recalled her first sight of the wounded at the Tishomingo Hotel. "Nothing that I had ever heard or read had given me the faintest idea of the horrors witnessed here," she wrote. "I do not think the words are in our vocabulary expressive enough to represent to the mind the realities of that sad scene. Certainly, none of the glories of the war were presented here."[99] Cumming took special interest in two wounded Confederates, including a member of the 2nd Texas, twenty-one–year-old Pvt. Elisha P. Wasson (Co. C), who had lost a leg from the battle yet was expected to recover. He had happily related stories about his family and home in Texas to her, but in a few days, his condition turned dire, and he died. Cumming, who knew Wasson just a few days, felt an emotional tie to him nonetheless, and was devastated to learn of his death. She had agreed to write a letter to Wasson's mother of his condition, and "inform her that he had made his peace with God, and hoped to meet her in that land where all is peace and happiness."[100]

---

[97] Roberts, *Star of Destiny*, 313–314; and Ron Rozelle, *Exiled: The Last Days of Sam Houston* (College Station: Texas A & M University Press, 2017), 154, n1. Word of Houston's imprisonment made its way into the press by the end of April. See, for example, *The Tri-Weekly Telegraph* (Houston, TX), April 28, 1862, which reported that he was alive but imprisoned. He recuperated in a private home and then spent several months imprisoned at Camp Douglas in Chicago. He was exchanged in September 1862, and returned home to convalesce. After his discharge from the 2nd Texas, he eventually re-enlisted and served in the 26th Texas Cavalry Regiment. See Roberts, *Star of Destiny*, 317–318; 334; also Sam Houston, CMSR, War Department Collection of Confederate Records, RG 109, NARA, accessed via fold3.com. Nurse Annie Wittenmyer recounted tending to Houston soon after the battle, writing: "The young Houston was severely wounded in the thigh." See Annie Wittenmyer, *Under the Guns: A Woman's Reminiscences of the Civil War* (Boston, MA: E. B. Stillings,1895), 34. Updates on his condition (as well as other POWs from Shiloh), continued into September. See, for example, *The Tri-Weekly Telegraph* (Houston, TX), September 22, 1862.

[98] Seale, *Sam Houston's Wife*, 220.

[99] Kate Cumming, *A Journal of Hospital Life in the Confederate Army of Tennessee from the Battle of Shiloh to the End of the War; with Sketches of Life and Characters, and Brief Notices of Current Events during that Period* (Louisville, KY: John P. Morton, 1866), 12.

[100] Cumming, *A Journal of Hospital Life in the Confederate Army*, 16. Wasson died on April 17, 1862. His mother, Jane Rebecca Thrash Wasson, was widowed, and he had nine siblings, including two brothers who served alongside him in the 2nd Texas. See Elisha Wasson, CMSR, War Department Collection of Confederate Records, RG 109, NARA, accessed via fold3.com; and Eighth Census of the United States, 1860: Population Schedule, Western District, Grimes County, TX, Records of the Bureau of the Census,

Cumming was essentially assuring Wasson's family that he had died a "Good Death."

William P. Doran also tried to comfort those grieving slain soldiers in his reporting for the *Telegraph*. "To those who may have to weep for lost friends, remember that the dead of the battle will have their memories enshrined in the hearts of a grateful people," he maintained. "They fell," he affirmed, "in the best cause a mortal could die for. May God comfort the mourners, and the survivors will visit a terrible vengeance upon the cowardly invaders."[101] He remained upbeat about the regiment, describing the men as being "in the best of spirits, and as anxious as ever to fight the Yankees again." Unsure of their future campaigns, they were, Doran insisted, confident in their generals, who would "bring us out all right."[102]

These were Texas soldiers after all, men assumed to be innately tenacious and courageous fighters. Not unlike the Fire Zouaves, there was an underlying assumption that they were natural warriors. A column in the *Memphis Daily Avalanche* a few weeks after Shiloh celebrated Captain Smith, who was recuperating in that city, as a "soldier for the war." Smith, the writer stated, "fought like a tiger, as did the whole forces from Texas." He continued: "Texans never fail to win laurels upon every battle field where they have fought since the war began. For talents, endurance, and daring and intrepid courage, Texas ranks second to no State in the South or the North – yea, of the world! They are characteristic for their prowess, heroism and devotion to the South and her institutions. 'Victory or death' is the motto of Texans."[103]

In a similar vein, news of Sam Houston Jr.'s status in the press provided another opportunity to tout not only the young private's assumed courage, but also that of his regiment. During his convalescence in Memphis, Captain Smith told a local judge that Houston "fought nobly, always in front," and that "Moore's regiment never flinched. – They stood their

RG 29, NARA; accessed via ancestry.com; and "Elisha Wasson," findagrave.com. Another account of Wasson's "noble death" aligning with Cumming's story but apparently based on a letter from an unnamed minister appeared in *The Tri-Weekly Telegraph* on September 3, 1862. See Chapter Six for more on this version of Wasson's death.
[101] "Sioux," Letter to the Editor, April 18, 1862, *The Tri-Weekly Telegraph* (Houston, TX), May 9, 1862.
[102] "Sioux," Letter to the Editor, April 18, 1862, *The Tri-Weekly Telegraph* (Houston, TX), May 9, 1862.
[103] The *Memphis Daily Avalanche* (Memphis, TN) excerpted in *The Tri-Weekly Telegraph* (Houston, TX), April 23, 1862; and *The Civilian and Gazette* (Galveston, TX), April 27, 1862.

ground like heroes."[104] About this same time, Col. George M. Flourney wrote to CSA Texas Senator Williamson S. Oldham with a plan to organize all "troops leaving & to leave Texas for the seat of war [to] be organized into a division" under command of P. O. Hébert. Flourney offered that these troops, including the 2nd Texas, would then "be separately and distinctly known in the war and will get full credit for the numbers and courage of her gallant sons who have entered the service for the war."[105]

At home, there was still the expectation that Texas soldiers would behave valorously. If not, shame and humiliation awaited them. Mary E. Smith, writing from Austin, expressed her views in a poem dated March 28, 1862, about the dilemma of a "Soldier's Wife" waiting and worrying and "sad to be alone, in a deserted home!" Her choice was a stark one: would she rather have her husband home safe or dead in battle? She responded:

> *I'd be a brave dead soldier's love;*
> *Before a coward's wife.*[106]

---

[104] See *The Tri-Weekly Telegraph* (Houston, TX), April 23, 1862; also Extract of Letter from "Judge Love," *Dallas Daily Herald* (Dallas, TX), May 3, 1862. I have not been able to identify who Judge Love was. Cushing consistently reminded readers of the storied deeds of Texas revolutionaries and their "unflinching zeal and courage," tying that celebrated heritage to Texas Confederates. See for example, *The Tri-Weekly Telegraph* (Houston, TX), April 23, 1862.

[105] George Flourney to Williamson S Oldham, April 19, 1862, in P. O. Hébert CMSR, War Department Collection of Confederate Records, RG 109, NARA, accessed via fold3.com. Flourney was born in Georgia in 1832 and moved to Texas in 1854. He served as the state attorney general and was avidly pro-secessionist, helping to co-author Texas' declaration of secession. He organized the 16th Texas Infantry, which became part of Walker's Texas Division, an all-Texas unit and The "only division in Confederate service composed, throughout its existence, of troops from a single state." See Lester Newton Fitzhugh, "Walker's Texas Division," Handbook of Texas Online, www.tshaonline.org. For more on Flourney see Thomas W. Cutrer, "Flourney, George M.," Handbook of Texas Online, www.tshaonline.org. Davis was amenable to this idea of creating brigades from the same state. In June 1862, Samuel Cooper informed Earl Van Dorn that it was the "wish of the President" to organize the troops "so that each brigade shall be composed of regiments from the same state." He recommended Moore take command of the second brigade. See Samuel Cooper to Earl Van Dorn, June 11, 1862, OR, Ser. 1, Vol. 17, pt. 2, 592. Moore gained command of the Second Brigade in the Army of the West under Bragg, but it was not made up of solely Texas units, instead (as of June 30, 1862) it included Mississippi, Missouri, and Arkansas troops, along with the 2nd Texas.

[106] Mary E. Smith, "The Soldier's Wife," March 28, 1862, *The Tri-Weekly Telegraph* (Houston, TX), April 16, 1862; emphasis from original. I have been unable to identify Smith in the census or other available sources. These were commonly expressed sentiments by southern white women, particularly soldiers' wives (and widows), although certainly not by all Confederate women and less so as the war dragged on. See Angela Esco Elder, *Love and Duty: Confederate Widows and the Emotional Politics of Loss*

A few weeks later, after the news of the Confederate defeat at Shiloh, Smith doubled down with a new poem, "Faint Heart Never Won Fair Lady." She urged "brave men" to go to war, vowing:

> For Texas girls will never take
> Pledges of love from souls that quake[107]

These sentiments contrasted sharply with the real loss and suffering soldiers and their families endured after Shiloh. It had not been all glory and celebrated sacrifice and that realization was just starting to sink in.

"OUR PERSEVERANCE"

By early May 1862, another large-scale battle seemed imminent at Corinth. Confederates had remained concentrated in the town and Union troops were encircling it. Soldier-journalist Doran penned a long letter to the *Telegraph*, trying again to be optimistic, despite recent setbacks. He listed six members of the regiment promoted "for gallantry on the field at Shiloh," and emphasized that "[t]hese gallant fellows distinguished themselves so as to command the admiration of our Generals on that bloody field." Anticipating another fight that Doran believed would be "one the bloodiest battles ever fought in the civilized world," he declared: "To all those who have friends in this regiment, let me say that the Generals and all the troops who saw us in the battle of Shiloh accord us praise for gallantry, and we shall avenge the death of our comrades before the battle is over." Still, Doran conceded that the regiment was depleted, not just from its losses at Shiloh, but from continual sickness. He estimated that "of 850 brave, healthy men who left Houston," there were maybe 200 who were "able to go into the fight" now. On the one hand Doran ridiculed Union troops as cowardly and "not yet cured of the habit of running." On the other hand, he related an incident in which his company, acting as skirmishers, faced an onslaught of Union cavalry which "came sweeping down on two sides of us in overwhelming numbers." He admitted, "our only chance was to escape the best way we could by the rear road," fleeing "like wild cats, our gallant Captain (old Joe

(Chapel Hill, NC: University of North Carolina Press, 2022); Faust, *Mothers of Invention*; and McCurry, *Confederate Reckoning*.
[107] Mary E. Smith, "Faint Heart Never Won Fair Lady," May 12, 1862, *The Tri-Weekly Telegraph* (Houston, TX), May 28, 1862.

Smith) bringing up the rear." "The scene," he deemed, "was ludicrous. There we were imitating the Yankees at foot races, and we Texians too."[108]

On the same day Doran wrote his long letter, Capt. William Christian corresponded with the mayor of Houston, T. W. House, bemoaning the loss of two of the "best men" from his company who had recently died from disease. He lamented: "They braved the balls of Shiloh like heroes, returned to camp and were cut down by sickness." Christian, though, was equally boastful and disdainful toward the enemy, bragging about the "hot work at Shiloh" that made Union soldiers fearful to engage with them at all.[109]

On May 9, Confederates and Federals collided in a "sharp little fight" near the town of Farmington, Mississippi, about ten miles east of Corinth.[110] Confederates halted the advance of Federal forces under command of Maj. Gen. John Pope, driving, as one soldier summarized glibly, "the entire force of the Yankees before us like frightened sheep."[111]

---

[108] Doran claimed that although each company had "thinned ranks," John Müller's "German company" (Co. F) "shows a force" and "are brave, and rush in as impetuous as any of our army. They do their duty, and Capt. Muller is winning the praises of all." See "Sioux," Letter to the Editor, May 6, 1862, *Tri-Weekly Telegraph* (Houston, TX), May 30, 1862; also *The Weekly Telegraph* (Houston, TX), June 4, 1862. The effective strength of the regiment in the weeks immediately following Shiloh is unclear due to "imperfect returns." The OR lists the 2nd Texas as having "aggregate present" 840 men and officers on both April 15 and May 4, 1862, which is clearly inaccurate. See "Abstract from Morning Report of the Trans-Mississippi District, commanded by Maj. Gen. Earl Van Dorn, April 15, 1862," OR, Ser. 1, Vol. 13, 818; and "Organization of the Army of the West, commanded by Maj. Gen. Earl Van Dorn, at Corinth Miss., May 4, 1862," OR, Ser. 1, Vol. 10, pt. 2, 489. An account by Capt. Edward R. Tarver published in the *Telegraph* later in May stated that the regiment was "down to 250 effective men" due to illness and no doubt the losses from Shiloh. See *The Tri-Weekly Telegraph* (Houston, TX), May 16, 1862; also *The Weekly Telegraph* (Houston, TX), May 21, 1862. Edward Rex Tarver was born in 1840, enlisted as private, promoted to captain, and served as staff officer for General H. P. Bee. After the war, Tarver was a member of the Texas legislature. See Legislative Reference Library of Texas, lrl.texas.gov. Charles Evans wrote that these losses were especially acute in Co. E with its captain and three lieutenants dying within two weeks later. See Evans, "The Second Texas Infantry," 581.

[109] William Christian to T. W. House, May 6, 1862, published in *The Tri-Weekly Telegraph* (Houston, TX), May 30, 1862; also *The Weekly Telegraph* (Houston, TX), June 4, 1862. The two men referenced by Christian as dead were Pvts. John White and John Miner. "Miner" does not appear in the existing CMSR, although there is a John "Miney" cross-listed as Murray but a different soldier who was paroled at Vicksburg; there's little information on White that can be corroborated given the commonness of his name.

[110] Smith, *Corinth 1862*, 43.

[111] Excerpt from the *Memphis Daily Appeal* reprinted in *The Tri-Weekly Telegraph* (Houston, TX), May 30, 1861. J. H. Cravey similarly remembered: "We sent them back quicker then thay [sic] came." See Cravey, "Reminiscences," THM.

For the 2nd Texas, at that time part of Col. James F. Fagen's Fourth Brigade, it was a relatively successful foray. The regiment suffered no casualties at all from the skirmish, chasing the Federals through a "bog and water almost waist-deep with several parting volleys sent after them." In addition, they plundered the enemy's discarded knapsacks, which "contained many treasures of which the Texans stood in great need."[112]

They also were in "great need" of praise for their performance in a battle and this they got, despite the small size of the fight. Their brigade commander Colonel Fagen reported: "The Second Texas, commanded by Lieutenant-Colonel Smith, behaved well, officers and men keeping at all times in good order, though marching rapidly and under fire."[113]

Conditions, though, were worsening in Corinth with nearly half of Beauregard's forces on the sick list. On the night of May 29, Confederates evacuated the town, slipping away south before Federals realized they were gone.[114] The 2nd Texas along with the rest of Beauregard's army moved some fifty miles to Tupelo, Mississippi, where it would remain for the next three months, concentrating on drilling and refilling its vacant ranks with new recruits.[115] Here, J. H. Cravey recollected, "We had a good time."[116]

Their new camp, about two miles from town, had easy access to clean water and abundant fruit trees.[117] With the time and space to refocus on instruction, officers touted the Texan's reputation as "a well drilled and disciplined Regiment," another counter to the festering rumors from

[112] Evans, "The Second Texas Infantry," 582; see also OR, Ser. 1, Vol. 10, pt. 1, 811; The 2nd Texas served under James F. Fagen along with the 1st Arkansas Infantry Regiment, 38th Tennessee Infantry Regiment, Ketchum's Alabama Battery, and Hoxton's Tennessee Battery.

[113] James F. Fagan to Roy Mason Hooe, May 11, 1862, OR Ser. 1, pt. 1, 830. Ashbel Smith commanded the regiment in place of Rogers, who served as an aid to Van Dorn during the fight. See William P. Rogers to Martha Rogers, June 3, 1862, Rogers Collection, DBC; also Pace, "Diary and Letters of William P. Rogers," 288–289. Smith was promoted to lieutenant colonel on June 5, 1862. See Ashbel Smith CMSR, War Department Collection of Confederate Records, RG 109, NARA, accessed via fold3.com.

[114] Smith, *Corinth*, 72; 82; 89–91.

[115] Evans, "The Second Texas Infantry," 583. Chance writes that initially the 2nd Texas moved to Camp Ingraham "forty miles south of Corinth on the Mobile and Ohio Railway." Here Chance notes, "several promotions were authorized for the regiment" including Moore's promotion to brigadier-general, although he still awaited formal approbation from Confederate Congress. See Chance, *The Second Texas Infantry*, 48.

[116] Cravey "Reminiscences," THM.

[117] "Sioux," Letter to the Editor, June 10, 1862, *The Tri-Weekly Telegraph*, July 4, 1862.

Shiloh.[118]At Tupelo there were also reunions with soldiers returning to
the regiment. When Ralph Smith and seventeen other members of the
unit appeared in camp, an emotional Colonel Moore met them, grasping
"each of us by the hand and with tears trickling down his cheeks spoke to
us of the joys he felt at seeing us back again safe and sound and congratulated us upon our perseverance in overcoming so many obstacles in our
efforts to array ourselves once more under the flag of our beloved Second
Texas."[119]

Ashbel Smith, recovered from his wound and very happy to be reunited
with the men, proclaimed, "The Second Texas is the bully regiment of this
army – it is acknowledged to have no rival, or rather no equal." He
admitted that it "was terribly torn to pieces at Shiloh," but now "recently
uniformed anew" it marched with a "stately tramp and arms glittering in
the sun as they move to the stirring music of our new band," with "a
display full of glory." Smith pronounced: "It is often said that it is better to
be a Captain in the Second Texas than to command many of the other
regiments."[120]

The regiment's sense of unit identity was strengthening to be sure, but
Smith's words underplayed the very real problems it would continue to
face.

"THE PEN OF THE FUTURE HISTORIAN"

Negative rumors about the regiment were circulating, but some sought to
dismiss them, especially in the local press. Editor Cushing repeatedly
praised the 2nd Texas, determined to preserve their reputation. In
a column defending attacks on General Hébert, and the exit of Texas
troops to the front, he avowed that at Shiloh, the men proudly "carried the

[118] George W. L. Fly, "Before, during and after the Battle of Iuka," 2nd Texas Infantry,
Regimental Files, CCWIC. Fly also recounted a story of the 2nd Texas competing with
the 3rd Louisiana Infantry Regiment over which unit was "the better drilled" with $500
paid by the winning colonel. The wager was apparently called off, but Fly told the story to
"show the standing of the 2d Texas." Timothy Smith refers to both units as being "well
known for their skill on the parade field." See Smith, *Corinth*, 120.
[119] Smith, *Reminiscences*, 5.
[120] Ashbel Smith to John Bowers, July 31, 1862, Ashbel Smith Letters, Truman G. Blocker,
Jr. History of Medicine Collections, Moody Medical Library, University of Texas
Medical Branch, Galveston, TX. John Henry Bowers (Bauers) (1817–1907) was
a French physician and friend of Sam Houston who "became a protégé of Dr. Ashbel
Smith with whom he studied medicine and who sent him to the University of Louisiana
(later Tulane University), where he received a degree in medicine." See Anonymous,
"Bowers, John Henry," Handbook of Texas Online, www.tshaonline.org.

banner of Texas where her honor and her past history required it should be, in the thickest of the fight."[121] He further criticized New Orleans' newspapers for only heralding Louisiana troops when it was the 2nd Texas that "did about the best fighting that was done on that field, making five desperate charges in one day." Exaggerating accounts of the 2nd Texas participating in the surrender of Union General Prentiss, he asserted: "That regiment was acknowledged as unsurpassed in appearance by any other before the battle; and we have a thousand evidence that it was gallant in the fight at it was elegant in drill." "If anything more were needed," he declared, "we have but to add that ten days after the fight, every field officer of the regiment was promoted one grade, a compliment that with all their boastings we do not see that our New Orleans contemporaries have yet claimed for any of their regiments."[122] Pvt. William Doran, in his capacity as special correspondent to the *Telegraph*, continued posting encouraging accounts of the regiment too, insisting, "In every instances when the Texians charged the Federals run. This has been so ever since I have here."[123]

Nevertheless, the troubling rumors remained. And perhaps the person most pained by the allegations of cowardice was William P. Rogers. He was after all the officer leading the regiment on the second day at Shiloh, and these incriminations were a direct attack on his honor as a white southern man. On May 1, Rogers wrote his wife with conflicting messages of hope and despair. He talked of a pending promotion – not to full colonel but to brigadier general. And he affirmed that the "gallantry of our Reg. is spoken by all." Rogers had taken sick and was on furlough at his mother's plantation in Mississippi and deeply worried about the

[121] *The Weekly Telegraph* (Houston, TX), August 27, 1862.

[122] *The Tri-Weekly Telegraph* (Houston, TX), April 28, 1862; also *The Weekly Telegraph* (Houston, TX), April 30, 1862. Cushing was exaggerating here – every field officer of the regiment was *not* promoted nor is it true that the regiment had anything directly to do with Prentiss' surrender, although this was a repeated story from the battle. Still, there were a number of promotions, including Moore's, Roger's, and, according to Doran, three lieutenants promoted to captain; two sergeants promoted to second lieutenant; and a private promoted to second lieutenant. See "Sioux," Letter to the Editor, May 6, 1862, *The Tri-Weekly Telegraph* (Houston, TX), May 30, 1862; also *The Weekly Telegraph* (Houston, TX), June 4, 1862. Moore stated that the 2nd Texas was near Prentiss' capture, but not directly responsible for it. See John C. Moore, "Shiloh Issues Again," *Confederate Veteran*, Vol. X (July 1902): 317. Evans alleges that Capt. John W. Hood (Co. G) accepted Prentiss' surrender, and his men were then "turned over to a regiment of cavalry, who escorted them to the rear." See Evans, "The Second Texas Infantry," 579

[123] "Sioux," Letter to the Editor, June 3, 1862, *The Tri-Weekly Telegraph* (Houston, TX), June 20, 1862.

condition of his men. "Our soldiers are badly treated & unless the war soon closes I fear very much for the future," he told Martha. "God only knows my dear Wife what is ahead of us – For the future of our country I greatly fear – All is gloomy now all is despondency among the people – You meet with [no] smiling face nor joyous brow." He had even considered resigning and going home, and told Martha, "if our prospects do not brighten soon I shall do so."[124]

After the Battle of Farmington, Rogers was still thinking about resigning and returning to Texas. But, for now, he felt a duty to his men to remain with them as long as there was prospect of battle. "I am more popular with the Reg. now [more] than ever and they implore me to stay with them," he wrote. The regiment's health was still precarious but slowly improving and he wanted Martha to assure their friends "that the battle flag of the 2nd Texas will ever be at the post of honor."[125]

Several weeks went by, however, and the accusations of the 2nd Texas' poor performance at Shiloh were spreading.[126] William P. Doran composed an impassioned defense of the regiment on June 10, explaining that he would have done it sooner, but he had fallen ill. He was blunt: "Some of our enemies, actuated by envy and malice, have cast imputations upon our regiment as to our conduct on the field; but these men who started these slanders were under arrest for cowardice. The 2d Texas never faltered." Doran went on to explain the moment on Monday morning when "ordered to charge upon an open field, and while charging were ordered to halt, and received a murderous fire from the enemy lying in ambush. Our loss in ten minutes was greater than the whole Sunday." "This," Doran insisted, "is where the slander started. The pen of the future historian will yet do the Texians justice." Although not yet paid, and still recovering from the waves of sickness, the regiment, Doran judged was, in "good spirits" and ready to fight again soon.[127]

---

[124] William P. Rogers to Martha Rogers, May 1, 1862, Rogers Collection, DBC.

[125] Rogers further wrote: "I think I have lost about 100 men by sickness since Shiloh, I have now barely 200 men for duty but as the warm weather advances the[ir] health is improving." See William P. Rogers to Martha Rogers, June 3, 1862, Rogers Collection, DBC. See also Pace, ed., "Diary and Letters of William P. Rogers," 288–289.

[126] Chance asserts that these "ugly rumors will never surface in print at home," which is untrue as evidenced by examples from the *Telegraph* discussed in this chapter. See Chance, *Second Texas*, 51.

[127] It is not clear whom Doran was referring to here as being under "arrest for cowardice," but it may have been Lieutenant Foster, whom Moore had singled out in his report. This author has found no other mention of specific individuals arrested. Doran bitterly complained that some correspondents recklessly "follow the army, ready to divulge

Another member of the regiment calling himself "Confederate" wrote a letter to editor Cushing a few weeks later, acknowledging that "our peace of mind has been rather disturbed by reports which have reached us from home, derogatory to a regiment which has been a favorite with Texians, and has won the good opinion of all, *worthy of notice*, it has been brought in contact with." "Confederate" went on to recount the story of the 2nd Texas breaking on the second day and refusing to rally even when pleaded to do so by its officers. "No one," he affirmed, "who was with our regiment on that eventful day can, with truth, make the statement that they dared not follow, where any dared to lead." Echoing the same defense others had offered, the soldier recounted their arduous journey from Texas to the front and their multiple charges on the first day of battle and the praise they received from others. He closed: "The fact that our field officers were promoted immediately after the battle and that we received an order from Head Quarters to inscribe the word 'Shiloh' on our battle-flag show honors seldom granted to a 'pack of cowards.'"[128]

Martha Rogers first heard the disturbing accounts about the 2nd Texas directly from Hal Runnels. Her husband William was astounded and urged her not to repeat any of the "falsehoods" to anyone else. Runnels was bitter, Rogers averred, for not gaining promotion and implied that this was why Runnels was casting aspersions on the entire unit. Rogers ruefully observed: "He has gratified my Reg. one and all by resigning – he was not promoted and one of my Capts was and so have I been. Facts speak for themselves. He never has been at any time even for one hour in command of the Reg."[129] Rogers had been solely in command of the regiment on April 7, reiterating that the regiment "did not run." Instead, "it fell back 2 or 3 hundred yards. I with others of my officers led it again to the fight and for its conspicuous gallantry I have been by General Beauregard authorized to inscribe Shiloh on my flag." All of his

everything they hear, and publish it to the world," puffing up the exploits of other officers and units in exchange for food and "luxuries and money." He was equally incensed over the lack of pay to the men in the ranks, telling readers: "I say you will agree with me that a wrong has been inflicted on the 2nd Texas Regiment." "Sioux," Letter to the Editor, June 10, 1862, *The Tri-Weekly Telegraph* (Houston, TX), July 4, 1862.

[128] "Confederate," Letter to the Editor, June 28, 1862, *Tri-Weekly Telegraph* (Houston, TX), July 16, 1862.

[129] Runnels had in fact resigned on June 3, but he said it was due to the "rupture of an old wound." Surgeon Benjamin F. Eads verified Runnels' injury, affirming that he was "incapable of performing the duties of a soldier." See Hal G. Runnels to Samuel Cooper, June 3, 1862, in Hal Runnels, CMSR, War Department Collection of Confederate Records, RG 109, NARA, accessed via fold3.com.

officers and men "were conspicuous for their gallantry – and indeed none of them were wanting in deeds of valor." His promotion and the regiment's designation as "advance sharp shooters" verified his assertions. "I deal in truth," he declared, "when I say that the 2nd Texas stands today ahead of all others in drill and discipline, and behind none in deeds of daring, valor and gallantry." His disgust was palpable, closing his letter exclaiming: "2nd Texas run – My God – it has bled [on] every field," and "250 of her braves are now in their graves."[130]

A few weeks earlier, Beauregard had instructed Earl Van Dorn to forward to him "for publication in orders, the names of those officers and privates of his regiment who shall have most distinguished themselves, as well as those who shall have abandoned their colors on the field of battle." He further announced that regiments "whose gallantry and bravery shall have been most conspicuous will be allowed to inscribe on their banners the name of the battle-field on which they were engaged." But, he added, any "regiments misbehaving in action will be deprived of their colors until they have shown themselves worthy of defending them." Beauregard, in a clear reference to the chaos of Shiloh, reminded his officers on every level that if ever "without orders or at a loss to know what to do in action they must rapidly advance in the direction of the heaviest firing; for the art of war consists of concentration of masses." "Their motto," he wrote, "should be FORWARD AND ALWAYS FORWARD!"[131]

On June 9, 1862, the 2nd Texas formally received word that: "For conspicuous gallantry in the battle of Shiloh the 2d Texas Regiment will have Shiloh inscribed on its battle flag."[132] A few weeks later, on June 20,

---

[130] Rogers was counting not just the killed from Shiloh, but those who died from disease. He wrote: "About 250 of my Reg. have been killed and died, and I have been at times as low in men for duty as one hundred. I now have 400. Their health is greatly improving now and I shall do the best I can for them – Ours is a hard life but our country is in peril." See William P. Rogers to Martha Rogers, June 19, 1862, in Pace, ed., "Diary and Letters of William P. Rogers," 289–290. There is no handwritten original in the Rogers collection at DBC, only a typescript with slight differences from Pace's edited version.

[131] P. G. T. Beauregard to Earl Van Dorn, May 10, 1862, OR, Ser. 1, Vol. 10, pt. 2, 508–509. Capitalization from original. Timothy Smith explains that Beauregard issued these circulars to "boost the army's sagging morale." See Smith, *Corinth*, 36.

[132] "By order of Brig. Gen. Comand'g Division (D. H. Maury), F. W. Floweree A. A. General," June 9, 1862, Folder: "Military Orders and Reports," Box 2G236, Ashbel Smith Papers, DBC. Charles Evans distinctly remembered hearing the order read aloud to the regiment during dress parade. See Evans, "The Second Texas Infantry," 580. "Farmington" was also stitched into the fabric of the regimental battle flag along with "Shiloh." See Chapter 6 for more discussion on the flag's fate after Corinth.

FIGURE 5.1 Flag of the 2nd Texas Infantry. Artist rendition by Bradley Smith.

the day after Rogers had written his wife about Runnels' allegations, the regiment received orders that it had been "designated the Sharp Shooters for Moore's Brigade" by special orders from Gen. D. H. Maury.[133] As Rogers noted himself, it made no sense that a regiment guilty of misconduct on the battlefield would be allotted these honors. What's more, serving as sharpshooters meant the Texans would be front and center of active campaigning.[134]

Rogers, though, continued to write his wife multiple times over the ensuing weeks referencing the charges. He was clearly upset, seeking to not only challenge them but to figure out why he and his men were being disparaged. One of his men later recalled: "No man was ever prouder of his Regiment than was Col. Rogers."[135] But it was more than simple pride; for an elite white southern male of Rogers' stature, this humiliating censure of his command was a direct attack on his personal reputation

[133] D. H. Maury, Special Orders No. 27, June 20, 1862, Folder: "Military Orders and Reports," Box 2G236, Ashbel Smith Papers, DBC. This order also appeared in print in *The Tri-Weekly Telegraph* (Houston, TX) on August 6, 1862.

[134] A former member of the 3rd Louisiana Infantry, which was also designated as sharpshooters for the brigade, recognized that this position placed them "in front of every battle," and certainly a "tribute to their efficiency." The Louisianans "acknowledged the compliment, but did not much relish the situation." See William H. Tunnard, *A Southern Record: The History of the Third Regiment, Louisiana Infantry. Containing a Complete Record of the Campaigns in Arkansas and Missouri; the Battles of Oak Hills, Elk Horn, Iuka, Corinth; the Second Siege of Vicksburg, Anecdotes, Camps, Scenery, and Description of the Country through Which the Regiment Marched, Etc., Etc.* (Baton Rouge, LA: "Printed for the Author," 1866), 174.

[135] Fly, "Before, during and after the Battle of Iuka," 2nd Texas Infantry, Regimental Files, CCWIC.

and manly honor. He could not let these allegations go. "We were all astonished," he told Martha, "to hear that we had been slandered by reports prejudiced to our gallantry, for we really thought we had fought well and our Generals thought so too for they have complimented us by authorizing us to put *Shiloh* on our flag as a badge of *conspicuous gallantry* & as yet, I am told that no other Reg – engaged in that battle has a similar honor." He again raised the fact that he and Moore, as well as other officers in the regiment, had gained promotion, and their new classification as sharp shooters. "Now if all these," he wrote, "do not give the lie to our enemies we can say no-more." He further urged his wife not to repeat any of the vile slander. Although these incriminations clearly pained him, Rogers emphasized, too, how well his regiment was doing since early May, despite the hard losses from battle and disease: "The men are all cheerful & happy – In a few days I will have them well uniformed again and then you would be proud of the old Reg."[136]

Still, Colonel Rogers was determined to counter these insults publicly. In late July, he reached out to a prominent Houston physician, Dr. William McCraven, to help quash the rumors, asking him to publish a defense of the unit in the local papers. McCraven was more than happy to oblige, admitting: "I have so many friends in the regiment and feel so warm an interest in its success that I sometimes almost fancy myself a member of it and that a portion of its laurel wins were encircling my own brow." But given prohibitions on publishing details about military matters, he could not disclose all the information Rogers asked for. Still, McCraven reassured the colonel of the strong affection people in Harris County felt toward the 2nd Texas, calling it "our *pet* Regiment." McCraven admitted that there had been troubling speculations circulating about their

---

[136] William P. Rogers to Martha Rogers, n.d., (July 1862) typescript copy, Rogers Collection, DBC; emphasis from original typescript; see also Pace, "Diary and Letters of William P. Rogers," 290–291. On July 31, Rogers wrote the editor of the *Telegraph* to "thank the ladies of Austin and Walker counties, and also to the Rev. Mr. Seat and J. W. Shipman for the sum of four hundred dollars kindly contributed to them for the benefit of the sick and wounded of this Regiment." He added: "Remembrances of this sort serve to assure the men of the Regiment that their services are appreciated by those whose esteem they hold dearer than life – the noble and patriotic women of their own loved State – and is an additional incentive to renewed and continued exertions for the defence of their homes and ours." See William P. Rogers to E. H. Cushing, July 31, 1862, in *The Weekly Telegraph* (Houston, TX), August 20, 1862. Rogers also referenced "medicines and money sent by the ladies" arriving "at a most propitious moment" in a letter to his wife in June. See William P. Rogers to Martha Rogers, June 3, 1862, Rogers Collection, DBC; transcribed with some errors in Pace, ed., "Diary and Letters of William P. Rogers," 288–289.

performance at Shiloh and he could only assume that they had "arisen either from misconception or exaggeration." He blamed "a few persons connected with discontented parties in or from the regiment," seeming to infer Runnels was again the culprit. "You may rest satisfied that those leaving the regiment from disappointed aspirations can never tarnish its glory no matter with what animus they may be impelled," McCraven affirmed. "The glory of *your regiment* is something we would not willingly let die." Saving the missive and sending it to his wife, Rogers added a note at the bottom: "This is from a gentleman of high standing and great influence in Texas. Please preserve it for me. It shows that I have *enemies* as well as friends in Texas. It is sent to explain the slander & to be preserved by you for me."[137] Rogers responded to McCraven, thanking him profusely, and recounting that when he shared the doctor's letter with other officers in the regiment, they cried.[138]

McCraven was true to his word. Soon after he drafted his letter to Rogers, a column appeared on the front page of *The Tri-Weekly Telegraph* entitled: "The Second Texas." Echoing many of Rogers' statements, it noted the "high encomiums from the commanding officers" bestowed on them which no "other regiment in the service" had received, including inscribing "Shiloh" on their banner. "This fact alone," the paper declared, "would suffice to silence the tongue of slander which for

---

[137] William McCraven to William P. Rogers, July 29, 1862, Rogers Collection, DBC, emphasis from original. McCraven, a native of South Carolina, was a wealthy doctor and slave-owner, and based on this letter, a devoted supporter of the Confederacy. In August 1865, McCraven petitioned directly to President Johnson for a pardon, stating that although he had advocated secession, he believed that the "Northern portion of the United States would permit the South to separate in peace." He stated: "No one deprecated war more strongly; or regretted it more when it became a reality"; and that he had "never taken the oath of allegiance to the so called Confederate States or Served the same, in any capacity except as examining Surgeon for Conscripts." McCraven died in 1872, with his obituary heralding him as "a true Southern gentleman" and "one of our most eminent and successful physicians." See *Galveston Daily News* (Galveston, TX), December 1, 1872; and Case Files of Applications from Former Confederates for Presidential Pardons, 1865–1867, RG 94, NARA, accessed via ancestry.com; and Eighth Census of the United States, 1860: Population and Slave Schedule, Houston Ward 3, Harris County, TX, Records of the Bureau of the Census, RG 29, NARA; accessed via ancestry.com.

[138] William P. Rogers to William McCraven, August 14, 1862, Rogers Collection, DBC; also in Pace, ed., "Diary and Letters of William P. Rogers," 294–295. Rogers described the letter as "long and encouraging," and called the doctor "very warmly my friend." See William P. Rogers to Martha Rogers, August 14, 1862, Rogers Collection, DBC. See also Pace, ed. "Diary and Letters of William P. Rogers, 291–292. There are again variations between the printed and unpublished letters.

awhile [sic] sought to detract from their well earned reputation." Their designation as sharpshooters was equally notable, since this was an honor markedly reserved for "the bravest and the best men of their respective Brigades." Following Rogers' instructions to Dr. McCraven, the paper published extracts from three different orders, including General Orders No. 39 issued by General Van Dorn, which stated in no uncertain terms that the specially selected corps of sharpshooters would be *"made of chosen men,* all of whom must be able bodied and active, good rifle shots, and *of tried courage."* Cushing added his own endorsement: "We feel proud of the Second Regiment, and are glad to be able to record such proofs of their prowess." They "stand a head and shoulders above all other regiments from this State," Cushing asserted, but he was quick to add that he fully expected every other Texas regiment to prove their mettle, too.[139]

Rogers was relieved to see the public defense of his regiment in the pages of the *Telegraph.* He wrote Dr. McCraven: "My object has been attained & the results hoped for more than received in the deep and generous interest you take in our behalf." Despite E. H. Cushing's constant praise of the 2nd Texas, Rogers insisted that they "had no newspaper eulogists & I hope will never have at least in her own ranks, *as some others have.*" Citing Proverbs 27: "'Let not mine own tongue praise thee'" as "if not the quickest, at least the most dignified and honorable road to fame," he reiterated that the 2nd Texas "is still esteemed equal in valor & superior in drill & discipline to all others without exception." Rogers took stock of the Confederate war effort and felt "cheered with the hope," telling the doctor "that the star of our destiny is rising & that no distant day will see us a proud and happy people secure in our liberties."[140]

Nevertheless, the anonymous soldier "Confederate" confessed: "The romance of soldiering has pretty nearly worn off, and it has become reduced to facts and figures."[141] The men of the 2nd Texas were tired and sickly, their white uniforms filthy, and they had not yet been paid. By

[139] Along with the editorial commentary, the paper published extracts from D. H. Maury, General Orders No. 5, June 10, 1862; Earl Van Dorn, General Orders No. 39, June 11, 1862; and D. H. Maury, General Orders, No. 27; as well as Maury's orders from June 9 allowing the regiment to inscribe Shiloh on their battle flag. See *The Tri-Weekly Telegraph* (Houston, TX), August 6, 1862. The column appeared under the date July 30, 1862, but was published in the August 6 edition of the paper.

[140] William P. Rogers to William McCraven, August 14, 1862, Rogers Collection, DBC; also in Pace, ed., "Diary and Letters of William P. Rogers," 294–295.

[141] "Confederate," Letter to the Editor, June 28, 1862, *The Tri-Weekly Telegraph* (Houston, TX), July 16, 1862.

mid-July, there were only about 200 healthy men in the regiment "fit for duty."[142] Despite the efforts of their defenders, they still bore the burden of lingering allegations of cowardice. Unlike the 11th New York, however, there would be more battles to come, and thus, more chances to prove themselves as heroes and not cowards. Their colonel, William P. Rogers, anxiously awaited that opportunity.

[142] James Cowling, Letter to the Editor, n.d., *The Tri-Weekly Telegraph* (Houston, TX), July 7, 1862. Cowling, who visited the 2nd Texas in camp at Corinth, also noted that the regimental surgeon was "entirely out of a large class of medicines, and in consequence the sick suffering."

6

"A Skeleton of Itself": Mississippi and Texas

September 1, 1862, marked the anniversary of the 2nd Texas' formal mustering into military service for the Confederate States of America. The regiment had endured tremendous upheaval in this first year. Many of its original officers were gone: dead, resigned, or discharged. Some deserted, like Captain Williams, who never returned to duty after furlough. What began as an estimated 1,300 strong when the 2nd Texas left Houston in early March 1862 was by mid-August reduced to less than half that number, with only "about 500 effective men" remaining.[1] These losses were due not just to the considerable casualties the regiment endured at Shiloh, but in the subsequent weeks that followed. Men were dying from their battle wounds and disease; others left the ranks because of disability discharges, resignations, and desertion.[2]

Conditions in camp had improved, however, since the regiment moved to Tupelo. Ashbel Smith offered an optimistic assessment of the troops, telling the *Houston Telegraph* that the army was "in excellent health and

---

[1] William P. Rogers to William McCraven, August 14, 1862, Rogers Collection, DBC; also Pace, ed., "Diary and Letters of William P. Rogers," 294–295.

[2] The *Houston Weekly Telegraph* printed a list of 117 soldiers dead, hospitalized, and missing from the 2nd Texas including names and locations of deaths, dating from April 14 to July 19, 1862. Company E had the most listed with twenty-nine total; and Company F with only two. See *The Tri-Weekly Telegraph* (Houston, TX), August 20, 1862. A separate post a few weeks later from Lt. James D. McCleery of Company B counted thirteen soldiers in the hospital and four dead dating from mid-June to early August. See James D. McClerry (McCleery) to E. H. Cushing, August 9, 1862, *The Weekly Telegraph* (Houston, TX), September 10, 1862.

discipline – full of confidence and anxious to receive the expected order to move forward. Rations [are] of good quality and in sufficient quantity." He added that the "2nd Texas is completely uniformed and every man supplied with a long range gun, or as it is commonly called a Minie Musket."[3] Soldiers still lacked other necessities, especially blankets, for the colder fall and winter months. Sam Houston in private correspondence, though, had heard his son's company, "the Bayland Guards," was "nearly naked and destitute, having lost all at the battle of Shiloh."[4]

Nevertheless, active campaigning was ongoing as summer turned to fall, and "skeleton regiments" – a term Braxton Bragg used to describe units like the 2nd Texas – needed to quickly replenish their empty ranks.[5] With the Conscription Law in place, Lt. Col. Ashbel Smith returned to Texas with orders to gather new recruits.[6] Colonel Rogers was disgusted with the prospect, telling his wife that he hoped Smith would be unsuccessful, threatening if "Gen. Price forces them upon me I shall get mad."[7] Rogers repeated these sentiments in a letter to Dr. McCraven, vowing: "I will not have them if I can help it." He asserted, "I do not want to command men who have been forced by the law into the ranks. No, give me the brave men who made a free offering of their services to their country." If compelled, he would demand a reduction in rank and transform his regiment into a battalion, "notwithstanding," he stressed, his

---

[3] Ashbel Smith quoted in the *Houston Telegraph Extra*, August 27, 1862; See also *The Weekly Telegraph* (Houston, TX), September 3, 1862.

[4] Sam Houston to Swante Magnus Swenson, August 14, 1862, in Williams and Baker, eds., *Writings of Sam Houston*, Vol. 8: 321–322. See also "H.W." to E. H. Cushing, September 3, 1862, *The Tri-Weekly Telegraph* (Houston, TX), October 1, 1862. It is not clear who "H.W." was as there were at least three different members of the regiment with those initials including Privates Henry Webster (Co. G), Henry Wehmeir (Co. H), and H. Witter (Co. I). This soldier complained that the regiment lacked blankets and "under-clothing" after having to leave such items behind in their evacuation from Corinth. There were determined efforts at home to supply the troops in the field by "private enterprise." See *The Weekly Telegraph* (Houston, TX), September 3, 1862; and "An Appeal to the Ladies of Texas, by a Texas Lady," in *The Tri-Weekly Telegraph* (Houston, TX), September 3, 1862.

[5] Bragg used this term in a letter to the CSA War Department complaining about the reduced numbers in much of his army and the lack of officers to command them as he prepared his Kentucky Campaign. See Braxton Bragg to Samuel Cooper, August 8, 1862, OR, Ser. 1, Vol. 17, pt. 2, 671–672.

[6] Sterling Price, Special Orders No. 8, August 13, 1862; and D. H. Maury, Special Orders No. 64, August 13, 1862, in Ashbel Smith, CMSR, War Department Collection of Confederate Records, RG 109, NARA, accessed via fold3.com.

[7] William P. Rogers to Martha Rogers, August 14, 1862, Rogers Collection, DBC; see also Pace, ed. "Diary and Letters of William P. Rogers," 291–292.

"*Cols. spurs were won at Shiloh & Farmington.*" Then he seemed to think better of this idea, conceding: "If they still force them upon me, why I must take the fellows & do the best I can with them."[8]

Rogers and his fellow officers would have to do the best they could as the Confederacy prepared two ambitious campaigns that fall of 1862. Bragg's Army of the Mississippi was to invade Kentucky; while Robert E. Lee's Army of Northern Virginia would march into Maryland. Their goal was both military and political: Bragg sought to draw Union forces out of northern Alabama and western Tennessee, but also to "liberate" the Bluegrass state.[9] Lee anticipated bolstering Confederate sympathizers in Maryland and amassing needed food and other supplies for his troops. A unified show of military strength would, Confederates hoped, encourage European recognition of their nascent state, and stir antiwar sentiment in the North.[10]

On August 27, 1862, Bragg notified Sterling Price and Earl Van Dorn to be prepared to "dispose of" federal forces in northern Mississippi as he advanced toward Kentucky.[11] On that same day, Price wrote Van Dorn about his "proposition to unite our forces for an aggressive campaign." "We must," Price urged Van Dorn, "attack the enemy before they begin to receive their new levies and while they are still discouraged by their late reverses. We ought to avail ourselves, too, of the moral force which we would gain by participating in the great forward movement which our armies are now making everywhere."[12]

The prospect of a "great forward movement" exhilarated the men of the 2nd Texas. It was not just an opportunity to leave the stagnant

---

[8] William P. Rogers to William McCraven, August 14, 1862, Rogers Collection, DBC; also in Pace, ed., "Diary and Letters of William P. Rogers," 294–295. Emphasis from the original with some corrections from the Pace transcription.

[9] Kenneth W. Noe, *Perryville: This Grand Havoc of Battle* (Lexington, KY: The University Press of Kentucky, 2011), 37; see also 26–27.

[10] Sterling Price to George G. Garner, September 26, 1862, OR, Ser. 1, Vol. 17, pt. 1, 120–121. For a broader discussion of Bragg's campaign and its strategic significance, see Noe, *Perryville*.

[11] Braxton Bragg to Sterling Price, August 27, 1862, OR, Ser. 1, Vol. 17, pt. 2, 688; OR adds note: "Similar letter of same date to Van Dorn at Tupelo." See also Earl Van Dorn to (Samuel Cooper), October 20, 1862, OR, Ser. 1, Vol. 17, pt. 1, 376; and Smith, *Corinth*, 119–120.

[12] Sterling Price to Earl Van Dorn, August 27, 1862, OR, Ser. 1, Vol. 17, pt. 2, 687. Van Dorn outranked Price, which would lead to confusion and frustration on both men's parts. Even Davis weighed in to clarify the hierarchy of command. See, for example, George W. Randolph to Earl Van Dorn, September 11, 1862, OR, Ser. 1, vol. 17, pt. 2, 699; and Jefferson Davis to Earl Van Dorn, September 11, 1862, OR, Ser. 1, vol. 17, pt. 2, 700.

monotony of camp life, but a chance to silence any lasting doubts about their bravery. One soldier predicted, "our gallant regiment (the 2d), under the command of the much loved and brave W. P. Rogers, will have met the vandal hordes of Lincoln, and make them feel what it is to resist the charge and fury of true Southerners."[13]

Rogers shared his soldiers' enthusiasm, writing his wife from Tupelo on August 3 that it was "highly probable" his regiment would soon march "in a northerly direction." Informed of Bragg's plans to advance into Kentucky, Rogers expected that federal troops under Don Carlos Buell would choose "either to intercept Bragg in his advance through Tennessee and Ky or to fall back to the Miss. river & thus allow Bragg to reconquer Ky and camp on the Ohio river." "If he attempts to intercept Bragg," Rogers predicted, "we will move to Bragg's support [and if] he falls back to the Missi river we will stay here to protect Mississippi." Either course cheered the colonel and he anticipated that "by the 1st of December we may look for glad tidings." He still felt the need to add: "You in Texas have but a feint idea of the horrors of war, You will have to be in a country whose soil has been crimsoned with the blood of patriots and mighty enemies have met in the shock of battle properly to appreciate its horrors."[14] More than a week later, Rogers remained confident, assuring Martha: "We hope now by the 1st of Nov to be in Yankee Land."[15]

Rogers was also heartened to learn that several of his "brother officers" from Texas and Arkansas had advocated for his appointment to major-general. Rogers worried, though, about continued bad blood with Jefferson Davis, whom he feared was "still vindictive to me" and might block his promotion. It was reassuring to Rogers, upset by the shameful accusations from Shiloh, that his fellow officers who had served with him in the "shock of battle" had such trust in his leadership.[16] The letter, signed by fourteen officers from the two states and addressed to the "Senators and Representatives from Texas and Arkansas," stated that Rogers merited the promotion because the signees were "satisfied that he

---

[13] H. W. to E. H. Cushing, September 3, 1862, *The Tri-Weekly Telegraph* (Houston, TX), October 1, 1862.

[14] William P. Rogers to Martha Rogers, August 3, 1862, Rogers Collection, DBC; also in Pace, ed., "Diary and Letters of William P. Rogers," 294–295; Pace misdates the letter August 30, 1862.

[15] William P. Rogers to Martha Rogers, August 14, 1862, Rogers Collection, DBC; see also Pace, ed. "Diary and Letters of William P. Rogers," 291–292.

[16] William P. Rogers to Martha Rogers, August 3, 1862, Rogers Collection, DBC; also in Pace, ed., "Diary and Letters of William P. Rogers," 294–295.

possesses the requisite qualifications and experience for so important a position besides having the confidence of those who will be likely to be placed under his command." Four Congressmen, including Texas Senator William S. Oldham, endorsed the letter and referred it to Davis.[17]

There was hopefulness in the air as the 2nd Texas prepared for renewed campaigning. They and their colonel believed combat could make everything right again.

"NO SUPERIOR IN POINT OF BRAVERY"

Meanwhile, the propaganda of war-making continued. The Confederate army had endured severe losses and units like the 2nd Texas had not always performed well. But at least publicly, most military and political leaders heralded Confederate soldiers' bravery, contrasting it with the enemy's alleged inherent cravenness. In a column sarcastically titled "Reward of Merit," *The Weekly Telegraph* maintained that in the past, "nations have relied mainly upon generalship and the bravery of their troops." The United States, however, the paper attested, "have inaugurated a new system. For generalship they put lying; and for bravery they use long-range guns, spades, iron-clad gunboats, and steel vests."[18] The insinuation was clear: US soldiers feared combat and sought ways to avoid it. By contrast, President Davis, in an address to the Confederate Congress in mid-August, unilaterally praised the "gallantry and good conduct of our troops," "illustrated on hard fought fields, marked by exhibitions of individual prowess which can find but few parallels in ancient or modern times." These "battle-stained soldiers" would triumph in the end, as superior men, and superior combatants.[19] Lt. Col. Ashbel Smith echoed similar sentiments, avowing the "acknowledged valor of our glorious Texians," to attract conscripts to those "now veteran regiments."[20]

---

[17] Samuel G. Earle, et al. to "The Senators and Representatives from Texas and Arkansas," August 24, 1862, in William P. Rogers CMSR, War Department Collection of Confederate Records, RG 109, NARA, accessed via fold3.com. It is not clear what Davis' reaction was since Rogers died several weeks later in early October. E. H. Cushing claimed that Rogers was promoted before Corinth but "had not yet received his commission"; however, there appears to be no corroboration of this. See *The Tri-Weekly Telegraph* (Houston, TX), December 5, 1862.

[18] *The Weekly Telegraph* (Houston, TX), August 13, 1862.

[19] Jefferson Davis, "President's Message," August 18, 1862, in *The Weekly Telegraph* (Houston, TX), September 10, 1862.

[20] Ashbel Smith to E. H. Cushing, September 15, 1862, in *The Tri-Weekly Telegraph* (Houston, TX), September 17, 1862. When there was push-back and confusion about

Telegraph editor E. H. Cushing remained determined to ensure that, at least in the pages of his newspaper, the 2nd Texas would stand out as the model of exceptional Confederate martialism. When Smith arrived in Houston on his recruiting mission, the paper told its readers: "This noble regiment has gained the greatest honor since it has been in the field, and it should be a matter of pride for any one to belong to it."[21]

To underscore the heroism and sacrifice of the regiment further, Cushing published excerpts from a letter by an unnamed minister who, like nurse Kate Cumming, witnessed Pvt. Elisha Wasson's death back in April. The letter-writer described Wasson's deep Christian faith and "superior nerve," refusing chloroform when his leg was amputated and calmly accepting his dire fate, all the while maintaining his unshakable commitment to the Confederacy. The minister stated: "I can but say to his parents and relatives, cheer up, for your son died – using his own language – 'fighting in a good cause, the cause of my country, which I would do again, if permitted.'"[22]

In the same issue that this dramatic description of Wasson's "Noble Death" appeared, Cushing penned a long editorial about the importance of "well drilled soldiers," complimenting several Texas regiments, but again singling out the 2nd Texas as "the best drilled regiment in the Confederate service. Is [It] certainly has no superior in point of bravery, at [as] was evinced in the field of Shiloh." And yet, Cushing, who had repeatedly stressed the value of training and leadership, offered a bit of a check to the boastful jingoisms that "Texas troops are as good without drill as others are with it." He argued that a well-drilled regiment would suffer fewer casualties in battle – a somewhat surprising concession given the nearly universal rhetoric (as witnessed by numerous columns in his own newspaper) about heroic deaths in combat.[23]

With or without drill, Confederate troops were about to demonstrate how superior they really were in the active campaigning of the fall of 1862. In early September, as Price waited with his army at Tupelo to unite

the law and which units these conscripts could join, Smith repeatedly defended the policy. See for example, "M" to E. H. Cushing, September 22, 1862, *The Tri-Weekly Telegraph* (Houston, TX), September 24, 1862; Ashbel Smith to E. H. Cushing, September 30, 1862, *The Tri-Weekly Telegraph* (Houston, TX), October 1, 1862; see also *The Weekly Telegraph* (Houston, TX), October 8, 1862; and *The Tri-Weekly Telegraph* (Houston, TX), October 15, 1862.

[21] *The Tri-Weekly Telegraph* (Houston, TX), September 1, 1862; also in *The Weekly Telegraph* (Houston, TX), September 3, 1862.

[22] Letter excerpted in *The Tri-Weekly Telegraph* (Houston, TX), September 3, 1862.

[23] *The Tri-Weekly Telegraph* (Houston, TX), September 3, 1862.

with Van Dorn, he received orders from Bragg to "move rapidly for Nashville."[24] Price raced northward from Tupelo toward Corinth, "pushing his columns," a member of the 2nd Texas described, "on it rapidly."[25] On September 19, Price clashed with William S. Rosecrans' troops at the Battle of Iuka in a "a sharp fight" that lasted throughout the day, resulting in a rather empty Union victory.[26] Combat was, in Price's words, "waged with severity which I have never seen surpassed."[27] Confederate losses were high but it could have been far worse if the phenomenon of an "acoustic shadow" had not muted the sounds of the battle and thus stalled Union Maj. Gen. Edward O. C. Ord from moving in support of Rosecrans. The next morning Price discovered an undefended route allowing him to slip out of town and retreat southward toward Baldywn, Mississippi.

The 2nd Texas did not participate in the battle, instead acting as skirmishers and then as a rear guard for Price's retreat. Despite their missing out on the main action, the regiment had a "spirited exchange" with federal skirmishers, displaying skills they had been practicing during their regular drills, including "some maneuvers never before attempted in the face of the enemy."[28] On their retreat, division commander Brig. Gen. Dabney H. Maury recounted that about 8 miles outside of Iuka, "the pursuing enemy was drawn into an ambuscade, admirably planned and executed by General Armstrong, Colonel Rogers, and Captain Bledsoe." The 2nd Texas and Bledsoe's battery fired on them "at short range, and were charged by McCulloch's cavalry and utterly routed." Pvt. J. Henry Cravey remembered Rogers exhorting the 2nd Texas to "give them hell boys"; they responded by doing "good work with our rifels."[29] Maury lauded his entire division, reporting that they "without exception conducted themselves on every occasion as disciplined soldiers."[30]

---

[24] Sterling Price to Earl Van Dorn, September 9, 1862, OR, Ser. 1, Vol. 17, pt. 2, 698. See also Sterling Price to Earl Van Dorn, September 5, 1862, OR, Ser. 1, Vol. 17, pt. 2, 692.

[25] "Lance Corporal," to E. H. Cushing, September 9, 1862, *The Weekly Telegraph* (Houston, TX), October 1, 1862. The identity of this soldier is unknown. George W. L. Fly remembered the "hard march" with the "last five miles at a Double-Quick," arriving at Iuka "[a]lmost exhausted," just as the federals abandoned the town. See Fly, "Before, during and after the Battle of Iuka," 2nd Texas Infantry, Regimental Files, CCWIC.

[26] U.S. Grant to Henry W. Halleck, September 20, 1862, OR, Ser. 1, Vol. 17, pt. 1, 64. Timothy Smith estimates total losses for the Union to be 790 and Confederates 525, but "probably higher" for Price's army. See Smith, *Corinth*, 126.

[27] Sterling Price to George G. Garner, September 26, 1862, OR, Ser 1, Vol. 17, pt. 1, 122.

[28] Evans, "The Second Texas Infantry," 584.

[29] Cravey, "Reminiscences," 3, THM.

[30] Dabney H. Maury to Thomas L. Snead, September 24, 1862, OR, Ser. 1, Vol. 17, pt. 1, 137.

Rogers remained keenly self-conscious of his regiment's reputation. At one point when covering Price's retreat, George Fly distinctly remembered Rogers addressing the Texans with a spirited speech to rally them forward: "Men, again you are called to the post of danger, which is the post of honor. 'Do your duty like men.'" Fly maintained: "After this short speech there was not a man of the Regiment but would have died rather than disappoint the expectations of our beloved Colonel."[31] Rogers wrote a letter to his wife underscoring how well he thought the regiment performed as skirmishers "with few exceptions." In the rear-guard action, he recounted ordering his men to "present a wall of fire between the enemy & our retreating army." Alongside Bledsoe's battery, his Texans easily defeated the Federals in a matter of minutes. Rogers asked his wife to share his positive assessments with his friend Dr. McCraven and have him publish them as he saw fit. "In all of these engagements," Rogers affirmed, "the Reg displayed the cool, obstinate & determined bravery of veterans and the Counties of Harris, Burleson, Robertson, Galveston, Gonzales, & Jackson may well be proud of them." Still, he admitted the regiment's reduced numbers, and the fact that they lacked basic supplies. With the weather turning cold and wet, he acknowledged, "the men are suffering."[32] Martha took her husband's instructions to heart, sharing it with the doctor, who made a few edits and submitted it for publication to the *Telegraph* where it appeared a few weeks later as a "private letter from an officer in the 2nd Texas."[33]

Sterling Price had avoided complete destruction of his army and masterfully escaped federal pursuit, but his troops suffered notable losses, leaving behind their sick and wounded at Iuka. In their retreat, "Morale was bad," historian Peter Cozzens writes, "discipline lax, and straggling heavy. Soldiers looted homes and robbed crops."[34] J. Henry Cravey "remembered well [there] was near two days without eney thing to

---

[31] Fly, "Before, during and after the Battle of Iuka," 2nd Texas Infantry, Regimental Files, CCWIC.

[32] Rogers counted 551 total men in his regiment, but of that number 128 were on sick leave and seventy-one on detached service "as teamsters, mechanics &c leaving me really only 342 fighting men." See William P. Rogers to Martha Rogers, September 24, 1862, Rogers Collection, DBC; also Pace, ed., "Diary and Letters of William P. Rogers, 1846–1862," 296–298.

[33] The letter appeared in the *Tri-Weekly Telegraph* (Houston, TX), October 8, 1862, less than a week after Roger's death at Corinth.

[34] Peter Cozzens, *The Darkest Days of the War: The Battles of Iuka and Corinth* (Chapel Hill, NC: The University of North Carolina Press, 1997), 132.

eat."[35] Iuka was not quite the opportunity for redemption the 2nd Texas sought. But that moment was coming in the weeks to follow.

"REMEMBER SHILOH!"

On September 28, Price finally united with Van Dorn to form the newly named "Army of West Tennessee," with Van Dorn at the helm.[36] The brash Van Dorn turned his attention back to Corinth, where Rosecrans had withdrawn most of his troops, planning what he proposed would be a decisive attack, not only to retake the town and drive the enemy out of northern Mississippi, but also to invade Tennessee. "No army," Van Dorn pronounced, "ever marched to battle with prouder steps, more hopeful countenances, or with more courage than marched the Army of West Tennessee out of Ripley on the morning of September 29 on its way to Corinth."[37] Yet, as proud and hopeful his army may well have been, many soldiers in the ranks, especially in Price's command, were still recovering from the hardships of the past several weeks.

Within Van Dorn's inner circle, few of his own officers understood just what his plan was at first, and when they did, historian Timothy Smith writes, they were "distraught and doubtful."[38] Rosecrans, realizing Van Dorn was advancing, moved to gather his forces and augment his defense of the town.[39] Van Dorn, failing to properly reconnaissance the ground his troops would soon fight upon, did not anticipate the additional fortifications the Union had constructed since Confederates abandoned Corinth in May. Van Dorn's scheme was starting to unravel even before the actual fighting commenced.[40]

---

[35] Cravey, "Reminiscences," 3, THM.

[36] The 2nd Texas remained part of D. H. Maury's Division and J. C. Moore's Second Brigade, alongside the 42nd Alabama Infantry Regiment, 35th Mississippi Infantry Regiment, 15th Arkansas Infantry Regiment, 23rd Arkansas Infantry Regiment, and Bledsoe's Battery. It is unclear when the name "Army of West Tennessee" became official, however. Nearly two weeks after Corinth, orders were issued for this designation, but Van Dorn was no longer commander. See General Orders 54, October 16, 1862, OR, Ser. 1, Vol. 17, pt. 2, 729–730. By the end of the month, the army was again "The Army of the West," under Price. See OR, Ser. 1, Vol. 17, pt. 2, 733.

[37] Earl Van Dorn to (Samuel Cooper), October 20, 1862, OR, Ser. 1, Vol. 17, pt. 1, 378.

[38] Smith, *Corinth*, 136–137; also 131–132.

[39] Rosecrans later stated that by October 1, he knew Van Dorn was preparing to attack and the only question was where he would "strike the main blow." See William S. Rosecrans to John A. Rawlins, October 25, 1862, OR, Ser 1, Vol. 17, pt. 1, 166.

[40] Smith, *Corinth*, 137.

Van Dorn was determined to attack anyway. On the morning of October 3, men from the 2nd Texas along with a company of the 35th Mississippi were deployed as skirmishers, and soon became "briskly engaged with those of the enemy."[41] At some point, the 42nd Alabama Infantry Regiment, which had never been in battle before, mistook the Confederate skirmishers for the enemy, and killed seven members of the 2nd Texas, including Lt. Joseph M. B. Haynie.[42] Lt. Charles C. Labruzan of the 42nd Alabama recalled the horror when "suddenly almost stunned by a tremendous fire seemingly in our face," he was shocked to realize they were firing into their own ranks.[43]

As the fight continued, the teenage son of the colonel, Halbert Rogers, was severely wounded. Learning of his son's injury, Rogers rode toward him distraught exclaiming, "my poor boy[,] my poor boy." Private Cravey heard the colonel declaring that if Halbert should perish, "let him dye for the good of his country." Drawing his revolver, Rogers turned his horse back toward the fray and "shouted come my brave boys let us have revenge."[44] Rogers spent the rest of the day frantically rallying his men.

---

[41] Dabney H. Maury to J. M. Loughborough, October 10, 1862, OR, Ser. 1, Vol. 17, pt. 1, 393.

[42] Cravey erroneously blamed the 35th Mississippi Volunteer Infantry for the fratricide, stating, "the old 2 never did like the 35 after would," but it was the 42nd Alabama Volunteer Infantry that made what Moore called the "unfortunate mistake." See John C. Moore to D. W. Flowerree, October 13, 1862, OR, Ser. 1, Vol. 17, pt. 1, 397–398; and Cravey, "Reminiscences," 4, THM. In his report, Moore praised the 42nd Alabama for advancing on October 3 "with remarkable steadiness, this being their first engagement," The unit mustered into service in May 1862, but most of its ranks were made up of former members from the 2nd Alabama Infantry Regiment, which had been stationed at Fort Morgan for much of its prior service. See "History of the 42d Alabama Infantry," Regimental Files, Alabama Department of Archives and History Digital Collections, digital.archives.alabama.gov. See also Smith, *Corinth*, 161–162.

[43] Charles C. Labruzan's diary is quoted in Smith, *Corinth*, 161. One historian of the Alabama regiment claimed that even though this was an "unfortunate friendly fire incident," the 42nd Alabama "reacted well to its baptism of fire, suffering less than ten wounded." See Samuel L. Askew III, "An Analysis of Unit Cohesion in the 42nd Alabama Infantry," MA Thesis. US Army Command and General Staff College (Fort Leavenworth, KS, 2003), 15.

[44] Cravey, "Reminiscences," 5, THM. Edmund H. Cummins on Maury's staff remembered Rogers telling him his son was dead. Halbert was shot in the mouth but survived and lived until 1894. See Joseph E. Chance, "William Peleg Rogers: A Short Biography," unpublished copy; and undated clipping from *The Sub-Soiler & Democrat* (Corinth, MS), January 4, 1895, in 2nd Texas Infantry, Regimental Files, CCWIC. Pvt. Mathias Conklin described Halbert's wound "in the mouth, the ball coming out at the shoulder." Conklin carried him and Adj. James W. Mangum, who was also injured, "off the field in my blanket." See excerpt from Mathias Conklin Letter, October 11, 1862, *Tri-Weekly Telegraph* (Houston, TX), October 24, 1862. Cummins' postwar account of Corinth appears in *The Cincinnati Enquirer* (Cincinnati, OH), March 29, 1885.

Intense fighting raged throughout the unseasonably hot October day with federals slowly withdrawing to the inner line of their fortifications at nightfall. "Our troops," a Union soldier surmised, were "rather rudely pushed back."[45] The 2nd Texas was in the thick of it, exhausted and having withstood heavy losses beyond the casualties of the morning. The physical and mental strain on the regiment was severe, but Charles Evans claimed that he and his comrades "slept soundly in the face of the enemy, without anything to eat."[46] Van Dorn, boastful and confident, informed Richmond that his army had "driven the enemy from every position." He assessed: "So far all is glorious and our men behaved nobly." Still, he conceded, "The loss, I am afraid is heavy."[47]

At dawn on October 4, Van Dorn determined to continue his attack, even though he had relinquished the two things central to his original scheme: surprise and close coordination of his forces. Rosecrans had concentrated his position, more than matching Van Dorn's 22,000 troops with some 25,000 men.[48] In the dark morning hours, artillery fired into the Union position, which was supposed to be followed up by a resumption of Van Dorn's advance. Federals responded in kind, and a "lively duel continued until some time after daylight."[49] Division commander Louis Hébert stalled, delaying what was supposed to be a synchronized attack all along the lines. Confederates in the ranks could only wait and watch – something one Texan later remembered as more difficult than actual combat. It was during such pauses in the killing, he wrote, "the men were subjected to the most intense mental strain, as all old soldiers know that the suspense of waiting just on the eve of battle is more trying

[45] Unnamed Union soldier's letter excerpted from the *Cincinnati Daily Commercial* (Cincinnati, OH) in the *Milwaukee Daily Sentinel* (Milwaukee, WI), October 16, 1862. Cravey also recalled that he never saw so many federals shot in the back. See Cravey, "Reminiscences," 5, THM.

[46] Evans, "The Second Texas Infantry," 586.

[47] "Official Dispatch" from Van Dorn quoted in *The Tri-Weekly Telegraph* (Houston, TX), October 17, 1862. Confederates swept Union troops back behind the outerworks of defenses into the town itself. See Smith, *Corinth*, 154–160.

[48] Rosecrans reported that he was severely outnumbered "probably two to one" into October 4, stating that Confederates "according to their own authorities" totaled 38,000 men. He wrote: "We signally defeated them with little more than half their numbers, and they fled, leaving their dead and wounded on the field." See William S. Rosecrans to John A. Rawlins, October 25, 1862, OR, Ser 1, Vol. 17, pt. 1, 168; 170. Van Dorn, however, stated his strength to be 22,000. See Earl Van Dorn to (Samuel Cooper), October 20, 1862, OR, Ser. 1, Vol. 17, pt. 1, 378.

[49] Evans, "The Second Texas Infantry," 586.

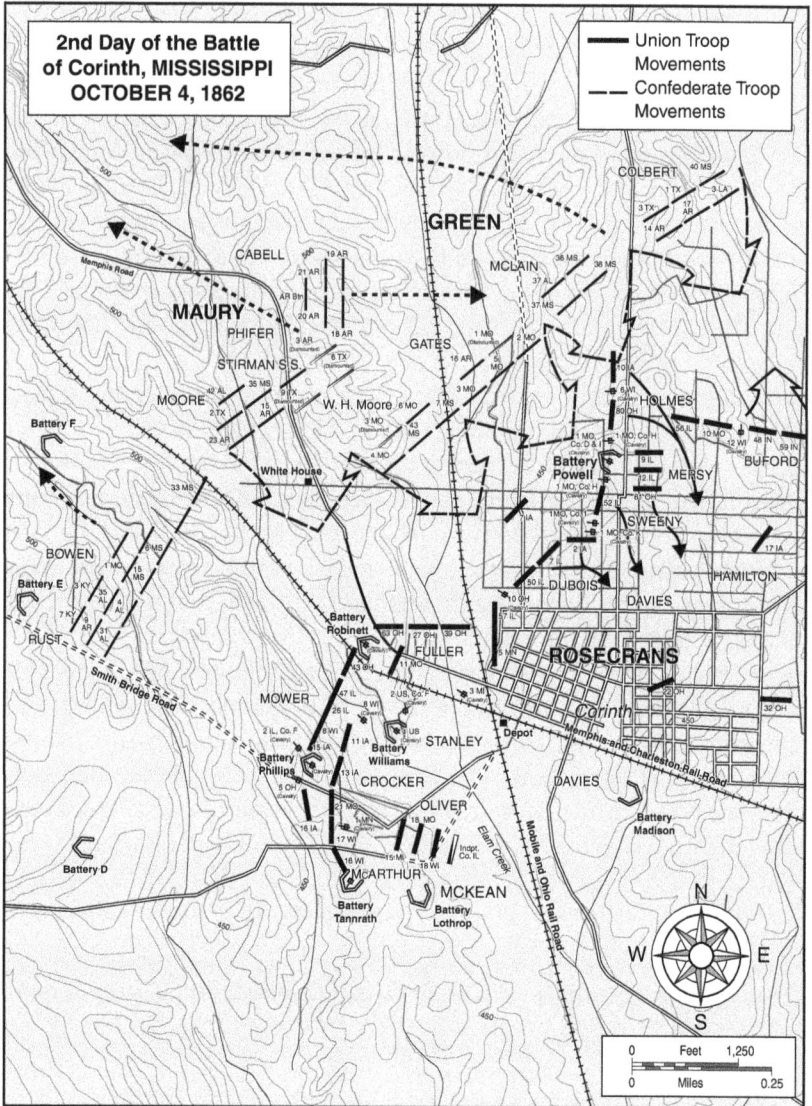

MAP 6.1 Map of the second day of the Battle of Corinth, October 4, 1862.

on the nerves than the actual conflict, in which men seem to lose the power of reflection amid the excitement and dangers of combat."[50]

[50] Evans, "The Second Texas Infantry," 587.

Around 10:00 AM, the Confederate advance finally resumed. By this time, Rogers was in command of a make-shift brigade compromising his own 2nd Texas, as well as the 6th Texas Infantry Regiment, the 9th Texas Infantry Regiment, a portion of the 35th Mississippi Infantry Regiment, and one company of the 42nd Alabama Infantry Regiment.[51] Over the next several hours, this combined force participated in successive attempts to take Battery Robinett at the center of the Union defenses. Rogers, atop his horse appeared to be everywhere at once. A Union officer recounted that it seemed the Confederate colonel lived a "charmed life."[52] After four color bearers fell in succession, Rogers snatched the 2nd Texas' regimental flag, decorated with the battle honors of "Shiloh" and "Farmington," and waved it furiously, exhorting his men to follow. The space they were to transverse was a killing field. Lieutenant Labruzan described "every foot of the ground covered with large trees and brush cut down to impede our progress." "I saw," the Alabamian wrote, "men running at full speed, stop suddenly and fall upon their faces, with their brains scattered all around; others, with legs and arms cut off shrieking with agony."[53] The day's scorching heat only added to the soldiers' misery.

After successive tries, and even some brutal hand-to-hand combat, Rogers and a small remnant of his men got close enough to mount the breastworks. Facing overwhelming numbers and unrelenting cannon and

---

[51] Stephen Sylvia notes that the large number of men Rogers led at Corinth may explain why Rogers was later misidentified as a brigadier general in post-battle accounts. It is ironic, of course, that Rogers, who desperately wanted to gain promotion to brigadier general, was credited with the rank only after his death. See Stephen Sylvia, "Battery Robinett: Relics of Col. Rogers," *North South Trader's Civil War* Vol. 32, No. 6 (2007): 32. Some sources suggest that Rogers volunteered to lead the "forlorn hope" of about 2,000 men when Price asked for volunteers to capture the battery, yet Price makes no mention of this in his report. See the account from a correspondent for the *Chicago Daily Tribune*, dated October 7, 1862, and excerpted in the *Milwaukee Daily Sentinel* (Milwaukee, WI), October 11, 1862. The *Tribune* report credited Confederate prisoners with the story of Rogers' volunteering to lead the attack.

[52] John Crane to Mrs. A. R. Howard, November 27, 1906, 2nd Texas Infantry, Regimental Files, CCWIC. Crane's full account of Corinth also appears in the *Confederate Veteran*, Vol. 15, No. 6 (June 1907): 245–246. Crane was adjutant of the 17th Wisconsin Volunteer Infantry. Evans also used this phrase ("charmed life") in his regimental history of the unit. See Evans, "The Second Texas Infantry," 608.

[53] Charles C. Labruzan, "A Rebel Officer's Account of His Experiences in the Fight at Corinth, Lieutenant Labruzan of the 42nd Alabama," included in David P. Jackson, ed., *The Colonel's Diary: Journals Kept during the Civil War by the Late Colonel Oscar L Jackson of New Castle, Pennsylvania, sometime Commander of the 63rd Regiment, O. V.I.* (Sharon, PA: n.p., 1922), 86. Jackson described the screaming rebels descending on his position, writing: "I have never lived through moments of such intense excitement. Events happened quicker than I can record them." See Jackson, ed., *Colonel's Diary*, 74.

rifle fire, the colonel hesitated. He turned to his men, waved a white handkerchief, and shouted for them to cease firing and surrender. But, as one soldier related, "We did not stop."[54] Charles Evans later speculated that the enemy either did not see him gesturing to surrender or refused to accept it; but it also appears that in the chaos of the fight, some of his men

[54] Mathias Conklin Letter, October 11, 1862, *The Tri-Weekly Telegraph* (Houston, TX), October 24, 1862. James A. McKinstry, with the 42nd Alabama, credited Capt. George W. Foster from his regiment with waving a handkerchief and ordering the men to cease fire, rather than Rogers. McKinstry, who was seventeen at the time of the battle, blamed himself for both officers' deaths, reasoning "I have always thought that perhaps if I had not fired my last shot that day we might have been permitted to surrender without being fired upon." It may well have been that both Rogers and Foster urged their men to cease firing. McKinstry described "whole bags of buckshot" and even "hand grenades" unleashed on the Confederates as they pressed forward on Battery Robinett. See J. A. McKinstry, "With Col. Rogers When He Fell. Thrilling Recollections of Fort Robinette," *Confederate Veteran* Vol. 4, No. 7 (July 1896): 221–222. John L. Mayo, another soldier from the 42nd Alabama, described Captain Foster with "a look of despair," urging his men "you had better get away from here." See *Confederate Veteran*, Vol. 4, No. 2 (February 1896): 58. Charles Labruzan Jr. with the 42nd Alabama claimed: "Someone placed a white handkerchief on Sergeant Buck's musket and took it to a porthole, but the Yankees snatched it off and took him prisoner." See, Labruzan, "A Rebel Officer's Account," 86–87. Sources further claim that Rogers attached the handkerchief to a ramrod "handed him by a soldier." See G. W. Dudley, *The Battle of Corinth, October 3–4, 1862. Including also the battle of Davis' Bridge, on Hatchie, and Skirmish at the Tuscumbia, October 5, 1862* (Iuka, MS: Vidette Press, 1899), 10. Evans stated that Pvt. Ben Weed (Co. I) "bore the flag of the regiment from the field when it fell from the nerveless grasp of the gallant Rogers." Weed died from disease three weeks later. See Evans, "The Second Texas Infantry," 590; and Ben Weed, CMSR War Department Collection of Confederate Records, RG 109, NARA, accessed via fold3.com. There was an ongoing controversy about the location flag and whether an Ohio unit captured it. See for example *The Dallas Morning News* (Dallas, TX), March 13, 1892; Charles I. Evans, Letter to the Editor, March 15, 1892, *The Dallas Morning News* (Dallas, Tx), March 17, 1892; and T. M. Church, Letter to the Editor, March 21, 1892, *The Dallas Morning News* (Dallas, TX), March 26, 1892, transcribed copies in 2nd Texas Infantry, Regimental Files, CCWIC. In 1894, Evan also identified William Weed from the 15th Arkansas as the man who saved the flag and later gave it to Clifton Parker, who then, according to Evans, resided in Bryan, Texas. However, this author has not been able to verify Weed as a member of the 15th Arkansas nor who Clifton Parker was – Parker does not appear in any roster of the 2nd Texas. See Charles I. Evans Letter to the Editor, November 3, 1894, *The Dallas Morning News* (Dallas, TX), November 9, 1894, transcribed copies in 2nd Texas Infantry, Regimental Files, CCWIC. Another source claims that it was Sgt. John Lloyd (Co. E) who "brought out with his regiment the flag, which was pierced by bullets several times while in his hands." See *History of Texas together with a Biographical History of Milam, Williamson, Bastrop, Travis, Lee and Burleson Counties* (Chicago, IL: The Lewis, 1893), 540. Whoever saved it, the banner was temporarily housed at the Texas Civil War Museum in Fort Worth, Texas, before its closing in December 2023. See Don Barnhart, "2nd Texas Flag and Rogers' Sword on Display," "Warriors of the Lone Star State Blog Spot," warriorsofthelonestar.blogspot.com.

did not know that he wanted them to capitulate. Rogers then proclaimed: "we will sell our lives as dearly as possible."[55]

And sell their lives dearly they did. Charles Labruzan "could see men failing as they attempted to run, some of their heads torn to pieces and some with the blood streaming from their backs." "It was," he lamented, "horrible."[56] Nearly every man in Rogers' small squad was killed. Seventeen-year-old Alabamian James McKinstry was shot three times but made it back safely behind Confederate lines.[57] Those unable to escape pleaded with the enemy, "shouting to spare them 'for God's sake.'"[58] Rogers' body, riddled with bullets and shrapnel wounds, was left in a ditch near the fort. Federal soldiers stripped him of his sword, scabbard, belt, blood-stained overcoat, and his boots.[59]

There is a lot to unpack in these final moments of Rogers' life and certainly some contradictions among the varying first-hand accounts. Yet, in the days and weeks leading up to Corinth, we know that Rogers was intensely aware of the accusations of cowardice made against his regiment. We know, too, that as late as one week prior to the battle, Rogers wrote his wife, concerned enough about the regiment's reputation that he wanted the 2nd Texas' participation in the Battle of Iuka, as minimal as it was, highlighted in the press. During the bloody fight on October 4, Pvt. Mathias Conklin distinctly heard the colonel exhorting his men: "Remember Shiloh!"[60] Clearly, Rogers knew, even in the din and chaos

[55] Evans, "The Second Texas Infantry," 589. Capt. George A. Williams with the 1st US Infantry, contended that the federals did see the white handkerchief allowing Rogers and a handful of his men "to come into the fort," but that the Confederates then reformed and continued fighting, implying surrendering was a ruse. See George A. Williams to H. G. Kennett, October 16, 1862, OR, Ser. 1, Vol. 17, pt. 1, 248.

[56] Labruzan, "A Rebel Officer's Account," 87.

[57] McKinstry, "With Col. Rogers When He Fell," 222.

[58] *Cincinnati Daily Commercial* (Cincinnati, OH) excerpted in the *Milwaukee Daily Sentinel* (Milwaukee, WI), October 16, 1862.

[59] Sylvia, "Battery Robinett," 29–34; Evans, "The Second Texas Infantry," Vol. 2. NPS Ranger and historian Tom Parsons tries to sort through two dozen accounts of Rogers' death, some contemporary and some postwar, to establish exactly how and where he died, concluding "they all attest to his bravery." See Tom Parsons, "The Many Deaths of Col. William P. Rogers," *Daily Corinthian* (Corinth, MS), September 8, 2013.

[60] Mathias D. Conklin Letter, October 11, 1862, published in *The Tri-Weekly Telegraph* (Houston, TX), October 24, 1862; See also *The Tri-Weekly Telegraph*, December 5, 1862. Conklin's sequence of events is a bit disjointed, and it is not entirely clear when Rogers yelled this, either on October 3 or 4, but Conklin wrote the letter just a week after the battle, so this was not a later embellishment. Conklin, a clerk from Houston, was nineteen years old when he enlisted, surviving the war, and dying in 1873, only thirty years old. See Mathias D. Conklin, CMSR, War Department Collection of Confederate

of combat, that those charges had to be addressed, and his actions suggest that the colonel equated his and his regiment's performance at Corinth to salvaging their reputations. Corinth was his opportunity to silence those humiliating allegations once and for all.

An additional anecdote highlights the extent to which the charges of cowardice haunted the 2nd Texas. In his initial report of Shiloh, John C. Moore had singled out Lt. James E. Foster as the sole exception to the rest of the company officers, whom he judged had "performed their respective parts bravely." Subsequently, he had placed Foster under arrest.[61] Capt. George W. Henry from the 11th Missouri Volunteer Infantry, years later related helping to remove bodies from the ditch, including Rogers, whom he had admiringly watched fight and fall in front of his unit's position. Henry, explaining that he was anxious to "know the name of so desperately gallant a soldier," retrieved a letter inside one of the colonel's pockets. Reading it, Henry realized it was addressed to Rogers from Lt. James Foster's wife, telling of "a report in Texas of her husband's alleged cowardice on the Shiloh field, and appealed to Rogers as a gentleman whose honor and integrity were of such high order that whatever he might say would be received absolutely true among the people of Texas."[62] That Rogers carried this letter with him into battle further underscores his awareness that such accusations went beyond harming his personal reputation or that of his regiment. Allegations of cowardice affected soldiers' families, too, like Foster's wife, who was concerned enough to ask for his help to clear her husband's name. Rogers was a man on a mission when he led those successive, but ultimately suicidal charges on Battery Robinett. He had also pinned

Records, RG 109, NARA, accessed via fold3.com; and Eighth Census of the United States, 1860: Population Schedule, Ward 4, Houston, Texas, Records of the Bureau of the Census, RG 29, NARA; accessed via ancestry.com. Thirty years after the battle, J. I. McGinnis alleged that Rogers also had his promotion on his mind (and his feud with Jefferson Davis), telling McGinnis the night of October 3: "Capt. McGinnis, to-morrow Jeff Davis must allow my promotion, or to-morrow I die." McGinnis said Davis had "a lurking dislike" of Rogers dating to the Mexican-American War. See J. I. McGinnis, Letter to the Editor, n.d., *The National Tribune* (Washington, DC), November 1, 1894.
[61] John C. Moore to J. B. Cummings, April 19, 1862, OR, Ser. 1, Vol 10, pt. 1, 563.
[62] *The National Tribune* (Washington, DC), June 28, 1894. Henry mistakenly believed Lt. James Foster was Capt. George W. Foster from the 42nd Alabama who died with Rogers. Foster, though wounded, survived the fight and would go on to gain promotion as captain. Foster's death in 1885 seemed to be under suspicious circumstances; see *The Galveston Daily News* (Galveston, TX), March 7, 1885.

a piece of paper under his uniform "giving his name, age, rank, command, and address" – evidence that he well understood the danger he faced.[63]

Yet there were also signs of doubt about Rogers' desire to sacrifice his life at Corinth. When first ordered to attack the fort, Rogers questioned staff officer Edmund Cummins, querying: "Are you sure I am ordered to take this battery?" When Cummins confirmed that he was, Rogers bellowed, "Second Texas, forward!"[64] Enmeshed in the violence, however, he appeared to realize that his misgivings were justified, and he hastily sought to save himself and his men. Waving the white flag of surrender would not have been something he or any of his fellow Texas soldiers would have anticipated when they waited anxiously for battle that morning. Surrendering did not match the militant rhetoric of war-making, nor the code of southern honor expressed by high-ranking military and political leaders, newspaper editors, and white southern women.[65] Nor did it appear to be the kind of behavior Rogers sanctioned when he told his wife Martha that he only wanted brave men to lead. But on a very human level, it was certainly understandable that Rogers would have reacted in this way; he did not want to die – even if it meant a martyr's death. But die he did.

Yet another detail revealed after federals stripped Roger's body raises additional questions. Union soldiers discovered Rogers wore body armor that fateful day an iron vest – something ridiculed in the Texas press just a few months prior. As writer David McCormick observes, "the stigma of cowardice attached itself to those wearing the vests." Nonetheless, the armament, which Rogers purchased or perhaps acquired from the battlefield at Shiloh, failed to protect him. The dented and pierced armor plate was not just a trophy for the unknown federal soldier who pilfered it from his dead body; it also speaks to Roger's mentality that

---

[63] *Richmond Daily Dispatch* (Richmond, VA), January 1, 1863. See also *The Tri-Weekly Telegraph* (Houston, TX), November 19, 1862.

[64] Rogers quoted by Cummins account in *The Cincinnati Enquirer* (Cincinnati, OH), March 29, 1885.

[65] Kenneth Greenberg emphasizes the desire of white elite southern men like Rogers to never submit or concede power, which is what surrendering in battle was in its essence. See Greenberg, *Honor and Slavery*, 91–92. For more on the concept and act of surrendering, see David Silkenat, *Raising the White Flag: How Surrender Defined the American Civil War* (Chapel Hill, NC: University of North Carolina Press, 2019). The *Telegraph* tried to shift the story by claiming that Rogers waved the white flag as the signal to cease firing, but the "cowardly and disgraceful" enemy refused to honor it. See *The Tri-Weekly Telegraph* (Houston, TX), November 12, 1862.

fateful day.[66] Rogers' body armor and attempt to surrender complicate
the portrait of the gallant Confederate soldier willing to die for his cause in
order to display, as historian Kenneth Greenberg writes, "mastery over
the fear of death."[67] One has to wonder, if captured, would Rogers have
faced further allegations of cowardice for waving the white flag and trying
to stay alive?

This we will never know. The fact of the matter was that the officers
and men of the 2nd Texas fought hard at Corinth and suffered severely.
Their colonel died in a violent, doomed assault. The question now was
whether this was enough to free them of disapprobation.

"IT WAS A MISTAKE"

For the Confederates, the battle was one of a series of unmitigated disas-
ters. Taken in combination with their defeat at the Battle of Perryville,
Kentucky, and Lee's failed campaign in Maryland culminating with the
bloody stalemate at Antietam, the fall of 1862 was a dark one for the
Confederacy. On October 11, Daniel Ruggles described the survivors of
Price's army of "about 12,000 men" as entirely "demoralized."[68] There
were several reports that captured Confederates, particularly those from
Price's command, were starving. On October 6, Col. Isham N. Haynie
wrote Gen. U. S. Grant that he had captured rebels from Moore's brigade,
including one from the 2nd Texas. "They are a miserable, squalid starved
set," Haynie told Grant.[69] Van Dorn had to concede the loss, writing
Richmond: "Exhausted from loss of sleep, wearied from hard marching
and fighting, companies and regiments without officers, our troops – let
no one censure them – gave way. The day was lost."[70]

Facing severe criticism for the defeat, Van Dorn demanded a Court of
Inquiry where he forcefully defended himself, maintaining that his plan

[66] McCormick reasons that Rogers wore the "gear" "without the imputation of cowardice."
But that is only, I would argue, because Rogers died in battle. Nor did it seem widely
known initially that Rogers wore the armor. See David McCormick, "Knights in Binding
Armor," *America's Civil War Magazine* (March 2010), www.historynet.com. See also
Sylvia, "Battery Robinett," 34. A portion of the steel vest is currently housed at the
Wisconsin Historical Society.
[67] Greenberg, *Honor & Slavery*, 88. To be sure, there are doubters that Rogers actually wore
the body plate. NPS Ranger Tom Parsons dismisses the story as myth on the Shiloh
National Military Park Facebook page, May 23, 2020, facebook.com.
[68] Daniel Ruggles to Earl Van Dorn, October 11, 1862, OR Ser. 1, Vol. 17, pt. 2, 726.
[69] I. N. Haynie to U. S. Grant, October 6, 1862, OR, Ser. 1, Vol. 17, pt. 2, 267.
[70] Earl Van Dorn to (Samuel Cooper), October 20, 1862, OR, Ser. 1, Vol. 17, pt. 1, 380.

was neither hasty nor impulsive, but carefully planned and that only the enemy's reinforcements quashed his victory. He blamed his men for being *too brave*, claiming that they "were greatly exhausted by heat, by thirst, and by the fatigue which excess of valor created." Although acquitted of all charges, including mistreating his men and inebriation, Van Dorn never commanded an army again.[71]

All of this seemed so pointless. Charles Labruzan from the 42nd Alabama, who was captured in the desperate fight for Robinett, wrote despairingly: "For the first time in many years, I cried to see our brave men slaughter so. I have never felt so bad in all my life. It is now said that our brigade was never ordered to charge such a place, and that it was a mistake. If so, it was a sad one."[72] For Pvt. J. Henry Cravey, memories of Corinth made his "blood run cold."[73]

The 2nd Texas' casualties were markedly high for a regiment already reduced to less than a third of its original strength.[74] Not only was their colonel dead, but so was Maj. John Müller, the fiery German immigrant from Galveston, killed, according to one account, "twenty steps from the breastwork of Battery Robinet[t] by a discharge of grape from a 24-pounder, while gallantly leading his regiment." Another officer, Capt. Edmond Daly (Co. D), wounded in the thigh by grapeshot, was captured and later died in a hospital in January 1863.[75] Casualties totaled 166, and

---

[71] The Court of Inquiry met in Jackson, Mississippi, over several weeks in November 1862. See OR, Ser. 1, Vol. 17, pt. 1, 414–459; quote from p. 457.

[72] Labruzan, "A Rebel Officer's Account," 88.

[73] Cravey, "Reminiscences," 6, THM. Confederate press reports were grim. One example is the *Mobile Advertiser and Register* calling Corinth "a serious disaster" and demanding a "searching investigation by the Government." See the *Mobile Advertiser and Register* (Mobile, AL), October 10, 1862; reprinted in the *Abingdon Virginian* (Abingdon, VA), October 24, 1862.

[74] *The Telegraph* reported that the regiment "went into action" at Corinth with an estimated 326 soldiers. See *The Weekly Telegraph* (Houston, TX), November 5, 1862. Evans calculated that the regiment lost "about fifty percent in killed and wounded." See Evans, "The Second Texas Infantry," 590. Capt N. L. McGinnis tallied a lower number of 125 total casualties, broken down as ten killed, thirty-nine wounded, and seventy-six missing. See N. L. McGinnis, "Recapitulation" of casualties, October 14, 1862," in "Confederate States Army Casualties: Lists and Narrative Reports, 1861–1865," War Department Collection of Confederate Records, RG 109, NARA, accessed via ancestry.com; also see *The Tri-Weekly Telegraph* (Houston, TX), November 12, 1862, for a lower number of 110 killed, wounded, and missing.

[75] "H" to E. H. Cushing, October 20, 1862, in *The Tri-Weekly Telegraph* (Houston, TX), November 10, 1862. See also Edmond Daly, CMSR, War Department Collection of Confederate Records, RG 109, NARA, accessed via fold3.com. "H" is described as a "correspondent in Price's army."

of that number, 122 were listed as missing – no doubt mostly taken prisoner, but some deserted.[76] At least six soldiers captured on the field later took the oath of allegiance to the United States.[77]

For members of the regiment who survived, their lack of basic necessities such as shoes and clothing was now critical. "This little band of heroes," one soldier described, "are in a very sad condition; at least one-third of them are actually barefooted, one half are without blankets and all are without tents."[78] Two weeks after Corinth, a mere sixty soldiers from the 2nd Texas participated in dress parade. "Our regiment," concluded Private Conklin, "is badly used up."[79]

In the weeks, months, and years following Corinth, the harsh reality of what happened to the 2nd Texas and the ambiguities about Rogers' role in the attack slowly faded from the public record.[80] Instead, a narrative coalesced around the slain Texas colonel and his "little band of heroes" dying valiantly for the Confederacy. In contrast to the Fire Zouaves at Bull Run, this plotline was unabashedly celebratory, muting any doubts about the Texas regiment and cleansing them of the stench of cowardice. Rogers became the lead protagonist, celebrated on both sides for his hero's death. Divisional commander Dabney H. Maury, in a private letter later made

---

[76] OR, Ser. 1, Vol. 17, pt. 1, 383.

[77] The defectors included three soldiers from Company A: Pvts. James Carter, Harrison Tims, and Robert Watson; one private from Company C: Aaron Morrell; and three members of Company D: Cpl. John Banks and Pvts. Charles A. Callais and John Smith; Four additional names of three men from Company A (James Dougherty, Newton M. Davis, Morse Newell) and one from Company F (Fred Gropp) were also listed as defectors in a letter to the *Telegraph*, but I have not been able to confirm this in the CMSR or other available sources. See "H" to E. H. Cushing, October 20, 1862, in *The Tri-Weekly Telegraph* (Houston, TX), November 10, 1862.

[78] "H" to E. H. Cushing, October 20, 1862, in *The Tri-Weekly Telegraph* (Houston, TX), November 10, 1862. Another letter sent to the *Telegraph* from an unidentified civilian in Mississippi stated: "The regiment suffered dreadfully." See "N" to E. H. Cushing, October 11, 1862, in *The Texas Almanac – Extra* (Austin, TX), October 30, 1862. See also "Rover," Letter to the Editor, October 19, 1862, *The Tri-Weekly Telegraph* (Houston, TX), November 3, 1862. Cushing made public the fact that Hal Runnels' mother sent the regimental hospital lint bandages, linen, pins, and some clothing in late November. See O. A. Runnels to E. H. Cushing, n.d., *The Tri-Weekly Telegraph* (Houston, TX), November 26, 1862.

[79] Mathias Conklin Letter, October 11, 1862, excerpted in *The Tri-Weekly Telegraph* (Houston, TX), October 24, 1862.

[80] Descriptions of Rogers' waving "a flag of truce" appeared in a few venues, including a letter from a soldier to editor Cushing. See "H" to E. H. Cushing, October 20, 1862, in *The Tri-Weekly Telegraph* (Houston, TX), November 10, 1862. This letter reappeared in *The Texas Almanac – Extra*, November 11, 1862; and *The Weekly Telegraph* (Houston, TX), November 12, 1862.

public, tried to console Rogers' widow Martha by assuring her of the "gallant manner" in which her "brave husband died."[81] Earl Van Dorn was hesitant to single out any individual soldier or officer in his official report of the battle, yet could not "refrain here from mentioning the conspicuous gallantry of a noble Texan, whose deeds at Corinth are the constant theme of both friends and foes. As long as courage, manliness, fortitude, patriotism, and honor exist, the name of Rogers will be revered and honored among men." Van Dorn added: "He fell in the front of battle, and died beneath the colors of his regiment, in the very center of the enemy's stronghold. He sleeps, and glory is his sentinel."[82]

Several Union soldiers, including high-ranking officers, mentioned seeing Rogers; stark images of him riding across the open space toward the fort, his death, and the sight of his body in the ditch clearly made an impression. Brig. Gen. Thomas A. Davies observed, though, that the Confederates' "brave and noble bearing," as impressive as it was, deserved "a better cause."[83] Even privately, the macabre scene affected Union soldiers. Iowan Cyrus Boyd, for example, confessed in his diary: "Although they are enemies of our government and our flag, I could not help but *pity* these poor fellows who thus went into *certain* and *sure destruction* here." "Such bravery has never been excelled in any field as the useless assaults on Robinette," he soberly stated.[84]

Northern press accounts – including excerpts from soldiers' letters– further added to the emerging narrative. Like Davies' and Boyd's observations, there was admiration but also disapproval and censure. They praised Rogers and his men for their "noble exhibition of desperate daring," but also reproached them for their foolhardiness.[85] An anecdote

[81] Dabney H. Maury to Martha Rogers, October 22, 1862, published in *The Tri-Weekly Telegraph* (Houston, TX), December 8, 1862.
[82] Earl Van Dorn to (Samuel Cooper), October 20, 1862, OR, Ser. 1, Vol. 17, Pt. I, 381.
[83] Thomas A. Davies to H. G. Kennett, October 18, 1862, OR, Ser. 1, Vol. 17, pt. 1 262. Lt. Kinzie Bates from the 1st US Infantry used similar phrasing in describing Rogers leading the attacks on Robinett, writing: "Rushing down at a run, they came on with a gallantry worthy of a better cause." Bates also claimed that he helped bury Rogers: "I gave the gallant Colonel a decent burial on the spot where he lost his life, but buried his men in one trench." See Kinzie Bates to George C. Bates, October 6, 1862, published in the *New York Daily Tribune*, October 13, 1862.
[84] Mildred Throne, ed., "The Civil War Diary of C.F. Boyd, Fifteenth Iowa Infantry. Part III," *Iowa Journal of History* Vol. 50, No. 3 (July 1952): 244.
[85] "noble exhibition" from *Cincinnati Daily Commercial* (Cincinnati, OH) excerpted in the *Milwaukee Daily Sentinel* (Milwaukee, WI), October 16, 1862; see also a *Chicago Daily Tribune* report published in the *Milwaukee Daily Sentinel* (Milwaukee, WI), October 11, 1862.

circulated that it was a Union drummer boy who shot Rogers, contrasting the desperation of the federal troops with the seemingly superhuman Rogers. Yet such a story, which is difficult to corroborate, also implied that a mere boy was able to take down this foolhardy rebel.[86] An officer in the 26th Illinois Volunteer Infantry Regiment found himself cheering Rogers on, admitting in a letter published in the *Springfield Daily Republican*: "Oh! For a few such men to lead our men as he did. I felt proud of that man just then, and I would have given worlds, just then, if he could have taken the fort and held it. I thought he deserved it."[87] "Let no intelligent man call the rebel cowards," another northerner proclaimed. "In the engagement they displayed a desperate courage seldom equaled and never surpassed."[88]

A letter from George W. Driggs, a private in the 8th Wisconsin Volunteer Infantry, perhaps best represents these mixed reactions. Writing his hometown newspaper, Driggs called the rebels: "Daring, bold, desperate and unflinching, they led on their men, while shells were bursting all around them, and bullets flying thick as hailstones into their ranks."[89] After the fight, he described seeing "rebel dead actually lay in

[86] The story seems to have originated from a column by "Ajax" entitled "What I saw at the Battle of Corinth," which described two "rebel Colonels" riding "right up to our trench," and Lieutenant Robinett taking down one of them; and then "one of the drummer boys shot down him (Rogers) from the other embrasure." See the *Milwaukee Daily Sentinel* (Milwaukee, WI), November 12, 1862. Rosecrans repeated this story in his postwar account of Corinth. See William S. Rosecrans, "The Battle of Corinth," in Robert Underwood Johnson and Clarence Cough Buel, eds. *Battles and Leaders of the Civil War: Being for the Most Part Contributions by Union and Confederate Officers. Based upon the Century War Series.* 4 Vols. (New York: The Century, 1884–1888), Vol. 2: 752. Illustrator W. C. Jackson also produced an artist's rendition of the drummer boy shooting Rogers.

[87] The unnamed lieutenant's letter originally appeared in the *Springfield Daily Republican* (Springfield, MA), and was reprinted in the *Cincinnati Daily Commercial* (Cincinnati, OH), November 20, 1862. See transcribed copy, 2nd Texas Infantry, Regimental Files, CCWIC.

[88] Letter from R. K. Miller to the *Daily State Register* (Des Moines, IA), October 29, 1862; quoted in Mildred Throne, ed., *The Civil War Diary of Cyrus F. Boyd, Fifteenth Iowa Infantry, 1861–1865* (Reprint, 1953; Baton Rouge, LA: Louisiana State University Press, 1998), 75, n7. Northern accounts appeared in southern newspapers, too, including those in Texas. See for example, "Acknowledgment of Confederate Bravery," citing a northern correspondent from Corinth praising Rogers in *The Tri-Weekly Telegraph* (Houston, TX), November 19, 1862.

[89] George W. Driggs, *Opening of the Mississippi; or Two Years Campaigning in the South-West: A Record of the Campaigns, Sieges, Actions and Marches in Which the 8th Wisconsin Volunteers Have Participated together with Correspondence by a Non-Commissioned Officer* (Madison, WI: Wm. J. Park & Co., Book and Job Printers, 1864), 109. For the original letter published in his local newspaper, see George

heaps." "I counted twenty-one bodies," he wrote, "some with their heads shot off, others with their legs and arms completely blown off. There they lay, a ghastly bloody mass of human bodies, who had forfeited their lives for their reckless and daring spirit." When Driggs spotted "an artist taking a picture" of the bodies, including Rogers, he was aghast.[90]

That "artist" was photographer Nicholas Brown, who had come to Corinth from St. Louis during the Union's occupation of the town. Brown toured the battlefield shortly after the rebel defeat and took a picture of Rogers slumped alongside other Confederate bodies near Battery Robinett. "Few other photographs of the dead," historian Earl Hess has remarked, "reveal the stark brutality of war like this one."[91] Images of deceased soldiers, reproduced and printed in popular northern newspapers, conveyed war visually in new and visceral ways. Matthew Brady and his team of assistants traveled to battlefields in the eastern theater, staging scenes to display in his New York studio. Brown was one of a handful of independent photographers in the western theater, and his picture of Rogers is one of the few wartime photographs that identifies the dead body in the image. Brown's apparently unstaged photograph of the slain Confederates sold individually and was also converted to engravings and published widely, adding to the notoriety of Rogers and his men at Corinth.[92] When this image began to circulate in print, appearing first in *Frank Leslie's Illustrated Newspaper* on November 15, 1862, and

---

W. Diggs, Letter to the Editor, October 9, 1862, *Wisconsin Daily Patriot*, (Madison, WI), October 15, 1862, accessed via Mississippians in the Confederate Army, mississippiconfederates.wordpress.com.

[90] Driggs, *Opening of the Mississippi*, 110. Driggs repeated the false rumor that Price's men "were to be issued whiskey mixed with powder to make them brave and desperate – so it was told since by one of the prisoners we took" (109).

[91] Earl J. Hess, *Banners to the Breeze: The Kentucky Campaign, Corinth and Stones River* (Lincoln, NE: University of Nebraska Press, 2010), 102.

[92] Two Union veterans later recounted purchasing copies of Brown's photographs during the war and still having them in their possession years later. Ohioan W. J. Lindsey said he bought a copy of the photo for $5; and Dr. C. W. Buvinger, who had served as surgeon with the 30th Ohio Volunteer Infantry, and conversed with Brown on the battlefield, still had a set in 1886. See *The National Tribune* (Washington, DC), July 22, 1886; and March 1, 1906. Jerome I. McGinnis recalled obtaining a copy of the photo from Union soldiers at Vicksburg after their surrender. See J. I. McGinnis, "Corinth to Vicksburg. A 2d Tex. Man Recalls a Few Incidents of that Campaign," *The National Tribune* (Washington, DC), June 28, 1894, 3; see also Bob Zeller, *The Blue and Gray in Black and White: A History of Civil War Photography* (Westport, CT: Greenwood, 2005), 87; 207, n.11); and Frances Osborn Robb, *Shot in Alabama: A History of Photography 1839–1941 and a List of Photographers* (Tuscaloosa, AL: University of Alabama Press, 2016), 61; 294–295.

described by the editors as "an exact copy of the photograph sent to us by an officer in our Western army," the emphasis began to shift from the war's brutality to Rogers' heroism. The caption accompanying *Frank Leslie's* quoted a Michigan cavalryman who heralded the rebel officer as "a brave man," "killed while planting the Confederate flag upon the parapet of the fort, from which the enemy were finally repulsed with great slaughter."[93]

These published words and visualizations helped to reconfigure the story of Rogers' death at Corinth and eventually silence any uncertainties about him or his men. *Harper's Weekly* "special artist" Alexander Simplot, who was also at Corinth, sketched a reimagined Rogers and his men breaching the ramparts of the Battery, with the rebel colonel, his head and chest thrust backward, still clutching the 2nd Texas flag, moments, it would seem, before he fell to his death.[94] Accompanying Simplot's sketch was an account by a correspondent from the *New York Tribune* who declared: "I doubt whether history has ever recorded a charge character-ized by such determined valor and bravery."[95]

Perhaps the person most instrumental in propagating the myth of Rogers at Corinth was Union Brig. Gen. William S. Rosecrans. Upon learning about the charge and the colonel's death, he ordered him buried with military honors, something commented upon repeatedly by press accounts as well as Confederate commanders. Rosecrans would continue to recite this hagiographic story of the rebel officer's fate in the years to follow, too.[96] But it may well have been that Rosecrans sought to use the example of these "gallant" rebel troops to make a point about his own army. Somewhat like Hardee's reaction at Shiloh, Rosecrans had con-fronted one of his division commanders on the battlefield, Thomas A. Davies, and angrily castigated him and his men as a "set of cowards,"

---

[93] *Frank Leslie's Illustrated Newspaper* (New York), November 15, 1862. Cushing at the *Tri-Weekly Telegraph* claimed that the "officer in command" at Corinth was so impressed with Rogers' heroism that he "had his daguerreotype taken after he was dead, as that of the bravest man he ever saw." See *The Tri-Weekly Telegraph* (Houston, TX), November 17, 1862.

[94] *Harper's Weekly*, November 1, 1862.

[95] *New York Daily Tribune* correspondent quoted in *Harper's Weekly*, November 1, 1862. Brooks Simpson notes that most "images of combat moved quickly to idealize the experience for the consumption of those at home." See Brooks D. Simpson, "The Changing Face of Battle: Corinth, October 4, 2012," Crossroads, cwcrossroads.word-press.com.

[96] Rosecrans, "The Battle of Corinth," in Johnson and Buel, eds. *Battles and Leaders of the Civil War*, Vol. 2: 752.

FIGURE 6.1 Photograph of Col. William P. Rogers and other Confederate dead at Corinth by Nicholas Brown. Rogers' body is in the foreground. Image courtesy of the Prints and Photograph Division, Library of Congress, Washington, DC.

vowing "that they never should have any military standing" in his command until they had redeemed themselves in combat. Davies bitterly complained to Rosecrans that his chastisement, which circulated in the press, had "a demoralizing effect upon the brave men," causing "injury to them throughout the country."[97] After Davies filed his official report of the battle, Rosecrans retracted his accusation, conceding that he would: "overlook the cowardly stampeding of those under my immediate observation on the second day, which gave rise to the public indignation I expressed in your presence and in theirs." He further assured Davies

---

[97] Thomas A. Davies to William S. Rosecrans, October 23, 1862, OR, Ser. 1, Vol. 17, pt. 1, 267. A month prior, Rosecrans had singled out the 17th Iowa Volunteer Infantry for "disgraceful stampeding" at Iuka, expecting that "on the first opportunity, by conspicuous gallantry, to wipe out the stain of their fair fame." See H. G. Kennett, General Orders No. 130, September 28, 1862, OR, Ser. 1, Vol. 17, pt. 1, 76. The same day that Davies complained to Rosecrans of the allegations against his division, Rosecrans pronounced that the Iowans had in fact "amply atoned for its misfortune at Iuka," and were then "among the honored regiments of his command." See William S. Rosecrans, General Orders No. 145, October 23, 1862, OR, Ser. 1, Vol. 17, pt. 1, 171.

FIGURE 6.2 "The Battle of Corinth fought October 4, 1862." Image courtesy of *Harper's Weekly*, November 1, 1862.

that he would do all he could to counter any reproachful assertions against the division.[98]

William P. Rogers, like Elmer E. Ellsworth, quickly became a wartime martyr, his death celebrated in poems and eulogies. But increasingly lost in the visualizations and exhortations of his bravery were the very human details of his life, and the worries and fears he expressed before he led that fateful charge.

"CAN WE EVER FORGET COL. ROGERS?"

For those who knew Rogers, keeping his memory alive was vitally important. A few weeks after Corinth, the officers of the 2nd Texas drafted "resolutions of respect to the memory of our late Colonel W. P. Rogers." "He was," the officers affirmed, "fast winning a glorious

---

[98] William S. Rosecrans to Thomas A. Davies, n.d., OR, Ser. 1, Vol. 17, 267. In his official report of Corinth, Rosecrans briefly referred to Rogers' leading his men "gallantly" in their attack on Robinett, but he still described his "personal mortification of witnessing" the "untoward and untimely stampede" by Davies' division. See William S. Rosecrans to John A. Rawlins, October 25, 1862, OR, Ser. 1, Vol. 17, pt. 1, 169–170.

reputation in this army and has woven for himself a crown of laurels, which shall remain green in the memories of the remnant of 'Moore's Brigade.'" Including praise from Union Gen. Thomas Davies, their resolution closed with a line from a dirge originally written for President John Tyler: "he is free from all Pain."[99]

Editor E. H. Cushing penned a lengthy tribute to the dead colonel, claiming to take details of Corinth from a "reliable letter" to portray the 2nd Texas commander as solicitous of his men and undeniably fearless. "When told to surrender he replied, 'Never! Surrender is not the Texan's motto! We conquer or die!'" Cushing alleged, conflicting with the accounts of Rogers trying to give up and save himself and his men. After he fell dead, Cushing wrote, the federals "rushed up to see the brave man, preserved his body from the slain, which was the admiration of all his enemies, and by the Yankee General buried with uncommon honors. Gen. Rosencrans [sic], though an enemy, acknowledged his bravery, and pronounced him 'the bravest of the brave in the Southern army,' and said he should be buried as 'a gentleman and a hero.'" Rogers' noble "example and revenge for his fall" would prove an inspiration for all Confederate soldiers. "History will record his gallant bearing whilst fighting against great odds," he prophesied, "and the spot upon which he fell, crimsoned with his heart's blood, will be a sacred spot to every Southerner."[100]

These accolades extended, it would appear, to the entire regiment. As one member proclaimed: "the 2d Texas has covered itself with imperishable honor, and won the esteem and admiration of the whole army."[101] And the way "Sioux," the correspondent for the *Telegraph*, saw things, northern praise of Rogers included not just to his regiment but all Texans, "whose prowess," he maintained, "has shone upon every battle field they have been placed, receive praises even from our enemy for gallant deeds and bravery."[102]

[99] The resolutions were dated October 18, 1862, but not published until December 1862. See *The Tri-Weekly Telegraph* (Houston, TX), December 19, 1862; Excerpt from Sarah S. Smith, "A Dirge: On the Death of President Taylor," in *Amaranth Blooms: A Collection of Embodied Poetical Thoughts* (Utica, NY: J. W. Fuller, 1853), 69.

[100] *The Tri-Weekly Telegraph* (Houston, TX), December 5, 1862.

[101] See "H" to E. H. Cushing, October 20, 1862, in *The Tri-Weekly Telegraph* (Houston, TX), November 10, 1862. Another tribute to Rogers is "A Friend," Letter to the Editor, October 15, 1862, in *The Tri-Weekly Telegraph* (Houston, TX), November 19, 1862.

[102] "Sioux," Letter to the Editor, November 26, 1862, *The Tri-Weekly Telegraph* (Houston, TX), November 28, 1862.

A poem aptly titled "Can We Ever Forget Col. Rogers?" praised him for his "deeds of valor," vowing to seek revenge for his death. It ended with a direct plea to his commanders:

> Forget our patriot at Corinth, I ask
> Where his daring courage surprised the foe?
> No Maury, No Moore, be this your task
> To laud his service where ere you go.[103]

Maury certainly followed this directive in his official report and emotional letter to Rogers' wife.[104]

The 2nd Texas former colonel John C. Moore, however, wrote nothing of the regiment or Rogers' dramatic death in his official report of the battle. He praised the 42nd Alabama for "rushing to the embrasures" and "driving the enemy from their guns, and then entering the work mounted the parapet" and claimed (erroneously it seems) that it was the Alabamians who planted "their flag on the walls." Similar to his reports of Shiloh, Moore also switched to the first-person plural pronoun "we" to conclude: "After entering the works we found ourselves opposed by an overwhelming force and being without support and our lines broken and disordered in the assault, we had no alternative left but to fall back, which was done." Acknowledging that his losses were "very severe," he added: "I can bear testimony to the coolness and gallantry with which our men and officers made this assault. I do not believe that any troops ever displayed greater courage in so desperate a charge." He commended his brigade's officers "one and all," for doing "their duty," declining to single out individuals, for if he mentioned "one in this connection I must mention all or do injustice." Nonetheless, he named Cpl. James A. Going, a color-bearer for the 42nd Alabama, for "particular notice."[105]

Surprisingly, Moore made no mention at all of Rogers. His failure to recognize his former regiment, and seeming confusion about which unit planted its regimental flag on the ramparts, are significant. Was it because

---

[103] "Can We Ever Forget Col. Rogers?" *The Tri-Weekly Telegraph* (Houston, TX), December 22, 1862.

[104] Maury would also make mention of Rosecrans burying Rogers with the "honors of war" in his postwar memoirs. See Dabney Herndon Maury, *Recollections of a Virginian in the Mexican, Indian and Civil Wars.* 2nd ed. (New York: Charles Scribner's, 1894), 171.

[105] John C. Moore to D. W. Flowerree, October 13, 1862, OR, Ser. 1, Vol. 17, pt. 1, 399–400. In his report, Moore condemned the behavior of the 35th Mississippi, which broke down and deserted after the fight at Hatchie (or Davis) Bridge on October 5, calling their conduct "astonishing and unaccountable."

he did not want to be associated with the Texans due to the scandalous rumors of their failure at Shiloh? Was there some kind of tension between Moore and Rogers, in the aftermath of his varying attempts to explain the Texans' performance at that battle? Might he have had incorrect or incomplete information on the fight when he filed his report only nine days from its end? It is not clear.

Whatever motives Moore had for failing to mention Rogers or the 2nd Texas at Battery Robinett, he was not yet free of his association with them. Though he claimed the rank of brigadier general in his report and commanded a brigade at Corinth, his promotion remained stymied in the Confederate Congress where it had been tabled for several weeks.[106] The most likely reason for this was William Hardee, who was still intent on besmirching the regiment's reputation and by default Moore's, too. Unlike Rosecrans in his allegations against Davies' division, Hardee refused to recant any of his allegations even after Rogers' celebrated death at Corinth; instead, he doubled down.

The timing of all of this is noteworthy. While the celebratory narrative of Rogers at Corinth was gaining traction and Moore's promotion sat dormant in Richmond, Hardee sent a letter to Confederate Adjutant and Inspector General Cooper, formally putting in writing his allegations against the 2nd Texas. Senator Louis Wigfall had heard about the rumors of the 2nd Texas' failings at Shiloh and, in turn, issued his own challenge against Hardee as the source of the rumors. Hardee set out to defend himself, explaining that he previously relayed his account orally to Generals Beauregard and Bragg, as well as Mississippi Senator James Phelan. Earlier in the summer, while reviewing a dress parade in Tupelo, Hardee spotted "Shiloh," in his words "conspicuously emblazoned on the colors of the Second Texas Regiment." This prompted him to disclose to Brig-Gen. Lewis H. Little "the facts concerning the conduct of this regiment at Shiloh," requesting Little to ask Moore for an explanation, which Hardee said he would have welcomed. Aware that Moore's promotion was stalled in Richmond, Hardee denied having any memory of requesting Senator Phelan to oppose it.[107]

---

[106] Secretaries of War G. W. Randolph and James Seddon, along with President Davis, supported Moore's promotion, but Congress repeatedly tabled it, stretching the process into the spring of 1863. See *Journal of the Congress of the Confederate States of America, 1861–1865*, 7 Vols., (Washington, DC: Government Printing Office, 1904–1905), September 19, 1862, Vol. 2: 299; 343; 392–393; 461; April 13, 1863, Vol. 3: 282; 289.

[107] William J. Hardee to Samuel Cooper, October 29, 1862, OR, Ser. 1, Vol. 10, pt. 1, 572.

In his letter to General Cooper, Hardee detailed how he had ordered the Texans into action the morning of April 7, and standing close to their position, watched in disgust as they "broke and fled disgracefully from the field." Hardee recounted how he had dispatched Capt. William Clare from his staff "to pursue and rally the regiment." Clare, however, told Hardee the Texans "could not be rallied; that a portion of the regiment swore they would not return to the field, and when told that I would call them a 'pack of cowards,' said they did not care a damn what I might call them."[108] Clare, who offered his own testimony to support Hardee's letter to Cooper, recalled one officer hiding behind a tree with other members of the unit. Shocked to witness Texas troops behaving so shamefully, he upbraided the officer for his poor conduct, relating Hardee's anger to him; the officer "replied that he didn't care a damn."[109]

Why was William J. Hardee so intent on singling out the 2nd Texas repeatedly, especially after Corinth? Some of it may have to do with Hardee's own history. As a West Point-trained officer in the Mexican-American War, Hardee had been accused of dishonorable conduct himself when Mexicans troops captured him and a small contingency of US dragoons. Recriminations against him circulated soon after the incident, alleging that Hardee had "deserted his commanding officers" and "carried off 25 men with him," resulting in his surrender. Eventually, a Court of Inquiry exonerated him, but in his lengthy defense, Hardee described how "painful and mortifying" it was to have to disprove attacks on his conduct.[110] By the second year of the Civil War, Hardee had risen quickly

---

[108] William J. Hardee to Samuel Cooper, October 29, 1862, OR, Ser. 1, Vol. 10, pt. 1, 571–572.

[109] Clare was wounded right after this heated exchange with the Texans. See William Clare to W. J. Hardee, October 29, 1862, OR, Ser. 1, Vol. 10, pt. 1, 572–573. Clare was a captain in the 7th Alabama Infantry Regiment, serving on Hardee's staff as a volunteer aid-de-camp. Clare's CMSR is full of effusive praise from military and political officials, including Mississippi Sen. James Phelan, who seemed to be referencing the 2nd Texas when he recounted Clare "whilst attempting to rally a regiment was again shot thru the foot" at Shiloh and Hardee's praise of Clare for his "distinguished gallantry" at Shiloh. See James Phelan to James A. Seddon, (April 1863); and William Hardee to Samuel Cooper, April 9, 1863, in William Clare, CMSR, War Department Collection of Confederate Records, RG 109, NARA, accessed via fold3.com.

[110] The complete transcript of the Court of Inquiry can be found in Lamont Wood, *Thornton's Luck: How America Almost Lost the Mexican-American War* (Guilford, CT: Lone Star Books, 2017), 128–162. For quotes above, see 144; 161–162. See also Nathaniel Cheairs Hughes, *General William J. Hardee: Old Reliable* (Baton Rouge, LA: Louisiana State University Press, 1965), 28–30. Hughes writes that this incident "tarnished" Hardee's reputation, but he was determined to "blot out this damaging episode with distinguished service in the coming campaigns" (30).

through the ranks of the Confederate army, proving himself as a corps commander. Yet there were doubts about his abilities the higher up the command scale he went. He was someone, his biographer writes, who "loved the color, the ceremony, the glamor, and the 'fight' of war" but generally "disliked" the "responsibilities of war."[111] Hardee took perceived slights to heart and cared a lot about the performative nature of soldiering; he had written the famed *Hardee's Tactics*, after all, the popular and widely used manual on light infantry training and drill that Elmer Ellsworth had sought to emulate with his Zouaves. Hardee admitted to telling numerous people about what he witnessed at Shiloh; and perhaps he worried that somehow with all the tributes to Rogers, the 2nd Texas' bad conduct at Shiloh would be overlooked.

To make matters worse, Senator Phelan, who had interjected himself into the dispute, conflated a separate incident that Hardee related about another Confederate regiment firing at the general at Shiloh after his attempt to rally them, insinuating that the 2nd Texas tried to kill him. Now Senator Louis Wigfall, a man with a violent history of dueling and angry outbursts, had Hardee in his sights, seeking to defend the 2nd Texas and the honor of his home state. Hardee, just as he had done decades earlier, was set on clearing his own name publicly and ensuring that what happened at Shiloh would not be forgotten.[112]

John C. Moore received a copy of Hardee's letter to Samuel Cooper in December, endorsed by President Davis "with the remark that unless I gave some satisfactory explanation, action would be taken in my case." Moore sat down to respond, methodically laying out his defense

[111] Hughes, *General William J. Hardee*, 184.
[112] Nothing else has come to light to shed light on Wigfall's charges either way, but it is worth noting that Hardee was on a parallel track to promotion at the same time as Moore, and while Moore's promotion lay dormant for months, the Confederate Congress promptly approved Hardee's. Both Texas senators, Wigfall and William Oldham, along with three others, opposed Hardee's promotion. See *Journal of the Congress of the Confederate States of America*, October 11, 1862, Vol. 2: 470. Wigfall's most recent biographer calls the senator "a violent, mercurial man," but does not reveal any additional information about this incident with Hardee either. See Edward S. Cooper, *Louis Trezevant Wigfall: The Disintegration of the Union and Collapse of the Confederacy* (Madison, NJ: Fairleigh Dickinson University Press, 2012), xi; also 101–102. Ken Noe has noted in conversation with the author that late October 1862 was also the time when Hardee was dealing with the disappointment and fallout of Bragg's failed Kentucky campaign, only adding to his discontent with the army. See also Smith, *Shiloh*, 305–307. Hardee's clarification that it was another regiment that fired on him at Shiloh and not the 2nd Texas is included in William J. Hardee to Samuel Cooper, October 29, 1862, OR, Ser. 1, Vol. 10, pt. 1: 572.

as former colonel of the 2nd Texas. He sought to correct Hardee on several errors, including the fact that Moore was not in command of the regiment on April 7; nor was the regiment ever part of Little's brigade. It was Rogers, "who died so gallantly at Corinth," leading the regiment that fateful day. Here, unlike in his report of Corinth, Moore commended the slain colonel, writing that "no braver man" had "fallen during the War." "That the Regt was repulsed and fell back in great confusion is set forth in my report," Moore stated, "but this was not confined to the Regt. but extended to the whole line; and why the Genl singles out this Regt and pronounces its members 'cowards' he can best explain." It also irked Moore that all of this seemed so backhanded: "Neither Genl Hardee nor any other officer as far as I know has openly charged me as wanting in the discharge of my duty on that occasion." He admitted that he could not rally the men, but nor could anyone else. He had witnessed "enough on that morning to satisfy me that the advance and the attack of our Brigade was a bungling, ill-managed affair." Moore had further learned that "when my name was presented to the Senate for confirmation as Brig. Genl an Honorable Senator stated that he was authorized by Genl Hardee to say that I and my Regt ran at the battle of Shiloh and thus refuted the ratification of my appointment." Recognizing that he lacked the same standing as Hardee – a friend of the president with powerful allies in Richmond – Moore could only hope "that I have sustained a good name with those of my commanding officers who know me most intimately and in their judgment and testimony I am willing to stand or fall." He asked that his letter, along with his previous reports of Shiloh, be presented to the Senate for their review.[113]

[113] John C. Moore to Samuel Cooper, December 18, 1862, Folder, "(Letters) to General Cooper, 1862–1864," John C. Moore Papers, DBC. There are three different versions of this letter in the Moore papers, including a typed copy with handwritten notes. Beyond Moore's letter indicating that Davis requested an explanation from him, this author has been unable to find Davis referencing the 2nd Texas at Shiloh directly in his correspondence. In a letter to Wigfall in September, Davis expressed his support for Moore commanding a brigade "at large" or one of all Texans, explaining: "My opinion is in this case it was in that of Hood, that the Brigade is more interested in the qualification than in the residency of its commander." See Jefferson Davis to Louis Wigfall, September 25, 1862, Folder: "Correspondence of Louis T. Wigfall, 1858–1862," Wigfall Papers, LC; see also Editors' notes, Crist, ed., *Papers of Jefferson Davis*, Vol. 8: 404. There is a cryptic letter to Wigfall and Oldham from Davis in October asking them to "confer with him on a matter of general importance and of special interest of Texas." See Jefferson Davis to William S. Oldham and Louis Wigfall, October 7, 1862, Folder: "Correspondence of Louis T. Wigfall, 1858–1862," Wigfall Papers, LC. Coincidentally, just a week after Moore wrote his letter, Davis visited Grenada, Mississippi, where Moore and the 2nd Texas

Nothing materialized from Wigfall's challenge, but Hardee was not done. In his formal report of Shiloh, filed four months later, he reiterated the story again, and although he noted other units faltering under his command, he homed in on the 2nd Texas, explaining that it would be "unjust to my brave and enduring soldiers, who stood by their colors to the end if I did not mention that many straggled from their ranks or fell back without orders." He wrote damningly that the 2nd Texas "seemed appalled, fled from the field without apparent cause, and were so dismayed that my efforts to rally them were unavailing." "It would be unjust to my brave and enduring soldiers," he added, "who stood by their colors to the end, if I did not mention that many straggled from their ranks or fell back without orders."[114]

Rogers' violent death, recast as inspirational and courageous, had not entirely redeemed the 2nd Texas. In December 1862, about the time Moore sought to defend himself in his letter to the War Department, Hal G. Runnells, the 2nd Texas' former major, wrote President Davis seeking a new commission. He stated the reason he resigned from the 2nd Texas was due to disability and not disgruntlement with his command, as implied by Rogers' letter to his wife. Runnells, though, was well "aware that a prejudice has been against the Regiment to which I was attached," but "with regard to that," he wrote, "I shall enter into no explanation." As far as his own "individual conduct on the battle field of Shiloh," Runnels directed Davis to General Withers' report of the battle, which commended him.[115]

There were contrasting stories afloat about the 2nd Texas and its officers. The veneration of Rogers would continue but Hardee's refusal to retract his allegations meant the taint of cowardice still hung heavy over the entire regiment.

were encamped. Charles Evans remembered that when Davis reviewed the troops "not a word was uttered until General Price approached, and then cheering and hurrahing for 'Old Pap' marked his course along the line of the army," displaying it would seem the soldiers' preference for Price over Davis. See Evans, "The Second Texas Infantry," 592; and Chance, *The Second Texas*, 86.

[114] William J. Hardee to Samuel Cooper, February 7, 1863, OR, Ser. I, Vol. 10, Pt. 1, 570. In the same report, Hardee listed a number of individual officers, praising them profusely for their courage. See 568–569.

[115] Hal G. Runnels to Jefferson Davis, December 23, 1862, Hal Runnels, CMSR, War Department Collection of Confederate Records, RG 109, NARA, accessed via fold3.com. Runnels became a volunteer aid on Moore's staff and was paroled at Vicksburg. His service after that is unclear. See Aragorn Storm Miller and David Park, "Runnels, Henry George (Hal)," Handbook of Texas Online, www.tshaonline.org.

"Shattered and Thinned"

Back home in Texas, news traveled slowly, not all of it accurate, in the days and weeks that followed the Confederate defeat. Civil War soldiers repeatedly complained about not getting enough letters from home; but correspondence from them to their family and friends was a valuable commodity, too, read and reread to glean bits of information about loved ones. In Jackson County, where a good number of the soldiers' families resided, Maj. Maurice Simons' wife Elizabeth learned "our men [were] driven back from Corinth. Maury's Div'n cut to pieces." "Oh," she lamented, "I dread to get letters now! Who, who are the victims[?]"[116] No word came for several days, and it seemed, Elizabeth wrote: "All who have friends in the 2nd Tx. [are] filled with gloomy forebodings[.]"[117] It was not until October 25 that Elizabeth received letters from her husband and brother confirming they were both safe; but she learned that Lt. Joseph M. B. Haynie, the victim of friendly fire on October 3, was "killed shot to pieces," and word of Colonel Rogers and other officers' deaths.[118]

In the ensuing days, a steady stream of neighbors visited the Simons' home to hear her read the letter aloud, and it was Elizabeth who notified Haynie's father, "a poor old man," that his son was dead.[119] Another letter from Maurice came a few weeks later with "an account of the suffering of the poor soldiers," inducing Elizabeth to "cut up my carpet to make blankets for some of them."[120] Elizabeth sought to cast her "burden on the Lord" and "found some comfort but felt sad."[121] Married to a Confederate officer, with enslaved people helping her run the household and care for their young daughter, Elizabeth still despaired.

---

[116] Diary Entry, October 18, 1862, Brandt, "Civil War Diary" 43. Elizabeth referenced brothers in the Confederate army, but it is not clear who they were and what unit. The 2nd Texas roster lists R. J. Hatcher in Co. D. as a conscript.

[117] Diary Entry, October 18, 1862, Brandt, "Civil War Diary," 45.

[118] Diary Entry, October 25, 1862, Brandt, "Civil War Diary," 47. Moore was also reported dead, a false rumor from the early weeks after Corinth.

[119] Diary Entry, October 26, 1862, Brandt, "Civil War Diary," 47. When Haynie left for the war, he signed his will, leaving four enslaved men, John (twenty-three), George (thirty), and Albert (thirty), and a boy Ned (thirteen) "slaves for life" to his wife Bettie; and bequeathed to his "personal effects & property" to his father, James. The four enslaved men and boy had been a "deed Gift" from his father. See Jackson County Court, Texas, *Probate Minutes, 1837–1912*, accessed via Ancestry.com. Simons mentioned various family members and soldiers of the 2nd Texas visiting her in the weeks after Corinth, including Ralph Smith, who was home recuperating. See Brandt, "Civil War Diary," 49–55.

[120] Diary Entry, November 11, 1862, Brandt, "Civil War Diary," 54.

[121] Diary Entry, November 16, 1862, Brandt, "Civil War Diary," 56.

She worried about her husband and brother but was also terrified there might be a slave uprising nearby. "God deliver us," she wrote in her diary, "from the horrors of an insurrection!"[122]

In Mississippi things looked bleak, too. Confederates consolidated forces and retreated southward along the railroad lines, which Grant sought to seize in his initial attempts to move toward Vicksburg. One member of 2nd Texas in a letter from Grenada complained of trudging through slush and mud, and giving up "nearly one fourth of the State." This *"new change of base,"* he scoffed, was shameful behavior and evidence of a man "who would rather run than fight." "There was to be no more retreating," he insisted, "right here we were to decide the fate of the State; so it was read to us on dress parade, by order of Gen. Pemberton."[123] In a speech at the state capital a few weeks later, President Davis tried to both cajole and bolster his fellow white Mississippians, telling them that they had yet to experience "the horrors of the war," as he had seen in other parts of the Confederacy; affirming, too, that Mississippians had a reputation to "never run." The question was a stark one, Davis asked: "will you be slaves or will you be independent?"[124] In other words, would Confederate soldiers and civilians be brave and stand firm; or run and retreat like a coward and a powerless slave?

Ashbel Smith, meanwhile, was actively trying to stir enlistments using his own lofty and martial rhetoric. He missed out on the fight at Corinth while in Texas on recruiting duty and trying to convince critics that the draft was necessary and beneficial. He reasoned that the "old regiments in the field," like the 2nd Texas, "have their glory already acquired to maintain and this spirit is felt by every fresh recruit who enters their ranks; they are commanded too for the most part by officers who at least are experienced." Any new recruit would then be joining these

[122] Diary Entry, November 29, 1862, Brandt, "Civil War Diary," 61. Rumors circulated of a "plot" "in which negroes from Hallettsville to Lavacca are implicated." David Gleason explores the trope of slave insurrection in Georgia and the ways in which politicians exploited such manufactured fears, but concludes that at least in that state, "real servile insurrection fears were rare." See David T. Gleason, "The Rhetoric of Insurrection and Fear: The Politics of Slave Management in Confederate Georgia," *The Journal of Southern History* Vol. 89, No. 2 (May 2023): 239.

[123] "W.H.W." to E. H. Cushing, December 10, 1862, *The Tri-Weekly Telegraph* (Houston, TX), January 19, 1863. The letter writer was most likely Sgt. William H. Walton (Co. G); but could have been Pvt. W. H. Woodall (Co. C) or Pvt. William H. Wherry (Co. B). The 2nd Texas arrived in Grenada on December 5, 1862.

[124] Jefferson Davis, "Speech at Jackson," December 26, 1862, Crist, ed., *The Papers of Jefferson Davis*, Vol. 8: 565–579.

"gallant old regiments, shattered and thinned in many a bloody, glorious battle," but keeping them from disappearing from the rolls.[125] Smith was largely successful, at least in a numerical sense, returning to Mississippi in December with nearly 200 recruits.[126]

Smith's faith in the regiment was unchanged, despite its thinned ranks. He wrote a friend: "the death of Col. Rogers places me in command of the 2d Reg. Texas. It is a glorious regiment. The best, I really believe, west of the mountains – inferior to no one in the whole army."[127] Gen. Dabney H. Maury also defended them in a letter to Smith soon after he became colonel, praising the Texans for their "drill, discipline and gallantry." "The regiment has served with me since the evacuation of Corinth, and I have no hesitation in stating that in camp, on the march, on the field of action, it was always one of the very best and staunchest regiments in my command," Dabney wrote.[128]

These were dark days that followed Corinth, but the Confederacy fought on, and so too did the 2nd Texas. It remained a skeleton of its former self; but it was also evolving into a hardened, elite unit to be reckoned with.

"WE CAN NOT HOLD OUT"

The rhetoric of cowardice and heroism remained omnipresent. Politicians and soldiers still used it to shame and to inspire men to battle, but also to bolster the spirits of those at home. A joint resolution issued by the Texas state legislature in February 1863 – soon after Hardee issued his formal report of Shiloh – "formally and sincerely tender[ed]

---

[125] Ashbel Smith to E. H. Cushing, October 14, 1862, in *The Tri-Weekly Telegraph* (Houston, TX), October 17, 1862. Smith, though, insisted that he was "not recruiting." Instead, he stated, "I come simply to receive from the authorities of Texas the men required to keep up the regiments of Texas in the field." See Ashbel Smith to E. H. Cushing, October 14, 1862, in *The Tri-Weekly Telegraph* (Houston, TX), October 17, 1862. A critic named "Ranger," attacked Smith for his "wounded" and "egotistic vanity" after a series of heated letters to the *Telegraph* on this matter. See "Ranger," Letter to the Editor, October 20, 1862, *Houston Telegraph Supplement*, November 7, 1862.

[126] Siverthrone, *Ashbel Smith of Texas*, 152. Evans was more complimentary toward the conscripts than others, calling them "good men, worthy of the State, and fit comrades of the brave men who made the reputation of the gallant Second Texas." See Evans, "The Second Texas Infantry," 594.

[127] Ashbel Smith to John Henry Bowers, n.d., Ashbel Smith Letters, Truman G. Blocker, Jr. History of Medicine Collections, Moody Medical Library, University of Texas Medical Branch, Galveston, TX.

[128] Dabney H. Maury to Ashbel Smith, January 14, 1863, OR, Ser. 1, Vol. 52, pt. 2, 409.

to the Officers and Privates in the Military Service of the country, from the State of Texas, the thanks and praises they have so justly merited, by their self-sacrificing devotion to their country, and their many deeds of valor upon every battle-field of the Confederacy." The tribute was extended to the people at home, too: "In the name of a gallant State and a gallant people we thank you."[129] Yet, despite these sentiments, the 2nd Texas was woefully understrength and taking further losses from illness, death, and desertions, as well as officer resignations.[130] Evans recalled many of the men barefoot and poorly clad to withstand the colder weather.[131]

In late December 1862, in skirmishing after the Battle of Chickasaw Bayou where Maj. Gen. William T. Sherman's troops were stymied from advancing toward Vicksburg, Lt. Col. William Timmons was mortally wounded. It was an additional blow to the regiment, losing another one of their original officers who had helped raise Company B in the early months of the war. Just prior to Timmons' death, special correspondent and former member William P. Doran reflected soberly on the regiment's past year, asking, "The noble, brave, chivalrous Rogers and Muller, where are they? Where are the noble martyrs of the old 2nd Texas Regiment, who left Houston a few months ago, so full of hope for the future?" They were gone, killed in battle or dead from disease, many filling "unknown graves."[132]

[129] "Joint Resolution," Texas State Legislature, February 21, 1863, copy in Governor Francis Richard Lubbock Records, Letterpress Book, Outgoing Correspondence, April 1862–February 1863, 501, TSLAC; Accessed via Texas Digital Archives, tsl.access.preservica.com.

[130] For example, in December 1862, two soldiers from Co. G, John F. Boren and George W. Randolph, deserted, and Captain McGinnis offered a reward for their "apprehension and delivery." See *The Tri-Weekly Telegraph* (Houston, TX), December 31, 1862. Based on their respective CMSRs, Boren and Randolph returned to the regiment to serve out their terms until the war ended. Capt. James D. McCleery (Co. B), an Irish immigrant who in November boastfully wrote a letter published in a Belfast newspaper that the Confederacy would never be "even partially subjugated," resigned in January 1863, deemed by a surgeon "completely unfit for duty." See James D. McCleery's letter to his father published in the *Belfast News* (Belfast, Antrim, Northern Ireland), April 4, 1863; and James D. McCleery, CMSR, War Department Collection of Confederate Records, RG 109, NARA, accessed via fold3.com. McCleery's letter seemed purposefully designed for publication, with him declaring Lincoln a tyrant who planned "almost imaginable horrors" "wherein white women and children would be the first victims."

[131] Evans, "The Second Texas Infantry," 591. Evans also described the men having little to eat except sweet potatoes, which he complained caused terrible heartburn.

[132] William P. Doran to E. H. Cushing, December 26, 1862, in *The Weekly Telegraph* (Houston, TX), December 31, 1862. Evans estimated that there were about 300 men in

Ashbel Smith, who returned to the regiment in January, was no William P. Rogers. He earned the grudging respect of the regiment, but his explosive temper became legendary, earning him the nickname "Jingle box." Ralph Smith explained: "These bursts of anger soon passed off but while they lasted the Colonel danced, swore, jangled his sword and denounced the object of his wrath in words that burned holes in the surrounding atmosphere."[133] Colonel Smith accepted the nickname from his volunteers, but one morning a conscript casually addressed him with it, and Smith "leaped from his stool as if shot at, grabbed the fellow by the collar, wheeled him around and began kicking him, exclaiming between kicks, 'Volunteer members to of 2nd Texas may call me Jingle but no damned conscript can do it.'"[134] Many of the "damned" conscripts that Ashbel Smith himself was so instrumental in recruiting were in his own words "the most pitiful shirks and invalids."[135] Ralph Smith likened the situation to "a team composed of a lazy mule and a spirited horse, when combined in the same regiment" with wholly different motivations to serve. "Our conscripts," Smith maintained, "never amalgamated with the 'boys' as the Colonel always called the remnant of the original volunteers, which was no doubt rather our fault than theirs, for we considered ourselves their superiors, an opinion even in which our officers shared."[136]

Unlike 11th New York, the 2nd Texas survived, with this infusion of conscripts, as an active combat unit.[137] In action at Chickasaw

the regiment by the end of December 1862, in line to fight at Chickasaw Bluffs, although there had been a good deal of straggling en route. See Evans, "The Second Texas Infantry," 592–593.

[133] Smith, *Reminiscences*, 8–9. Ralph Smith also recounted a story about Colonel Smith raging at the entire regiment when one of the soldiers "disfigured the mane and tail of the Colonel's black charger to such an extent that we were unable to recognize him." Smith threatened that "if the dastard who did this unholy deed did not come forward to be hung immediately he would throw the whole regiment in irons and make the last one of them draw for a black bean and shoot the man who got it for an example" (10).

[134] Smith, *Reminiscences*, 8–9; 12; see also Smith, "To the Daughters of the Confederacy," in *Reminiscences*, 20.

[135] Ashbel Smith described the majority of the conscripts he was transporting to Mississippi as sickly with a wide array of ailments. Of the few able-bodied men, about twenty deserted before he left Texas. See Ashbel Smith to A. G. Dickinson, December 27, 1862, in Ashbel Smith, CMSR, War Department Collection of Confederate Records, RG 109, NARA, accessed via fold3.com.

[136] Smith, *Reminiscences*, 8. Henry Cravey was more charitable toward the conscripts, at least in retrospect, estimating that Smith brought "350 brave good boys to fill the plases (*sic*) of the brave boys that had fallen in battel (*sic*)." See Cravey, "Reminiscences," 8, THM.

[137] Smith reported a strength of 468 men on May 17, 1863 – the majority of new members no doubt the conscripts he supplied a few months earlier. See OR, Ser. I, Vol. 24, 394.

Bayou in January, they received notable praise from several commanders including, John C. Pemberton, D. H. Maury, and Stephen. D. Lee, calling them "noble," "the most gallant Regiment," and "much spoken of by those who observed them."[138] Charles Evans related that when the unit marched through Vicksburg, local white women lined the streets and exclaimed: "Thank God, there's the Second Texas! They'll never desert us!"[139]

By mid-May 1863, the 2nd Texas manned a lunette along the Confederate lines outside of Vicksburg. In a reversal of roles from Corinth, this time the Texans acted as defenders of their fort against desperate frontal assaults by the Union troops. There were successive waves of attack on the lunette on May 22; cotton bags used to bolster the fort's protection were smashed apart, the cotton scattered and set ablaze by the gunfire. But the Texans held, shooting their rifles with methodical and deadly precision. Repeating the phrase Rogers had used in a letter to his wife, Ashbel Smith called their position "the place of danger; the post of honor."[140] He reported: "Our men mowed down the enemy terribly. Their men recoiled occasionally & as often returned to the

---

[138] "The noble Second Texas," from John C. Pemberton to Samuel Cooper, February 1863, OR, Ser. 1, Vol. 17, pt. 1, 668; "the most gallant Regiment," from Stephen D. Lee to James R. Currell, January 6, 1863, OR, Ser. 1, Vol. 17, pt. 1, 684–685; "much spoken of by those who observed them," from Dabney H. Maury to J. J. Reeve, January 5, 1863, OR, Ser. 1, Vol. 17, pt. 1, 679–680. Both Lee and Maury's reports were published in *The Tri-Weekly Telegraph* (Houston, TX), February 23, 1863. Maury and Pemberton also praised the slain Timmons, and regimental officers passed a motion commending his gallantry, noting, "it has pleased Almighty God to take from the regiment, within a short period of time, another of its gallant commanders." The motion appeared in *The Tri-Weekly Telegraph*, February 23, 1862. A few months later, Maj. Gen. William W. Loring praised Ashbel Smith and the 2nd Texas for defending Fort Pemberton "with great gallantry and skill" and stopping the enemy from turning their flank. See William W. Loring to R. W. Memminger, March 22, 1863, OR, Ser. 1, Vol. 24, pt. 1, 417. Other examples of individuals from the regiment publicly praised for their bravery include an obituary by William P. Doran of Capt. Edmond Daly, who died from his wounds from Corinth; and the story of two members of the 2nd Texas saving civilians, including an enslaved man, from a destroyed steamer. The Texans were labeled "gallant" and "brave." See *The Tri-Weekly Telegraph* (Houston, TX), March 30, 1863; and The *Dallas Daily Herald*, April 8, 1863.

[139] Evans, "The Second Texas Infantry," 596.

[140] Ashbel Smith to J. M. Loughborough, July 10, 1863, OR, Ser. 1, Vol. 24, pt. 2, 385. Ed Bearss echoes Ashbel Smith's words that the lunette was "the place of danger; the post of honor; the key to the center of the Southern lines." See Edwin C. Bearss, "Texas at Vicksburg," unpublished manuscript (September 1956), Vicksburg National Military Park, Vicksburg, MS (hereafter referred to as VNMP).

charge with increasing numbers." For the Texans it was "almost certain death to raise one's head for an instant above the parapet."[141]

At one point Colonel Smith yelled out: "Volunteers to clear the embrasure!" from the enemy swarming on their right. Four men, William T. Spence, T. E. Bagwell, J. A. Stewart, and Smith's nephew Ashbel Smith Kittredge, sprang into action, "discharging their guns within 5 paces of the muzzles of the assailants, [and] hurled them back headlong into the ditch outside." "The repulse was decisive"; but Bagwell and Spence were dead.[142] As the Federal attack faltered, a lone color bearer of the 99th Illinois Volunteer Infantry made his way into their fortifications. The Texans responded: "Don't shoot at that man again; he is too brave a man to be killed that way." They did not, Charles Evans maintained, want him "shot down like a dog." Instead, they cheered his "manly courage" and took him prisoner. Rather than kill the Yankee color bearer in a manner analogous to Colonel Rogers' brutal death at Corinth, the Texans felt compelled to save his life.[143] A bit of a brouhaha emerged when General

[141] Ashbel Smith to James M. Loughborough, July 8, 1863, Fold "1863," Box 2G224, Ashbel Smith Papers, DBC.

[142] William T. Spence enlisted in August 1861, was wounded slightly at Corinth, but shot in the head on May 22, dying a few days later; Twenty-five-year-old Pvt. Ashbel Smith Kittredge, who like his uncle was born in New England (in his case New Hampshire), had transferred from the 4th Tennessee Infantry in April 1863. His uncle later helped Kittredge obtain the position of instructor of tactics. After the war, Kittredge moved to California and became a judge, dying in 1899. T. E. Bagwell (also spelled "Baginell") enlisted in August 1862 and "fell dead on the platform." He is buried in the "Soldiers Rest" section of Cedar Hill Cemetery in Vicksburg. A. J. Stewart, a native of Boston and former sailor who had enlisted in August 1861, took one of the flags off the battlefield from the Union troops. See Ashbel Smith to James M. Loughborough, May 26, 1863, OR, Ser. 1, Vol. 24, pt. 3, 921; and Bagwell, Kittredge and Stewart's CMSR's, War Department Collection of Confederate Records, RG 109, NARA, accessed via fold3.com; and "T. E. Bagwell," and "Ashbel Smith Kittredge," findagrave.com.

[143] That color bearer, Thomas J. Higgins, was awarded the Congressional Medal of Honor in 1898, based on Evans' account. See *The Weekly Republican* (Newton, KS), November 19, 1897. Evans related the story publicly at a Confederate veterans' reunion in Dallas in 1896, and in his regimental history of the regiment. See Evans, "The Second Texas Infantry," 599; and *The Political Forum* (Holdrege, NE), June 10, 1896. "Thomas J. Higgins," Congressional Medal of Honor Society, www.cmohs.org. Ralph Smith also remembered the color-bearer's bravery: "Many of the boys who saw this said, 'This Yankee was loaded with gun powder and whiskey on the inside.'" In *Reminiscences* 13. Accounts of Evans' testifying in support of Higgin's medal are told by NPS staff at Vicksburg and recounted in a Facebook post marking the 200th anniversary of Pike County, Illinois. See Bob Norris, "Thomas Higgins, Medal of Honor Recipient," Pike County's 200th Birthday, Facebook Post, September 15, 2021, facebook.com. These types of stories, generalizing and abstracting the bravery of all Civil War soldiers, were part and parcel of postwar commemorations. The 2nd

Pemberton singled out Stephen Lee's brigade for praise for the fight on May 22, issuing a tortured follow-up statement that the circular "was not intended to compliment General Lee's brigade to any greater extent than any of the troops engaged in the trenches. No distinction can be drawn, all the troops having behaved with the greatest gallantry."[144]

Not everyone agreed that all Confederate soldiers were heroes. Some months prior, in December 1862, Senator Louis Wigfall had proposed that the Confederate War Department find ways to better establish "the meaning of the words 'valor and skill,'" contending that there were far too many officers who fell "out of the ranks when the fire becomes hot, throwing away arms & quitting the colors to plunder." Wigfall believed men gained promotion based purely on seniority and not on their conduct and abilities.[145]

Enduring this kind of unrelenting warfare, though, demanded more than displaying valor or possessing skills; it meant combating starvation, exposure, and disease. Officers needed to keep their men motivated but also keep them healthy. The 2nd Texas, like many Confederate troops participating in the campaigns of 1863, still lacked basic necessities, including sufficient food, clean water, and decent shoes.[146] Encamped at Grenada, J. Henry Cravey recounted that he and his comrades often would go out at night to scour for shoes to rob from dead bodies. One morning he woke up to a terrible smell: one of his comrades had stolen boots from a dead Yankee and in doing so "the skin slipped off" so when he put them on, they reeked of rotting flesh.[147]

After the failed attacks on May 22, Grant determined to lay siege to the city. Manning the trenches at Vicksburg proved an especially grueling experience: artillery fire was incessant day and night, making the threat of

---

Texas captured another enemy flag, requesting they be allowed to keep it "as a memorial of the hard day's fight." It is not clear that they were permitted to do that. See John H. Forney to R. W. Memminger, May 26, 1863, OR, Ser. 1, Vol. 24, pt. 3, 921; Ashbel Smith to James M. Loughborough, May 26, 1863, OR, Ser. 1, Vol. 24, pt. 3, 921; John C. Moore to R. W. Memminger, May 26, 1863, OR, Ser. 1, Vol. 24, pt. 3, 921.

[144] R. W. Memminger to Joh S. Bowen, John H. Forney, Martin Luther Smith, May 23, 1863, OR, Ser. 1, Vol. 24, pt. 3, 909; see also R. W. Memminger to Marlin L. Smith, May 24, 1863, OR, Ser. 1, Vol. 24, pt. 3, 913.

[145] Louis T. Wigfall to James A. Seddon, December 5, 1862, Letters Received by the Confederate Adjutant and Inspector General, 1861–1865, War Department Collection of Confederate Records RG 109, NARA; accessed via fold3.com.

[146] Smith, "Reminiscences," 12.

[147] Based on Cravey's other comments, it appears that this anecdote dates from the time the 2nd Texas was stationed at Grenada, Mississippi, in early December 1862. Cravey noted that when Smith returned to the regiment in January, he brought a large supply of donated clothes and blankets. See Cravey, "Reminiscences," 7–8, THM.

death constant. Soldiers improvised weapons with makeshift grenades – a cannon shell, manually lit, and thrown over the trench; and "fire-balls" – bullets wrapped in rags soaked with turpentine and then shot out of a musket.[148] Rations were low, fresh water scarce, and space cramped. In addition to the constant shelling, men were exposed to blistering heat and pouring rains. At times, the trenches filled completely with water, only adding to the soldiers' discomfort and inability to sleep. Colonel Smith reported that his men, already "[d]irty and ragged" when they arrived in Vicksburg, had but one blanket "to bivouac in the mud."[149] It was difficult to stay mentally alert let alone physically safe. Almost every day, a member of the 2nd Texas was killed or wounded, often shot in the head as that was the part of the body most exposed to enemy fire. On June 26, twenty-three-year-old Sgt. Alexander Frazier (Co. E) recorded: "This is the fortieth day we have lain in these ditches with the enemys deadly missels passing in showers over our heads and their deadly canon battering away at our works and about one hundred of our Regt. have been killed and wounded, and still no succor is at hand yet I think we can not hold out but few days more[.]"[150] Major Simons despaired that all "this suffering of human life" made men "deaf to every feeling of

---

[148] General Forney described Lt. William Allen of the 2nd Texas throwing these "turpentine fire-balls" with great effect. See John H. Forney to R. W. Memminger, July 2, 1863, OR, Ser. 1, Vol. 24, pt. 2, 364–365. See also John H. Forney to R. W. Memminger, July 21, 1863, OR, Ser. 1, Vol. 24, pt. 2, 367.

[149] Ashbel Smith to J. M. Loughborough, July 10, 1863, OR, Ser. 1 Vol. 24, pt. 2, 392.

[150] Alex Frazier Diary, June 26, 1863, McCardle Research Library, Old Warren County Courthouse, Vicksburg, MS. Spelling retained from original (hereafter referred to as OWCC). Frazier recorded men killed or wounded nearly every day, counting 106 total (forty-six killed and sixty wounded) in his entry for, July 8, 1863. The official casualty returns from the regiment list thirty-nine officers and enlisted men killed and sixty-four wounded, with a total of 103. The 2nd Texas had the most aggregate casualties in their brigade and the second most in their division (after the 3rd Louisiana Infantry). See OR, Ser. 1, Vol. 24, pt. 2, 369. Ashbel Smith offered a much higher estimate with fifty-three killed, seventy-three wounded, and fifteen missing out of an aggregate of 468. See Ashbel Smith to J. M. Loughborough, July 10, 1863, OR, Ser. 1, Vol. 24, pt. 2, 394; and "Report of the Killed, wounded and missing and died of disease or privation of the 2d Regt. Texas Vol. Inf. in the siege of Vicksburg." N.d. in Folder "Military Orders and Reports," Box 2G236, Ashbel Smith Papers, DBC. In contrast to Smith's calculations, an unidentified member of the unit going by "H.P." wrote *The Tri-Weekly Telegraph*: "This regiment went into Vicksburg with two hundred and seventy-eight men, and came out with one hundred and seventy-two. Killed, wounded and missing, one hundred and six." H.P. included an incomplete list of the regiment's killed and wounded from regimental chaplain Thomas H. Brenan. See *The Tri-Weekly Telegraph* (Houston, TX), July 24, 1863. Pvt. James Holliday (Co. A) also provided a detailed list of regimental casualties (totaling 106), printed in *The Tri-Weekly Telegraph* (Houston, TX), July 27, 1863.

humanity," except to seek "his brothers blood." Simons could only pray to God that he would "raise thy mighty army in our defense & cause this dreadfull war to ceas[e]."[151]

Siege warfare was ruthless. It reconfigured the very meaning of heroism and cowardice. Whereas Chaplain Foster mused candidly about Vicksburg "making cowards of the bravest men," Ralph Smith recalled a good number of "parsons" disappearing from the lines. "I suppose that their prayers of our success might ascend to the throne of grace unmixed with the unholy sound of war," he mused bitterly.[152] Referring to lowly "third Lieutenants," who abruptly felt the need to volunteer for detached service, Smith dismissed them derisively as "dog robbers."[153] Hal Runnells' behavior during the siege, though, left a lasting impression on the private. The man whom Rogers had castigated and blamed for spreading malicious rumors about the regiment at Shiloh was now a staff officer under Moore. Smith remembered Runnels seeming "to court death daily." There was one location on the lines that the rest of the men deemed especially dangerous and steadfastly avoided, but Runnels, Ralph Smith wrote, "in passing from headquarters to the trenches, walked this death trap as calmly as if he were taking a walk in a quiet garden far from the scenes of war." This did not seem like heroism to Smith. Instead, he reasoned, that the major had "been under special protection of the god of war."[154]

When Pemberton polled his officers to ask if their troops had the ability to evacuate the lines in lieu of a surrender, they demurred. The regimental commanders in Moore's brigade stated: "In our opinion, the physical condition and general health and strength of our men are not such as to enable them to make the marches and undergo the fatigues necessary

[151] Braudaway, "The Civil War Journal," 67. Chaplain Foster described life in the trenches in his letter to his wife. See Urquhart, ed., Vicksburg, 47–48; See also Evans, "The Second Texas Infantry," 603.

[152] Chaplain Foster spent most of the siege tending to the wounded and sick in makeshift hospitals. He described escaping to a cave for safety for one night but determined that it was too claustrophobic and uncomfortable, so he took his chances in the open lines. See Urquhart, ed., Vicksburg: Southern City under Siege, 38. The 2nd Texas Chaplain Thomas H. Brenan, a native South Carolinian and veteran of the Texas Revolution, had two sons serving with him, Eugene Brenan and David R. Brenan. See The Houston Post (Houston, TX), July 31, 1905; and Galveston Daily News (Galveston, TX), June 2, 1895; see also the David R. Brenan, CMSR, War Department Collection of Confederate Records, RG 109, NARA, accessed via fold3.com.

[153] Smith, Reminiscences, 13.

[154] Smith, Reminiscences, 14

to accomplish the successful evacuation of Vicksburg."[155] General Pemberton sought terms for surrender on July 3; the next day, the siege was over and the Union triumphant in one of the most important victories of the entire war. For all his earnest prayers for peace, Major Simons found it "truly disgusting to see" the enemy "walking the streets with negroes as if there was no distinction in the races."[156]

In addition to the jolt to their sense of white supremacy, the Texans complained of an inherent unfairness in this type of warfare. Runnels' recklessness aside, how could Confederate soldiers display their manly valor when everything came down to a matter of grinding attrition? Private Cravey refused to concede that General Grant and his army defeated them: "They starved us out. Thay was not abel to whyp or run over us so they stareved us out."[157] "Only those who were a near witness of the siege of Vicksburg will ever have a true conception of the endurance and suffering of these men," Colonel Moore affirmed. Only those "who stood at their post until overpowered, not by the enemy, but by the wants of nature," could relate to this experience. His "former regiment, "the veteran and gallant" 2nd Texas, endured this particularly well, he judged, with good cheer.[158]

Ashbel Smith viewed Vicksburg as continuing the redemption story for the 2nd Texas. Emphasizing their bravery and the significance of their position at the lunette, Smith described:

Up to the last moment of the siege, the men bore with unrepining cheerfulness and undaunted spirit the fatigues of almost continual position under arms, of frequent working parties by night and day, the broiling of the midday sun in summer with no shelter, the chilling night dews, the cramped inaction at all times in the trenches, short rations, at times drenched with rain and bivouacking in the mud, together with the discomforts inseparable from their having no change of clothing and an insufficient supply of water for cleanliness, tired, ragged, dirty, barefoot, hungry, covered with vermin, with a scanty supply of ammunition, almost hand to hand with the enemy, and beleaguered on every side, with no prospect and little hope of relief – when I think of their cheerfulness and buoyant courage under these

---

[155] William S. Barry, J. F. Dowdell, W. B. Corbet, Ashbel Smith, John H. Higley, Thomas C. Lanier to John C. Moore, July 2, 1863, OR, Ser. 1, Vol. 24, pt. 2, 383.

[156] Braudaway, "The Civil War Journal," 92–93.

[157] Cravey, "Reminiscences," 10.

[158] John. C. Moore to S. Croom, July 8, 1863, OR, Ser. 1, Vol. 24, pt. 2, 382. Evans in his postwar account built on these sentiments, writing: "Many had met death with a smile upon their lips, all had cheerfully encountered danger, and without a murmur had been borne privations and hardships well calculated to test their manhood. They had made a heroic defense." See Evans, "The Second Texas Infantry," 604.

circumstances, the alacrity with which they performed every duty, it appears to me no commendation of these soldiers can be too great.[159]

More than a year after the campaign had ended, Smith was still smarting over what he perceived to be continued disrespect toward his regiment in some quarters of the Confederate high command. Worried that his original reports of the Vicksburg campaign were lost, he asked that an extra copy of the longer one he had penned on July 10 be sent to Richmond, explaining that it was "necessary that my regiment may have its proper status and repute in the War Department."[160] In his second report, he vaguely acknowledged individual exceptions to his glowing assessments of Texans' good behavior; and yet, despite the "misfortune" of the surrender, he insisted that the failed campaign was "not a wholly unredeemed disaster," certainly not for his command. In language that appeared to reference questions about the regiment's bravery, Smith declared: "The Second Texas Infantry achieved one victory – they utterly destroyed any prestige which the enemy might have heretofore felt when the soldiers they should encounter should be Texans." This, he argued, "was evinced in the marked and special respect with which the enemy, officers and men, after the surrender, during our stay in Vicksburg, were wont to treat and speak of the members of the Second Texas Infantry." He declared: "When the Second Texas Infantry marched through the chain of the enemy's sentinels, the spirits of most of the men were even then at the highest pitch of lightening valor."[161]

If Corinth did not silence questions over the 2nd Texas' bravery, surely Vicksburg did. At least that was what Smith and others were determined to prove. The regiment, though, would never participate in another campaign.

"VIRTUALLY DISORGANIZED"

Rather than wait out their exchange, the bulk of the 2nd Texas unceremoniously went home. A northern journalist described the moment when the regiment reached Warrenton, Mississippi, on its way to parole camp,

---

[159] Ashbel Smith to J. M. Loughborough, July 10, 1863, OR, Ser. 1, Vol. 24, pt. 2, 393.

[160] Ashbel Smith to John C. Pemberton, July_1864, OR, Ser. 1, Vol. 24, pt. 2, 384.

[161] Smith wrote two reports on the Vicksburg campaign, one dated July 8, 1863, and the second, far lengthier account on July 10, 1863 – the latter one is included in the OR; and the former is found in his personal papers. See Ashbel Smith to James M. Loughborough, July 8, 1863, Folder "1863," Box 2G224, Ashbel Smith Papers, DBC; and Ashbel Smith to J. M. Loughborough, July 10, 1863, OR, Ser. 1, Vol. 24, pt. 2, 394. In the second report, Smith listed casualties from the Vicksburg campaign as thirty-eight killed, seventy-five wounded, fifteen missing, and eleven dead from disease, totaling 139.

and then abruptly "refused to go any further, and without halting turned off from the Jackson road, leaving the three field officers to represent their regiment." Those officers, "had no real way to stop them," as the men, "coolly took their own course in spite of threats and expostulations." The men refused to listen. "The Confederacy was played out, they said; they wanted to go home and were determined to do so," reported the correspondent.[162] In echoes of what happened to the 11th New York and their virtual disbandment after Bull Run, the Texans became "virtually disorganized" and scattered into small groups.[163] Henry Cravey, along with his brother Bill and Sylvester Head, set out on their own, constructing a crude boat to cross the Mississippi, feeling "like birdes [*sic*] let out of a cage." "We was," he remembered, "on our way home."[164] Not everyone, however, welcomed them back. They were

---

[162] The Texans were not the only ones who refused to go to the parole camp in Demopolis, Alabama. Three other regiments, most of the 3rd and 26th Missouri Infantry and 26th Louisiana Infantry, according to this report, followed suit and went home, too. The journalist is identified as the "Vicksburg correspondent of the N.Y. *Tribune*." See the *Milwaukee Daily Sentinel* (Milwaukee, WI), August 1, 1863; also *Richmond Daily Dispatch* (Richmond, VA), August 3, 1863. Another report listed more than a dozen regiments and batteries that "returned to their homes after the surrender of Vicksburg." See OR, Ser. 1, Vol. 24, pt. 1060. John C. Pemberton complained to Jefferson Davis that his men had been "misled by many officers," and "insist on going home." Powerless to stop them without the threat of arms, he stated: "It is not to avoid a camp for paroled prisoners, but a determination to see their families." He estimated that all the troops from the Trans-Mississippi and Mississippi went home, and he expected those from Georgia, Alabama, and Tennessee to follow. To mitigate the losses, Pemberton asked to issue furloughs confident that "it will bring back nine-tenths of the men who will not otherwise return." See John C. Pemberton to Jefferson Davis, July 17, 1863, OR, Ser. 1, Vol. 24, pt. 3, 1010. Ralph Smith erroneously claimed that he and his comrades had authorization "to go where we pleased and command ourselves according to our own free will, with the exception that we were not to take up arms against the United States." See Smith, *Reminiscences*, 15. Ashbel Smith repeatedly defended the regiment for going home, insisting that formally issuing individual furloughs was impractical given the circumstances. See Ashbel Smith to S. S. Anderson, September 25, 1863, Ashbel Smith, CMSR, War Department Collection of Confederate Records, RG 109, NARA, accessed via fold3.com.

[163] Unnamed newspaper clipping (October 13, 1907), 2nd Texas Infantry, Regimental Files, VNMP. Frazier described: "we all scatered and went our own way," with his "crowd" heading south to Warrenton, Mississippi, and building a makeshift raft to the Mississippi River. See Frazier Diary, July 11 and 12, 1863, OWCC. Spelling retained from the original.

[164] Cravey, "Reminiscences," 11, THM. Three other soldiers from Co. A joined them: Henry O. Graves, Wash Herring, and Lem S. Ward. Herring notably was fifty-one years old and joined in October 1862 in Houston, and may have been a conscript. He served as a cook to regimental officers. See Wash Herring, CMSR, War Department Collection of Confederate Records, RG 109, NARA, accessed via fold3.com.

dirty, raw and hungry. At Beaumont, people slammed doors in their faces when Craven and his comrades begged for food. A "grate big fellow" Craven identified as "Jo Porter" of Co. K, seized a commissary captain by the throat and threatened that "he would wipe the ground up with him right there" if he did not provide them with something to eat.[165]

Meanwhile, John C. Moore was still enmeshed in the fallout from Hardee's Shiloh incriminations. There is no evidence that Moore received a response to his December 1862 letter to Richmond and then, in the aftermath of the reorganization of the army after Vicksburg, he found himself under Hardee's rule again when Hardee was assigned to the parole camp at Demopolis. Upon taking command, Hardee issued a bombastic statement, urging those men who had not yet rejoined their units to do so: "Come to your colors and stand beside your comrades, who, with heroic constancy, are confronting the enemy." It was again a stark choice: "Choose now between the glory of successfully defending all that entitles you to the name of men, and the infamy of creeping abjectly to the feet of a foe who will spurn your submission and despise your cowardice."[166] Moore, though, despised Hardee and desperately hoped to find a way out of serving with him ever again. His ally Dabney H. Maury repeatedly requested that Moore be reassigned to his District of the Gulf defending Mobile, Alabama, contending: "He has no real command nor important duty. His ability, skill, and experience will be most important to me at

---

[165] Cravey, "Reminiscences," 12–13, THM. There was no "Jo Porter" in Co. K; the only Joseph M. Porter was in Co. I. However, Sgt. John A. Porter from Co. I was listed as six foot two inches in his CMSR, War Department Collection of Confederate Records, RG 109, NARA, accessed via fold3.com. To get control of the dispersed troops, Pemberton ordered Smith on July 17 to return to Texas to "collect & organize his regiment" and then "report with it at Demopolis." Still, there was confusion over the furloughs and who was authorized to allot them. Smith ended up issuing a forty-day furlough to his entire regiment, ordering them to then gather at their new headquarters in Texas in late August or "they will be considered as deserters." See John C. Pemberton Orders to Ashbel Smith, July 17, 1863, Folder "1863"; Box 2G224, Ashbel Smith Papers, DBC; and Ashbel Smith, General Orders, July 17, 1863, Folder "Military Orders and Reports," Box 2G236, Ashbel Smith Papers, DBC. In December 1863, only twenty-nine men from the regiment were accounted for in the parole camp in Enterprise, Mississippi: "The large majority of the officers and men have crossed the Mississippi River." See "Abstract from paroled and exchange prisoners," December 1, 1863, OR, Ser. 1, Vol. 31, pt. 3, 773. See also Ashbel Smith to Samuel Cooper, February 27, 1864, Letters Received by the Confederate Adjutant and Inspector General, 1861–1865, RG 109, NARA, accessed via fold3.com.

[166] William J. Hardee quoted in the *Richmond Daily Dispatch* (Richmond, VA), September 10, 1863.

this time."[167] Orders for his reassignment were finally issued in November 1863, but then reversed without explanation one month later; he was simply told to "to rejoin his former brigade in Lieutenant-General Hardee' command."[168]

Moore grudgingly accepted his fate, fighting under Hardee at the Battle of Lookout Mountain, but then opted to resign rather than withstand the continued humiliation of serving with a man who accused him of cowardice in combat. When his resignation was rejected, he visited Richmond to make his case personally to President Davis. His resignation was finally accepted on February 3, 1864. Officers from the 40th and 42nd Alabama in Moore's brigade issued a resolution expressing their "unfeigned regret" at the loss of their commander. They praised his "fidelity to the duties of his high office, his impartial administration of justice, his courtesy in the private walks of life and his coolness and gallantry on the field that won our admiration and deeply endeared him to us all." The soldiers saw Moore's resignation as a painful loss not just to them but to the Confederacy as a whole. He was, they affirmed: "An officer who has attested his devotion to her cause on every battlefield in the west from Shiloh to Missionary Ridge."[169]

Later that spring, Maj. Gen. John H. Forney, who had served with Moore at Vicksburg, wrote Samuel Cooper on Moore's behalf: "The causes which, (as he conceived) compelled him to tender his resignation are I suppose known to you. Although the tender of his resignation was voluntary, I am satisfied he would not have taken the step, could he have felt that he could

---

[167] Dabney H. Maury to Samuel Cooper, September 9, 1863, OR, Ser. 1, Vol. 31, pt. 3, 852; see also Dabney H. Maury to Joseph E. Johnston, August 31, 1863, OR, Ser. 1, Vol. 26, pt. 2, 190. Simons mentioned Moore's keen desire to go to Mobile and take him along, but Simons refused. He also referenced Moore's disappointment that the 2nd Texas was no longer part of his brigade, seeming to blame Hardee, but at that time (late August 1863), the regiment had largely dissolved after their parole. See Braudaway, "The Civil War Journal," 101–102; 108.

[168] See Special, Orders, No. 278, November 23, 1863, OR, Ser. 1, Vol. 31, pt. 3, 741; Special Orders No. 117, December 10, 1863, OR, Ser. 1, Vol. 31, pt.3, 852–853; and "Abstract from returns of the Department of the Gulf, Maj. Gen. Dabney H. Maury, C. S. Army, commanding, for December 17, 1863; headquarters, Mobile, Ala.," OR, Ser. 1, Vol. 26, pt. 2, 511; Dabney H. Maury to Samuel Cooper, December 21, 1863, OR, Ser. 1, pt. 3, 851–852; Samuel Cooper to Dabney H. Maury, December 23, 1863, OR, Ser. 1, Vol. 26, pt. 2, 527; and Samuel Cooper, "Indorsement," December 23, 1863, OR, Ser. 1, Vol. 31, pt. 3, 849.

[169] Resolutions from Officers in Moore's Brigade, Stewart's Division, Hardee's Corps, Army of Tennessee, March 7, 1864, Folder, "(Letters) to General S. Cooper, 1862–1864," Moore Papers, DBC.

retain his self respect and longer remain in the Corps in which he was thus serving." Forney urged Moore to seek help from Senator Wigfall to "put the ball in motion" or other prominent politicians to obtain him a commission in Lee's army.[170] But nothing came of Forney's efforts, and it is not known if Moore communicated with Wigfall at all. Essentially, his career in the Confederate army ended under the cloud of Shiloh.[171]

In September 1863, the 2nd Texas was formally exchanged, and Colonel Smith received orders to reorganize the unit in Houston in preparation for service with Maj. Gen. John B. Magruder at Sabine Pass. Smith declared that this offered a new chance for the regiment to defend their home state and prepare "again *for duty in the field*."[172] But Smith disappointedly reported that his men were returning "very slowly and reluctantly." He blamed the unclear status of their exchange. Without acknowledging that so many of the unit had gone home against orders, Smith contended that a "large number of the men have at all times since the surrender at Vicksburg expressed the greatest readiness and desire to return to active service on being exchanged, many of them have engaged recruits to accompany them on rejoining their command." He pledged that upon confirmation of their exchange, "the entire regiment will flock to their old standard with the greatest alacrity," affirming: "At no moment have they been in the slightest degree demoralized; they have been full of fight from the surrender of Vicksburg to the present time." Still, Smith warned that unless the men believed they had to report or faced any sort of punishment, he was unwilling to force the issue.[173]

---

[170] John H. Forney to Samuel Cooper, May 11, 1864, Moore Papers, DBC; John H. Forney to John C. Moore, May 11, 1864, Moore Papers, DBC.

[171] There is some confusion over whether Moore returned to service. His CMSR indicates that he was reappointed as Lieutenant Colonel in the Confederate States Army commanding "Local Defense Troops" in August and later assigned to defending the Selma, Alabama, arsenal. But there are some discrepancies with dates, and it is not clear that this is the same Moore. See John C. Moore, CMSR, War Department Collection of Confederate Records, RG 109, NARA, accessed via fold3.com; and Evans, "The Second Texas Infantry," 606; also Chance, *The Second Texas*, 89.

[172] Special Order No. 252, September 17, 1863, Ashbel Smith, CMSR, War Department Collection of Confederate Records, RG 109, NARA, accessed via fold3.com; emphasis from original. See also *Richmond Daily Dispatch* (Richmond, VA), September 14, 1863. In late August, Smith had asked for an extension to the furloughs he issued the men who had gone home to Texas, and that once reformed, the 2nd Texas "be retained for duty this the Western side of the Mississippi River." Ashbel Smith to S. S. Anderson, August 29, 1863, Folder "1863," Box 2G224, Ashbel Smith Papers, DBC.

[173] Ashbel Smith claimed that other unnamed regiments had deserted without repercussions. See Ashbel Smith to Albert N. Mills, September 24, 1863; also Ashbel Smith to

By October 1863, Smith had command of a reconstituted 2nd Texas Infantry Regiment quartered at its old camp just outside of Houston. The contrast to its prior self was stark. Two years earlier, the Texans were confident and boastful, convinced they could "wipe the best brigade of Yankees that ever entered the field off the face of the earth any morning before breakfast." But now, after combat, disease, and other deprivations, and those searing charges of cowardice, it was a very different regiment. "We had learned," one member reflected, "many things about war that tended to lesson our zeal for glory." Less zealous for combat than they were when they enlisted, Smith admitted: "Orders that met our approval we obeyed but others we evaded as all old soldiers know well how to do."[174]

Signs of despair were apparent. At one point, officers of the regiment accepted a Sibley tent from Margaret M. Houston, Sam Jr's mother and widow of Sam Houston. Houston told Colonel Smith that her "object is to provide as far as I can for the comfort of those in the command who would otherwise suffer from the want of cover in wet and cold."[175] In December, William P. Doran recounted a story about several members of the regiment disguising themselves as militia guarding a distillery in order to steal barrels of whiskey. The regiment, whom Doran stated "everybody knows," was pilfering alcohol as a "keen trick."[176] A few months later, Pvt. Larkin Sweeney (Co. D) offered information to the Provost Marshall in Houston about a "gang of Deserters (9) Thieves & Conscripts (20) who have banded themselves together" and were hiding out around the city

---

S. S. Anderson, September 25, 1863; Ashbel Smith, CMSR, War Department Collection of Confederate Records, RG 109, NARA, accessed via fold3.com. Ralph Smith referred to doubts about their proper exchange but stated that "all the old members fit for duty reported as soon as the order reached them." He added that he and his comrades were more worried about the severe punishment they might face for breaking parole. This was probably a postwar embellishment as the regiment already defied the terms of parole by going home without authorization. See Smith, *Reminiscences,* 16.

[174] Smith, *Reminiscences,* 16. The regiment's composition continued as a hybrid of conscripts and volunteers. In January 1864, men who were serving as state troops but "liable" for conscription were encouraged to join the 2nd Texas, among other CSA units. See John B. Magruder, Special Orders No. 27, January 27, 1864, Folder "Military Orders and Reports," Box 2G236, Ashbel Smith Papers, DBC.

[175] Margaret M. Houston to [Ashbel Smith], October 26, 1863, Folder "1863" Box 2G224, Ashbel Smith Papers, DBC. One Sibley tent could cover about a dozen men. See Bell Irvin Wiley, *Billy Yank: The Common Soldier of the Union,* Reprint 1952 (Baton Rouge, LA: Louisiana State University Press, 2008), 55.

[176] "Sioux," Letter to the editor, December 28, 1863, *The Tri-Weekly Telegraph* (Houston, TX), December 30, 1863.

and in swamps. It would not be surprising if the miscreants Sweeney identified were his comrades in the 2nd Texas.[177]

Through it all, Ashbel Smith remained intent on defending his regiment's reputation. In February 1864, Colonel Smith was "mortified and surprised" to hear that the 2nd Texas, "including myself, has been reported absent without leave." Smith detailed the history of the unit and the "misapprehensions of the obligations" his men had about their parole status after Vicksburg. He felt obligated to state the high number of casualties the regiment had suffered since its formation, "upwards of 600 and accounted for as dead in the service as either disabled or wounded," affirming that despite these losses and depravations the 2nd Texas was still a "well-disciplined, obedient, gallant regiment," "attested by the Colors presented to it lately by its former Division Commander, Maj. Genl Maury bearing on their fold Shiloh, Iuka, Tallahatchie, Corinth, Greenwood, Vicksburg." Still acutely sensitive to the unit's standing in the CSA War Department, he closed, "I respectfully ask that the status of the 2d Texas Vol. Inf. in your Department be rectified and that the reproach of absence without leave whether imparted through ignorance or misplaced punctilio be utterly expunged."[178]

In the Spring of 1864, the 2nd Texas garrisoned on Galveston Island along with a smattering of state troops and encountered entirely new adversaries far from the field of battle.[179] By this time, the unit totaled

---

[177] Sweeny offered to act as a guide to reveal the deserters' hideouts in exchange for an extension of his furlough. See E. Keyser to W. K. Foster, April 2, 1864 in Larkin Benjamin Sweeney, CMSR, War Department Collection of Confederate Records, RG 109, NARA, accessed via fold3.com. Sweeny, from Harris County, volunteered in the 2nd Texas in August 1861 at the age seventeen; he was counted as a deserter on April 4, 1864; and authorized for this "special duty" on April 9, 1864; but then listed as "Joined from desertion" on April 25, 1864. It would make sense that he would identify fellow soldiers in the 2nd Texas since they were stationed in Houston at this time, although certainly not the only unit. It is difficult to estimate just how many desertions the 2nd Texas suffered, especially after Vicksburg when the regimental records are sparser, but again, there was a wave of desertions after Corinth, including those who became "galvanized Yankees" and joined the Union army.

[178] Ashbel Smith to Samuel Cooper, February 27, 1864, Letters Received by the Confederate Adjutant and Inspector General, 1861–1865, RG 109, NARA, accessed via fold3.com; Smith submitted documents to support his statements including special orders from Pemberton dated July 17, 1863; also see copies in Folder "1864," Box 2G224, Ashbel Smith Papers, DBC.

[179] There was an attempt to convert the regiment to mounted infantry, but General Magruder argued against it, reasoning that it would prove inefficient for the needs of his command and because there were no horses "to be had." Magruder recognized the brigade, which included not just the 2nd Texas, but Waul's Legion and the 3rd Texas, as

"no more than 250 men," and continued to accept conscripts to try to bolster its numbers.[180] Ashbel Smith was on extended detached service as "President of Examiners for disabled and disqualified officers," absenting him from the regiment he had so fiercely defended for so long.[181] In September 1864, a yellow fever epidemic hit Galveston and swept the ranks of the already depleted regiment, weakening and killing many who had survived the sufferings of combat and imprisonment. In October, things got so bad that the 2nd Texas was ordered to quell an angry mob which included "resident soldiers and their families" demanding "government issue rations" to feed "starving wives and children."[182] The regiment was, an inspector judged in December 1864, "only a skeleton of itself."[183]

The heroism required to withstand these trials was markedly different from the kind most volunteers had gone to war envisioning: "No surging

"splendidly drilled infantry – the best brigade in my command." See John B. Magruder to W. R. Boggs, November 30, 1863, OR, Ser. 1, Vol. 26, pt. 2, 460–461.

[180] John B. Magruder to W. R. Boggs, May 20, 1864, OR, Ser. 1, Vol. 34, pt. 3, 833–834. Even though the unit was nowhere near full strength, it retained its regimental designation and Magruder continued to compliment them as the "gallant Second Texas." Abstracts for the months of May, June, and August 1864 reported 233, 243, and 243 officers and men "present for duty" respectively, out of 414 "aggregate present and absent." See "Abstract from return of the First Sub-District, Galveston," for May and June 1864, OR, Ser. 1, Vol. 34, pt. 4, 638; OR, Ser. 1, Vol. 34, pt. 4, 701. In October, Samuel Cooper noted that regiments "west of the Mississippi," including the 2nd Texas, "can only be approximated, as the returns of division generals do not give the regimental strength, and no recent rolls or returns have been received from any above." He estimated an average of 400 aggregate per regiment. See Samuel Cooper to (James Seddon), October 10, 1864, OR, Ser. 1, Vol. 41, pt. 2, 1056–1057.

[181] Ashbel Smith, CMSR War Department Collection of Confederate Records, RG 109, NARA, accessed via fold3.com.

[182] Smith, *Reminiscences*, 18.

[183] Lt. J. T. Scott, acting Inspector General report from December 1, 1864, quoted in an unnamed newspaper clipping (October 13, 1907), in Shettles Scrapbook, 1886–1909, 2nd Texas Volunteer Infantry Regimental Files, VNMP. Scott also called their company and battalion drill "deficient," noting that "due to the prevalence of yellow fever at this post, by which the regiment suffered severely, all drills were suspended." Some members were boarding with family members in town and the lack of equipment (in both quantity and quality) remained abysmal. Abstracts for regimental strength in December 1864 and January 1865 listed 231 and 234 officers and men "present for duty" respectively. See "Abstract from field returns of the Defenses of Galveston," OR, Ser. 1, Vol. 41, pt. 4, 1139; OR, Ser. 1, Vol. 48, Pt. 1, Section 2, 1355. By April 1865, regimental numbers had increased to 420 officers and men "Present for duty"; "Aggregate present" was 492; and "Aggregate present and absent," was 783. See "Abstract from return of the Defenses of Galveston," April 1865, OR, Ser. 1, Vol. 48, pt. 2, 1292. The final abstract from May 10, 1865, reported 370 officers and men "Present for duty." See "Abstract from Field Return of the Defenses of Galveston," OR, Ser. 1, Vol. 48, pt. 2, 1297.

crowds of men to urge one on to victory or death," Ralph Smith remembered, "yet now what heroic bravery it required to sit alone through the sad silent watches of the night besides a plague-stricken comrad[e]'s bed and minister to the dieing [*sic*] wants of one who's very breath exhaled death into the surrounding atmosphere." Here, he maintained, "during the epidemic was displayed equally as much heroism if not more than its required to go into battle both by soldiers and also the good women of the city, true heroines indeed who so kindly cared for and ministered to the sick and dieing [*sic*] soldiers."[184] The regiment suffered "considerable loss from yellow fever but," Charles Evans wrote, "it fought no more battles."[185] In May 1865, Confederates evacuated Galveston, and some soldiers looted the town as they left.[186] When formal surrender came on June 2, 1865, in Galveston, most of the unit had already disbanded for good.[187]

In a decidedly unheroic coda, two veterans of the regiment tried to disarm an artillery shell discovered in the Buffalo Bayou near Galveston in 1867. According to a newspaper account, the men "took it ashore and commenced operations on it with coldchisels and hammers, in order to break it open, when the shell exploded, blowing the men up and horribly mutilating them." Neither survived the explosion. The paper added: "We were unable to obtain their names, but we understand that they both did good service in the 'Lost Cause,' and were worthy members of the gallant 2nd Texas." The column ended with a warning to readers not to tamper with "old

---

[184] Smith, *Reminiscences*, 18–19. In addition, accusations of disloyalty were made against J. I. McGinnis, one of the original commissioned officers from 1861. More than two dozen officers from the regiment signed a statement avowing his loyalty and noting: "To the contrary, he was one of the first among us to discountenance the project of reconstruction as agitated amongst the soldiers, whilst others with less of policy could not see its disorganization tendencies." Petition from officers of the 2nd Texas, February 2, 1865, in J. I. McGinnis, CMSR, War Department Collection of Confederate Records, RG 109, NARA, accessed via fold3.com.

[185] Evans, "The Second Texas Infantry," 605.

[186] Chance, *The Second Texas Infantry*, 143–144.

[187] Sterling Fisher, "The Amenities of War," *Blue and Gray: The Patriotic American Magazine*, Vol. 1 (1893): 321–323. Fisher's account further stresses the sentimentalized bonds between North and South, claiming that wounded Union troops were "astonished" to have Texas soldiers treat them kindly. Chance states: "Rather than surrender at the cessation of hostilities, the men mutinied in May 1865 and disbanded to return to their homes, after service distinguished by gallantry under fire and devotion to duty." See Joseph E. Chance, "Second Texas Infantry," Handbook of Texas Online, tshaonline.org.

fire arms, shells and the like."[188] This was all a rather anticlimactic end to the "gallant" 2nd Texas' war story.

Most postwar histories, nevertheless, stressed their bravery and self-sacrifice and the martyred loss of Colonel Rogers at Corinth, rather than any embarrassing allegations of cowardice, disloyalty, or recklessness.[189] Rogers' death became a staple in the Lost Cause propaganda that flourished in the decades to follow. His daughter Mary, echoing much of the postwar sentiment toward him, stated decisively that her father's "courage and his heroic death on Corinth's blood-stained field are matters of history."[190] Appeals called for "aid in erecting a monument to Anglo-Saxon courage, in honor of brave" Rogers and "his no less brave followers, who died at Corinth."[191] Such references to "Anglo Saxon courage" reinforced the sentiments pronounced by Confederates throughout the war, emphasizing their belief in white supremacy. Such rhetoric took on renewed meaning in the 1890s with the entrenchment of racist segregation and pernicious violence against African Americans, fusing with white Christian American nationalism.

The result was two monuments: one placed in downtown Corinth in 1896, featuring a single generic soldier cast in zinc high atop a marble base, dedicated to Rogers and all "Confederate patriots who fell at the Battle of Corinth in October 1862." Van Dorn's praise of Rogers from his report of the battle is inscribed on one side of the monument; on another are stanzas from a poem, "The Virginians of the Valley" by Francis Orray Ticknor, that partially reads: "They were. The Knightliest of the Knightly Race." In 1912, the United Daughters of the Confederacy along with members of Rogers, family and "admiring friends" erected a separate granite obelisk on Rogers'

---

[188] *The Civilian and Gazette* (Galveston, TX) excerpted in *The Dallas Daily Herald* (Dallas, TX), March 2, 1867; see also *The Galveston Daily News* (Galveston, TX), February 12, 1867. The two veterans, Henry D. Donnellan (Co. B) and F. Richter (Co. F), operated a Houston tin business and it seems likely they were seeking to extract the metal from these shells – a large amount of them had been dumped into the bayou by the Federal army.

[189] A few examples include George F. Williams, *Memorial War Book as Drawn from Historical Records and Personal Narratives of the Men Who Served in the Great Struggle* (New York: Lovell Brothers, 1894), 340; Wittenmyer, *Under the Guns*, 82–83; Byron Cloyd Bryner, *Bugle Echoes: The Story of the Illinois 47th* (Springfield, IL: Phillips Bros., Printers and Binders, 1905), 63.

[190] Mary Rogers Bolton, "Sketch of Col. W. P. Rodgers," included in Dudley. *The Battle of Corinth*, 22.

[191] George W. Bynum, quoted in Luther Coyner, Letter to the Editor, January 31, 1895, *Galveston Daily News* (Gavlveston, TX), February 3, 1895.

grave site. In 2010, the state of Texas placed yet another marker at Corinth, close to the colonel's grave, to recognize all Texas units that fought there, affirming: "Texas Remembers the Valor and Devotion of its Sons."[192]

Few veterans of the 2nd Texas challenged this generic war story of bravery and sacrifice. If ex-members referenced charges of cowardice at all, they did not dwell on them in any meaningful way.[193] John C. Moore, in a postwar column about Lookout Mountain that took direct aim at his old nemesis William Hardee, referred to an incident where troops panicked in the battle, acknowledging that this behavior was not uncommon at all. He observed, "sometimes a body of men of well-tried and undoubted bravery become panic-stricken from really trifling causes, losing all presences of mind and self control." He may or may not have been thinking of his former regiment when he wrote this.[194]

---

[192] *Confederate Veteran*, Vol. 2, No. 8 (August 1894), 249; *Confederate Veteran*, Vol. 15, No. 6. (June 1907), 245–247. See also Luther Coyner, Letter to the Editor, January 31, 1895, *Galveston Daily News* (Galveston, TX), February 3, 1895; and Tom Parsons, "Rogers Monuments Tell Unique Corinth Story," *Daily Corinthian* (Corinth, MS), January 6, 2013.

[193] There were continued debates among veterans, including those of the 2nd Texas, discussing Rogers' final moments and the fate of the 2nd Texas' flag. See for example, William G. Wood, Letter to the Editor, *The Houston Post* (Houston, TX), July 27, 1896; and *The Houston Post* (Houston, TX) December 6, 1903; transcribed copy in 2nd Texas Infantry, Regimental Files, CCWIC. See also *The National Tribune* (Washington, DC), August 18, 1898; and August 31, 1899.

[194] John C. Moore, "The Battle of Lookout Mountain," *Confederate Veteran*, Vol. 6, No. 9 (September 1898): 428. In another story, Moore appeared to mock the assumed bravery of white Texans when a "countryman" appeared at his headquarters in Galveston, eager to fight Yankees armed only with a bowie knife. Moore agreed, shook the man's hand, and authorized him to raise a company to do just as he suggested. After vowing to return, the "bloodthirsty friend never reported." See *Galveston Daily News* (Galveston, TX), July 2, 1911.

CONCLUSION

"When Cowards Shrink and Brave Men Die"

Sam Houston, Jr.'s connection to the 2nd Texas essentially ended at Shiloh. After his release from prison and recovery from his wounds, he re-enlisted in a Texas cavalry unit and served the rest of the war. In early February 1864, while stationed at Cedar Lake, Texas, he penned a poem called "The Southern Flag," later published in the *Houston Daily Telegraph*, which referred to the battlefield "red with Southern heroes gore." The final stanza reads:

> And when death's dreadful missiles fly
> When cowards shrink and brave men die.
> 'Tis, then, bright flag, thy splendors shine,
> Flag of the South, thy fate is mine![1]

Houston's poem is typical of much of the jingoistic militaristic rhetoric churned out during the conflict which stressed the notion that there could only be two choices in war: heroes who died and cowards who shrank and ran away. And yet, we know even from Houston himself, who years later wrote "Shiloh Shadows," that war was – and is – rarely so black and white. Sometimes men expected to behave bravely in battle faltered and failed, and faced humiliating charges of cowardice. And they did not simply move on, as suggested by some historians, without such failings affecting them. Nor was it necessarily a handful of individuals grappling with these humiliations, but entire units of men, with lasting repercussions reverberating back upon their families, home communities, and beyond. The soldiers' experiences described in these pages reveal a good deal of

---

[1] Sam Houston, Jr., "The Southern Flag," *The Houston Daily Telegraph*, March 9, 1864, reprinted in Bill Winsor, *Texas in the Confederacy: Military Instillations, Economy and People* (Hillsboro, TX: Hill Jr. College Press, 1978), 89.

ambiguity, confusion, and fear, challenging abstracted ideals of heroism that were omnipresent in the milieu of the Civil War era. Human behavior under pressure of such extreme violence does not register as simply courageous or cowardly; often it is something in between.

For both the 11th New York and 2nd Texas, allegations of cowardice directly affected their military service. Their officers were acutely aware of the shame associated with these charges, and along with the men in the ranks, sought to challenge and defy them. It did not really matter whether these accusations were accurate or fair; they stuck and were nearly impossible to shake off. The only real way to bring some element of redemption was through bloody, preferably deadly combat – but even that was not a guarantee. In the aftermath of the war, few if any of these veterans referenced these charges at all. Instead, they, along with successive generations of historians, helped craft a postwar narrative of manly heroism and triumph, where soldiers on both sides of the conflict were unquestionably brave.

The lived experiences of the Fire Zouaves were not so celebratory. Their very beginnings were fraught with controversy and drama due to the hurried nature of their founding and the celebrity of their colonel. After Ellsworth's shocking death, factors within and without the regiment exacerbated the problems it already faced. The men continued to balk at attempts to tame their defiant identity as firemen and as Zouaves. When battle came, they were as ill-prepared as nearly all the Union troops that fought at Bull Run. Their assumed physical courage – seemingly innate and already proven as volunteer firemen – could not save them; they suffered deep humiliation when publicly shamed for cowardice in the press and by Congress. It is hard to imagine how any regiment could have fully recovered.

A close look at the 2nd Texas reveals a more complicated story, too. They had several opportunities to redeem themselves, and on the surface it would seem they did just that by making a near-suicidal assault at Corinth, and losing their colonel in the attempt. But like the Fire Zouaves, there were other factors at play that weakened the regiment. By the time of the surrender at Vicksburg, they had earned a reputation as hard-fighting veterans. But the siege was grueling, making them question what bravery even meant anymore. After their parole, the unit dispersed, with only a fragment reassembled to serve out the final days of the war suffering from disease and want of food.

Both the Union and Confederacy grappled with the question of what made effective and resilient soldiers, particularly for a conflict waged within a single nation. Overly optimistic assumptions about the innate bravery of white manhood and citizen-soldiers fell to the wayside once the pragmatic pressures of war revealed the limitations of hasty training, battlefield inexperience, and flawed leadership. The men studied here were assumed to be brave and thus "instant soldiers." The reality of this terrible war proved that this was often a false supposition. When leadership broke down, combined with a lack of experience and chaos of battle, the result, at least for these two regiments, was abject failure. And yet, even for the 2nd Texas, after they gained proficiency as sharpshooters, earned the battle scars of combat, and had inspired leadership, it was still hard, if not impossible, to shed the ignominy of cowardice.

Confederate Alfred H. Colquitt predicted in 1862 that the "secret history of the fight" – specifically soldiers acting cowardly in battle – would remain hidden from public view. In the history books, this is largely true. But more of these stories exist, sometimes covered by layers of militarized rhetoric and postwar mythology. We can find them by listening to the men themselves. And when we do, we see chinks in the glorified bombast of war-making.

Bibliography

MANUSCRIPT COLLECTIONS

Albany, New York
  New York State Archives
    Bureau of Military Statistics
      Administrative Correspondence Files (Series A4111)
      Telegrams Received and Sent by the Governor's Office (Series A4149)
      Civil War Muster Roll Abstracts of New York State Volunteers, United
      States Sharpshooters, and United States Colored Troops [ca. 1861–1900]
  New York State Library
    Elmer Ephraim Ellsworth Collection
Austin, Texas
  The University of Texas
    Dolph Briscoe Center for American History
      Edward Clark Papers
      George G. Fisher Collection
      Sam Houston, Jr. Papers
      John Creed Moore Papers
      Ashbel Smith Papers
  Texas General Land Office
    Dudley Ward Papers
  Texas State Library and Archives Commission
    "Autobiography of Major William P. Doran (Sioux) Confederate Soldier
    in the Battles of Galveston, Shiloh, Vicksburg, Mansfield, Pleasant Hill,
    and Forty Skirmishes along Red River in 1864," Typescript, n.d.
    Governor Francis Richard Lubbock Records
    Texas Confederate Pension Applications, 1899–1975
Corinth, Mississippi
  Shiloh National Military Park
    Corinth Civil War Interpretive Center

Regimental Files
2nd Texas Infantry Regiment
Galveston, Texas
Moody Medical Library, University of Texas Medical Branch
Truman G. Blocker, Jr. History of Medicine Collections,
Ashbel Smith Letters
Hillsboro, Texas
Historical Research Center, Texas Heritage Museum, Hill College
J. Henry Cravey, "Reminiscences" (typescript copy)
Indianapolis, Indiana
Indiana State Library, Rare Books and Manuscripts
Frank E. Brownell Papers
Kenosha, Wisconsin
The Civil War Museum
Elmer E. Ellsworth Archival Collection
Kingsville, Texas
The South Texas Archives & Special Collections, James C. Jernigan Library,
Texas A&M University-Kingsville
Simons Family Collection
Lubbock, Texas
Special Collections Library, Southwest Collection, Texas Tech University
Temple Houston Morrow: Sam Houston Family Papers
Manassas, Virginia
Manassas National Battlefield Park
11th New York Volunteer Infantry Regimental File
Montgomery, Alabama
Alabama Department of Archives and History
Confederate Regimental History Files
19th Alabama Infantry Regiment
42nd Alabama Infantry Regiment
New York, New York
New York Historical Society
Edward Riley, "Song of the Zouaves"
G. B. De Wolfe, "Columbia Mourns for Ellsworth"
Palo Alto, California
Huntington Library
Sparks Family Papers
Philadelphia, Pennsylvania
The Rosenbach Museum
Elmer E. Ellsworth Papers
Providence, Rhode Island
John Hay Library, Brown University
Elmer E. Ellsworth Papers
Saratoga Springs, New York
New York State Military Museum and Veterans Research Center
11th New York Voluntary Infantry Collection
Elmer Ephraim Ellsworth Collection

Shiloh National Military Park, Tennessee
  Regimental Files
    2nd Texas Infantry Regiment
Springfield, Illinois
  Abraham Lincoln Presidential Papers
  Elmer Ephraim Ellsworth Papers
St. Paul, Minnesota
  Minnesota Historical Society
    Frank E. Brownell Papers
Vicksburg, Mississippi
  McCardle Research Library, Old Warren County Courthouse
    Alexander Frazier Diary
  Vicksburg National Military Park
    Edwin C. Bearss, "Texas at Vicksburg," unpublished manuscript
      (September 1956)
    2nd Texas Infantry Regimental File
Washington, DC
  Manuscript Division, Library of Congress
    Confederate States of America Records
      Letters Sent, CSA War Department
    William J. Hardee Letters
    Samuel Peter Heintzelman Papers
    Louis T. Wigfall Family Papers
National Archives and Records Administration
  RG 15, Department of Veterans Affairs
    Historical Register of National Homes for Disabled Volunteer Soldiers,
      1866–1938.
  RG 29, Records of the Bureau of the Census
    Sixth Census of the United States, 1840
    Seventh Census of the United States, 1850
    Eighth Census of the United States, 1860
    Ninth Census of the United States, 1870
  RG 94, Records of the Adjutant General's Office
    Case Files of Applications from Former Confederates for Presidential
      Pardons, 1865–1867
    Compiled Military Service Records
    Regimental Returns
      Volunteer Organizations
        11th New York Volunteer Infantry
  RG 109, War Department Collection of Confederate Records
    Confederate States Army Casualties: Lists and Narrative Reports, 1861–1865
    Compiled Military Service Records
    Letters Received by the Confederate Adjutant & Inspector General, 1861–
      1865
    Selected Records of the War Department Relating to Confederate Prisoners
      of War, 1861–1865

NEWSPAPERS

Abingdon Virginian (Abingdon, VA)
The Advance (Ogdensburgh, NY)
Alexandria Gazette and Virginia Advertiser (Alexandria, VA)
Baltimore Sun (Baltimore, MD)
Belfast News (Belfast)
The Budget (Troy, NY)
The Buffalo Commercial (Buffalo, NY)
Buffalo Courier (Buffalo, NY)
The Boston Evening Transcript
Boston Herald
Brooklyn Daily Eagle (Brooklyn, NY)
Charleston Mercury
Chicago Daily Tribune
Chicago Times
Christian Recorder (Philadelphia, PA)
Cincinnati Daily Commercial (Cincinnati, OH)
The Cincinnati Enquirer (Cincinnati, OH)
The Citizens (Columbus, TX)
The Civilian and Gazette (Galveston, TX)
Cleveland Daily Herald (Cleveland, OH)
Daily Corinthian (Corinth, MS)
Daily Picayune (New Orleans, LA)
The Daily Pittsburgh Gazette (Pittsburgh, PA)
Daily Register (Raleigh, NC)
Daily Richmond Examiner (Richmond, VA)
Daily State Register (Des Moines, IA)
Daily True Delta (New Orleans, LA)
Dallas Daily Herald (Dallas, TX)
The Dallas Morning News (Dallas, TX)
Elmira Weekly Advertiser (Elmira, NY)
The Evening Republican (Meadville, PA)
The Evening Star (Washington, DC)
Frank Leslie's Illustrated Newspaper (New York, NY)
The Freedman's Champion (Atchison, KS)
Galveston Daily and Weekly News (Galveston, TX)
Geneva Daily Gazette (Geneva, NY)
The Graphic News (Cincinnati, OH)
The Hartford Courant (Hartford, CT)
Harper's Weekly (New York, NY)
The Houston Post (Houston, TX)
Illinois Daily State Journal (Springfield, IL)
The Irish American (New York, NY)
Lansing State Republican (Lansing, MI)
Lexington Gazette (Lexington, VA)
Malden City Press (Malden, MA)

Memphis Daily Appeal (Memphis, TN)
The Memphis Daily Avalanche (Memphis, TN)
Milwaukee Daily Sentinel (Milwaukee, WI)
Mobile Advertiser and Register (Mobile, AL)
Monroe Sentinel (Monroe, WI)
The Nashville Union American (Nashville, TN)
The National Tribune (Washington, DC)
New Orleans Daily Crescent
New York Albion
New York Atlas
New York Commercial
New York Daily News
New York Daily Tribune
New York Evening Post
New York Herald
New York Illustrated News
New York Leader
New York Sunday Mercury
The New York Times
New York World
North American and United States Gazette (Philadelphia, PA)
The Press (Philadelphia, PA)
The Political Forum (Newton, KS)
Railroad Gazette (New York)
The Raleigh Register (Raleigh, NC)
Richmond Daily Dispatch (Richmond, VA)
Richmond Enquirer (Richmond, VA)
San Antonio Light (San Antonio, TX)
Semi-Weekly Citizen (Des Arc, AR)
Southern Intelligencer (Austin, TX)
Springfield Daily Republican (Springfield, MA)
St. Louis Globe Democrat (St. Louis, MO)
St. Paul Daily Press (St. Paul, MN)
The Sub-Soiler & Democrat (Corinth, MS)
The Sugar Planter (West Baton Rouge, LA)
The Sun (New York, NY)
The Sunbury Gazette (Sunbury, PA)
The Sunday Herald (Chicago, IL)
The Texas Almanac – Extra (Austin, TX)
The Times Union (Brooklyn, NY)
Troy Observer (Troy, NY)
Union (Galveston, TX)
Union and Dakotaian (Yankton, SD)
The Weekly and Tri-Weekly Telegraph (Houston, TX)
The Weekly Times (Philadelphia, PA)
Weekly Republican (Newton, KS)
Wisconsin Daily Patriot (Madison, WI)

GOVERNMENT DOCUMENTS AND PUBLICATIONS

Confederate States of America War Department, *Articles of War for the Government of the Army of the Confederate States*. Montgomery, AL: Barrett, Wimbish, Printers and Binders, 1861.

Jackson County Court. *Probate Minutes, 1837–1912*. Texas.

Journal of the Congress of the Confederate States of America, 1861–1865. Vols. 7, Washington, DC: Government Printing Office, 1904–1905.

Journal of the Senate of the General Assembly of the State of Illinois at Their Regular Session, Begun and Held at Springfield, January 7, 1861. Springfield, IL: Bailhache & Baker Printers, 1861.

The Medical and Surgical History of the War of the Rebellion (1861–65). Vols. 6. Washington, DC: Government Printing Office, 1870–1888.

Official Records of the Union and Confederate Navies in the War of the Rebellion. Vols. 30. Washington, DC: Government Printing Office, 1894–1922.

Reports and Documents of the Union Defense Committee of the Citizens of New York. Board of Alderman, September 9, 1861. Document No. 18. New York: Edmund Jones, Printers of the Corporation, 1861.

State of New York. *A Record of the Commissioned Officers, Non-Commissioned Officers and Privates, of the Regiments which were Organized in the State of New York and Called to the Service of the United States to Assist in Suppressing the Rebellion caused by the Secession of Some of the Southern States from the Union, A.D. 1861, As Taken from the Muster-In Rolls on File in the Adjutant General's Office, State of New York*. Vols. 8. Albany, NY: Comstock & Cassidy, Printers, 1864–1868.

State of New York. *Annual Report of the Adjutant General of the State of New York*. Albany, NY: C. Van Benthuysen, Printer, 1862.

State of New York. *Annual Report of the Adjutant General of the State of New York for the Year 1899. Registers of the Sixth, Seventh, Seventh Veterans, Eighth, Ninth, and Eleventh Regiments of Infantry Transmitted to the Legislature February 5, 1900. Serial No. 18 Included in Documents of the Assembly of the State of New York, One Hundred and Twenty-Third Session*. Albany, NY: James B. Lyon, State Printer, 1900, Vol. X, No. 58, Part 3: 1073–1222.

State of New York. *Annual Report of the Adjutant General, Transmitted to the Legislature, January 31, 1868*. Vols. 2. Albany, NY: Printing House of Charles van Benthuyson, 1868, Vol. 1: 115.

State of New York. *Fifth Annual Report of the Chief of the Bureau of Military Statistics*. Albany, NY: C. Van Benthuysen Steam Printing House, 1868.

State of New York. *Some of the Southern States from the Union, A. D. 1861, as Taken from the Muster-In Rolls on File in the Adjutant General's Office, State of New York*. Vols. 8. Albany, NY: Comstock & Cassidy, Printers, 1864–1868.

State of New York. *Third Annual Report of the Bureau of Military Record of the State of New York*. Albany, NY: G. Wendell Printer, 1866.

US Congress. *Report of the Joint Committee on the Conduct of the War in Three Parts*. Washington, DC: Government Printing Office, 1863.

United States War Department. *Revised United States Army Regulations, 1861. With an Appendix Containing the Changes and Laws Affecting Army Regulations and Articles of War to June 25, 1863.* Washington, DC: Government Printing Office, 1863.

War of the Rebellion: A Compilation of the Official Records of the Union and Confederate Armies. Vols. 128. Washington, DC: Government Printing Office, 1880–1901.

BOOKS

Adams, Michael C. C. *Fighting for Defeat: Union Military Failure in the East, 1861–1865.* Lincoln, NE: University of Nebraska Press, 1992.

Adams, Michael C. C. *Living Hell: The Dark Side of the Civil War.* Baltimore, MD: Johns Hopkins University Press, 2014.

Aldrich, Thomas M. *The History of Battery A, First Regiment Rhode Island Light Artillery in the War to Preserve the Union, 1861–1865.* Providence, RI: Snow & Farnham, Printers, 1904.

Anbinder, Tyler. *Five Points: The Nineteenth Century New York City Neighborhood.* New York: Simon and Schuster, 2012.

Andreas, Alfred Theodore. *A History of Chicago: From 1857 until the Fire of 1871.* Vols. 3. Chicago, IL: A. T. Andes, 1885.

Andrews, J. Cutler. *The North Reports the Civil War.* Pittsburgh, PA: University of Pittsburgh Press, 1955.

Ashcroft, Allan C. *Texas in the Civil War: A Résumé History.* Austin, TX: Texas Civil War Centennial Commission, 1962.

Askew III, Samuel. *An Analysis of Unit Cohesion in the 42nd Alabama Infantry.* Auckland: Pickle Partners, 2015.

Baker, John Walter. *A History of Robertson County, Texas.* Waco, TX: Robertson County Historical Survey Committee, 1970.

Ballard, Ted, ed. *Staff Ride Guide: Battle of First Bull Run.* Washington, DC: Center of Military History United States Army, 2007.

Barron, Samuel B. *The Lone Star Defenders: A Chronicle of the Third Texas Cavalry, Ross' Brigade.* New York The Neale, 1908.

Basler, Roy P., ed. *The Collected Works of Abraham Lincoln.* Vols. 8. New Brunswick, NJ: Rutgers University Press, 1953.

Bederman, Gail. *Manliness and Civilization: A Cultural History of Gender and Race in the United States, 1880–1917.* Chicago, IL: University of Chicago Press, 1995.

Biographical Encyclopedia of Texas. New York: Southern, 1880.

Blackford, William W. *Wars Years with Jeb Stuart.* Reprint, 1945. Baton Rouge, LA: Louisiana State University Press, 1993.

Branda, Eldon Stephen, ed. *The Handbook of Texas: A Supplement.* Vol. III. Austin, TX: Texas State Historical Association, 1976.

Brown, John G., Henry S. Nourse, and Lucian Crooker. *The Story of the Fifty-Fifth Regiment Illinois Volunteer Infantry in the Civil War 1861–1865 by a Committee of the Regiment.* Clinton, MA: W. J. Coulter, 1887.

Bruce, Susannah Ural. *The Harp and the Eagle: Irish American Volunteers and the Union Army, 1861–1865*. New York: New York University Press, 2006.

Bryner, Byron Cloyd. *Bugle Echoes: The Story of the Illinois 47th*. Springfield, IL: Phillips Bros., Printers and Binders, 1905.

Burke, Eric Michael. *Soldiers from Experience: The Forging of Sherman's Fifteenth Corps, 1862–1863*. Baton Rouge, LA: Louisiana State University Press, 2022.

Burt, Silas W. *My Memoirs of the Military History of the State of New York during the War for the Union, 1861–1865*. Albany, NY: J. B. Lyon Company, 1902.

Butts, Joseph Tyler, ed. *A Gallant Captain of the Civil War: Being the Record of the Extraordinary Adventures of Frederick Otto, Barron Von Fritsch, Comp. from His War Record in Washington and His Private Papers*. New York: F. Tennyson Neely, 1902.

Callenda, Frank. *The 14th Brooklyn Regiment of the Civil War: A History and Roster*. Jefferson, NC: McFarland, 2013.

Carmichael, Peter S. *The Last Generation: Young Virginians in Peace, War and Reunion*. Chapel Hill, NC: University of North Carolina Press, 2005.

Carter III, Samuel. *The Final Fortress: The Campaign for Vicksburg, 1862–1863*. New York: St. Martin's Press, 1980.

Censer, Jane Turner, ed. *The Papers of Frederick Law Olmsted: Defending the Union: The Civil War and the U.S. Sanitary Commission, 1861–1863*. Vol. IV. Baltimore, NC: Johns Hopkins University Press, 1986.

Chance, Joseph E. *Jefferson Davis's Mexican War Regiment*. Jackson, MS: University Press of Mississippi, 1991.

Chance, Joseph E. *The Second Texas Infantry: From Shiloh to Vicksburg*. Austin, TX: Eakin Press, 1984.

Clark, Emmons. *History of the Second Company of the Seventh Regiment (National Guard) N. Y. S. Militia*. New York: J. G. Gregory, 1864.

Clark, Emmons. *History of the Seventh Regiment of New York 1806–1889*. Vols. 2. New York: Published by the Seventh Regiment, 1890.

Comings, Harrison H. *Personal Reminiscences of Co. E. N. Y. Fire Zouaves; Better Known as Ellsworth's Fire Zouaves*. Malden, MA: J. Gould Tilden Steam Book and Joe Printer, 1886.

Conklin, Ryan A. *The 18th New York Infantry in the Civil War: A History and Roster*. Jefferson, NC: McFarland, 2016.

Cooper, Edward S. *Louis Trezevant Wigfall: The Disintegration of the Union and Collapse of the Confederacy*. Madison, NJ: Fairleigh Dickinson University Press, 2012.

Corcoran, Michael. *The Captivity of General Corcoran, the Only Authentic and Reliable Narrative of the Trial and Sufferings Endured, during His Twelve Months' Imprisonment in Richmond and Other Southern Cities, by Brig. General Michael Corcoran, the Hero of Bull Run*. Philadelphia, PA: Barclay, 1862.

Costa, Dora L., and Matthew E. Kahn. *Heroes and Cowards: The Social Face of War*. Princeton, NJ: Princeton University Press, 2008.

Costello, Augustine E. *Birth of the Bravest: A History of the New York Fire Department from 1609 to 1887.* Abridged from 1887 version. New York: Tom Doherty Associates, 2002.

Costello, Augustine E. *Our Firemen: A History of the New York Fire Department.* New York: Augustine E. Costello, 1887.

Cotham, Jr., Edward T. *Battle on the Bay: The Civil War Struggle for Galveston.* Austin, TX: University of Texas Press, 1998.

Cozzens, Peter. *The Darkest Days of the War: The Battles of Iuka and Corinth.* Chapel Hill, NC: University of North Carolina Press, 1997.

Creighton, Margaret. *The Colors of Courage: Gettysburg's Forgotten History: Immigrants, Women and African Americans in the Civil War's Defining Battle.* New York: Basic Books, 2005.

Crist, Lynda Lasswell, ed. *The Papers of Jefferson Davis.* Vols. 14. Baton Rouge, LA: Louisiana State University Press, 1971–2015.

Cudworth, Warren H. *First Regiment (Massachusetts Infantry), from the 25th of May to the 25th of May 1864: Including Brief References to the Operations of the Army of the Potomac.* Boston, MA: Walker, Fuller, 1866.

Cumming, Kate. *A Journal of Hospital Life in the Confederate Army of Tennessee from the Battle of Shiloh to the End of the War; with Sketches of Life and Characters, and Brief Notices of Current Events during that Period.* Louisville, KY: John P. Morton, 1866.

Cumming, Kate. *Gleanings from Southland: Sketches of Life and Manners of the People of the South Before, During and After the War of Secession, with Extracts from the Author's Journal and An Epitome of the New South.* Birmingham, AL: Roberts &. Son, 1895.

Cunliffe, Marcus. *Soldiers and Civilians: The Martial Spirit in America, 1775–1865.* Boston, MA: Little Brown, 1968.

Cunningham, O. Edward, *Shiloh and the Western Campaign of 1862.* Edited by Gary D. Joiner and Timothy B. Smith. El Dorado Hills, CA: Savas Beatie, 2007.

Daniel, Larry J. *Shiloh: The Battle that Changed the Civil War.* New York: Simon and Schuster, 1997.

Davenport, Alfred. *Camp and Field of the Fifth New York Volunteer Infantry (Duryee Zouaves).* New York: Dick and Fitzgerald, 1879.

Davis, Washington. *Camp-fire Chats of the Civil War: Being the Incident, Adventure and Wayside Exploit of the Bivouac and Battle Field, as Related by Veteran Soldiers Themselves. Embracing the Tragedy, Romance, Comedy Humor and Pathos in the Varied Experiences of Army Life.* Chicago, IL: The Lewis, 1888.

Davis, William C. *Battle at Bull Run: A History of the First Major Campaign of the Civil War.* New York: Doubleday, 1977.

Davis, William C., and Julie Hoffman, eds. *The Confederate General.* Vols. 6. Harrisburg, PA: National Historical Society, 1991.

Dawes, James. *The Language of War: Literature and Culture in the U.S. from the Civil War through World War II.* Cambridge, MA: Harvard University Press, 2005.

Debray, Xavier Blanchard. *A Sketch of the History of Debray's (26th) Regiment of Texas Cavalry.* Reprint, 1884. Waco, TX: Waco Village, 1961.

Driggs, George W. *Opening of the Mississippi; or Two Years Campaigning in the South-West. A Record of the Campaigns, Sieges, Actions and Marches in which the 8th Wisconsin Volunteers Have Participated, by A Non-Commissioned Officer.* Madison, WI: Wm. J. Park, 1864.

Dudley, G. W. *The Battle of Corinth, October 3–4, 1862. Including also the battle of Davis' Bridge, on Hatchie, and Skirmish at the Tuscumbia, October 5, 1862.* Iuka, MS: Vidette Press, 1899.

Dudley, G. W. *The Lost Account of the Battle of Corinth and the Court-Martial of Gen. Van Dorn by an Unknown Author.* Monroe F. Cockrell, ed. Jackson, TN: McCowat-Mercer Press, 1955.

Duncan, Thomas, *Recollections of Thomas D. Duncan: A Confederate Soldier.* Nashville, TN: McQuiddy, 1922.

Dyer, Frederick. *A Compendium of the War of the Rebellion.* Des Moines, IA: The Dyer, 1908.

Elder, Angela Esco. *Love and Duty: Confederate Widows and the Emotional Politics of Loss.* Chapel Hill, NC: University of North Carolina Press, 2022.

Elliot, Isaac H. *History of the Thirty-Third Regiment Illinois Veteran Volunteer Infantry in the Civil War 22nd August, 1861 to 7th December, 1865.* Gibson City, IL: Gibson Courier, 1902.

Evans, Clement A., ed. *Confederate Military History.* Vols. 12. Atlanta: Confederate Publishing, 1899.

Exercises Connected with the Unveiling of the Ellsworth Monument at Mechanicville, May 27, 1874. Albany, NY: Joel Munsell, 1875.

Fahs, Alice. *The Imagined Civil War: Popular Literature of the North & South, 1861–1865.* Chapel Hill, NC: University of North Carolina Press, 2001.

Faust, Drew Gilpin. *Mothers of Invention: Women of the Slaveholding South in the American Civil War.* Chapel Hill, NC: University of North Carolina Press, 1996.

Faust, Drew Gilpin. *This Republic of Suffering: Death and the American Civil War.* New York: Knopf, 2008.

Field, Ron. *Union Infantryman vs Confederate Infantryman: Eastern Theater 1861–65.* Oxford: Osprey, 2013.

Fitzhugh, Lester N. *Texas Batteries, Battalions, Regiments, Commanders and Field Officers, Confederate States Army, 1861–1865.* Midlothian, TX: Mirror Press 1959.

Fleischman, Flavia. *Old River Country: A History of West Chambers County.* Fort Worth, TX: Worth Bindery, 1976.

Folmar, John Kent, ed. *From That Terrible Field: Civil War Letters of James M. Williams, Twenty-first Alabama Infantry Volunteers.* Tuscaloosa, AL: University of Alabama Press, 1981.

Foote, Lorien. *The Gentlemen and the Roughs: Violence, Honor and Manhood in the Union Army.* New York: New York University Press, 2010.

Fox, William F. *Regimental Losses in the American Civil War, 1861–1865: A Treatise On The Extent And Nature Of The Mortuary Losses In The Union Regiments, With Full And Exhaustive Statistics Compiled From The Official Records On File In The State Military Bureaus And At Washington.* Albany, NY: Albany Publishing, 1889.

Frank, Joseph Allen, and George A. Reaves. *"Seeing the Elephant": Raw Recruits at the Battle of Shiloh.* Westport, CT: Greenwood Press, 1989.

Franklin, John Hope. *The Militant South, 1800–1861.* Cambridge, MA: Harvard University Press, 1956.

Furneaux, Holly. *Military Men of Feeling: Emotion, Touch and Masculinity in the Crimean War.* Oxford: Oxford University Press, 2016.

Gallman, J. Matthew. *Defining Duty During the Civil War: Personal Choice, Popular Culture, and the Union Homefront.* Chapel Hill, NC: University of North Carolina Press, 2015.

Gilham, William. *Manual of Instruction for the Volunteers and Militia of the State of Texas; taken from Gilham's Manual of Instruction for the Volunteers and Militia of the United States.* Galveston, TX: Richardson, 1861.

Glatthaar, Joseph T. *General Lee's Army: From Victory to Collapse.* New York: Free Press, 2008.

Gleeson, David T. *The Green and the Gray: The Irish in the Confederate States of America.* Chapel Hill, NC: University of North Carolina Press, 2013.

Goodheart, Adam. *1861: The Civil War Awakening.* New York: Alfred E. Knopf, 2011.

Gordon, Lesley J. *A Broken Regiment: The 16ᵗʰ Connecticut's Civil War.* Baton Rouge, LA: Louisiana State University Press, 2014.

Grant, Ulysses S. *Personal Memoirs of U.S. Grant,* Vols. 2. New York: Charles L. Webster, 1885.

Grear, Charles David. *Why Texans Fought in the Civil War.* College Station, TX: Texas A&M University Press, 2010.

Greenberg, Amy. *Cause for Alarm: The Volunteer Fire Department in the Nineteenth Century City.* Princeton, NJ: Princeton University Press, 1998.

Greenberg, Amy. *Manifest Manhood and the Antebellum American Empire.* Cambridge: Cambridge University Press, 2005.

Greenberg, Kenneth S. *Honor & Slavery: Lies, Duels, Noses, Masks, Dressing as a Woman, Gifts, Strangers, Humanitarianism, Death, Slave Rebellions, the Proslavery Argument, Baseball, Hunting, and Gambling in the Old South.* Princeton, NJ: Princeton University Press, 1996.

Greenberger, Scott S. *The Unexpected President: The Life and Times of Chester A. Arthur.* New York: Da Capo Press, 2017.

Griffith, Paddy. *Battle Tactics of the Civil War.* New Haven, CT: Yale University Press, 1989.

Grimsley, Mark, and Steven E. Woodworth. *Shiloh: A Battlefield Guide.* Lincoln, NE: University of Nebraska Press, 2006.

Groeling, Meg. *First Fallen: The Life of Colonel Elmer Ellsworth, the North's First Civil War Hero* El Dorado Hills, CA: Savas Beatie, 2021.

Halttunen, Karen, and Lewis Perry, eds. *Moral Problems in American Life: New Perspectives in Cultural History.* Ithaca, NY: Cornell University Press, 1998.

Harrison. Carole E., and Thomas J. Brown. *Zouave Theaters: Transnational Military Fashion and Performance.* Baton Rouge, LA: Louisiana State University Press, 2024.

Hartje, Robert G. *Van Dorn: The Life and Times of a Confederate General.* Reprint, 1967. Nashville, TN: Vanderbilt University Press, 1994.

Hay, John. *Inside Lincoln's White House: The Complete Diary of John Hay.* Michael Burlingame, and John R. Turner Ettlinger, eds. Carbondale, IL: Southern Illinois Press, 1997.

Haynes, Sam W. *Unsettled Land: From Revolution to Republic, The Struggle for Texas.* New York: Basic Books, 2022.

Haynie, Henry. *The Nineteenth Illinois: A Memoir of a Regiment of Volunteer Infantry Famous in the Civil War of Fifty years ago for its Drill, Bravery and Distinguished Services.* Chicago: M.A. Donohue, 1912.

Heck, Timothy G., and Walker D. Mills, eds. *Armies in Retreat: Chaos, Cohesion and Consequences.* Fort Leavenworth, KS: Army University Press, 2023.

Heineman, Kenneth J. *Civil War Dynasty: The Ewing Family of Ohio.* New York: New York University Press, 2012.

Henderson, Harry McCorry. *Texas in the Confederacy.* San Antonio, TX: The Naylor Company, 1955.

Hennessy, John. *The First Battle of Manassas: An End to Innocence, July 18–21, 1861,* Revised ed. Mechanicsburg, PA: Stackpole Books, 2015.

Hess, Earl J. *Banners to the Breeze: The Kentucky Campaign, Corinth and Stones River.* Lincoln, NE: University of Nebraska Press, 2010.

Hess, Earl J. *Braxton Bragg: The Most Hated Man of the Confederacy.* Chapel Hill, NC: University of North Carolina Press, 2016.

Hess, Earl J. *Civil War Infantry Tactics: Training, Combat and Small-Unit Effectiveness.* Baton Rouge: Louisiana State University Press, 2015.

Hess, Earl J. *Storming Vicksburg: Grant, Pemberton and the Battles of March 19–22, 1863.* Chapel Hill, NC: University of North Carolina Press, 2020.

Hess, Earl J. *The Union Soldier in Battle: Enduring the Ordeal of Combat.* Lawrence, KS: University Press of Kansas, 1997.

Hesseltine, William B. *Civil War Prisons: A Study in War Psychology.* Reprint, 1930. Forward by William Blair. Columbus, OH: Ohio State University Press, 1998.

Hewett, Janet B., ed. *Texas Confederate Soldiers 1861–1865.* Vols. 2. Wilmington, NC: Broadfoot, 1997.

History of Texas Together with a Biographical History of Milam, Williamson, Bastrop, Travis, Lee and Burleson Counties. Chicago: The Lewis, 1893.

House, Edward H. *Biography of Col. E. E. Ellsworth.* Cincinnati, OH: Mumford, 1864.

Houston: A History and Guide. Compiled by Workers of the Writer's Program of the Work Projects Administration in the State of Texas. Houston, TX: The Anson Jones Press, 1942.

Howe, George Frederick. *Chester A. Arthur: A Quarter Century of Machine Politics.* New York: Frederick Ungar, 1935

Howell, Kenneth W., ed. *The Seventh Star of the Confederacy: Texas During the Civil War.* Denton, TX: University of North Texas Press, 2009.

Hudson, Frederic. *Journalism in the United States, from 1690–1872.* New York: Harper and Brothers, 1873.

Hughes, Nathaniel Cheairs. *General William J. Hardee: Old Reliable.* Baton Rouge, LA: Louisiana State University Press, 1965.

Hutchinson, Louise Daniel. *The Anacostia Story, 1608–1930*. Washington, DC: U.S. Govt. Printing Office, 1977.

Ingraham, Charles. *Elmer E. Ellsworth and the Zouaves of '61*. Chicago: University of Chicago Press, 1925.

Jackson, David P., ed. *The Colonel's Diary: Journals Kept During the Civil War by the Late Colonel Oscar L Jackson of New Castle, Pennsylvania, sometime Commander of the 63rd Regiment, O.V.I*. Sharon, PA: N.p., 1922.

James, Marquis. *The Raven: A Biography of Sam Houston*. New York: Blue Ribbon Books, 1929.

Jeffery, William H. *Richmond Prisons, 1861–62, Compiled from the original Records kept by the Confederate Government. Journals kept by Union Prisoners of War Together with the Name, Rank, Company, Regiment and State of the Four Thousand Who Were Confined There*. St. Johnsbury, VT: Caledonia County, 1893.

Jewett, Clayton E., ed. *Rise and Fall of the Confederacy: The Memoir of Senator Willamson S. Oldham, CSA*. Springfield, MO: University of Missouri Press, 2006.

Jewett, Clayton E. *Texas in the Confederacy: An Experiment in Nation Building*. Columbia, MO: University of Missouri Press, 2002.

Johnson, Robert Underwood and Clarence Cough Buel, eds. *Battles and Leaders of the Civil War: Being for the Most Part Contributions By Union and Confederate Officers. Based Upon The Century War Series*. Vols. 4. New York: The Century, 1884–1888.

Johnston, William Preston. *The Life of Gen. Albert Sidney Johnston Embracing His Services in the Armies of the United States, the Republic of Texas, and the Confederate States*. New York: D. Appleton, 1878.

Jones, J. W., ed. *The Story of American Heroism: Thrilling Narratives of Personal Adventures During the Great Civil War, as Told by the Medal Winners and Roll of Honor Men*. Springfield, OH: J. W. Jones, 1897.

Keegan, John. *The Face of Battle*. New York: Viking Press, 1976.

Kennon, Donald, and Paul Finkleman, eds. *Congress and the People's Contest: The Conduct of the Civil War*. Athens, OH: Ohio University Press, 2018.

Kerman, Frank. *Reminiscences of the Old Fire Laddies and Volunteer Departments of New York and Brooklyn Together with a Complete History of the Paid Departments in Both Cities*. New York: M. Crane, 1885.

Lanman, Charles, ed. *Journal of Alfred Ely, A Prisoner of War in Richmond*. New York: D. Appleton, 1862.

Levin, Kevin M. *Searching for Black Confederates: The Civil War's Most Persistent Myth*. Chapel Hill, NC: University of North Carolina Press, 2019.

Linderman, Gerald F. *Embattled Courage: The Experience of Combat in the American Civil War*. New York: The Free Press, 1987.

Lindley, Ernest R., Comp. *Biographical Directory of the Texan Conventions and Congresses, 1832–1845 of Texas*. Austin: Book Exchange, 1941.

Longacre, Edward G. *The Early Morning of War: Bull Run, 1861*. Norman, OK: University of Oklahoma Press, 2014.

Lonn, Ella. *Foreigners in the Confederacy*. Chapel Hill, NC: University of North Carolina Press, 1940.

Manning, James H. *Albany Zouave Cadets: Fifty Years Young*. Albany, NY: Weed-Parsons, 1910.

Marr, Timothy. *The Cultural Roots of American Islamicism*. Cambridge: Cambridge University Press, 2006.

Maury, Dabney Herndon. *Recollections of a Virginian in the Mexican, Indian and Civil Wars*. 2nd ed. New York: Charles Scribner's Sons, 1894.

McCaslin, Richard B. *Portraits of Conflict: A Photographic History of South Carolina in the Civil War*. Little Rock, AR: University of Arkansas Press, 1995.

McCurry, Stephanie. *Confederate Reckoning: Power and Politics in the Civil War South*. Cambridge, MA: Harvard University Press, 2010.

McDonough, James Lee. *Shiloh: In Hell Before Night*. Knoxville, TN: University of Tennessee Press, 1977.

McPherson, James. *For Cause and Comrades: Why Civil War Soldiers Fought in the Civil War*. New York: Oxford University Press, 1997.

McWhiney, Grady, and Perry Jamieson. *Attack and Die: Civil War Military Tactics and the Southern Heritage*. Tuscaloosa: University of Alabama Press, 1982.

Meier, Kathryn Shively. *Nature's Civil War: Common Soldiers and the Environment in 1862 Virginia*. Chapel Hill, NC: University of North Carolina Press, 2013.

Military Order of the Loyal Legion, Commandery of the State of Illinois. *Military Essays and Recollections: Papers Read before the Commandry of the State of Illinois, Military Order of the Loyal Legion of the United States*. Vols. 2. Chicago, IL: A.C. McClurge, 1891–1894.

Military Order of the Loyal Legion, Commandery of the State of Ohio. *Sketches of War History 1861–1865: Papers Read Before the Ohio Commandery of the Military Order of the Loyal Legion of the United States, 1886–1888*. Vols. 2. Cincinnati, OH: Robert Clarke, 1886–1888.

Miller, Brian Craig. *Empty Sleeves: Amputation in the Civil War South*. Athens, GA: University of Georgia Press, 2015.

Miller, Daniel J. *American Zouaves, 1859–1959: An Illustrated History*. Jefferson, NC: McFarland Press, 2019.

Miller, Francis Trevelyan., ed. *Photographic History of the Civil War in Ten Volumes*. New York: The Review of Reviews, 1911.

Moe, Richard. *The Last Full Measure: The Life and Death of the First Minnesota Volunteers*. Reprint, 2001, St. Paul, MN: Minnesota Historical Society. New York: Henry Holt, 1993.

Moore, Albert B. *Conscription and Conflict in the Confederacy*. New York: Macmillan, 1924.

Moore, Frank, ed. *The Rebellion Record: A Diary of American Events, with Documents, Narratives, Illustrative Incidents, Poetry, etc*. Vols. 12. New York: G. P. Putnam, 1861–1868.

Morford, Henry. *The Days of Shoddy: A Novel of the Great Rebellion in 1861*. Philadelphia, PA: J. B. Person & Brothers, 1863.

Morgan, William H., *Personal Reminiscences of the War of 1861-5*. Lynchburg, VA: J. P. Bell, 1911.

Morrison, John H. *History of American Steam Navigation*. New York: W. F. Sametz, 1903.

Murray, R. L. *"They Fought Like Tigers": The 11th New York Fire Zouaves, 14th Brooklyn and Irish 69th New York at First Bull Run. Army of the Potomac Journal, Volume Two*. Wolcott, NY: Benedum Books, 2005.

Nash, Eugene Arus. *A History of the Forty-Fourth Regiment New York Volunteer Infantry in the Civil War, 1861–1865*. Chicago, IL: R.R. Donnelley, 1911.

Neely, Jr., Mark E. *The Union Divided: Party Conflict in the Civil War North*. Cambridge, MA: Harvard University Press, 2002.

Nevins, Allan and Milton Halsey Thomas, eds. *The Diary of George Templeton Strong: The Civil War, 1860–1865*. New York: The Macmillan, 1952.

The New Excelsior Dictionary, Containing Every Useful Word in the English Language With Its Correct Spelling, Accurate Pronunciation, and Exact Meaning According to Webster and Worcester. To which is Added an Encyclopedia of Valuable Information, Also a Complete Supplement of New Words. Nashua, NH: C. C. Parker, 1889.

Noe, Kenneth W. *Perryville: This Grand Havoc of Battle*. Lexington, KY: The University Press of Kentucky, 2011.

North, Thomas. *Five Years in Texas; What You did not Hear During the War from January 1861-January 1866. A Narrative of his travels, experiences, and Observations in Texas and Mexico*. Cincinnati, OH: Elm Street Printing, 1871.

Pohanka, Brian C. and Patrick A. Schroeder, eds. *With the 11th New York First Zouaves in Camp, Battle, and Prison: The Narrative of Private Arthur O'Neil in the New York Atlas and Leader*. Lynchburg, VA: Schroeder Publications, 2011.

Phisterer, Frederick. *New York in the War of the Rebellion, 1861 to 1865*. Albany, NY: Wee, Parsons, 1890.

Porter, David Dixon. *The Naval History of the Civil War*. New York: The Sherman, 1886.

Purcell, Sarah J. *Spectacle of Grief: Public Funerals and Memory in the Civil War Era*. Chapel Hill, NC: University of North Carolina Press, 2022.

Rable, George C. *Civil Wars: Women and the Crisis of Southern Nationalism*. Champaign, IL: University of Illinois Press, 1989.

Rable, George C. *Damn Yankees!: Demonization and Defiance in the Confederate South*. Baton Rouge, LA: Louisiana State University Press, 2015.

Raines, Cadwell W., ed. *Six Decades in Texas: Or Memoirs of Francis Richard Lubbock, Governor of Texas in War Time, 1861–63. A Personal Experience in Business, War and Politics*. Austin, TX: B. C. Jones, 1900.

Randall, Ruth Painter. *Colonel Elmer Ellsworth: A Biography of Lincoln's Friend and First Hero of the Civil War*. Boston, MA: Little, Brown, 1960.

Reardon, Carol. *With a Sword in One Hand and Jomini in the Other: The Problem of Military Thought in the Civil War North*. Chapel Hill, NC: University of North Carolina Press, 2012.

Reynolds, John P. *"In Her Hour of Sore Distress and Peril": The Civil War Diaries, Eighth Massachusetts Volunteer Infantry*. Edited by Jeffery Patrick. Jefferson, NC: McFarland, 2013.

Rich, Joseph W. *The Battle of Shiloh*. Iowa City, IA: The State Historical Society of Iowa, 1911.

Robb, Frances Osborn. *Shot in Alabama: A History of Photography 1839–1941 and a List of Photographers*. Tuscaloosa, AL: University of Alabama Press, 2016.

Roberts, Madge Thornall., ed. *The Personal Correspondence of Sam Houston*. Vols. 4. Denton, TX: University of North Texas Press, 1996–2001.

Roberts, Madge Thornall. *Star of Destiny: The Private Life of Sam and Margaret Houston*. Denton TX: University of North Texas Press, 1993.

Robertson, James I. *Soldiers Blue and Gray*. Columbia, SC: University of South Carolina Press, 1988.

Roman, Alfred. *The Military Operations of General Beauregard*. Vols. 2. New York: Harper & Brothers, 1884.

Rozelle, Ron. *Exiled: The Last Days of Sam Houston*. College Station, TX: Texas A&M University Press, 2017.

Rubin, Anne Sarah, *A Shattered Nation: The Rise and Fall of the Confederacy, 1861–1868*. Chapel Hill, NC: University of North Carolina Press, 2005.

Sacher, John M., *Confederate Conscription and the Struggle for Southern Soldiers*. Baton Rouge, LA: Louisiana State University Press, 2021.

Sanders, Jr., Charles W. *While in the Hands of the Enemy: Military Prisons of the Civil War*. Baton Rouge, LA: Louisiana State University Press, 2005.

Schmidt, James M. *Galveston and the Civil War: An Island City in the Maelstrom*. Cheltenham: History Press, 2012.

Scott, Robert Garth, ed. *Forgotten Valor: The Memoirs, Journals and Civil War Letters of Orlando B. Willcox*. Kent, OH: Kent State University Press, 1999.

Seale, William. *Sam Houston's Wife: A Biography of Margaret Lea Houston*. Norman, OK: University of Oklahoma Press, 1970.

Sheehan-Dean, Aaron. *Why Confederates Fought: Family and Nation in Civil War Virginia*. Chapel Hill, NC: University of North Carolina Press, 2007.

Sheldon, George W. *The Story of the Volunteer Fire Department of the City of New York*. New York: Harper & Brothers, 1882.

Shiels, Damian. *The Irish in the American Civil War*. Dublin: The History Press of Ireland, 2013.

Sifakis, Stewart. *Compendium of the Confederate Armies: Texas*. New York: Facts on File, 1995.

Silkenat, David. *Raising the White Flag: How Surrender Defined the American Civil War*. Chapel Hill, NC: University of North Carolina Press, 2019.

Silverthorne, Elizabeth. *Ashbel Smith of Texas: Pioneer, Patriot and Statesman, 1805–1886*. College Station, TX: Texas A&M University Press, 1982.

Simpson, Harold B. *Texas in the War, 1861–1865*. Hillsboro, TX: Texas Hill Junior College Press, 1965.

Smart, Richard W. *History of the 19th Alabama Infantry Regiment, Army of Tennessee. C. S. A.* Madison, AL: R. W. Smart, 1991.

Smart, Richard W., ed. *They Bore Every Burden: History of the 19th Alabama Regiment, Army of Tennessee, C.S.A.* Madison, AL: R. W. Smart, 1995.

Smith, Ashbel. *Address Delivered in the Chapel at West Point, Before the Officers and Cadets of the United States Military Academy, by the Hon. Ashbel Smith of Texas and Col. A. W. Doniphan, of Missouri. June 16,*

1848. New York: Published by Order of the First Class of the United States Corps of Cadets, 1848.

Smith, Ashbel. *An Address Delivered in the City of Galveston on the 22d of February,1848, The Anniversary of the Birth Day of Washington and the Battle of Buena Vista*. Galveston, TX: News Office, 1848.

Smith, Charles H. *The History of Fuller's Ohio Brigade, 1861–1865: Its Great March, with Roster Portraits, Battle Maps and Biographies*. Cleveland, OH: Press of A. J. Watt, 1909.

Smith, Mark A. *The Smell of Battle, the Taste of Siege: A Sensory History of the Civil War*. New York: Oxford University Press, 2014.

Smith, Ralph J. *Reminiscences of the Civil War and Other Sketches*. Reprint, 1911. Waco, TX: W. M. Morrison, 1962.

Smith, Sarah S. *Amaranth Blooms: A Collection of Embodied Poetical Thoughts*. Utica, NY: J. W. Fuller, 1853.

Smith, Timothy B. *Corinth 1862: Siege, Battle, Occupation*. Lawrence, KS: University Press of Kansas, 2012.

Smith, Timothy B. *Rethinking Shiloh: Myth and Memory*. Knoxville, TN: University of Tennessee Press, 2013.

Smith, Timothy B. *Shiloh: Conquer or Perish*. Lawrence, KS: University Press of Kansas, 2014.

Smith, Timothy B. *The Union Assaults at Vicksburg: Grant Attacks Pemberton, May 17–22, 1863*. Lawrence, KS: University Press of Kansas, 2020.

Smith, Timothy B. *The Untold Story of Shiloh*. Knoxville, TN: University of Tennessee Press, 2006.

Stevens, Walter Barlow. *A Reporter's Lincoln*. Edited by Michael Burlingame. Lincoln, NE: University of Nebraska Press, 1998.

Stocker, Jeffrey D., ed. *From Huntsville to Appomattox: R. T. Coles 4th Regiment Alabama Volunteer Infantry, C.S.A. Army of Northern Virginia*. Knoxville, TN: The University of Tennessee Press, 1996.

Speer, Lonnie R. *Portals of Hell: Military Prisons of the Civil War*. Lincoln, NE: University of Nebraska Press, 2005.

Sword, Wiley. *Southern Invincibility: A History of the Confederate Heart*. New York: St. Martin's Press, 1999.

Styple, William B., ed. *Writing and Fighting the Civil War: Soldier Correspondence to the New York Sunday Mercury*. Gettysburg, PA: Belle Grove, 2000.

Tap, Bruce. *Over Lincoln's Shoulder: The Committee on the Conduct of the War*. Lawrence, KS: University Press of Kansas, 1998.

Taylor, William R. *Cavalier and Yankee: The Old South and American National Character*. New York: George Braziller, 1961.

Tebeau, Mark. *Eating Smoke: Fire in Urban America, 1800–1950*. Baltimore, MD: Johns Hopkins University Press, 2012.

Tevis, C. V. Compiler. *The History of the Fighting Fourteenth: Published in Commemoration of the Fiftieth Anniversary of the Muster of the Regiment into the United States Service, May 23, 1861*. New York: Brooklyn Eagle Press, 1911.

Thomas, Emory M. *Bold Dragoon: The Life of J.E.B. Stuart*. New York: Harper and Row, 1986.

Throne, Mildred, ed. *The Civil War Diary of Cyrus F. Boyd, Fifteenth Iowa Infantry, 1861–1865*. Baton Rouge, LA: Louisiana State University Press, 1998.

Todd, William. *The Seventy-Ninth Highlanders New York Volunteers in the War of Rebellion 1861–1865*. Albany, NY: Press of Brandow, Barton, 1886.

Tunnard, William H. *A Southern Record: The History of the Third Regiment, Louisiana Infantry. Containing a Complete record of the Campaigns in Arkansas and Missouri; the Battles of Oak Hills, Elk Horn, Iuka, Corinth; the Second Siege of Vicksburg, Anecdotes, Camps, Scenery, and Description of the Country Through Which the Regiment Marched, etc*. Baton Rouge, LA: Printed for the Author, 1866.

Ural, Susannah J., ed. *Civil War Citizens: Race, Ethnicity and Identity in America's Bloodiest Conflict*. New York: New York University Press, 2010.

Ural, Susannah J. *Hood's Texas Brigade: The Soldiers and Families of the Confederacy's Most Celebrated Unit*. Baton Rouge, LA: Louisiana State University Press, 2017.

Urquhart, Kenneth Trist., ed. *Vicksburg: Southern City Under Siege: William Lovelace Foster's Letter Describing the Defense and Surrender of the Confederate Fortress on the Mississippi*. New Orleans, LA: The Historic New Orleans Collection, 1980.

Walsh, Chris. *Cowardice: A Brief History*. Princeton, NJ: Princeton University Press, 2014.

Warner, Ezra. *Generals in Gray: Lives of Confederate Commanders*. Baton Rouge, LA: Louisiana State University Press, 1959.

Waugh, John C. *Reelecting Lincoln: The Battle for the 1864 Presidency*. Cambridge, MA: De Capo Press, 2001.

Webb, Walter Prescott., ed. *The Handbook of Texas*. Vols. 2. Austin: Texas State Historical Association, 1952.

Weigley, Russell. *The American Way of War: A History of United States Military Strategy and Policy*. New York: Macmillan, 1973.

Whites, LeeAnn. *Gender Matters: Civil War, Reconstruction, and the Making of the New South*. New York: Palgrave Macmillan, 2005.

Wilcox, Arthur M. and Warren Ripley. *The Civil War at Charleston*. Charleston, SC: The News and Courier and the Evening Post, 1983.

Wiley, Bell Irvin. *The Life of Billy Yank: The Common Soldier of the Union*. Reprint 1952. Baton Rouge: Louisiana State University Press, 2008.

Wiley, Bell Irvin. *The Life of Johnny Reb: The Common Soldier of the Confederacy*. Indianapolis: Bobbs-Merrill, 1943.

Williams, Ameila W. and Eugene C. Baker, eds. *The Writings of Sam Houston, 1813–1863*. Vols. 8. Austin, TX: University of Texas Press, 1938–43.

Williams, George F. *Memorial War Book As Drawn from Historical Records and Personal Narratives of the Men Who Served in the Great Struggle*. New York: Lovell Brothers, 1894.

Williams, Timothy J. *Intellectual Manhood: University, Self and Society in the Antebellum South*. Chapel Hill, NC: University of North Carolina Press, 2015.

Winkler, Ernest William, ed. *Journal of the Secession Convention of Texas 1861*. Austin, TX: Texas Library and Historical Commission, 1912.

Wittenmyer, Annie. *Under the Guns: A Woman's Reminiscences of the Civil War*. Boston, MA: E. B. Stillings, 1895.

Wood, Lamont. *Thornton's Luck: How America Almost Lost the Mexican-American War*. Kingwood, TX: Lone Star Books, 2017.

Woodworth, Steven E. and Charles D. Grear, eds. *Vicksburg Besieged*. Carbondale, IL: Southern Illinois University Press, 2020.

Woodworth, Steven E., ed. *The Shiloh Campaign*. Carbondale, IL: Southern Illinois University Press, 2009.

Wooster, Ralph A. *Civil War Texas: A History and a Guide*. Austin, TX: Texas State Historical Association, 1999.

Wooster, Ralph A., ed. *Lone Star Blue and Gray: Essays on Texas in the Civil War*. Austin, TX: Texas State Historical Association, 1995.

Wooster, Ralph A. *Lone Star Regiments in Gray*. Austin, TX: Eakin Press, 2002.

Wooten, Dudley, ed. *A Comprehensive History of Texas, 1685–1897*. Vols. 2. Dallas, TX: William Scarff, 1898.

Wright, Marcus J. *Texas in the War, 1861–1865*. Edited by Harold Simpson. Hillsboro, TX: Junior College Press, 1965.

Wyatt-Brown, Bertram. *Southern Honor: Ethics and Behavior in the Old South*. New York: Oxford University Press, 1982.

Yearly, Mamie. *Compiler: Reminiscences of the Boys in Gray 1861–1865*. Reprint, 1912. Dayton, OH: Morningside, 1986.

Zeller, Bob. *The Blue and Gray in Black and White: A History of Civil War Photography*. Westport, CT: Greenwood, 2005.

ARTICLES

Braudaway, Douglas Lee. "A Texan Records the Civil War Siege of Vicksburg Mississippi: The Journal of Maj. Maurice Kavanaugh Simons, 1863," *The Journal of Southwest History* Vol. 105, No. 1 (July 2001): 92–131.

Carmichael, Peter S. "Relevance, Resonance, and Historiography: Interpreting the Lives and Experiences of Civil War Soldiers," *Civil War History* Vol. 62, No. 2 (June 2016): 170–185.

Cook, Joseph. "The Future of Civil War Soldier Studies: The Failure of Courage," *Saber and Scroll* Vol. 3, No. 4 (Fall 2014): 25–38.

Dickens, Charles. "American Volunteer Firemen," *All the Year Round*, March 16, 1861.

Dickens, Charles, "Naval and Military Traditions in America," *All the Year Round*, June 15, 1861.

Eisenschiml, Otto. "The 55th Illinois at Shiloh," *Journal of the Illinois State Historical Society* Vol. 56, No. 2, Civil War Centennial (Summer 1963): 193–211.

"Ellsworth Was 'Golden Boy': Death Made Him a Martyr of the North," *New York State and the Civil War* Vol. 2 No. 1 (June 1962): 1–17.

Emberton, Carole. "'Only Murder Makes Men': Reconsidering the Black Military Experience," *Journal of the Civil War Era* Vol. 2, No. 3 (September 2012): 369–393.

Fisher, Sterling, "The Amenities of War," *Blue and Gray Monthly Patriotic Magazine* Vol. 1 (1893): 321–323.

Gallagher, Gary W., and Kathyrn Shively Meier. "Coming to Terms with Civil War Military History," *Journal of the Civil War Era* Vol. 4, No. 4 (December 2014): 487–508.

Gleason, David T. "The Rhetoric of Insurrection and Fear: The Politics of Slave Management in Confederate Georgia," *The Journal of Southern History* Vol. 89, No. 2 (May 2023): 237–266.

Gordon, Lesley J. "'Deeds of Brave Suffering and Lofty Heroism': Martialised Rhetoric and Kentucky Soldiers," *Register of the Kentucky Historical Society* Vol. 117, No. 2 (Spring 2019): 179–195.

Gordon, Lesley J. "'Novices in Warfare': Elmer E. Ellsworth and Militia Reform on the Eve of Civil War." *Journal of Civil War Era* Vol. 11, No. 2 (June 2021): 194–223.

Hicks, John D. "The Organization of the Volunteer Army in 1861 with Special Reference to Minnesota," *Minnesota History Bulletin* Vol. 2, No. 5 (February 1918): 324–368.

Hsieh, Wayne. "'Go to Your Gawd Like a Soldier': Transnational Reflections on Veteranhood," *Journal of the Civil War Era* Vol. 5, No. 4 (December 2015): 551–577.

Hubbell, Finley L. "Diary of Lieut. Col. Hubbell, of 3d Regiment Missouri Infantry, C.S.A.," *The Land We Love* Vol. VI, No. 2 (December 1868): 97–105.

Ingraham, Charles. "Colonel Elmer E. Ellsworth: First Hero of the Civil War," *The Wisconsin Magazine of History* Vol. 1, No. 4 (June, 1918): 349–374.

Longacre, Edward G. "'Indeed We Did Fight': A Soldier's Letters Describe the First Minnesota Regiment before and during the First Battle of Bull Run," *Minnesota History* Vol. 47, No. 2 (Summer 1980), 63–70.

McKinstry, James A. "With Col. Rogers When He Fell: Thrilling Recollections of Fort Robinette." *Confederate Veteran* Vol. 4, No. 7 (July 1896): 220–222.

Meek, Clarence E. "The Fire Zouaves," *WNYF: With New York Firefighters* Vol. 22, No. 2 (Spring 1961): 12–13.

Metcalf, Lewis Herbert. "So Eager Were We All," *American Heritage* Vol. 16 (June 1965): 33–41.

Moore, John C. "Some Confederate War Incidents," *Confederate Veteran* Vol. 12, No. 3 (March 1904): 116–117.

Morton, Christopher S. "'The Star Spangled Banner in Triumph Shall Wave': The New York City Fire Department's Presentation Color Carried by Ellsworth's New York Zouaves, 1861," *Military Collector and Historian* Vol. 57, No. 2 (Summer 2005): 58–60.

Mulligan, John. "'Trial by Fire,' the Story of the Fire Zouaves," *WNYF: With the New York Firefighters* Vol. 48 (1987): 8–11.

Pace, Eleanor Damon, ed. "The Diary and Letters of William P. Rogers, 1846–1862," *Southwestern Historical Quarterly* Vol. 37, No. 4 (April 1929): 259–299.

Phillips, Jason. "Battling Stereotypes: A Taxonomy of Commons Soldiers in Civil War History," *History Compass* Vol. 6, No. 6 (November 2008): 1407–1425.

Riley, Jr., Harris D. "Colonel William P. Rogers: A Confederate Hero at Corinth," *Confederate Veteran* (March–April 1994): 21–29.

Smith, David P. "Civil War Letters of Sam Houston," *The Southwestern Historical Quarterly* Vol. 81, No. 4 (April 1978): 417–426.

Sternhell, Yael A. "Revisionism Reinvented? The Antiwar Turn in Civil War Scholarship," *The Journal of the Civil War Era* Vol. 3, No. 2 (June 2013): 239–256.

Sommerville, Diane Miller. "'A Burden too Heavy to Bear': War Trauma, Suicide and Confederate Soldiers," *Civil War History* Vol. 59, No. 4 (December 2013): 453–491.

Swart, Stanley L. "The Military Examination Board in the Civil War: A Case Study," *Civil War History* Vol. 16, No. 3 (September 1970): 227–245.

Thomas, Emory M. "Rebel Nationalism: E. H. Cushing and the Confederate Experience," *The Southwestern Historical Quarterly* Vol. 73, No. 3 (January 1970): 343–355.

Throne, Mildred, ed. "The Civil War Diary of C. F. Boyd, Fifteenth Iowa Infantry. Part III," *Iowa Journal of History* Vol. 50, No. 3 (July 1952): 239–270.

Walsh, Chris. "'Cowardice Weakness or Infirmity, Whichever It May be Termed': A Shadow History of the Civil War," *Civil War History* Vol. 59, No. 4 (December 2013): 492–526.

Warren, Richard, and Roger Sturckle. "The 11th New York Volunteer Infantry (Ellsworth's First New York Zouaves), 1861–1862," *Military Collector & Historian* Vol. 39 (1987): n.p. Plates No. 614 and 615.

Weitz, Mark A. "Drill, Training, and the Combat Performance of the Civil War Soldier: Dispelling the Myth of the Poor Soldier, Great Fighter," *Journal of Military History* Vol. 62, No. 2 (April 1998): 263–290.

Wheeler, Gerald E. "D'Epineuil's Zouaves," *Civil War History* Vol. 2, No. 4 (December 1956): 93–100.

DISSERTATIONS AND THESES

Askew, Samuel L. III. "An Analysis of Unit Cohesion in the 42nd Alabama Infantry." MA. Thesis. US Army Command and General Staff College, Fort Leavenworth, KS, 2003.

Brandt, Julie Lynn. "The Civil War Diary of Elizabeth Hatcher Simons: Life and Hardship in Texana, Texas." MA Thesis. Texas A & M University – Kingsville, 1999.

Braudaway, Douglas Lee. "The Civil War Journal of Major Maurice Kavanaugh Simons, A. C. S., together with an Account of His Life." MA Thesis. Texas A & M University – Kingsville, 1994.

Curlee, Abigail. "A Study of Texas Slave Plantations, 1822–1865." PhD Dissertation, University of Texas, Austin, TX, 1932.

ONLINE SOURCES AND SITES

Alabama Department of Archives and History Digital Collections. digital.archives
.alabama.gov.

Ancestry.com.

Artandpopularculture.com.

Aristotle, *Nicomachean Ethics* (1115b.7 to 1116a.15), from "What Is Courage
and How It Stands between Cowardice and Rashness," Aristotelian Philosophy,
translated by George Kotsalis, www.aristotelianphilsophy.com.

American Battlefield Trust. www.battlefields.org.

Barnhart, Don. "2nd Texas Flag and Rogers' Sword on Display," Warriors of the
Lone Star State Blog Spot. warriorsofthelonestar.blogspot.com.

Biography.com.

Bull Runnings: A Journal of the Digitization of a Civil War Battles. Bullrunnings
.wordpress.com.

CivilWartalk.com.

Congressional Medal of Honor Society. www.cmohs.org.

Essential Civil War Curriculum. www.essentialcivilwarcurriculum.com.

Facebook.com.

Faust, Drew Gilpin. "Telling War Stories: Reflections of a Civil War Historian,"
National Endowment for the Humanities Lecture (2011). www.neh.gov.

Findagrave.com.

Fold3.com.

Gilder Lehrman Institute of American History. gilderlehrman.org;

Gordon, Lesley J. "Civil War Regiments," in Jon Butler, ed., *Oxford Research
Encyclopedia of American History*. Oxford: Oxford University Press, 2021.
oxfordre.com/americanhistory.

The Handbook of Texas Online. www.tshaonline.org

Historynet.com.

Iowa Digital Library. digital.lib.uiowa`.edu.

"Irish Colonels: Henry F. O'Brian, 11th New York Infantry," irishamericancivil
war.com.

Kalu, Michael. "Fierce and Colorful – Zouave Regiments in the Civil War," War
History Online. www.warhistory.com.

Legislative Reference Library of Texas. lrl.texas.gov.

Library of Congress. loc.gov.

Lyons, Candice D. "Rage and Resistance at Ashbel Smith's Evergreen Plantation,"
notevenpast.org.

McCormick, David. "Knights in Binding Armor," *America's Civil War Magazine*
(March 2010), via www.historynet.com.

Mississippians in the Confederate Army. mississippiconfederates.wordpress.com

Molliemooredavis.org.

Newspapers.com.

New York State Military Museum and Veterans Research Center. museum.dmna
.ny.gov.

Senate.gov.

Simpson, Brooks D. "The Changing Face of Battle: Corinth," October 4, 2012," Crossroads, cwcrossroads.wordpress.com.
Soldiers and Sailors Database. nps.gov/civilwar/soldiers-and-sailors-database .htm.
Texas Digital Archives. tsl.access.preservica.com.
Texas State Library. www.tsl.texas.gov.
TNGenWEb.org.
Turpin, Zachary. "'Manly Health and Training' and the *New York Atlas*," Ed Folsom and Kenneth M. Price, eds., The Walt Whitman Archive, www.whitma narchive.org.

Index

Driggs, George W., 248–249, 249n90
Dunn, John W., 106, 106n67

Eddy, Hiram, 118, 119
Ellsworth, Elmer E., 7–10, 16n2, 17–20,
 17n8, 17n11, 18n12, 18n13, 19n14,
 19n15, 23–26, 25n23, 26n42, 27,
 27n45, 28n50, 29, 29n59, 29n60, 31–
 40, 37n100, 40n110, 40n112, 42–45,
 42n119, 44n128, 47, 48n143, 49–58,
 49n145, 49n146, 53n5, 54n8, 55–
 56n9, 57n20, 59–63, 59n28, 60n30,
 60n32, 60–61n34, 65–67, 70–71, 75,
 82, 87n55, 88, 95, 98–100, 105, 110,
 115, 118, 122, 126, 130, 132,
 132n197, 133-134, 133n197, 139,
 144n19, 167, 252, 257, 283
Ellsworth's Avenger. *See* Brownell, Frank
 E.
Ellsworth's Avengers/People's Ellsworth
 Regiment. *See* New York Troops, 44th
 Infantry
Ely, Alfred, 116, 116n117, 117n120, 118,
 119n128
Evans, Charles, 154, 162, 167–168,
 168n124, 181n174, 192n35,206n83,
 207n85, 215n108, 218n122,
 221n132,237, 239n52, 240, 240n54,
 245n74, 259n113, 262n126, 263,
 263n131, 263n132, 265, 266,
 266n143, 270n158, 279

Fagen, James F., 216, 216n112
Farmer, John W., 94
Farmington, Battle of (MS), 215–216, 219,
 221n132, 229, 239
Farnham, Noah L., 40n112, 42–43, 56, 57,
 62, 65–66, 66n57, 66n58, 67, 68–69,
 73, 73n90, 74, 75, 79, 95, 96, 106,
 109–110, 122, 129, 133
Farr, John R., 133n197
Faust, Drew Gilpin, 10, 11
Feeney, John H., 206, 207n86
Fergus, George H., 20n23, 67n60, 133
First Fire Zouaves
 Alexandria, Virginia, 8, 46n137, 48–50,
  52–59, 52n1, 53n3, 53n4, 61–63,
  63n49, 87, 92–93, 97, 97n28, 115, 129,
  139, 139n3
 Accusations of Cowardice, 7–8, 12, 37,
  86, 88–90, 92–94, 97–104, 105–108,

 110, 114, 124–127, 129, 131–135,
  139, 283–284
 Bull Run, First Battle of (VA), 8, 74–90,
  94–95, 97–102, 107–108, 112, 114–
  115, 122, 124–127, 129, 134, 139, 205,
  246, 283
 casualties, 62, 78, 85–86, 90, 94, 96, 101,
  103, 108
 congressional investigation of, *see* Joint
  Committee on the Conduct of War
 desertion, 24, 44n128, 66n58, 93, 93n8,
  96, 97, 101, 105–108, 112, 114, 122,
  128–129
 disease and illness, 48, 73, 94
 disbandment, 37n98, 96–97, 109, 122,
  130–131, 131n186, 132–133, 272
 drill and discipline, 16, 17–20, 22, 27n45,
  29, 32–34, 32n74, 37, 42–43, 45, 50,
  58, 67–68, 70, 98–101, 103, 107, 109–
  110, 112–115, 122–124, 128, 134
 Ellsworth's death, 8–10, 52–58, 61–63,
  62n43, 71, 87n155, 88, 98–99, 122,
  133–134, 283
 fire near Willard's Hotel, 39–40, 40n112
 formation, 7, 15–23, 37, 45, 139, 139n1
 Fort Monroe, VA, 113, 114, 115, 140
 identity as firemen, 7, 16–17, 19–23, 29–
  30, 34, 36–37, 45–46, 65, 67, 71, 88,
  92, 100, 102, 110–111, 119–120, 124,
  132–134, 283
 imprisonment, 26n41, 76n102, 86n150,
  85, 85n143, 87–88, 92, 103, 115–120,
  116n116, 117n120, 121n145, 122,
  129, 131, 140
 Irish immigrants, 8–9, 21, 21n27, 84–85,
  96n23, 134
 leadership and officers, 9–10, 16n2, 20,
  42–43, 56–58, 61–63, 65–70, 67n60,
  74–76, 79, 84–86, 86n143, 94–97, 99,
  103, 129, 130n185, 134, 283–284 *See
  also* Elmer E. Ellsworth, Noah
  L. Farnham, and Charles Leoser
 New York, NY, 12, 15–17, 19, 23–32, 93,
  104–109, 110–112, 128–129, 131, 132
 Newport News, VA, 120, 121, 130
 newspaper coverage of, 8, 15–17, 23n34,
  25–27, 35–36, 44, 47, 53n3, 60n34,
  62n41, 63–64, 74n93, 77n106, 78–79,
  81n129, 82, 88–89, 91, 98–104, 106,
  110, 124, 127, 134–135, 139–140, 283
 postwar, 58, 132–135, 283–284

lton Keynes UK
ram Content Group UK Ltd.
HW020101061124
708UK00006B/727

9 781108 729192